Prague

written and researched by

Rob Humphreys

with additional contributions by
Tim Nollen

**ROUGH
GUIDES**

www.roughguides.com

Introduction to

Prague

First things first: Prague is a very beautiful city. With some six hundred years of architecture virtually untouched by natural disaster or war, few other cities, anywhere in Europe, look as good. Straddling the winding River Vltava, with a steep wooded hill to one side, the city retains much of its medieval layout and the street facades remain smothered in a rich mantle of Baroque, Rococo and Art Nouveau, all of which successfully escaped the vanities and excesses of postwar redevelopment. Of course, while the Iron Curtain was still in place, Prague was seldom visited by westerners – since the 1990s, however, all that has changed. Prague is now one of the most popular city break destinations in Europe, and is enjoying the sort of economic boom not seen since the 1920s.

 Prague's emergence as one of Europe's leading cities, capital of a country poised to join the EU, has come as a surprise to many people – but not the Czechs. After all, Prague was at the forefront of the European avant-garde for much of the last century, boasting a Cubist movement second only to Paris, and, between the wars, a modernist architectural flowering to rival Bauhaus. With a playwright and human rights activist as their president, the Czechs easily grabbed the headlines in the 1990s. Even today, the country's athletes and models enjoy a very high profile, and its writers, artists and film directors continue to exert a profound influence on European culture, out of all proportion to their number.

Naturally, not everybody is happy with the changes. Like most central Europeans, Czechs love to moan, especially over a glass or two of beer.

Prices have gone up dramatically over the past ten years, with ever-increasing rents pushing locals out of the centre, and ever more expensive restaurants making the old town a no-go area for the average Praguer. Some argue that over-zealous restoration has turned central Prague into a theme park, that the arrival of the multinationals has made Prague like every other European city, and that the smartening-up of the city centre has made the place just like Vienna (a city universally disliked by Czechs).

Certainly, the exhilarating popular unity of the 1989 Velvet Revolution, and the feeling of participating in history itself, have now gone for ever. Few Czechs refer to the events of 1989 as a "revolution". Disorientation at the speed of change, disillusionment with modern politics and the first real taste of Western vices in the capital have taken their toll. The lifestyle gulf between Party and non-Party members has been replaced by the Western malaise of rich and poor. There's nothing new in this, but it does serve as a sobering footnote to the city's glowing image in the West.

What to see

With a population of just one and a quarter million, Prague (Praha to the Czechs) is relatively small as capital cities go. It originally developed as four separate self-governing towns and a Jewish ghetto, whose individual identities and medieval street plans have been preserved, more or less intact, to this day. Almost every-

thing of any historical interest lies within these compact central districts, the majority of which are easy to master quickly on foot. Only in the last hundred years has Prague spread beyond its ancient perimeter, and its suburbs now stretch across the hills for miles on every side. There's a cheap and efficient transport system on which to explore them – a decent map is all you need to find your way around.

> **Almost everything of any historical interest lies within Prague's compact central districts**

Prague is divided into two unequal halves by the **River Vltava**. The steeply inclined left bank is dominated by the castle district of **Hradčany** (Chapter 1), which contains the city's most obvious sight: Pražský hrad or **Prague Castle** (known simply as the Hrad in Czech), home to the city's cathedral, and the old royal palace and gardens, as well as a host of museums and galleries. Squeezed between the castle hill and the river are the picturesque Baroque palaces and houses of the "Little Quarter" or **Malá Strana** (Chapter 2) – around 150 acres of twisting cobbled streets and

v

secret walled gardens – home to the Czech parliament and most of the city's embassies, and dominated by the green dome and tower of the church of **sv Mikuláš**. At the southern end of Malá Strana, a funicular railway carries you out of the cramped streets to the top of **Petřín** hill, the city's most central leafy escape, with a wonderful view across the river.

The city's twisting matrix of streets is at its most confusing in the original medieval hub of the city, **Staré Město** (Chapter 3) – literally, the "Old Town" – on the right bank of the Vltava. The Karlův most, or **Charles Bridge**, its main link with the opposite bank, is easily the city's most popular historical monument, and the best place from which to view Prague Castle. Staré Město's other great showpiece is its main square, **Staroměstské náměstí**, where you can view Prague's famous astronomical clock. Enclosed within the boundaries of Staré Město is the former Jewish quarter, or **Josefov** (Chapter 4). The ghetto walls have long since gone and the whole area was remodelled at the turn of the century, but six synagogues,

House signs

As well as preserving their Gothic or Romanesque foundations, many houses throughout Prague retain their ancient **house signs**, which you'll see carved into the gables, on hanging wooden signs, or inscribed on the facade. The system originated in medieval times, and still survives today, though it's now used  predominantly by *pivnice* (pubs), restaurants and hotels. Some signs were deliberately chosen to draw custom to the business of the house, like *U zeleného hroznu* (The Green Bunch of Grapes), a wine shop in the Malá Strana; others, like *U železných dveří* (The Iron Door), simply referred to some distinguishing feature of the house, often long since disappeared. The pervasive use of *zlatý* (gold) in the house names derives from the city's popular epithet, *Zlatá Praha* (Golden Prague), which could either refer to the halcyon days of Charles IV, when the new Gothic copper roofing shone like gold, or to the period of alchemy under Rudolf II. Religious names, like *U černé Matky boží* (The Black Madonna), were popular, too, especially during the Counter-Reformation.

In the 1770s, the Habsburgs, in their rationalizing fashion, introduced a numerical system, with each house in the city entered onto a register according to a strict chronology. Later, however, the conventional system of progressive street numbering was introduced, so don't be surprised if seventeenth-century pubs like *U medvídků* (The Little Bears) have two numbers in addition to a house sign, in this case 7 and 345. The former, Habsburg number is written on a red background, the latter, modern number, on blue.

a medieval cemetery and a town hall survive as powerful reminders of a community that has existed here for over a millennium.

South and east of the old town is the large sprawling district of **Nové Město** (Chapter 5), whose main arteries make up the city's commercial and business centre. The nexus of Nové Město is Wenceslas Square (Václavské náměstí), focus of the political upheavals of the modern-day republic. Further afield lie various **suburbs**, most of which were developed only in the last hundred years or so. The single exception is **Vyšehrad**, one of the original fortress settlements of the newly arrived Slavs in the last millennium, now the final resting-place of leading Czech artists of the modern age, including the composers Smetana and Dvořák. To the east is the up-and-coming residential suburb of **Vinohrady**, peppered with parks and squares; and **Žižkov**, one of the city's poorer districts, whose two landmarks – the Žižkov monument and the futuristic TV tower – are visible for miles around. All of these areas are covered in Chapter 6.

Nineteenth-century suburbs also sprang up to the north of the city centre in **Holešovice**, now home to the city's chief modern art museum, **Veletržní palác**. The area also boasts two huge swathes of greenery: the Letná plain, overlooking the city; and the Stromovka park, beyond which lie the city chateau of **Troja** and the zoo. Further west, leafy interwar suburbs like **Dejvice** and **Střešovice**, dotted with modernist family villas, give an entirely different angle on Prague. All these places are covered in Chapter 7.

Prague's outer suburbs, where most of the population live, are more typical of Eastern Europe:

seemingly half-built, high-rise housing estates, known locally as *paneláky*, swimming in a sea of mud. However, once you're clear of the city limits, the traditional, provincial feel of **Bohemia** (Čechy) immediately makes itself felt. Many Praguers own a *chata*, or country cottage, somewhere in these rural backwaters, and every weekend the roads are jammed with folk heading for the hills. For visitors, few places are more than an hour from the city by public transport, making day-trips relatively painless.

The most popular destinations for foreign day-trippers are the castles of **Karlštejn** and **Konopiště**, both of which suffer from a daily swarm of coach parties, but make up for it by being surrounded by beautiful wooded countryside. Alternatively, you can head north, away from the hills and the crowds, to the wine town of **Mělník**, perched high above the confluence of the Vltava and Labe (Elbe) rivers. Further north is **Terezín**, the wartime Jewish ghetto that is a living testament to the Holocaust. One of the most popular day-trips is to the medieval silver-mining town of **Kutná Hora**, 60km to the east, which boasts a glorious Gothic cathedral and a macabre ossuary. Day-trips are covered in Chapter 8.

When to go

L ying at the heart of central Europe, Prague has a continental climate: winters can be pretty cold, summers correspondingly scorching. The best times to visit, in terms of weather, are late spring and early autumn. Summer in the city can be pretty stifling, but the real reason for avoiding the peak season is that it can get uncomfortably crowded in the centre

> **The best times to visit, in terms of weather, are late spring and early autumn**

– finding a place to eat in the evening, let alone securing a room, can become fraught with difficulties. If you're looking for good weather, April is the earliest you can guarantee at least some sunny days, and October is the last warm month. If you don't mind the cold, the city looks beautiful in the snowy winter months, though it can also fall prey to "inversions", which blanket the city in a grey smog for a week or more.

Average temperatures (°C), hours of sunshine and monthly rainfall

	Jan	Feb	Mar	Apr	May	June	July	Aug	Sept	Oct	Nov	Dec
Min °C	-4	-3	-0	2	8	11	12	13	9	3	0	-2
Max °C	1	2	8	12	18	21	22	23	18	12	5	1
Hours of sunshine	2	3	4	6	7	7	7	7	5	4	2	2
mm	18	17	25	35	58	68	66	64	40	30	28	22

20 things not to miss

It's not possible to see everything Prague has to offer on a short trip – and we don't suggest you try. What follows is a subjective selection of the city's highlights, from Art Nouveau masterpieces and medieval backstreets, to tranquil Baroque terraced gardens and great day-trip destinations around the city – all arranged in colour-coded categories to help you find the very best things to see, do and experience. All entries have a page reference to take you straight into the guide, where you can find out more.

01 **Karlův most (Charles Bridge)** • Page **78** Prague's wonderful medieval stone bridge, peppered with Baroque statuary, has been the main link between the two banks of the river for over five hundred years.

02 **Café Imperial** • Page **199** Unpretentious, Habsburg-era café with a stunning 1914 ceramic tiled interior and free doughnuts.

03 **Veletržní palác (Trade Fair Palace)** • Page **152** The city's chief gallery of modern art is housed in a functionalist masterpiece.

04 **Backstreets of Staré Město** • Page **75** Lose the crowds (and yourself) in the twisted matrix of Staré Město's backstreets.

05 **Staroměstské náměstí (Old Town Square)** • Page **85** Prague's busy showpiece square, dominated by the Art Nouveau Hus Monument, and best known for its astronomical clock.

06 **Josefov** • Page **99** Six synagogues, a town hall and a medieval cemetery survive from the city's fascinating former Jewish ghetto.

07 **Nightlife** • Page **211** From DJs to Dvořák, Prague boasts a surprisingly varied nightlife.

09 **Shopping in Prague's pasáže** • Page **116** The covered shopping malls, or *pasáže*, on and around Wenceslas Square, are just the place to do a bit of window-shopping.

08 **Vyšehrad** • Page **137** Leafy, riverside zig-zag fortress which houses the country's most exclusive cemetery, resting place of composers Dvořák and Smetana.

10 **Pražský hrad (Prague Castle)** • Page **37** The city's most spectacular landmark, and home to the cathedral, royal palace and a host of museums and galleries.

11 **Obecní dům** • Page **124** The largest and most impressive Art Nouveau building in the city houses a café, a bar, two restaurants, exhibition space and a concert hall.

12 **Petřín** • Page **72** Take the funicular up the wooded hill of Petřín, home to a mirror maze, an observatory and a miniature Eiffel Tower, as well as spectacular views across Prague.

13 **Bílkova vila** • Page **150** House and studio (now museum) of the maverick, turn-of-the-century Czech artist, Frantisek Bílek.

14 **Prague tea-houses** • Page **196** Prague's hippified, smoke-free tea-houses are the perfect place to chill out after tramping the streets.

16 Malá Strana's terraced gardens • Page **68** Hidden behind the palaces of Malá Strana, these terraced gardens are the perfect inner-city escape.

15 Terezín • Page **169** Habsburg fortress outside Prague, turned into a "model Jewish ghetto" by the Nazis and now a chilling memorial to the Holocaust.

17 Stavovské divadlo • Page **94** Venue for the premiere of Mozart's *Don Giovanni*, Prague's oldest theatre is worth visiting for its architecture alone.

18 **Church of sv Mikuláš** • Page **64** Experience the theatre of the High Baroque in this landmark of Malá Strana.

19 **Astronomická věž** • Page **84** The central tower of the former Jesuit College allows access to a frescoed Baroque library and the best viewing gallery in the Staré Město.

20 **Prague pubs** • Page **205** With the best beer in the world on tap, Prague's pubs are not to be missed.

Contents

Using the Rough Guide

We've tried to make this Rough Guide a good read and easy to use. The book is divided into eight main sections, and you should be able to find whatever you want in one of them.

Front section

The front **colour section** offers a quick tour of Prague. The **introduction** aims to give you a feel for the place and tells you the best times to go. Next, the author rounds up his favourite aspects of Prague in the **things not to miss** section – whether it's fantastic architecture, great day-trips or a special café. Right after this comes the Rough Guide's full **contents** list.

Basics

The basics section covers all the **pre-departure** nitty-gritty to help you plan your trip, and the practicalities you'll want to know once you're there. This is where to find out how to get there, what paperwork you'll need, what to do about money and insurance, how to get around – in fact just about every piece of **general practical information** you might need.

The City

This is the heart of the Rough Guide, divided into user-friendly chapters, each of which covers a city district or day-trip destination. Every chapter starts with an **introduction** that helps you to decide where to go, followed by a tour of the sights.

Listings

Listings contains all the consumer information you need to make the most of your stay, with chapters on **accommodation**, places to **eat and drink**, **nightlife** and **culture** spots, **shopping** and **sports**.

Contexts

Read Contexts to get a deeper understanding of what makes Prague tick. We include a brief **history**, and a further reading section that reviews dozens of **books** relating to the city.

Language

The **language** section offers useful guidance for speaking Czech and pulls together all the vocabulary you might need on your trip, including a comprehensive **menu reader**. Here you'll also find a **glossary** of words and terms peculiar to the Czech Republic.

Index + small print

Apart from a **full index**, which includes maps as well as places, this section covers publishing information, credits and acknowledgements, and also has our contact details in case you want to send in updates, corrections or suggestions for improving the book.

Colour maps

The back colour section contains ten detailed **maps and plans** to help you explore the city close up and locate the sights, hotels, restaurants, cafés and pubs recommended in the guide.

Map and chapter list

- Colour section
- Contents
- **Ⓑ** Basics
- **❶** Hradčany
- **❷** Mala Strána
- **❸** Staré Město
- **❹** Josefov
- **❺** Nové Město
- **❻** Vyšehrad and the eastern suburbs
- **❼** Holešovice and the western suburbs
- **❽** Out from the city
- **❾** Accommodation
- **❿** Eating and drinking
- **⓫** Clubs and live venues
- **⓬** The arts and festivals
- **⓭** Sports
- **⓮** Shopping
- **⓯** Directory
- **Ⓒ** Contexts
- **Ⓛ** Language
- **Ⓘ** Index

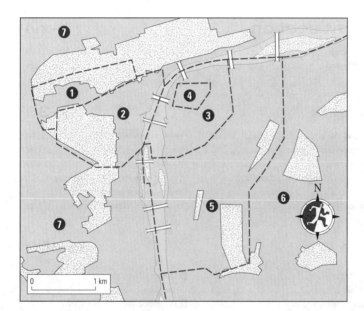

Contents

Contexts

Language

Index + small print

Colour maps

Map symbols

Maps are listed in the full index using coloured text

―――	Chapter division boundary	*(i)*	Information office
═══	Road	⊠	Post office
▬▬▬	Pedestrianized road	Ⓜ	Metro station
≋≋≋	Passageway	◉	Hotel
ⅢⅢⅢ	Steps	▣	Restaurant
-----	Path	▮	Building
―▬―	Railway	⊞	Church
– – –	Ferry route	✡	Synagogue
―――	Waterway	⊹	Christian cemetery
―――	Wall	⊡	Jewish cemetery
▲	Mountain peak	▨	Park
⊙	Statue		

Basics

Basics

Getting there

Unless you're coming from a neighbouring European country, the quickest and easiest way to get to Prague is by plane. There are direct flights from just about every European capital city, with flight time from London just under two hours. There are also one or two non-stop flights from North America, though you'll get a much wider choice – and often lower fares – if you fly via London or another European gateway.

Airfares depend primarily on availability, but they also vary with **season**, with the highest fares charged from Easter to October, and around Christmas and New Year. Fares will ordinarily be cheaper during the rest of the year, which is considered low season, though some airlines also have a shoulder season – typically April to mid-June and mid-September to October – and a correspondingly shorter high season. Note also that flying on weekends may add to the round-trip fare; price ranges quoted below assume midweek travel.

You can often cut costs by going through a **specialist flight agent** – either a consolidator, who buys up blocks of tickets from the airlines and sells them at a discount, or a **discount agent**, who in addition to dealing with discounted flights may also offer special student and youth fares and a range of other travel-related services such as travel insurance, rail passes, car rentals, tours and the like. Some agents specialize in **charter flights**, which may be cheaper than anything available on a scheduled flight, but again departure dates are fixed and withdrawal penalties are high.

Another option, if you're travelling from Britain or elsewhere in Europe, is to go by **train**, **bus** or car, though these usually take considerably longer than a plane and may not work out that much cheaper. For more details, see pp.13–15.

Booking flights online

Many airlines and discount travel websites offer you the opportunity to book your tickets online, cutting out the costs of agents and middlemen, and often giving you a discount at the same time. Good deals can often be found through discount or auction sites, as well as through the airlines' own websites.

Online booking agents and general travel sites

ⓦ **travel.yahoo.com** Incorporates a lot of Rough Guide material in its coverage of destination countries and cities across the world, with information about places to eat, sleep and other practicalities.

ⓦ **www.cheapflights.com** Bookings from the UK and Ireland only. Flight deals, travel agents, plus links to other travel sites.

ⓦ **www.cheaptickets.com** Discount flight specialists.

ⓦ **www.deckchair.com** Bob Geldof's online venture, drawing on a wide range of airlines.

ⓦ **www.etn.nl/discount.htm** A hub of consolidator and discount agent web links, maintained by the nonprofit European Travel Network.

ⓦ **www.expedia.com** Discount airfares, all-airline search engine and daily deals.

ⓦ **www.flyaow.com** Online air travel info and reservations site.

ⓦ **www.gaytravel.com** Gay online travel agent, concentrating mostly on accommodation.

ⓦ **goeasterneurope.about.com** US site with good links to discount airfares to, and accommodation in, Prague.

ⓦ **www.hotwire.com** Bookings from the US only. Last-minute savings of up to forty percent on regular published fares. Travellers must be at least 18 and there are no refunds, transfers or changes allowed. Log-in required.

ⓦ **www.lastminute.com** Offers good last-minute holiday package and flight-only deals.

ⓦ **www.orbitz.com** Discounted airline tickets from the US only.

ⓦ **www.priceline.com** Name-your-own-price website that has deals at around forty percent off standard fares. You cannot specify flight times (although you do specify dates) and the tickets are non-refundable, non-transferable and non-changeable.

ⓦ**www.skyauction.com** Bookings from the US only. Auctions tickets and travel packages using a "second bid" scheme. The best strategy is to bid the maximum you're willing to pay, since if you win you'll pay just enough to beat the runner-up regardless of your maximum bid.

ⓦ**www.smilinjack.com/airlines.htm** Lists an up-to-date compilation of airline website addresses.

ⓦ**www.travelocity.com** Destination guides, hot web fares and best deals for car hire, accommodation and lodging as well as fares. Provides access to the travel agent system SABRE, the most comprehensive central reservations system in the US.

ⓦ**www.travelshop.com.au** Australian website offering discounted flights, packages, insurance, online bookings.

Flights from Britain and Ireland

The most competitive airfares from Britain are with the no-frills **budget airlines**. At the time of going to press, Go was offering return fares from **Stansted** to Prague from around £100 upwards, with prices roughly the same from **Bristol** and **East Midlands** airports. British Midland's budget arm, bmibaby, was offering similar fares from East Midlands. Note, however, that the cheaper tickets need to be booked well in advance, and often apply to specific (early or late) flights on specific days, and are either non-refundable or only partially refundable, and non-exchangeable.

British Airways (BA) and Czech Airlines (ČSA) both have a wider choice of flight times from London to Prague; BA flies only from **Heathrow**, while ČSA flies from Heathrow, Stansted, **Birmingham** and **Manchester**. The national airlines are rarely the cheapest option, though their special offers can bring return fares down to as low as £120, though a fare between £150 and £200 is more common. ČSA operates a regular non-stop service from **Dublin** to Prague, costing around €350 return, though you may still find it cheaper to fly via London.

Finding the best deal involves ringing round, or checking the websites of a few of the discount specialist agents (see below), and comparing prices, routes and timings.

Students under 32 and those under 26 should enquire about discounts on scheduled flights, or contact the likes of STA Travel (see opposite). Note, however, that in peak season, discount flights are often booked up weeks in advance. If this is the case, it might be worth considering flying to a neighbouring European city such as Berlin, Leipzig or Vienna, all of which are around five hours' train ride away.

Numerous tour operators offer simple flight and accommodation **city breaks** to Prague, which for a short trip can often be much better value than travelling independently. Most of the companies listed below will put together some kind of package for you. Travelscene, for example, offers a three-night city break including flights and accommodation in a three-star hotel for around £350 in high season. If you're flying with Go, you can claim a discount if you book your accommodation through Hotel Connect.

Airlines

British Airways UK ☎0845/773 3377; Ireland ☎1800/626 747; ⓦwww.britishairways.com.
bmibaby UK ☎0870/264 2229; Ireland ☎01/407 3036; ⓦwww.bmibaby.com.
Czech Airlines (ČSA) London ☎020/7255 1898; Manchester ☎0161/489 0241; Ireland ☎01/814 4626; ⓦwww.csa.cz.
Go UK ☎0870/607 6543, www.go-fly.com.

Specialist agents and operators in Britain and Ireland

Bridgewater Travel ☎0161/703 3003, ⓦwww.bridgewater-travel.co.uk. Accommodation and package deals.
ČEDOK ☎020/7580 3778, ⓦwww.cedok.co.uk. Unreconstructed former state-owned tourist board offering flights, accommodation and package deals.
CIE Tours International Ireland ☎01/703 1888, ⓦwww.cietours.ie. General flight and tour agent.
Czech & Slovak Tourist Centre ☎020/7794 3263, ⓦwww.czech-slovak-tourist.co.uk. Accommodation, bus tickets, flights and lots more.
Czech Travel ☎01245/328 647, ⓦwww.czechtravel.freeuk.com. Rooms and flats for rent in Prague, plus flights.
Hotel Connect ☎020/8731 7000, ⓦwww.hotelconnect.co.uk. Accommodation in Prague.
Joe Walsh Tours Ireland ☎01/676 0991, ⓦwww.joewalshtours.ie. General budget fares agent.

Martin Randall Travel UK ☏020/8742 3355,
ⓦwww.martinrandall.com. Small-group cultural
tours led by experts on art, archeology and music.
McCarthy's Travel Ireland ☏021/427 0127,
ⓦwww.mccarthystravel.ie. General flight agent.
Neenan Travel Ireland ☏01/607 9900, ⓦwww
.neenantrav.ie. Specialists in European city breaks.
North South Travel UK ☏01245/608 291,
ⓦwww.northsouthtravel.co.uk. Friendly, competitive
travel agency, offering discounted fares worldwide –
profits are used to support projects in the developing
world, especially the promotion of sustainable tourism.
STA Travel UK ☏0870/1600 599, ⓦwww.statravel
.co.uk. Worldwide specialists in low-cost flights and
tours for students and under-26s, though other
customers welcome.
Student & Group Travel Ireland ☏01/677 7834.
Student and group specialists to Europe.
Trailfinders UK ☏020/7628 7628, Ireland ☏01/
677 7888, ⓦwww.trailfinders.com. One of the
best-informed and most efficient agents for
independent travellers.
Travelscene ☏0208/427 4445,
ⓦwww.travelscene.co.uk. Two-night breaks and
upwards in Prague.

Flights from the USA and Canada

Czech Airlines (ČSA) is the only airline to
offer non-stop flights from North America to
Prague. Its most frequent service is from
New York's JFK airport, with only a couple
of flights a week departing from **Toronto** and
Montréal. Flying time from New York to
Prague is about eight and a half hours;
Toronto to Prague is around ten hours. ČSA
occasionally code-shares with Delta, which
means through ticketing, good connections
and often competitive prices can be had
from other US cities such as Chicago, LA,
San Francisco and Washington.

Fares depend very much on the flexibility
of the ticket and on availability. Tickets tend
to be comparatively expensive if you buy
directly from ČSA, with an economy class
New York–Prague return costing between
$800 and $1000, and a Toronto–Prague
return rarely going below C$1200. By con-
trast, agents and consolidators regularly offer
New York–Prague return fares of between
$600 and $800, and Toronto–Prague return
fares of around C$1000. Note that the
cheaper fares usually mean that the ticket is
non-exchangeable and non-refundable.

You'll get a much wider choice of flights
and ticket prices if you opt for the **one- and
two-stop flights** offered by the major carri-
ers (a selection of which are listed below)
allowing you to depart from any number of
North American gateways via one of the
major European cities. Another option is to
fly into Berlin, Leipzig or Vienna, all of which
are around five hours by train from Prague. If
Prague is part of a longer European trip,
you'll also want to check out details of the
Eurail pass (see p.14).

Plenty of tour companies include a couple
of days in Prague as part of a whirlwind itinerary around the Czech Republic, but for a
more in-depth experience of Prague or the
surrounding region you'll want to join up with
a specialist group. Most of these offer independent **city breaks**; the cost per person for
a typical three-night stay sharing a double
room, with the round-trip airfare from New
York included, will start from around
$500–600.

Airlines

Air Canada ☏1-888/247-2262,
ⓦwww.aircanada.ca.
Air France US ☏1-800/237-2747; Canada
☏1-800/667-2747; ⓦwww.airfrance.com.
American Airlines ☏1-800/433-7300,
ⓦwww.aa.com.
Austrian Airlines ☏1-800/843-0002,
ⓦwww.aua.com.
British Airways ☏1-800/247-9297,
ⓦwww.britishairways.com.
Czech Airlines (ČSA) US ☏1-877/359-6629 or
☏212/765-6022; Canada ☏416/363-3174;
ⓦwww.czechairlines.com.
Delta Air Lines ☏1-800/241-4141,
ⓦwww.delta.com.
Lufthansa US ☏1-800/645-3880; Canada ☏1-
800/563-5954; ⓦwww.lufthansa-usa.com.
United Airlines ☏1-800/538-2929,
ⓦwww.ual.com.

Discount agents and tour operators

Airtech ☏1-877/247-8324 or ☏212/219-7000,
ⓦwww.airtech.com. Standby seat broker; also
deals in consolidator fares and courier flights.
Central Europe Holidays ☏1-800/800-8891,
ⓦwww.tourdeal.com/ceheurope. Tour packages to
Prague.

Council Travel ☎1-800/226-8624, ☏617/528-2091, ⊛www.counciltravel.com. Nationwide organization that mostly, but by no means exclusively, specializes in student/budget travel.

Escapade Tours ☎1-800/356-2405, ⊛www.isram.com. City breaks and multicity Czech packages.

Europe Train Tours ☎1-800/551-2085, ⊛www.ettours.com. Customized tours by rail, with special rates on Swiss Air and Finnair.

General Tours ☎1-800/221-2216, ⊛www.generaltours.com. City breaks to Prague.

New Frontiers/Nouvelles Frontières ☎1-800/677-0720, ⊛www.newfrontiers.com. French discount-travel firm based in New York City. Other branches in LA, San Francisco and Québec City.

Romantic Czech Tours ☎206/522-4559, ⊛www.romanticczechtours.com. Walking, biking, and customized tour operator specializing in Prague and Eastern Europe.

Skylink US ☎1-800/247-6659 or ☎212/573-8980; Canada ☎1-800/759-5465; ⊛www.skylinkus.com. Consolidator.

Summit International Travel ☎1-800/527-8664, ⊛www.summittours.com. Highly regarded specialists in the area. Walking, bicycling and car packages plus customized tours.

STA Travel ☎1-800/777-0112 or 1-800/781-4040, ⊛www.sta-travel.com. Worldwide specialists in independent travel; also student IDs, travel insurance, car rental, rail passes, etc.

TFI Tours International ☎1-800/745-8000 or ☎212/736-1140, ⊛www.lowestairprice.com. Consolidator.

Travac ☎1-800/872-8800, ⊛www.thetravelsite.com. Consolidator and charter broker with offices in New York City and Orlando.

Travel Avenue ☎1-800/333-3335, ⊛www.travelavenue.com. Full-service travel agent that offers discounts in the form of rebates.

Travel Cuts Canada ☎1-800/667-2887; US ☎1-866/246-9762; ⊛www.travelcuts.com. Canadian student-travel organization.

Flights from Australia and New Zealand

Flight time from **Australia and New Zealand** to Prague is over twenty hours, and can be longer depending on routes, with those flights touching down in Southeast Asia the quickest and cheapest on average. To reach Prague, you'll have to change planes in one of the main European gateways. Given the length of the journey involved, you might be better off including a night's stopover in your itinerary, and indeed some airlines include one in the price of the flight.

The cheapest direct scheduled flights to European gateways are usually to be found on one of the Asian airlines. Average return **fares** (including taxes) from eastern gateways to London are A$1500–2000 in low season, A$2000–2500 in high season (fares from Perth or Darwin cost around A$200 less). You'll then need to add A$100–200 onto all these for the connecting flight to Prague. Return fares from Auckland to London range between NZ$2000 and NZ$2500 depending on the season, route and carrier.

Airlines in Australia and New Zealand

Aeroflot Australia ☎02/9262 2233, ⊛www.aeroflot.com.

Air New Zealand Australia ☎13 24 76; New Zealand ☎0800/737 000; ⊛www.airnz.com.

Alitalia Australia ☎02/9262 3925, ⊛www.alitalia.com.

American Airlines Australia ☎1300/650 747, ⊛www.aa.com.

British Airways Australia ☎02/8904 8800; New Zealand ☎0800/274 847; ⊛www.britishairways.com.

Czech Airlines (ČSA) Australia ☎02/9247 7706, ⊛www.csa.cz/en.

Garuda Australia ☎02/9334 9970; New Zealand ☎09/366 1862; ⊛www.garuda-indonesia.com.

KLM Australia ☎1300/303 747; New Zealand ☎09/309 1782; ⊛www.klm.com.

Lauda Air Australia ☎02/9251 6155; New Zealand ☎09/522 5948; ⊛www.laudaair.com.

Lufthansa Australia ☎1300/655 727; New Zealand ☎09/303 1529; ⊛www.lufthansa.com.

Malaysia Airlines Australia ☎13 26 27; New Zealand ☎09/373 2741; ⊛www.mas.com.my.

Qantas Australia ☎13 13 13; New Zealand ☎09/661 901; ⊛www.qantas.com.au.

Singapore Airlines Australia ☎13 10 11; New Zealand ☎09/303 2129; ⊛www.singaporeair.com.

Sri Lankan Airlines Australia ☎02/9244 2234; New Zealand ☎09/308 3353; ⊛www.airlanka.com.

Swiss Australia ☎1800/221 339, ⊛www.swiss.com.

Thai Airways Australia ☎1300/651 960; New Zealand ☎09/377 3886; ⊛www.thaiair.com.

Virgin Atlantic Airways Australia ☎02/9244 2747; New Zealand ☎09/308 3377; ⊛www.virgin-atlantic.com.

Travel agents and tour operators in Australia and New Zealand

Australians Studying Abroad ☏ 02/9509 1955, ⊛ www.asatravinfo.com.au. Cultural, historical and political package tours of Prague and Bohemia.
Budget Travel New Zealand ☏ 09/366 0061 or ☏ 0800/808 040, ⊛ www.budgettravel.co.nz. Long-established agent with budget airfares and accommodation packages.
Destinations Unlimited New Zealand ☏ 09/373 4033. Discount fares with a good selection of tours and holiday packages.
Flight Centres Australia ☏ 13 31 33 or ☏ 02/9235 3522; New Zealand ☏ 09/358 4310; ⊛ www.flightcentre.com.au. Concentrates on discounted air fares.
Gateway Travel Australia ☏ 02/9745 3333, ⊛ www.russian-gateway.com.au. Packages to the Czech Republic.
Silke's Travel Australia ☏ 1800 807 860 or ☏ 02/8347 2000, ⊛ www.silkes.com.au. Gay and lesbian specialist travel agent.
STA Travel Australia ☏ 1300/733 035, ⊛ www.statravel.com.au; New Zealand ☏ 0508/782 872, ⊛ www.statravel.co.nz. Fare discounts for students and under-25s as well as student cards, rail passes and accommodation.
Student Uni Travel Australia ☏ 02/9232 8444, ⊛ australia@backpackers.net. Discounted airfares and student/youth travel specialists.
Trailfinders Australia ☏ 02/9247 7666, ⊛ www.trailfinders.com.au. Discounted flights, car rental, tailor-made tours, rail passes and RTW tours.

By train

You can travel from London to Prague overnight in around twenty hours by **train**. The fares, however, only really compete with standard scheduled airline tickets.

The routes

There are several possible routes from London to Prague via **Eurostar**. The quickest option is to catch the train just after 2pm from Waterloo, arriving in Brussels Midi an hour before the departure of the Brussels–Köln service. From **Köln**, there's an overnight service to Prague, which gets into the Czech capital just after 10am the following morning. If you set off a couple of hours earlier from Waterloo, and change at Brussels, Köln and **Frankfurt**, you can pick up an earlier

overnight service and arrive at around 8am in Prague.

Another option is to travel **via Berlin**. This route allows you to leave in the evening from Waterloo at around 7.30pm, picking up an overnight service from Brussels Midi and changing trains the following morning in Berlin, arriving in Prague in the middle of the afternoon. Travelling **via Paris** tends to be a bit more expensive, and with no direct nighttime service from Paris to Prague, you'll still have to change trains at Frankfurt to pick up the overnight service.

Although you can simply crash out on the seats on the overnight service from Köln to Prague, it makes sense to book a **couchette** which costs around £15 one-way in a six-berth compartment, rising to £20 in a four-berth compartment. Couchettes are mixed-sex and allow little privacy; for a bit more comfort, you can book a bed in a single-sex three-berth **sleeper** for around £35 one-way, or £45 for a two-berth compartment. You should be able to book your couchette or sleeper when you buy your ticket, but if you have any problems, contact German Railways (Deutsche Bahn) – see p.14. However you decide to sleep, you'll probably be woken up in the early hours of the morning when the train crosses the Czech border.

Tickets and passes

Fares for continental rail travel are much more flexible than they used to be, so it's worth shopping around for the best deal, rather than taking the first offer you get. The cheapest deals for a return ticket from London–Prague tend to hover around £200; tickets are usually valid for two months and allow as many stopovers as you want on the specified route. To qualify for the most heavily discounted fares, however, there are usually various restrictions: you may have to stay over a Saturday night, and your Eurostar ticket may be non-exchangeable and non-refundable. If you're travelling with one or more companions, you may be eligible for a further discount.

Those **under 26** can purchase discounted tickets from one of the rail agents listed on p.14, thus saving up to 25 percent on the return fare. Travellers **over 60** can also get discounts of up to thirty percent between, but not within, European countries by purchasing a **Rail Plus** card at a cost of £12. However, before you can buy this card, you must already possess a British Senior Rail Card (£18); both are valid for a year.

Virtually the only way **to buy** an international train ticket at the moment is via a travel agent or over the phone with one of the rail agents listed below. However, while Eurostar can book you as far as Paris or Brussels from any station in the UK, they can't book your onward travel; conversely, Rail Europe and the other national rail agents can only book your journey from London onwards – for travel within the UK, contact National Rail Enquiries (☎08457/484 950). Both European Rail and Trainseurope can book you from anywhere in the UK to anywhere in Europe. The only British stations that can sell you an international train ticket over the counter (further than Paris or Brussels) are Euston and Charing Cross in London.

If you're planning to visit Prague as part of a more extensive trip around Europe, it may be worth purchasing an **InterRail pass**, which gives you unlimited rail travel within certain countries; you must, however, have been resident in Europe for at least six months. InterRail tickets are currently zonal: to travel to Prague and back, you'll need at least a three-zone pass, costing £209 for one month for those under 26, and £299 a month for those aged 26 and over. Passes are not valid in the UK, though you're entitled to discounts in Britain and on Eurostar and cross-Channel ferries. Either way, though, you're only really going to get your money back if you do a lot of travelling.

North Americans, **Australians** and **New Zealanders** who don't qualify for the InterRail pass can obtain a **Eurail** pass, which comes in various forms, and must be bought before leaving home. For more information, and to reserve tickets, contact: Rail Europe in North America (US ☎1-877/456-7245; Canada ☎1-800/361-7245; ⊛www.raileurope.com); and CIT World Travel (☎02/9267 1255 or ☎03/9650 5510, ⊛www.cittravel.com.au) or Rail Plus (☎1300/555 003 or ☎03/9642 8644, ⊜info@railplus.com.au) in Australia.

Rail contacts

Belgian Railways UK ☎020/7593 2332, ⊛www.b-rail.be. Sells tickets from London across Europe, with discounts on journeys through Belgium.

European Rail ☎020/7387 0444, ⊛www .europeanrail.com. Rail specialists that consistently offer competitive prices on international rail tickets from anywhere in the UK.

Eurostar ☎0870/160 6600, ⊛www.eurostar.com. Latest fares and youth discounts (plus online booking) on the London–Paris and London–Brussels Eurostar service, and competitive add-on fares from the rest of the UK.

German Railways (Deutsche Bahn) UK ☎0870/243 5363, ⊛www.bahn.de. Competitive discounted fares for any journey from London across Europe, with very reasonable prices for those journeys that pass through Germany.

Rail Europe UK ☎0870/584 8848, ⊛www .raileurope.co.uk. SNCF-owned information and ticket agent for all European passes and journeys from London.

Trainseurope UK ☎020/8699 3654, ⊛www .trainseurope.co.uk. Agent specializing in organizing discounted international rail travel.

By bus

One of the cheapest ways to get to Prague is by **bus**. There are direct services from London's Victoria Station more or less daily throughout the year. Coaches tend to depart in the evening, arriving eighteen hours later in Prague's main bus terminal, Florenc, in the early afternoon. The journey is bearable (just about), but only really worth it if you absolutely can't find the extra cash for a budget flight. Prices between companies vary very slightly so it's worth ringing round to find the best deal; a return ticket can cost as little as £65. Addresses and telephone numbers for all current operators are given on p.15.

Another option worth considering if you're heading for other parts of Europe as well as Prague is a **Eurolines Pass**. The pass, which covers all the major cities in Europe (including Prague), is valid for fifteen days (£155/£130, over 26/under 26), thirty days (£229/£186) or sixty days (£267/£205). Prices outside the peak period (June to mid-Sept) are around thirty percent cheaper.

From mid-April to mid-October **Busabout** offers a hop-on, hop-off bus service, which calls at Prague, plus numerous other cities in western Europe. The **Consecutive Pass** allows unlimited travel from two weeks (£179/£159, over 26/under 26) to seven months (£699/£629); the **Flexible Pass** gives you anything from ten days' travel in two months (£169/£149) to 25 days in four months (£549/£449). There's a ten percent discount for those travelling before mid-May.

Bus contacts

Busabout ☎020/7950 1661, 🖱www.busabout .com. European bus passes. The passes are available from STA Travel (see p.12) in the US.
Capital Express ☎020/7243 0488, 🖱www.capitalexpressuk.com. Regular London to Prague services via Eurotunnel.
Eurolines UK ☎0870/514 3219; Republic of Ireland ☎01/836 6111; 🖱www.eurolines.co.uk. Tickets can also be purchased from any National Express agent – ☎0870/580 8080, 🖱www.gobycoach.com.
Kingscourt Express ☎0800/496 0001, 🖱www .kce.cz. Czech-based bus company running regular services from London to Prague via the ferry.

By car

With two or more passengers, **driving** to Prague can be relatively inexpensive. However, it is not the most relaxing option, unless you enjoy pounding along the motorway systems of Europe for the best part of a day and a night.

The **Eurotunnel** service through the Channel Tunnel doesn't significantly affect total travel times for drivers to the Czech Republic, though it does of course speed up the cross-Channel section of the journey. Eurotunnel operates a 24-hour service carrying cars, motorcycles, buses and their passengers to Calais. At peak times, services run every fifteen minutes, with the journey lasting 35 minutes. Off-peak fares start at around £300 return (passengers included) – no bargain, though special offers do appear from time to time.

The alternative cross-Channel options for most travellers are the conventional **ferry** links between Dover and Calais, Ostend or Zeebrugge. Fares vary enormously with the time of year, month and even day that you

travel, and the size of your car. If you book in advance, the cheapest off-peak summer fare on the Dover–Calais run, for example, can be as little as £170 return per carload. Journey times are usually around ninety minutes.

Once you've made it onto the Continent, you have some **1000km of driving** ahead of you. Theoretically, you could make it in twelve hours solid, but realistically it will take you longer. The most direct route from Calais or Ostend is via Brussels, Liège (Luik), Cologne (Köln), Frankfurt, Würzburg and Nuremberg (Nürnberg), entering the country at the **Waidhaus–Rozvadov** border crossing. Motorways in Belgium and Germany are free, but to travel on any motorways within the Czech Republic you need authorization in the form of a sticker or *dálniční známka*, which can be purchased from all border crossings and most garages and post offices. A ten-day sticker costs 100Kč, a month-long one costs 200Kč.

If you're travelling by car, you'll need proof of ownership, or a letter from the owner giving you permission to drive the car. A British or other EU driving licence is fine; all other drivers are advised to purchase an International Driving Licence. You also need a red warning triangle in case you break down, a first-aid kit (both these are compulsory in the Czech Republic), and a "Green Card" for third party insurance cover at the very least. An even better idea is to sign up with one of the national motoring organizations, who offer continental breakdown assistance and, in extreme circumstances, will get you and your vehicle brought back home if necessary.

Cross-Channel contacts

Eurotunnel ☎0870/535 3535, 🖱www.eurotunnel .com. Folkstone–Calais through the tunnel.
Hoverspeed ☎0870/240 8070, 🖱www .hoverspeed.co.uk. Dover to Calais and Ostend.
Norfolk Line ☎0870/870 1020, 🖱www.norfolkline .com. Dover to Dunkirk.
P&O Stena Line ☎0870/600 0600, 🖱www.posl.com. Dover to Calais and Zeebrugge.
Sea France ☎0870/571 1711, 🖱www.seafrance .com. Dover to Calais.

Red tape and visas

US, New Zealand and all EU nationals need only a full passport to enter the Czech Republic, though the passport itself must be valid for at least six months beyond your return date. US citizens can stay for up to thirty days; UK citizens can stay up to 180 days; all other EU citizens and New Zealanders can stay up to ninety days. All visitors must register with the police within three days of arrival (if you're staying in a campsite, hostel, pension or hotel, this will be done for you). Entry requirements do change, so if in doubt, check with your nearest embassy or consulate before you leave.

At the time of writing, Australians, Canadians and South Africans need a **visa** (valid for up to thirty days), which must be bought beforehand from a Czech embassy or consulate; prices vary (around £25 is the norm), and can take ten to fifteen working days to obtain by post. Along with your application form you'll need a valid passport and two passport photographs (four for a multiple entry visa) and a SAE if applying by post.

If you wish to extend your visa or your stay, you need to go to the Cizinecká policie (Foreigners' Police), Olšanská 2, Žižkov. You'll need either a really good excuse, or a **residence permit** (*občanský prükaz*), which is difficult to obtain unless you're studying in the country or have a job (and, therefore, a work permit). Many people avoid this bureaucratic nightmare – which can take up to six months – by simply leaving the country for a few days when their time runs out, making sure they get their passport stamped upon re-entry. However, the legality of this is somewhat doubtful, and the Prague police frequently clamp down on foreigners working or staying illegally.

Czech embassies and consulates abroad are listed below; for an updated list, plus their opening times, go to ⓦ www.mfa.cz. Foreign consulates and embassies in Prague are listed on p.232.

Czech embassies and consulates

Australia 169 Military Rd, Dover Heights, Sydney, NSW 2030 ☏ 02/9371 8887.
Austria Penzingerstrasse 11–13, 1140 Vienna ☏ 0222/894 2125.
Canada 541 Sussex Drive, Ottawa, Ontario K1N 6Z6 ☏ 613/562-3875; 1305 Avenue des Pins Ouest, Montréal, Quebec H3G 1B2 ☏ 514/849-4495.
Germany Wilhelmstrasse 44, 10117 Berlin ☏ 030/226 380.
Ireland 57 Northumberland Rd, Ballsbridge, Dublin 4 ☏ 01/668 1135.
New Zealand 48 Hair St, Wainuiomata, Wellington ☏ 44/939 1610.
South Africa 2 Fleetwood Ave, Claremont 7700, Cape Town ☏ 021/7979 835.
UK 26 Kensington Palace Gdns, London W8 4QY ☏ 020/7243 1115.
USA 3900 Spring of Freedom St, NW, Washington DC 20008 ☏ 202/274-9100; 1109 Madison Ave, New York, NY 10028 ☏ 212/535-8814; 10990 Wilshire Blvd, Suite 1100, Los Angeles, CA ☏ 310/473-0889.

Insurance

Even though EU health care privileges apply in the Czech Republic, you'd do well to take out an insurance policy before travelling to cover against theft, loss and illness or injury. Before paying for a new policy, however, it's worth checking whether you are already covered: some all-risks home insurance policies may cover your possessions when overseas, and many private medical schemes include cover when abroad. In Canada, provincial health plans usually provide partial cover for medical mishaps overseas, while holders of official student/teacher/youth cards in Canada and the US are entitled to meagre accident coverage and hospital in-patient benefits. Students will often find that their student health coverage extends during the vacations and for one term beyond the date of last enrolment.

After exhausting the possibilities above, you might want to contact a specialist travel insurance company, or consider the travel insurance deal we offer (see box). A typical travel insurance policy usually provides cover for the loss of baggage, tickets and – up to a certain limit – cash or cheques, as well as cancellation or curtailment of your journey. Most of them exclude so-called dangerous sports unless an extra premium is paid. Many policies can be chopped and changed to exclude coverage you don't need – for example, sickness and accident benefits can often be excluded or included at will. If you do take medical coverage, ascertain whether benefits will be paid as treatment proceeds or only after return home, and whether there is a 24-hour medical emergency number. When securing baggage cover, make sure that the per-article limit – typically under £500 – will cover your most valuable possession. If you need to make a claim, you should keep receipts for medicines and medical treatment, and in the event you have anything stolen, you must obtain an official statement from the police (see p.31).

Rough Guides travel insurance

Rough Guides offers its own travel insurance, customized for our readers by a leading UK broker and backed by a Lloyd's underwriter. It's available for anyone, of any nationality and any age, travelling anywhere in the world.

There are two main Rough Guide insurance plans: **Essential**, for basic, no-frills cover; and **Premier** – with more generous and extensive benefits. Alternatively, you can take out **annual multi-trip insurance**, which covers you for any number of trips throughout the year (with a maximum of sixty days for any one trip). Unlike many policies, the Rough Guides schemes are calculated by the day, so if you're travelling for 27 days rather than a month, that's all you pay for. If you intend to be away for the whole year, the Adventurer policy will cover you for 365 days. Each plan can be supplemented with a "Hazardous Activities Premium" if you plan to indulge in sports considered dangerous, such as skiing, scuba-diving or trekking.

For a policy quote, call the Rough Guide Insurance Line on UK freefone ☎0800/015 0906, US toll-free ☎1-866/220-5588 or, if you're calling from elsewhere ☎+44 1243/621 046. Alternatively, get an online quote or buy online at ⊛www.roughguidesinsurance.com.

ⓘ Information, websites and maps

If you want to do a bit of research on your trip before arriving in Prague, you should contact the Czech tourist board – known as the Czech Centre. The offices themselves have a handful of good maps and pamphlets to give away, and the staff are generally helpful and should be able to answer any queries you have about the country. There are also one or two fairly useful websites worth checking out (see below).

Tourist information offices

Once in Prague, the main tourist office is the **Prague Information Service** or **PIS** (Pražská informační služba), whose main branch is at Na příkopě 20, Nové Město (April–Oct Mon–Fri 9am–7pm, Sat & Sun 9am–5pm; Nov–March Mon–Fri 9am–6pm, Sat & Sun 9am–3pm; ⊛www.prague-info.cz). There are additional PIS offices in the main train station, Praha hlavní nádraží, and within the Staroměstská radnice on Staroměstské náměstí (same hours), plus a summer-only office in the Malá Strana bridge tower on the Charles Bridge. PIS staff speak English, but their helpfulness varies enormously; they can usually answer most enquiries, and can organize accommodation, sell maps, guides and theatre tickets.

PIS also distributes and sells some useful **listings** publications, including *Culture in Prague/Česká kultura* (⊛www.ceskakultura .cz), a monthly English-language booklet listing the major events, concerts and exhibitions, and a free fortnightly leaflet, *Do města/ Downtown* (⊛www.downtown.cz), which concentrates on cinema, art exhibitions and club listings. Another good source of information is the weekly **English-language paper**, *Prague Post* (⊛www.praguepost .com), which carries selective listings on the latest exhibitions, shows, gigs and events around the capital.

The PIS also sells the much vaunted **Prague Card**, which gives three days' free entry into over forty sights within the city for 490Kč. Given the average entry charge for a museum is only 50Kč, and the card doesn't include the sights of the Jewish Museum, you're not necessarily going to save much money. For another 200Kč, your Prague Card can also serve as a three-day public transport pass (see p.21), though again, it's worth it only if you're going to use the trams and metro a lot. All in all, the card may save you hassle, but probably not a lot of money.

Czech Centres abroad

Austria Herrengasse 17, 1010 Vienna ☏0222/535 2361.
Belgium Boulevard Leopold II Laan 262, 1080 Brussels ☏02/644 9527, ⊛www.czechcenter.be.
Germany Friedrichstrasse 206, 10969 Berlin ☏030/208 2592, ⊛www.czech-berlin.de.
Slovakia Hviezdoslavovo nám 8, 811 02 Bratislava ☏02/5920 3305, ⊛www.czc.sk.
UK 95 Great Portland St, London W1 5RA ☏020/7291 9920, ⊛www.czechcentre.org.uk.
USA 1109 Madison Ave, New York, NY 10028 ☏212/288-0830, ⊛www.czechcenter.com.

Useful websites

Czech language ⊛www.bohemica.com. Czech language and culture – especially language. You can learn it online and there are lots of links to Czech sites.
Directory ⊛www.pell-mell.cz. A directory of Prague-related web links.
Downtown/Do města ⊛www.downtown.cz. Prague's fortnightly listings leaflet online in English and Czech.
Maps ⊛www.mapy.cz. This site will provide you with a thumbnail map to help you find any hotel, restaurant, pub, shop or street in Prague (and elsewhere in the Czech Republic).
News ⊛www.praguedaily.com and ⊛www .ceskenoviny.cz/news. Daily online news from Prague, and weekly news from the Czech News Agency (ČTK).
Prague Post ⊛www.praguepost.cz. A very useful site, not just for getting the latest news, but also for

finding out what's on in Prague over the coming week.

Radio Prague www.radio.cz/english. An informative site well worth visiting, with updated news and weather as audio or text.

Tickets www.ticketpro.cz, www.ticketstream .cz or www.ticketsbti.cz. Three good sites for finding out what's on in Prague and booking tickets online.

Welcome to the Czech Republic www.czech .cz. Basic information on the country in English, and on the worldwide network of Czech Centres, run by the Czech Foreign Ministry.

Maps

For wandering round the centre of Prague, the **maps** in this book should be sufficient, but if you crave greater detail, or are staying out in the suburbs, you may wish to buy something more comprehensive. The best maps of Prague are produced by Kartografie Praha, whose 1:20,000 booklet (*plán města*) covers the whole city and includes the tram and bus routes, too. It's easy enough to get hold of maps once you've arrived in Prague, from the tourist office, bookstores or even your hotel, but if you want to buy one before you arrive, contact one of the map outlets listed opposite.

Arrival

Prague is one of Europe's smaller capital cities, with a population of just one and a quarter million, and its airport lies just over 10km northwest of the city centre, with only a bus link or taxi to get you into town. By contrast, both the international train stations and the main bus terminal are linked to the centre by the fast and efficient metro system.

By air

Prague's **Ruzyně** airport (☎220 111 111, www.csl.cz) is connected to the city by several local buses, the most direct of which is **bus #119** (daily 5am–midnight; every 15–20min; journey time 20min), which stops frequently and ends its journey outside Dejvická metro station. You can buy your ticket (see p.21) from the public transport (*DP*) information desk in arrivals (daily

7am–10pm), or from the nearby machines or newsagents. If you arrive after midnight, you can catch a night bus #510 to Divoká Šárka, the terminus for night tram #51, which will take you to Národní třída in the centre of town. More convenient if you've a lot of luggage is to take the ČEDAZ **express minibus service** (daily 5.30am–9.30pm; every 30min; ☎220 114 296), which stops first at Dejvická metro station, at the end of metro line A (journey time 20min), and ends up at náměstí Republiky (journey time 30min); the full journey currently costs 90Kč. The express minibuses will also take you straight to your hotel for around 360Kč per drop-off – a bargain if you're in a group.

Of course, it's easy enough to take a **taxi** from the airport into the centre, though Prague taxi drivers have a reputation for over-charging. If you do end up taking a taxi, head for "Airport Cars", which offer a "fixed price" system depending on your destination; fares start at 260Kč to the northwest of the city, but will be more like 350Kč for somewhere in the centre.

By train and bus

International trains arrive either at the old Art-Nouveau **Praha hlavní nádraží**, on the edge of Nové Město and Vinohrady, or at **Praha-Holešovice**, which lies in an industrial suburb north of the city centre. At both stations you'll find exchange outlets (there's even a branch of the PIS tourist office at Hlavní nádraží – see p.18), as well as a 24-hour left-luggage office and accommodation agencies (see p.183). Both stations are on metro lines, and Hlavní nádraží is only a five-minute walk from Václavské náměstí (Wenceslas Square). If you arrive late at night, there's a hostel in Hlavní nádraží itself (see p.190).

Domestic trains usually wind up at Hlavní

nádraží or the central **Masarykovo nádraží** on Hybernská, a couple of blocks east of náměstí Republiky. Slower trains and various provincial services arrive at a variety of obscure suburban stations: trains from the southwest pull into **Praha-Smíchov** (metro Smíchovské nádraží); trains from the east arrive at **Praha-Vysočany** (metro Českomoravská); trains from the west at **Praha-Dejvice** (metro Hradčanská); and trains from the south very occasionally rumble into **Praha-Vršovice** (tram #24 to Václavské náměstí).

If you're catching a **train out of Prague**, don't leave buying your ticket until the last minute, as the queues can be long and slow. You can buy international train tickets (*mezinárodní jízdenky*) at either Praha hlavní nádraží or Praha-Holešovice, or at the main office of ČEDOK on Na příkopě, in the centre of town.

Prague's main **bus** terminal is **Praha-Florenc** (metro Florenc), on the eastern edge of Nové Město, where virtually all long-distance international and domestic services terminate. It's a confusing (and ugly) place to end up, but it has a left-luggage office upstairs (daily 5am–11pm) and you can make a quick exit to the adjacent metro station. **Busabout buses** (see p.14) currently arrive at Arena Hostel, U výstaviště 1, Holešovice (metro Nádraží Holešovice).

City transport

The centre of Prague, where most of the city's sights are concentrated, is reasonably small and best explored on foot. At some point, however, in order to cross the city quickly or reach some of the more widely dispersed attractions, you'll need to use the city's cheap and efficient public transport system, comprising the metro and a network of trams and buses. To get a clearer picture, it's essential to invest in a city map (see p.19), which marks all the tram, bus and metro lines.

Prague's **public transport system** (*dopravní podnik* or *DP*; ❽ www.dp-praha .cz) used to have a simple ticketing system – not any more. Most Praguers simply buy monthly passes, and to avoid having to

understand the complexities of the single ticket system, you too are best off buying a travel pass (for more on which, see below). There are *DP* **information offices**, where you can also buy tickets and passes, at the airport (daily 7am–7pm), Nádraží Holešovice (Mon–Fri 7am–6pm) and the Můstek and Muzeum metro stations (daily 7am–9pm).

Tickets and passes

Probably the single most daunting aspect of buying a ticket is having to use the new ticket machines found inside all metro stations and at some bus and tram stops. Despite the multitude of buttons on the machines, for a single **ticket** (*lístek* or *jízdenka*) in the two central zones (*2 pásma*), there are just two basic choices. The 8Kč version (*zlevněná*) allows you to travel for up to fifteen minutes on the trams or buses, or up to four stops on the metro; it's known as a *nepřestupní jízdenka*, or "no change ticket", although you can in fact change metro lines (but not buses or trams). The 12Kč version (*plnocenná*) is valid for one hour at **peak times** (Mon–Fri 5am–8pm) – or an hour and a half off-peak – during which you may change trams, buses or metro lines as many times as you like, hence its name, *přestupní jízdenka*, or "changing ticket". Half-price tickets are available for children aged 6–14, bikes and other large objects; under-6s travel free.

If you're buying a ticket from one of the machines, you must press the appropriate button – press it once for one ticket, twice for two and so on – followed by the *výdej/enter* button, after which you put your money in. The machines do give change, but if you don't have enough coins, you may find the person on duty in the metro office by the barriers can give you change or sell you a ticket. Tickets can also be bought, en masse, and rather more easily, from a tobacconist (*tabák*), street kiosk, newsagent, PIS office or any place that displays the yellow *DP* sticker. When you enter the metro, or board a tram or bus, you must validate your ticket by placing it in one of the electronic machines to hand.

To save hassle, it's best to buy a **travel pass** (*časová jízdenka*). These are available for 24 hours (*na 24 hodin*; 100Kč), three days (*na 3 dny;* 200Kč), seven days (*na 7 dní*; 250Kč), fifteen days (*na 15 dní*; 280Kč), thirty days (*30 denní*; 560Kč), ninety days (*90 denní*; 1600Kč) or a year (*roční*; 5900Kč); no photos or ID are needed,

though you must write your name and date of birth on the reverse of the ticket, and punch it to validate when you first use it. All the passes are available from *DP* outlets, and the 24-hour pass is also available from ticket machines.

Most Praguers buy a monthly (*měsíční*), quarterly (*čtvrtletní*) or yearly (*roční*) pass, with an ID photo attached, which is why you see so few of them punching tickets. Passes with ID photos are slightly cheaper: 420Kč for the monthly; 1150Kč for the quarterly; 3800Kč for the yearly. To obtain one, simply present your ID and a passport-sized photo at the windows marked *DP* at major metro stations. There's nothing to stop people from freeloading on the system, of course, since there are no barriers. However, plain-clothes **inspectors** (*revizoři*) make spot checks and will issue an on-the-spot fine of 400Kč (800Kč if you don't cough up immediately) to anyone caught without a valid ticket or pass; controllers should show you their ID (a small metal disc), and give you a receipt (*paragon*).

Metro

Prague's futuristic, Soviet-built **metro** is fast, smooth and ultra-clean, running daily from 5am to midnight with trains every two minutes during peak hours, slowing down to every four to ten minutes by late in the evening. Its three lines (with a fourth planned) intersect at various points in the city centre and the route plans are easy to follow (see colour map at back of book).

The stations are fairly discreetly marked above ground with the metro logo, in green (line A), yellow (line B) or red (line C). The constant bleeping at metro entrances is to enable blind people to locate the escalators, which are a free-for-all, with no fast lane. Once inside the metro, it's worth knowing that *výstup* means exit and *přestup* will lead you to one of the connecting lines at an interchange. The digital clock at the end of the platform tells you what time it is and how long it was since the last train.

Trams

The electric **tram** (*tramvaj*) **system**, in operation since 1891, negotiates Prague's hills and cobbles with remarkable dexterity. Modern Škoda rolling stock is gradually being introduced, but many of Prague's trams (traditionally red, but often now plastered over with advertising) still date back to the 1950s. After the metro, trams are the fastest and most efficient way of getting around, running every six to eight minutes at peak times, and every five to fifteen minutes at other times – check the timetables posted at every stop (*zastávka*), which list the departure times from that specific stop. Note that it is the custom for younger folk (and men of all ages) to vacate their seat when an older woman enters the carriage.

Tram #22, which runs from Vinohrady to Hradčany via the centre of town and Malá Strana, is a good way to get to grips with the lie of the land, and a cheap way of sightseeing, though you should beware of pickpockets. From Easter to October, interwar **tram #91** runs from Výstaviště to náměstí Republiky via Malá Strana (Sat & Sun hourly 1–7pm) and back again; the ride takes forty minutes and costs 15Kč. **Night trams** (*noční tramvaje*; #51–58) run roughly every thirty to forty minutes from around midnight to 4.30am; the routes are different from the daytime ones, though at some point all night trams pass along Lazarská in Nové Město. For more tram routes, see the colour map at the back of the book.

Buses

You'll rarely need to get on a **bus** (*autobus*) within Prague itself, since most of them keep well out of the centre of town. If you're intent upon visiting the zoo or staying in some of the city's more obscure suburbs, though, you may need to use them: their hours of operation are similar to those of the trams (though generally less frequent), and route numbers are given in the text where appropriate. **Night buses** (*noční autobusy*) run just once an hour between midnight and 5am.

Out of Prague, you're more likely to find yourself using buses, though timetables are designed around the needs of commuters, and tend to fizzle out at the weekend. Most services are run by the state-owned **ČSAD** and depart from Prague's main bus terminal, Praha-Florenc (metro Florenc), which is run with train-like efficiency, though finding the right departure stand (*stání*) can be a daunting task. Some services, however, depart from Prague's suburban bus terminals; for example buses to Lidice (see p.179) depart from metro Dejvická. For most minor routes, simply buy your ticket from the driver; for popular long-distance routes, and for travel at peak times, it's best to try and book your seat in advance.

Bus **timetables** (@www.vlak-bus.cz) are even more difficult to figure out than train ones (see below), as there are no maps at any of the stations. In the detailed timetables, each service is listed separately, so you may have to scour several timetables before you discover when the next bus is. A better bet is to look at the departures and arrivals board. Make sure you check on which day the service runs, since many run only on Mondays, Fridays or at the weekend (see the section below on trains for the key phrases). Minor bus stops are marked with a rusty metal sign saying *zastávka*. If you want to get off, ask *já chci vystoupit?*; "the next stop" is *příští zastávka*.

Trains

The most relaxing way to day-trip from Prague is by **train** (*vlak*). Czech Railways, **České dráhy** or **ČD** (@www.cdrail.cz), runs two main types of train: *rychlík* (R) or *spěšný* (Sp) trains are the faster ones which stop only at major towns, while *osobní* (or *zastavkový*) trains stop at just about every station, averaging as little as 30kph. Fast trains are further divided into SuperCity (SC), which are first class only, EuroCity (EC) or InterCity (IC), for which you need to pay a supplement, and Expres (Ex).

Suburban *osobní* trains depart from a variety of stations (see arrival on p.20 for details). To buy a **ticket**, simply state your destination – if you want a return ticket (*zpáteční*), you must say so, though these are no cheaper than buying two singles. First-class carriages (*první třída*) exist only on fast trains. There are half-price **discount fares** for children under 16, and you can take two children under 6 for free (providing they don't take up more than one seat). There are even some "crèche carriages" on the slower trains, where those with children under 10 have priority over seats.

With very few English-speakers employed on the railways, it can be difficult getting **train information**. The larger stations have a simple airport-style arrivals and departures board, which includes information on delays under the heading *zpoždění*. Many stations have poster-style displays of arrivals (*příjezd*) and departures (*odjezd*), the former on white paper, the latter on yellow, with fast trains printed in red. All but the smallest stations also have a comprehensive display of **timings and route information** on rollers. These timetables may seem daunting at first, but with a little practice they should become decipherable. First find the route you need to take on the diagrammatic map and make a note of the number printed beside it; then follow the timetable rollers through until you come to the appropriate number. Some of the more common Czech notes at the side of the timetable are *jezdí jen v...* (only running on...), or *nejezdí v* or *nechodí v...* (not running on...), followed by a date or a symbol: a cross or an "N" for a Sunday, a big "S" for a Saturday, two crossed hammers for a weekday, "A" for a Friday and so on. Small stations may simply have a board with a list of departures under the title *směr* (direction) followed by a town. A platform, or *nástupiště*, is usually divided into two *kolej* on either side.

Boats

In the summer months there's a regular **boat** service on the River Vltava run by the PPS (*Pražská paroplavební společnost*; ☏224 930 017, ⊕www.paroplavba.cz) from just south of Jiráskův most on Rašínovo nábřeží. From April to October three or four boats a day run to Troja (see p.159) in the northern suburbs (April, Sept & Oct Sat & Sun; May–Aug daily). There are also very infrequent services north to Mělník (see p.168) and south to Slapy via Zbraslav.

In addition, the PPS also offers hour-long **boat trips** around Prague (April–Oct daily; 150Kč) – and less frequently to Slapy – on board a 1930s paddlesteamer. EVD (☏224 810 030, ⊕www.evd.cz), departing from Čechův most, near the *Hotel Intercontinental* at the far end of Pařížská, offers one-hour cruises (100Kč) or longer trips with food and drink thrown in. Another option is to hop aboard the much smaller boats run by Prague-Venice (☏221 108 407, ⊕www.prague-venice.cz), which depart for a half-hour meander over to the Čertovka by Kampa island (195Kč, including a free drink). The boats depart from the north side of the Charles Bridge on the Staré Město bank.

Taxis

Taxis come in all shapes and sizes, and, theoretically at least, are extremely cheap. However, if they think they can get away with it, many Prague taxi drivers will attempt to rip you off; the worst offenders, needless to say, hang out at the taxi ranks closest to the tourist sights. Officially, the initial fare on the meter should be 25Kč, plus 19Kč per kilometre within Prague. The best advice is to hail a cab or have your hotel or pension call you one, rather than pick one up at the taxi ranks. The following cab companies have fairly good reputations: Profitaxi ☏261 314 151; AAA ☏233 113 311.

Car rental

You really don't need a **car** in Prague, since much of the city centre is pedestrianized and the public transport system is so cheap and efficient. Should you want to drive out of Prague, however, **car rental** is easy to arrange, with all the major companies operating both downtown and out of Ruzyně airport. If you book in advance with a multinational you're looking at a whopping £60/$84 per day for a small car, £200/$280 a week. You'll get a much cheaper deal, however, if you go for a Škoda and book your car through a local agent (see p.24) once you've arrived in Prague; prices can be as low as £10/$14 a day, though language may be a problem. To drive a car in the Czech Republic, you need to be 18, but in order to rent a car, you'll need to be at least 21, have a clean licence, and have been driving for at least a year.

Rules and regulations on Czech roads are pretty stringent, with on-the-spot fines regularly handed out, up to a maximum of 500Kč. The basic rules are driving on the right (introduced by the Nazis in 1939); compulsory wearing of seat belts; headlights on at all times (Nov–March); no under-12s in the

B

front seat, and no alcohol at all in your blood when you're driving. Watch out for restricted streets, most notably Wenceslas Square, and give way to pedestrians crossing the road when turning left or right, even when you've been given a green light. Theoretically, Czechs are supposed to give way to pedestrians at zebra crossings, but few do. However, you must give way to trams, and if there's no safety island at a tram stop, you must stop immediately and allow passengers to get on and off.

Speed limits are 130kph on motorways, 90kph on other roads and 50kph in all built-up areas. In addition, there's a special limit of 30kph for level crossings (you'll soon realize why if you try ignoring it). If you want to use one of the motorways outside Prague, you must have a special tax disc (see p.15 for more details). As in other continental countries, a yellow diamond means you have right of way; a black line through it means you don't. If you have **car trouble**, dial ☎154 at the nearest phone and wait for assistance.

Petrol (*benzín*) is relatively inexpensive compared to the EU (and particularly the UK). It comes in two types: *super* (96 octane) and *special* (90 octane); diesel (*nafta*) is also available. **Lead-free** petrol (*natural* or *bezolovnatý*) is available from most petrol stations in and around Prague, many of which are open 24 hours.

Vehicle crime is on the increase and western cars are a favourite target – never leave anything visible or valuable in the car. The other big nightmare is **parking**. There are now three colour-coded parking zones, with pay-and-display meters: the orange zone allows you to park for up to two hours; the green zone allows you up to six hours; the blue zone is for locals only. Illegally parked cars will either be clamped or towed away – if this happens, phone ☎158 to find out the worst. If you're staying outside the centre, you'll have no problems; if you're at a hotel in the centre, they'll probably have a few parking spaces reserved for guests, though whether you'll find one vacant is another matter. Otherwise, your best option is to park near one of the metro stations out of the centre, several of which have park-and-ride schemes: try Hradčanská, Opatov or Skalka.

Rental agencies abroad

Alamo US ☎1-800/522-9696, ⊛www.alamo.com.
Auto Europe US ☎1-800/223-5555; Canada ☎1-888/223-5555; ⊛www.autoeurope.com.
Avis Australia ☎13 63 33; Canada ☎1-800/272-5871; Ireland ☎01/605 7500; New Zealand ☎0800 655 111 or ☎09/526 2847; UK ☎0870/606 0100; US ☎1-800/331-1084; ⊛www.avis.com.
Budget Australia ☎1300/362 848; Ireland ☎01/9032 7711; New Zealand ☎0800/652 227 or ☎09/976 2222; UK ☎0800/181 181; US ☎1-800/527-0700; ⊛www.budgetrentacar.com.
Hertz Australia ☎13 30 39; Canada ☎1-800/263-0600; Ireland ☎01/676 7476; New Zealand ☎0800/654 321; UK ☎0870/844 8844; US ☎1-800/654-3001; ⊛www.hertz.com.
Holiday Autos UK ☎0870/400 00 99; Ireland ☎01/872 9366; ⊛www.holidayautos.com.
National Australia ☎13 10 45; New Zealand ☎0800/800 115 or ☎03/366 5574; UK ☎0870/5365 365; US ☎1-800/227-7368; ⊛www.nationalcar.com.
Thrifty Australia ☎1300/367 227; New Zealand ☎09/309 0111; UK ☎01494/751 600; US ☎1-800/367-2277; ⊛www.thrifty.com.

Rental agencies in Prague

Avis Klimentská 46, Nové Město ☎221 851 229, ⊛www.avis.cz.
Cernis Opletalova 55, Nové Město ☎ 603 590 380.
Czechocar Kongresové centrum 5 května 65, Nusle ☎261 222 079, ⊛www.czechocar.cz.
Hertz Karlovo nám. 28, Nové Město ☎220 102 424, ⊛www.hertz.cz.

Cycling

Cycling is seen as more of a leisure activity in the Czech Republic than a means of transport. Prague has a handful of brave cycle couriers but the combination of cobbled streets, tram lines and sulphurous air is enough to put most people off. Facilities for **bike rental** are still not that widespread, but if you're determined to give cycling a go, head for City Bike, Králodvorská 5, Staré Město (☎776 180 284); they also organize group rides through Prague. A bike (*kolo*) needs a half-price ticket to travel on the metro or the train (they're not allowed on trams and buses); they travel in the guard's van on trains, and in the last carriage of the metro.

Costs, money and banks

In general terms, Prague is still incredibly cheap for westerners. The one exception is accommodation, which is comparable with many EU countries. At the time of writing, inflation was pretty much under control, though before you get to thinking everything is rosy in the Czech Republic, it's worth bearing in mind that the average monthly wage for Czechs is currently around 15,000Kč (£300/$450).

You'll find more precise costs for accommodation, food and drink in the relevant sections of the book: see "Accommodation" (p.182) and "Eating and Drinking" (p.192). At the bottom end of the scale, if you stay in a hostel and stick to pubs and takeaways, you could get by on as little as £10/$14 a day. If you stay in private accommodation or cheapish hotels, and eat in slightly fancier restaurants, then you could easily spend £25/$35 a day. The good thing about Prague, however, is that once you've accounted for your room, most restaurants, pubs, museums and galleries, beer and even taxis and nightclubs are far from expensive.

Tipping is normal practice in cafés, bars, restaurants and taxis, though this is usually done by simply rounding up the total. For example, if the waiter tots up the bill and asks you for 74Kč, you should hand him a 100Kč note and say "take 80Kč".

Czech currency

The currency in the Czech Republic is the Czech crown or *koruna česká* (abbreviated to Kč or CZK), which is divided into one hundred relatively worthless hellers or *halíře* (abbreviated to h). At the time of going to press there were around 50Kč to the pound sterling, 30Kč to the Euro and around 35Kč to the US dollar. For the most up-to-date exchange rates, consult the useful currency converter websites @www.oanda.com or @www.xe.com.

Notes come in 20Kč, 50Kč, 100Kč, 200Kč, 500Kč, 1000Kč and 2000Kč (less frequently 5000Kč) denominations; coins as 1Kč, 2Kč, 5Kč, 10Kč, 20Kč and 50Kč, plus 10h, 20h and 50h.

Travellers' cheques and credit cards

Although they are the traditional way to carry funds, **travellers' cheques** are no longer the cheapest nor the most convenient option – bank cards are better, see below – although they do offer safety against loss or theft. The usual fee for buying travellers' cheques is one or two percent, though this fee may be waived if you buy the cheques through a bank where you have an account. Be sure to keep the purchase agreement and a record of the cheques' serial numbers safe and separate from the cheques themselves. In the event that cheques are lost or stolen, the issuing company will expect you to report the loss forthwith to their office in Prague; most companies claim to replace lost or stolen cheques within 24 hours.

Credit cards are a very convenient way of carrying your funds, and can be used either in ATMs or over the counter. Mastercard, Visa and American Express are accepted just about everywhere. Remember that all cash advances are treated as loans, with interest accruing daily from the date of withdrawal; there may be a transaction fee on top of this. However, you may be able to make withdrawals from **ATMs** in Prague using your **debit card**, which is not liable to interest payments, and the flat transaction

Cancelling credit cards

To cancel lost or stolen credit cards whilst in Prague, phone the following numbers:
American Express ☎222 800 111.
Diners Club ☎267 314 485.
Mastercard/Access ☎261 354 650.
Visa ☎224 125 353.

fee is usually quite small – your bank will be able to advise on this. Make sure you have a personal identification number (PIN) that's designed to work overseas.

Changing money

The 24-hour exchange desk at the **airport** run by the Československá obchodní banka is, somewhat surprisingly, an excellent place to change money, regularly charging a mere one or two percent commission. Most Czech **banks** will be prepared to change travellers' cheques and give cash advances on credit cards – look for the window marked *směnárna*. Commissions at banks are fairly reasonable (generally under three percent), but the queues and the bureaucracy can mean a long wait. Quicker, but more of a rip-off in terms of either commission or exchange rate, are the exchange outlets which can be found on just about every street corner in the centre of Prague.

Banking hours are usually Monday to Friday 8am to 5pm, often with a break at lunchtime. Outside these times, you may find the odd bank open, but otherwise you'll have to rely on exchange outlets and international hotels.

Wiring money

Having money wired from home using one of the companies listed below is never conven-

ient or cheap, and should be considered a last resort. It's also possible to have money wired directly from a bank in your home country to a bank in the Czech Republic, although this is likely to take a couple of days and will cost around £25/$40 per transaction. If you can last out the week, then an **international money order**, exchangeable at any post office, is by far the cheapest way of sending money. If you're in really dire straits, get in touch with your **consulate** in Prague, who will usually let you make one phone call home free of charge, and will – in worst cases only – repatriate you, but will never, under any circumstances, lend you money.

Money-wiring companies

American Express Moneygram
Australia ☎1800/230 100; New Zealand
☎09/379 8243 or ☎0800/262 263; UK and
Republic of Ireland ☎0800/6663 9472; US and
Canada ☎1-800/926-9400;
ⓦwww.moneygram.com.
Thomas Cook Britain ☎01733/318 922; Canada
☎1-888/823-4732; Northern Ireland ☎028/9055
0030; Republic of Ireland ☎01/677 1721; US ☎1-
800/287-7362; ⓦwww.us.thomascook.com.
Western Union Australia ☎1800/649 565; New
Zealand ☎09/270 0050; Republic of Ireland
☎1800/395 395; UK ☎0800/833 833; US and
Canada ☎1-800/325-6000;
ⓦwww.westernunion.com.

☎ Post, phones and email

Czech telecommunications have come a long way in the last ten years. The phone system, in particular, has improved enormously and has recently undergone a radical overhaul, with all numbers within the country now made up of nine digits. Czechs are also keen web-users and access to the internet is possible in numerous cafés in Prague.

Post

The **main post office** (*pošta*) in Prague is at Jindřišská 14 (☎221 131 111), just off Wenceslas Square. Designed in ornate neo-Renaissance style, the building is open daily

7am to 8pm. The chief problem, once inside, is making sure you queue at the right counter – look for the appropriate sign in order to buy *známky* (stamps); *telefonní karty* (phone cards) or send *balíky* (parcels). For a

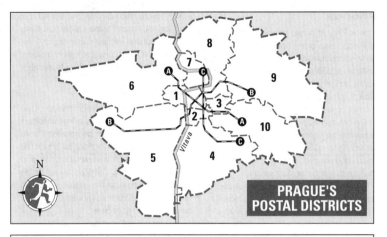

PRAGUE'S POSTAL DISTRICTS

1. Hradčany, Malá Strana, Staré Město, Josefov and Nové Město.
2. Nové Město, Vinohrady, Vyšehrad and Nusle.
3. Vinohrady and Žižkov.
4. Nusle, Podolí, Braník, Krč and the southeastern suburbs.
5. Smíchov and the southwestern suburbs

6. Dejvice, Střešovice, Břevnov and the northwestern suburbs
7. Holešovice, Bubeneč and Troja
8. Karlín, Libeň and the northern suburbs
9. Vysočany and the northeastern suburbs
10. Vršovice, Strašnice and the eastern suburbs

24-hour post office, go to Hybernská 15, by Masarykovo nádraží. Each postal district in Prague has several post offices, though these have far less comprehensive services, and are usually closed at the weekend.

Poste restante (pronounced as five syllables in Czech) letters to Prague will automatically arrive at the main post office mentioned above (the postcode is 110 00 PRAHA 1), though theoretically you may use any post office. Alternatively, American Express, at Václavské náměstí 56 (daily 9am–7pm), will hold mail for a month for credit card and cheque holders.

Outbound post is reasonably reliable, with letters or cards taking around five working days to Britain and Ireland, and one week to ten days to North America or Australasia.

You can buy **stamps** from newsagents, tobacconists and some kiosks, as well as at the post offices. Postal charges at the time of going to print were 9Kč for postcards within Europe and 12Kč to North America.

To send a **parcel over 2kg** (but below 15kg) you must go to the Pošta-Celnice customs parcel office at the junction of Plzeňská and Vrchlického in Prague 5 (tram #4, #7, #9 or #10 to stop Klamovka from metro Anděl). After filling in two separate forms for shipping and customs, you then have a choice of sending your parcel by ship, air or express. Alternatively, you can save a lot of hassle, and get the parcel there in no time at all, by paying considerably more at a courier company such as DHL (☎220 300 111, ⊛www.dhl.cz).

Addresses

The street name is always written before the number in Prague **addresses**. The word for street (*ulice*) is either abbreviated to *ul.* or missed out altogether – Celetná ulice, for instance, is commonly known as Celetná. Other terms often abbreviated are *náměstí* (square), *třída* (avenue), and *nábřeží* (embankment), which become *nám.*, *tř.* and *nábř.* respectively. Prague is divided into numbered **postal districts** (see map above) – these are too large to be very much help in orientation, so in this guide, we have generally opted for the names of the smaller historic districts as they appear on street signs, for example Hradčany, Nové Město, Smíchov, etc.

Phones

The majority of public phones in the centre of Prague take only **phone cards** (*telefonní karty*), currently available in 50, 100 and 150 units from post offices, tobacconists and some shops (prices vary). You can make international calls from all card phones, though be warned that rates are expensive. There are instructions in English, and if you press the appropriate button the language on the digital read-out will change to English. If you have any problems, ring ☎1181 to get through to international information.

In **coin-operated phones**, you need to insert a minimum of 3Kč to make a local call, 5Kč for long distance – if you stock up with enough coins, it is perfectly possible to make an international phone call. The **dialling tone** is a short followed by a long pulse; the **ringing tone** is long and regular; **engaged** is short and rapid (not to be confused with the connecting tone which is very short and rapid). The standard Czech response is *prosím*; the word for "extension" is *linka*.

You can also make phone calls (including reverse-charge or collect calls) from a **telephone exchange** like the one at Hybernská 15. Write down the town and number you want, leave a deposit of around 200Kč and wait for your name to be called out. Calls from a telephone exchange cost slightly less, but avoid making any calls from hotels, where the surcharge is usually outrageous.

Email

One of the best ways to keep in touch while travelling is to sign up for a **free internet email address** that can be accessed from anywhere, for example YahooMail or Hotmail – accessible through ⍟www.yahoo.com and ⍟www.hotmail.com. Once you've set up an account, you can use these sites to pick up and send mail from any internet café, or hotel with internet access

You can get online at numerous cafés and bars in Prague, including unlikely places such as the *Obecní dům* (see p.199) and *Bohemia Bagel* (see p.194). However, Prague's best specialist **cybercafé** is the funky *Terminal Bar*, Soukenická 6, Nové Město (daily 10am–2am; metro náměstí Republiky).

For details of how to plug your lap-top in when abroad, plus information on country codes around the world, and electrical systems in different countries, check out the useful website ⍟www.kropla.com.

Useful telephone numbers

Prague telephone numbers
In September 2002, all Czech regional prefixes became an integral part of telephone numbers. Thus in Prague, the first digit of all phone numbers is now **2** and it is necessary to dial this even when calling from within the city. All Prague numbers should therefore contain nine digits, beginning with a 2.

Phoning Prague from abroad
From Britain & Ireland: ☎00 + 420 (Czech Republic) + number.
From the USA & Canada: ☎011 420 (Czech Republic) + number.
From Australia & New Zealand: ☎0011 420 (Czech Republic) + number.

Phoning abroad from Prague
To the UK: ☎0044 + area code minus zero + number.
To the Republic of Ireland: ☎00353 + area code minus zero + number.
To the USA & Canada: ☎001 + area code minus zero + number.
To Australia: ☎0061 + area code minus zero + number.
To New Zealand: ☎0064 + area code minus zero + number.

The media

You'll find the full range of foreign newspapers at the kiosks on Wenceslas Square and elsewhere. They're generally a day old, though one that you can buy on the day of issue is the European edition of *The Guardian*, printed in Frankfurt (it arrives on the streets of Prague around mid-morning).

The Prague Post (🕸www.praguepost.com) is an English-language weekly aimed at the expat community, but good for visitors, too; it's a quality paper with strong business coverage and a useful pull-out listings section (for more on listings, see p.18). In the **magazine** market, you'll find the best coverage of contemporary Czech politics in English in *The New Presence/Nová přítomnost*, a bilingual current affairs magazine, directly inspired by the Masaryk-funded *Přítomnost*, which was one of the leading periodicals of the First Republic. Various arty magazines run by expats have come and gone over the years so it's worth calling in at one of Prague's English-language bookstores (see p.228) for the latest titles.

It's a sign of the times that the majority of **Czech newspapers** are German-owned. The only Czech-owned paper is the left-wing *Právo*, formerly the official mouthpiece of the Communist Party (when it was known as *Rudé právo* or "Red Justice"). Its chief competitor is *Mladá fronta dnes*, former mouthpiece of the Communist youth movement, now a very popular centre-right daily. *Lidové noviny* (the best-known *samizdat* or underground publication under the Communists and the equivalent of *The Times* under the First Republic) is now a much less respected right-wing daily, while the orange-coloured *Hospodáské noviny* is the Czech equivalent of the *Financial Times* or *Wall Street Journal*. The country's most popular tabloid is *Blesk*, a sensationalist tabloid with lurid colour pictures, naked women and reactionary politics. If all you want, however, is yesterday's (or, more often than not, the day before yesterday's) international sports results, pick up a copy of the daily *Sport*.

TV and radio

Česká televize's two state-owned **TV channels**, ČT1 and ČT2, have both been eclipsed as far as ratings go by the runaway success of the commercial channel, Nova. The latter features lots of American sitcoms dubbed into Czech, plenty of game shows, striptease weather and comprehensive coverage of Czech football. Prima, the other commercial channel, has yet to make any significant inroads into Nova's audience monopoly. ČT2 is your best bet for foreign films with subtitles; it also shows news in English from the BBC on Monday to Friday at 8am, and on Saturday and Sunday at 7am.

On the **radio**, the BBC World Service (🕸www.bbc.co.uk/worldservice) now broadcasts loud and clear on 101.1FM, mostly in English, with occasional bits of Czech programming. The state-run Český rozhlas has four stations: ČR1 Radiožurnál (94.6FM), which is mainly current affairs; ČR2 (91.3FM), which features more magazine-style programming; Regina (92.6FM), which features news and pop music; and ČR3 Vltava (105FM), which plays classical music. Havel broadcasts his presidential Sunday evening chat on ČR1; an English-language news summary goes out Monday to Friday at 5.30pm. The three top commercial channels are Evropa 2 (88.2FM), Radio Bonton (99.7FM) and Radio Kiss 98 FM (98FM), which dish out bland Euro-pop. More interesting is Radio 1 (91.9FM), which plays a wide range of indie rock.

Opening hours and public holidays

Shops in Prague are generally open Monday to Friday from 9am to 5pm, though most supermarkets and tourist shops stay open later, until 6 or 7pm. Smaller shops may close for lunch for an hour some time between noon and 2pm. Some shops close by noon or 1pm on Saturday, and only a few open on Sunday. Most traditional pubs tend to close between 10 and 11pm, with food often difficult to obtain after 9pm. However, there are plenty of late-night bars, where you can continue drinking, and restaurants that stay open much later.

Museums, galleries and churches

Opening hours for **museums and galleries** are generally 10am to 6pm every day except Monday (when they are closed) all year round. Full opening hours are detailed in the text. Ticket prices to museums and galleries range between 50Kč and 100Kč, and are listed in the text – one or two major sights charge a great deal more, most notably the sights of the Jewish Museum (see p.103).

Getting into **churches** can present more of a problem. Some of the more central ones operate in much the same way as museums and occasionally even have an entry charge. Most churches, however, are kept locked, with perhaps just the vestibule open, allowing you at least a glimpse of the interior, opening fully only for worship in the early morning (around 7 or 8am on weekdays, more like 10am on Sundays) and/or the evening (around 6 or 7pm). Sights of the Jewish Museum close before dusk on Friday, and re-open again on Sundays.

National holidays

National holidays were always a potential source of contention under the Communists, and they remain controversial even today.

May Day, once a nationwide compulsory march under dull Commie slogans, remains a public holiday, though only the skinheads, anarchists and die-hard Stalinists take to the streets nowadays. Of the other *slavné májové dny* (Glorious May Days), as they used to be known, **May 5**, the beginning of the 1945 Prague Uprising, has been binned, and VE Day is now celebrated along with the western Allies on **May 8**, and not on May 9, as it was under the Communists, and still is in Russia. September 28, the feast day of the country's patron saint, St Wenceslas, is now Czech State Day. Strangely, however, October 28, the day on which the First Republic was founded in 1918, is still celebrated, despite being a "Czechoslovak" holiday (and, for a while, Communist Nationalisation Day).

National holiday dates

January 1 New Year's Day
Easter Monday
May 1 May Day
May 8 VE Day
July 5 Introduction of Christianity
July 6 Death of Jan Hus
September 28 Czech State Day

"Closed for technical reasons"

Don't be too surprised if one or two of Prague's museums and galleries are "closed for technical reasons", "closed due to illness", or, more permanently, "closed for reconstruction". Notices are rarely more specific than that, but the widespread shortage of staff and funds is often behind the closure. It's impossible to predict what will be closed when, but it's a good idea to make alternative plans when visiting galleries and museums, just in case.

October 28 Foundation of the Republic
November 17 Battle for Freedom and Democracy Day
December 24 Christmas Eve

December 25 Christmas Day
December 26 St Stephen's Day

Trouble and the police

Prague has experienced a dramatic rise in crime since 1989. The Czech papers are full of the latest robbery, mafia shooting or terrorist intrigue. The police, meanwhile, are regarded by most Czechs as corrupt, incompetent and compromised by their Communist past. However, you shouldn't be unduly paranoid: the crime rate is still very low compared with most European or North American cities. Pickpockets are the biggest hassle, especially in summer around the most popular tourist sights and on the trams and metro.

There are two main types of police nowadays: the Policie and the Městská policie. The **Policie**, with white shirts, navy blue jackets and grey trousers, are the national force, with the power of arrest, and are under the control of the Ministry of the Interior. If you do need the police, though – and above all if you're reporting a serious crime – you should always go to the **Městská policie** (municipal police), run by the Prague city authorities, distinguishable by their all-black uniforms. The main central police station is at Bartolomějská 6, Staré Město (metro Národní třída).

In addition, there are various private security guards, who also dress in black – hence their nickname, *Černé šerií* (Black Sheriffs) – employed mostly by hotels and banks. They are allowed to carry guns, but have no powers of arrest, and you are not legally obliged to show them your ID.

Avoiding trouble

Almost all the problems encountered by tourists in Prague are to do with **petty crime** – mostly theft from cars and hotel rooms – rather than more serious physical confrontations. Sensible precautions include making photocopies of your passport, leaving passport and tickets in the hotel safe and noting down travellers' cheque and credit card numbers. If you have a car, don't leave anything in view when you park it, and take the

cassette/radio with you if you can. Vehicles are rarely stolen, but luggage and valuables left in cars do make a tempting target and rental cars are easy to spot.

In theory, you're supposed to carry some form of **identification** at all times, and the police can stop you in the street and demand it. In practice, they're rarely bothered if you're clearly a foreigner (unless you're driving). In any case, the police are now so deferential that they tend to confine themselves to socially acceptable activities like traffic control and harassing Romanies.

What to do if you're robbed

If you are unlucky enough to have something stolen, you will need to **go to the police** to report it, not least because your insurance company will require a police report. It's unlikely that there'll be anyone there who speaks English, and even less likely that your belongings will be retrieved but, at the very least, you should get a statement detailing what you've lost for your insurance claim. Try the phrase *byl jsem oloupen* (pronounced

Emergencies

Ambulance ☎155
Police ☎158
Fire ☎150

something like "bill sem ollo-pen)" or (if you're a woman) *byla jsem oloupena* – "I have been robbed".

Sexual harassment

As far as **sexual harassment** is concerned, things are, if anything, marginally less intimi-dating than in Western Europe, although without the familiar linguistic and cultural signs, it's easier to misinterpret situations. Specific places to avoid going after dark include Wenceslas Square, Uhelný trh, and the main train stations, Hlavní nádraží and nádraží Holešovice.

Travellers with disabilities

Under the Communists very little attention was paid to the needs of the disabled. Attitudes are slowly changing – since 1994 all new buildings have to provide dis-abled access – but there is still a long way to go, and the country's chronic short-age of funds makes matters worse.

Transport is a major problem, since buses and all except the newest trams are virtually impossible for wheelchairs, though some metro stations now have facilities for the dis-abled, and the two railway stations (Hlavní nádraží and nádraží Holešovice) actually have self-operating lifts. Prague's cobbles, and general lack of ramps, make life hard even on the streets.

At the time of writing, none of the **car rental** companies could offer vehicles with hand controls in Prague. For help and advice obtaining one, contact the local Association of Disabled People (*Sdružení zdravotné postižených*), Karlínské nám. 12 (☎224 816 997, ext 238). If you're driving to Prague, most cross-Channel ferries now have adequate facilities, as does British Airways for those who are flying.

For a list of wheelchair-friendly hotels, restaurants, metro stations and so forth, order the **guidebook** *Accessible Prague/Přístupná Praha* from the Prague Wheelchair Association (*Pražská organizace vozíčkářů*), Benediktská 6, Staré Město (☎224 827 210, ☻www.pov.cz). The asso-ciation can organize an airport pick-up if you contact them well in advance, and can help with transporting wheelchairs.

Contacts for travellers with disabilities

UK and Ireland

Access Travel 6 The Hillock, Astley, Lancashire M29 7GW ☎01942/888 844, ☻www.access-travel.co.uk. Tour operator that can arrange flights, transfer and accommodation. This is a small business, personally checking out places before recommendation. ATOL bonded, established seven years.

Holiday Care 2nd floor, Imperial Building, Victoria Rd, Horley, Surrey RH6 7PZ ☎01293/774 535, Minicom ☎01293/776 943, ☻www.holidaycare .org.uk. Provides free lists of accessible accommodation abroad. Information on financial help for holidays available.

Irish Wheelchair Association Blackheath Drive, Clontarf, Dublin 3 ☎01/833 8241, ☎833 3873, ☻iwa@iol.ie. Useful information provided about travelling abroad with a wheelchair.

Tripscope Alexandra House, Albany Rd, Brentford, Middlesex TW8 0NE ☎0845/7585 641, ☻www.justmobility.co.uk/tripscope, ☻tripscope@cableinet.co.uk. This registered charity provides a national telephone information service offering free advice on UK and international transport for those with a mobility problem.

US and Canada

Access-Able ⊛ www.access-able.com. Online resource for travellers with disabilities.

Directions Unlimited 123 Green Lane, Bedford Hills, NY 10507 ☎ 1-800/533-5343 or ☎ 914/241-1700. Tour operator specializing in custom tours for people with disabilities.

Mobility International USA 451 Broadway, Eugene, OR 97401, voice and TDD ☎ 541/343-1284, ⊛ www.miusa.org. Information and referral services, access guides, tours and exchange programmes. Annual membership $35 (includes quarterly newsletter).

Society for the Advancement of Travelers with Handicaps (SATH) 347 5th Ave, New York, NY 10016 ☎ 212/447-7284, ⊛ www.sath.org. Non-profit educational organization that has actively represented travellers with disabilities since 1976.

Travel Information Service ☎ 215/456-9600. Telephone-only information and referral service.

Twin Peaks Press Box 129, Vancouver, WA 98661 ☎ 360/694-2462 or ☎ 1-800/637-2256, ⊛ www.twinpeak.virtualave.net. Publisher of the *Directory of Travel Agencies for the Disabled* ($19.95), listing more than 370 agencies worldwide; *Travel for the Disabled* ($19.95); the *Directory of Accessible Van Rentals* ($12.95); and *Wheelchair Vagabond* ($19.95), loaded with personal tips.

Wheels Up! ☎ 1-888/389-4335, ⊛ www.wheelsup.com. Provides discounted airfare, tour and cruise prices for disabled travellers, also publishes a free monthly newsletter and has a comprehensive website.

Australia and New Zealand

ACROD (Australian Council for Rehabilitation of the Disabled) PO Box 60, Curtin ACT 2605 ☎ 02/6282 4333; Suite 103, 1st floor, 1–5 Commercial Rd, Kings Grove 2208 ☎ 02/9554 3666. Provides lists of travel agencies and tour operators for people with disabilities.

Disabled Persons Assembly 4/173–175 Victoria St, Wellington, New Zealand ☎ 04/801 9100. Resource centre with lists of travel agencies and tour operators for people with disabilities.

The City

The City

Hradčany

H RADČANY is wholly dominated by the city's omnipresent landmark, **Prague Castle**, or Pražský hrad, the vast hilltop complex that looks out over the city centre from the west bank of the River Vltava. Site of a Slav settlement in the seventh or eighth century AD, there's been a castle here since at least the late ninth century, and since then whoever has had control of the Hrad has exercised authority over the Czech Lands. It continues to serve as the seat of the president, though the public are free to wander round from the early hours until late at night, since the castle is also home to several museums and galleries.

The rest of the castle district, or Hradčany, has always been a mere appendage, its inhabitants serving and working for their masters in the Hrad. Even now, despite the odd restaurant or *pivnice* (pub) in amongst the palaces (and even in the Hrad itself), there's very little real life here beyond the stream of tourists who trek through the castle and the civil servants who work either for the president or the government, whose departmental tentacles spread right across Hradčany and down into neighbouring Malá Strana. All of which makes it a very peaceful and attractive area in which to take a stroll, and lose the crowds who crawl all over the Hrad.

Stretched out along a high spur above the River Vltava, Hradčany shows a suitable disdain for the public transport system. There's a choice of **approaches** from Malá Strana, all of which involve at least some walking. From Malostranská metro station, most people take the steep short cut up the Staré zámecké schody, which brings you into the castle from its rear end. A better approach is up the stately Zámecké schody, where you can stop and admire the view, before entering the castle via the main gates. The alternative to all this climbing is to take tram #22 from Malostranská metro, which tackles the hairpin bends of Chotkova with ease, and deposits you either at the Pražský hrad stop outside the Královská zahrada (Royal Gardens) to the north of the castle, or, if you prefer, at the Pohořelec stop outside the gates of the Strahovský klášter (monastery), at the far western edge of Hradčany.

Pražský hrad (Prague Castle)

Viewed from the Charles Bridge, **Pražský hrad** (known to the Czechs simply as the Hrad), stands aloof from the rest of the city, protected, not by bastions and castellated towers, but by a rather austere palatial facade – an "immense unbroken sheer blank wall", as Hilaire Belloc described it – above which rises the great Gothic mass of St Vitus Cathedral. It's the picture-post-

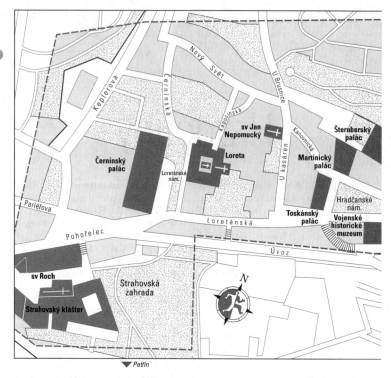

▼ Petřín

card image of Prague, and is spectacularly lit up at night, though for the Czechs the castle has been an object of disdain as much as admiration, its alternating fortunes mirroring the shifts in the nation's history. The golden age of Charles

Visiting the castle

Pražský hrad (@www.hrad.cz) is open daily April–October 5am–midnight, November–March 6am–11pm; sights within the castle (unless otherwise stated) are open daily April–October 9am–5pm, November–March 9am–4pm.

You can wander freely through most of the streets, courtyards and gardens of the castle and watch the changing of the guard without a ticket. A single ticket, costing 220Kč and valid for three days, will give you entry to four sights within the castle: the choir, crypt and tower of the cathedral; the Starý královský palác (Old Royal Palace); the Basilica of sv Jiří; the Zlatá ulička; and the Mihulka or Prašná věž (Powder Tower). Tickets which cover all the above sights except the Basilica cost 130Kč and tickets for just the Zlatá ulička cost 40Kč Tickets are available from the main information centre in the third courtyard, opposite the cathedral, where you can also hire an audioguide (in English) for another 145Kč for two hours.

The art collections of the Jiřský klášter and the Obrazárna Pražského hradu, the toys at the Muzeum hraček, the museum in the Lobkovický palác, and the exhibitions held in Císařská konírna and Jízdárna, all have different opening hours and separate admission charges.

Within the castle precincts there are several reasonably priced cafés and restaurants. If you simply want a quick cup of coffee, head for the *Café Poet*, which has tables outside and is hidden away in the peaceful and little visited Zahrada na baště.

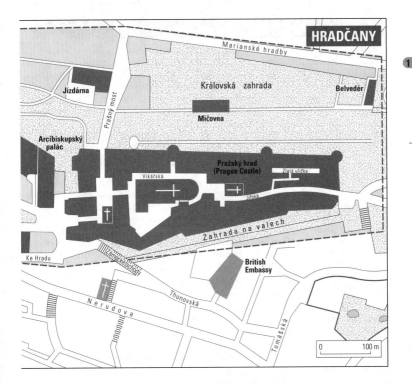

IV and Rudolf II and the dark ages of the later Habsburgs, interwar democracy and Stalinist terror – all have emanated from the Hrad. When the first posters appeared in December 1989 demanding "HAVEL NA HRAD" (Havel to the Castle), they weren't asking for his reincarceration. Havel's occupancy of the Hrad was the sign that the reins of government had finally been wrested from the Communist regime.

The site has been successively built on since the Přemyslid princes erected the first castle here in the ninth century, but two **architects** in particular bear responsibility for the present outward appearance of the Hrad. The first is **Nicolo Pacassi**, court architect to Empress Maria Theresa, whose austere restorations went hand in hand with the deliberate rundown of the Hrad until it was little more than an administrative barracks. For the Czechs, his grey-green eighteenth-century cover-up, which hides a variety of much older buildings, is unforgivable. Less apparent, though no less controversial, is the hand of **Josip Plečnik**, the Slovene architect who was commissioned by T.G. Masaryk, president of the newly founded Czechoslovak Republic, to restore and modernize the castle in his highly distinctive style in the 1920s (for more on Plečnik, see box on p.40).

The first and second courtyards

The **first courtyard** (první nádvoří), which opens onto Hradčanské náměstí, is guarded by Ignaz Platzer's blood-curdling *Battling Titans* – two gargantuan figures, one on each of the gate piers, wielding club and dagger and about to

Plečnik: a postmodernist before his day

Born in Ljubljana, **Josip Plečnik** (1872–1957) studied under the great Viennese architect Otto Wagner at the turn of the century, and was appointed chief architect to Prague Castle shortly after the foundation of the First Republic. Despite having the backing of the leading Czech architect Jan Kotěra, and of President Masaryk himself, controversy surrounded him as soon as the appointment was announced; his non-Czech background and, moreover, his quirky, eclectic style placed him at odds with the architectural establishment of the day. More recently, Plečnik's work, which happily borrows elements from any number of genres from classical to Assyrian architecture, has been compared with the work of postmodernists of the late 1980s and early 1990s, and as such has attracted a growing audience.

Plečnik's most conspicuous contributions to the castle are the fir-tree flag poles in the first courtyard and the granite obelisk in the third courtyard, but his light-hearted touch is to be seen throughout the castle grounds: check out the jokey palm tree with roped-on copper leaves outside the Jízdárna; the Bull Staircase, which leads down to the Zahrada na valech; or the impressive Sloupová síň (Hall of Columns), which contains the stairs going up to the Španělský sál, and can be peeked at through the glass doors between the first and second courtyards. Sadly, much of Plečnik's work – in particular the president's private apartments – remains hidden from public view, though thanks partly to Havel (a keen Plečnik fan), public access has been greatly increased.

inflict fatal blows on their respective victims. Below them stand a couple of impassive presidential sentries, sporting fancy-dress style navy blue and grey uniforms that deliberately recall those of the First Republic. They were designed by the Oscar-winning costume designer for Miloš Forman's film *Amadeus*, and chosen by Havel himself. The hourly **Changing of the Guard** is a fairly subdued affair, but every day at noon there's a much more elaborate parade, accompanied by a brass ensemble which appears at the first-floor windows to play local rock star Michal Kocáb's specially commissioned, gentle, slightly comical, modern fanfare.

To reach the **second courtyard** (druhé nádvoří), you must pass through the early Baroque Matyášova brána (Matthias Gate), originally a freestanding triumphal arch in the middle of the long-since defunct moat, now set into one of Pacassi's featureless wings. A grand stairway leads to the presidential apartments in the south wing, while to the north you can peek in at the beautiful Neoclassical lines of Plečnik's Hall of Columns, which leads to the two grandest reception rooms in the entire complex: the **Španělský sál** (Spanish Hall) and the **Rudolfova galerie** (Rudolf Gallery) in the north wing. Sadly, both are generally out of bounds, though concerts are occasionally held in the Španělský sál. Both rooms were redecorated in the 1860s with lots of gilded chandeliers and mirrors for Emperor Franz-Josef I's coronation, though in the end he decided not to turn up. Under the Communists, the Rudolfova galerie was the incongruous setting for Politburo meetings.

Surrounded by monotonous Pacassi plasterwork, the courtyard itself is really just a through-route to the cathedral, with an early Baroque stone fountain, the **Kohlova kašna**, and a wrought-iron well grille the only obvious distractions. The striking gilded sculpture of a winged leopard by Bořek Šípek, at the entrance to the east wing, is a postmodern homage to Plečnik. Occupying the southeast corner of the courtyard is Anselmo Lurago's **Chapel of sv Kříž**, whose richly painted interior, dating mostly from the mid-nineteenth century, can be entered via the information office in the vestibule. On the opposite side of the courtyard are the former **Císařská konírna** (Imperial Stables), which still boast their original, magnificent Renaissance vaulting dating from the reign of Rudolf II, and are now used to house temporary exhibitions (Tues–Sun 10am–6pm).

Obrazárna Pražského hradu (Prague Castle Picture Gallery)

The remnants of the imperial collection, begun by the Habsburg Emperor Rudolf II (see box on p.51), are housed in the nearby **Obrazárna Pražského hradu** (Prague Castle Picture Gallery; daily 10am–6pm; 100Kč). However, the best of what Rudolf amassed was either taken as booty by the marauding Saxons and Swedes, or sold off by his successors. Most sorely missed are the works of Giuseppe Arcimboldo, whose surrealist portraits – such as the one of Rudolf himself as a collage of fruit, with his eyes as cherries, cheeks as apples and hair as grapes – now reside in Vienna and Madrid. The surviving collection is definitely patchy, but it does contain one or two masterpieces that are well worth seeing, and visiting the gallery is a great way to escape the castle crowds.

One of the collection's finest paintings is Rubens' richly coloured *Assembly of the Gods at Olympus*, featuring a typically voluptuous Venus and a slightly fazed Zeus. The illusionist triple portrait of Rudolf (when viewed from the left), and his Habsburg predecessors (when viewed from the right), by Paulus Roy, is typical of the sort of tricksy work that appealed to the emperor. Elsewhere, there's an early, very beautiful *Young Woman at her Toilet* by Titian, and a superbly observed *Portrait of a Musician* by one of his pupils, Bordone. Veronese's best offering is his portrait of Jakob König, a German art dealer in Venice who worked for Rudolf II among others, and who was also a personal friend of the artist. Look out, too, for Tintoretto's *Flagellation of Christ*, a late work in which the artist makes very effective and dramatic use of light. Other works of note include excellent portraits and a fragment of an altarpiece by Cranach the Elder and Holbein's portrait of Lady Vaux.

St Vitus Cathedral

St Vitus Cathedral (chram sv Víta) is squeezed so tightly into the third courtyard that it's difficult to get an overall impression of this chaotic Gothic edifice. Its asymmetrical appearance is the product of a long and chequered history, for although the foundation stone was laid in 1344, the cathedral was not completed until 1929 – exactly 1000 years after the death of Bohemia's most famous patron saint, Wenceslas.

The site of the present cathedral was originally a sacrificial altar to the heathen fertility god **Svantovit**, which partly explains why the first church, founded in 929 by Prince Václav, was dedicated to St Vitus (svatý Vít in Czech). Vitus allegedly exorcized the Emperor Diocletian's son and was there-

---

Visiting the cathedral

Entry to the main nave, the Chapel of sv Václav and to all services is free; the cathedral is open for services only on Sunday until noon. To enter the chancel or crypt, where some of the most interesting monuments are located, you must have a castle ticket (see box on p.38), available from the box office in the south transept, or the information office opposite the cathedral.

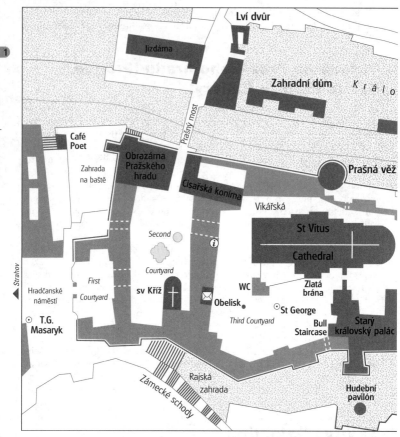

after known as the patron saint of epilepsy and of the convulsive disorder, Sydenham's chorea (hence its popular name, St Vitus' Dance). The inspiration for the medieval cathedral came from Emperor Charles IV (1346–78), who, while still only heir to the throne, not only wangled an independent archbishopric for Prague, but also managed to gather together the relics of St Vitus.

Inspired by the cathedral at Narbonne in France, Charles commissioned the Frenchman **Matthias of Arras** to start work on a similar structure. Matthias died eight years into the job in 1352, with the cathedral barely started, so Charles summoned **Peter Parler**, a precocious 23-year-old from a family of great German masons, to continue the work. For the next 46 years, Parler imprinted his slightly flashier, more inventive *SonderGotik* ("Unusual Gothic") style on the city, but the cathedral advanced no further than the construction of the choir and the south transept before his death in 1399.

Little significant work was carried out during the next four centuries and the half-built cathedral became a symbol of the Czechs' frustrated aspirations to nationhood. Not until the Czech national revival or *národní obrození* of the nineteenth century did building begin again in earnest, with the foundation,

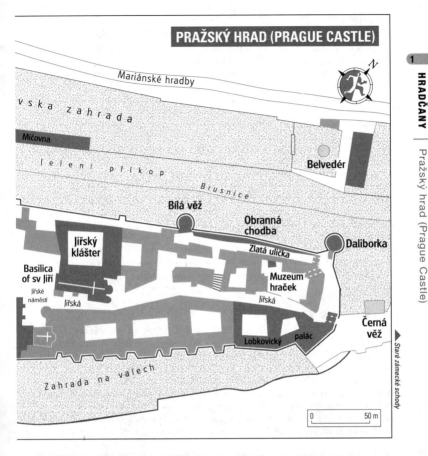

In the image: PRAŽSKÝ HRAD (PRAGUE CASTLE)

Mariánské hradby

vska zahrada

Míčovna

Jelení příkop

Brusnice

Belvedér

Bílá věž

Obranná chodba

Jiřský klášter

Zlatá ulička

Daliborka

Basilica of sv Jiří

Jiřské náměstí

Jiřská

Muzeum hraček

Jiřská

Lobkovický palác

Černá věž

Zahrada na valech

Staré zámecké schody

0   50 m

---

in 1859, of the **Union for the Completion of the Cathedral**. A succession of architects, including Josef Mocker and Kamil Hilbert, oversaw the completion of the entire west end, and, with the help of countless other Czech artists and sculptors, the building was transformed into a treasure-house of Czech art. The cathedral was finally given an official opening ceremony in 1929, though work, in fact, continued right up to and beyond World War II.

The exterior

The sooty Prague air has made it hard now to differentiate between the two building periods. Close inspection, however, reveals that the **western facade**, including the twin spires, sports the rigorous if unimaginative work of the neo-Gothic restorers (their besuited portraits can be found below the rose window), while the **eastern section** – best viewed from the Belvedere – shows the building's authentic Gothic roots. The south door, known as the Zlatá brána (see p.47), is also pure Parler. Oddly then, it's above the south door that the cathedral's tallest steeple reveals the most conspicuous stylistic join: Pacassi's Baroque topping resting absurdly on a Renaissance parapet of light stone, which is itself glued onto the blackened body of the original Gothic tower.

The nave

The cathedral is the country's largest and, once inside, it's difficult not to be impressed by the sheer height of the **nave**. This is the newest part of the building, and, consequently, is decorated mostly with twentieth-century furnishings. The most arresting of these are the cathedral's modern **stained-glass** windows, which on sunny days send shafts of rainbow light into the nave. The effect is stunning, though entirely out of keeping with Parler's original concept, which was to have almost exclusively clear-glass windows. The most unusual windows are those by František Kysela, which look as though they have been shattered into hundreds of tiny pieces, a mosaic-like technique used to good effect in the rose window over the west door with its kaleidoscopic *Creation of the World* (1921).

In keeping with its secular nature, two of the works from the time of the First Republic were paid for by financial institutions. The *Cyril and Methodius* window, in the third chapel in the north wall, was commissioned from Art Nouveau artist Alfons Mucha by the Banka Slavie, while on the opposite side of the nave, the window on the theme *Those Who Sow in Tears Shall Reap in Joy* was sponsored by a Prague insurance company.

One of the most striking later additions to the church is František Bílek's **wooden altar**, in the north aisle, whose anguished portrait of Christ on the cross breaks free of the neo-Gothic strictures that hamper other contemporary works inside.

Chapel of sv Václav

Of the cathedral's 22 side chapels, the grand **Chapel of sv Václav**, by the south door, is easily the main attraction. Although officially dedicated to St Vitus, spiritually the cathedral belongs as much to the Přemyslid prince, Václav (Wenceslas, of "Good King" fame; see box below), the country's patron saint, who was killed by his pagan brother, Boleslav the Cruel. Ten years later, in 939, Boleslav repented, converted, and apparently transferred his brother's remains to this very spot. Charles, who was keen to promote the cult of Wenceslas in order to cement his own Luxembourgeois dynasty's rather tenuous claim to the Bohemian throne, had Peter Parler build the present chapel on top of the

Good King Wenceslas

As it turns out, there's very little substance to the story related in the nineteenth-century English Christmas carol, *Good King Wenceslas looked out*, by J.M. Neale, itself a reworking of the medieval spring song *Tempus adest floridum*. For a start, **Václav** was only a duke and never a king (though he did become a saint); he wasn't even that "good", except in comparison with the rest of his family; Prague's St Agnes fountain, by which "yonder peasant dwelt", wasn't built until the thirteenth century; and he was killed a good three months before the Feast of Stephen (Boxing Day) – the traditional day for giving to the poor, hence the narrative of the carol.

Born in 907, Václav inherited his title at the tender age of thirteen. His Christian grandmother, Ludmila, was appointed regent in preference to Drahomíra, his pagan mother, who subsequently had Ludmila murdered in a fit of jealousy. On coming of age in 925, Václav became duke in his own right and took a vow of celibacy, intent on promoting Christianity throughout the dukedom. Even so, the local Christians didn't take to him, and when he began making conciliatory overtures to the neighbouring Germans, they persuaded his pagan younger brother, Boleslav the Cruel, to do away with him. On September 20, 929, Václav was stabbed to death by Boleslav at the entrance to a church just outside Prague.

△ Guard at castle gates

original grave; the lion's head **door-ring** set into the north door is said to be the one to which Václav clung before being killed. The chapel's rich, almost Byzantine decoration is like the inside of a jewel casket: the gilded walls are inlaid with approximately 1372 semiprecious Bohemian stones (corresponding to the year of its creation and symbolizing the New Jerusalem from the Book of Revelations), set around ethereal fourteenth-century frescoes of the Passion; meanwhile the tragedy of Wenceslas unfolds above the cornice in the later paintings of the Litoměřice school, dating from 1509.

Though a dazzling testament to the golden age of Charles IV's reign, it's not just the chapel's artistic merit which draws visitors. A door in the south wall gives access to a staircase leading to the coronation chamber (only very rarely open to the public), which houses the **Bohemian crown jewels**, including the gold crown of St Wenceslas, studded with some of the largest sapphires in the world. Closed to the public since 1867, the door is secured by seven different locks, the keys kept by seven different people, starting with the president himself – like the seven seals of the holy scroll from Revelations. The tight security is partly to prevent any pretenders to the throne trying on the head-gear, an allegedly fatal act: the Nazi *Reichsprotektor* Reinhard Heydrich tried it, only to suffer the inevitable consequences (see p.130). Replicas of the crown jewels are on display in the nearby Lobkovický palác (see p.46).

The chancel

Having sated yourself on the Wenceslas Chapel, buy a ticket from the nearby box office, and head off to the north choir aisle – the only place where you can currently enter the **chancel**. Following the ambulatory round, make sure you check out the high-relief seventeenth-century wooden panelling between the arcading on the right, which glories in the flight of the "Winter King" (he's depicted crossing the Charles Bridge), following the disastrous Battle of Bílá hora in 1620. The remains of various early Czech rulers are scattered throughout the side chapels, most notably those of Přemysl Otakar I and II, in the Saxon Chapel (the fifth one along), whose limestone tombs are the work of Peter Parler and his workshop; you can also pay your respects to Rudolf II's internal organs, buried in the chapel vault.

St John of Nepomuk

Where Emperor Charles IV sought to promote Wenceslas as the nation's preferred saint, the Jesuits, with Habsburg backing, replaced him during the Counter-Reformation with another Czech martyr, **John of Nepomuk** (Jan Nepomucký). The latter had been arrested, tortured, and then thrown – bound and gagged – off the Charles Bridge in 1393 on the orders of Václav IV, allegedly for refusing to divulge the secrets of the queen's confession. A cluster of stars was said to have appeared over the spot where he drowned, hence the halo of stars on every subsequent portrayal of the saint. The Jesuits, in order to ensure his canonization, exhumed his corpse and produced what they claimed to be his tongue – alive and licking, so to speak (it was in fact his very dead brain).

The more prosaic reason for John of Nepomuk's death was simply that he was caught up in a dispute between the archbishop and the king over the appointment of the abbot of Kladruby, and backed the wrong side. John was tortured on the rack along with two other priests, who were then made to sign a document denying that they had been maltreated; John, however, died before he could sign, and his dead body was secretly dumped in the river. The Vatican finally admitted this in 1961, some 232 years after his canonization.

Slap bang in the middle of the ambulatory, close to the Saxon Chapel, is the perfect Baroque answer to the medieval chapel of sv Václav, the **Tomb of St John of Nepomuk**, plonked here in 1736. It's a work of grotesque excess, designed by Johann Bernhard Fischer von Erlach's son, Johann Michael, and sculpted in solid silver with free-flying angels holding up the heavy drapery of the baldachin. On the lid of the tomb, back-to-back with John of Nepomuk himself, a cherub points to the martyr's severed tongue (see box on p.46).

Between the tomb of St John of Nepomuk and the chapel of sv Václav, Bohemia's one and only Polish ruler, Vladislav Jagiello, built a **Royal Oratory**, connected to his bedroom in the royal palace by a covered bridge. The balustrade sports heraldic shields from Bohemia's (at the time) quite considerable lands, while the hanging vault is smothered in an unusual branch-like decoration, courtesy of Benedikt Ried. To the left, the statue of a miner is a reminder of just how important Kutná Hora's silver mines were in funding such artistic ventures.

Imperial Mausoleum, Royal Crypt and Hlavná věž

Before you leave the chancel, check out the sixteenth-century marble **Imperial Mausoleum**, situated in the centre of the choir, and surrounded by a fine Renaissance grille on which numerous cherubs are irreverently larking about. It was commissioned by Rudolf II and contains the remains of his grandfather Ferdinand I, his Polish grandmother, and his father Maximilian II, the first Habsburgs to wear the Bohemian crown.

Rudolf himself rests beneath them, in one of the two pewter coffins in the somewhat cramped **Royal Crypt** (Královská hrobka), whose entrance is beside the Royal Oratory. Rudolf's coffin (at the back, in the centre) features yet more cherubs, brandishing quills, while the one to the right contains the remains of Maria Amelia, daughter of the Empress Maria Theresa. A good number of other Czech kings and queens are buried here, too, reinterred this century in incongruously modern 1930s sarcophagi, among them the Hussite King George of Poděbrady, Charles IV and, sharing a single sarcophagus, all four of his wives. The exit from the crypt brings you out in the centre of the nave.

In the summer months (April–Oct daily 9am–4.15pm), you can get a great view over the castle and the city from the cathedral's **Hlavná věž** (Great Tower), the entrance to which is in the south aisle – be warned, there are around three hundred steps before you reach the top.

The third courtyard and the Starý královský palác

The rest of the **third courtyard** (třetí nádvoří) reveals yet more of Pacassi's monotonous plasterwork. Plečnik's deliberately priapic granite **monolith** is, in fact, a stunted and unfinished monument, originally designed to complement the granite bowl in the Jižní zahrady (South Gardens). Close by is a fourteenth-century **bronze statue**, executed by a couple of Transylvanian Saxon sculptors, and depicting a rather diminutive St George astride a disturbingly large horse (actually two hundred years younger than the rest of the ensemble), slaying an extremely puny dragon – the original is in the Lapidárium (see p.157).

The other reason for hanging about in the third courtyard is to clock Parler's **Zlatá brána** (Golden Gate), decorated with a remarkable fourteenth-century mosaic of the *Last Judgement*, which has been restored to something like its original, rich colouring – it remains to be seen how it fares in Prague's polluted atmosphere. For the moment, you can clearly see the angels helping the dead out of their tombstones, and the devils dragging off the wicked by a golden rope towards the red flames of hell. On the opposite side of the courtyard is Plečnik's **Bull Staircase**, which leads down to the Jižní zahrady or South Gardens (see p.52), and also to the newly opened **Tereziánské křídlo** (Theresian Wing), now used for temporary exhibitions (Tues–Fri & Sun 10am–6pm, Sat 10am–7pm).

Starý královský palác (Old Royal Palace)

Across the courtyard from the Zlatá brána, the **Starý královský palác** (Old Royal Palace) was home to the princes and kings of Bohemia from the eleventh to the sixteenth century. It's a sandwich of royal apartments, built one on top of the other by successive generations, but left largely unfurnished and unused for the last three hundred years. The original Romanesque palace of Soběslav I now forms the cellars of the present building, above which Charles IV built his own Gothic chambers; these days you enter at the third and top floor, built at the end of the fifteenth century.

Immediately past the antechamber is the bare expanse of the massive **Vladislavský sál** (Vladislav Hall), the work of Benedikt Ried, the German mason appointed by Vladislav Jagiello as his court architect. It displays some remarkable, sweeping rib-vaulting which forms floral patterns on the ceiling, the petals reaching almost to the floor. It was here that the early Bohemian kings were elected, and since 1918 every president from Masaryk to Havel has been sworn into office in the hall. In medieval times, the hall was also used for banquets and jousting tournaments, which explains the ramp-like **Riders' Staircase** in the north wing (now the exit). At the far end of the hall, to the right, there's an outdoor **viewing platform**, from which you can enjoy a magnificent view of Prague (at its best in the late afternoon). You can also look down onto the chapel of **Všech svatých**, which Parler added to Charles IV's palace, but which had to be rebuilt after the 1541 fire, and has since been Baroquified. Its only point of interest is the remains of the Czech saint, Procopius, which are contained within an eighteenth-century wooden tomb along the north wall.

From a staircase in the southwest corner of the hall, you can gain access to the Ludvík Wing. The rooms themselves are pretty uninspiring, but the furthest one, the **Bohemian Chancellery**, was the scene of Prague's **second defenestration**. After almost two centuries of uneasy coexistence between Catholics and Protestants, matters came to a head over the succession to the throne of the Habsburg archduke Ferdinand, a notoriously intolerant Catholic. On May 23, 1618, a posse of more than one hundred Protestant nobles, led by Count Thurn, marched to the chancellery for a showdown with Jaroslav Bořita z Martinic and Vilém Slavata, the two Catholic governors appointed by Ferdinand I. After a "stormy discussion", the two councillors (and their personal secretary, Filip Fabricius) were thrown out of the window. As a contemporary historian recounted: "No mercy was granted them and they were both thrown dressed in their cloaks with their rapiers and decoration head first out of the western window into a moat beneath the palace. They loudly screamed *ach, ach, oweh!* and attempted to hold on to the narrow window-ledge, but Thurn beat their knuckles with the hilt of his sword until they were both obliged to let go." There's some controversy about the exact window from which they were ejected, although it's agreed that they survived to tell the tale, landing in a medieval dung heap below, and – so the story goes – precipitating the Thirty Years' War.

Back down in the Vladislavský sál, to the right of the Riders' Staircase, a door leads into the vaulted room of the **Diet**, whose (purely decorative) ribs imitate those of the Vladislavský sál. The room is laid out as if for a seventeenth-century session of the Diet: the king on his throne, the archbishop to his right, the judiciary to his left, the nobility facing him, and representatives from towns across Bohemia (with just one collective vote) confined to the gallery by the window.

A staircase to the left of the Riders' Staircase will take you up to the sparsely furnished rooms of the New Land Rolls, whose walls are tattooed with coats-of-arms. More rewarding, though, is the quick canter down the Riders' Staircase to the **Gothic and Romanesque chambers** of the palace, equally bare, but containing a couple of interesting models showing the castle at various stages in its development. Also on display are copies of busts by Peter Parler's workshop, which are virtually hidden from view in the triforium of the cathedral. As well as the architect's remarkable self-portrait, there are portraits of Charles IV and his four wives, including his formidable fourth spouse, Elizabeth of Pomerania, who used to bend horseshoes and tear chained mail to shreds with her bare hands.

The Basilica and Convent of sv Jiří

The only exit from the Royal Palace is via the Riders' Staircase, which deposits you in Jiřské náměstí. Don't be fooled by the russet-red Baroque facade of the **Basilica of sv Jiří** (St George) which dominates the square; inside is Prague's most beautiful Romanesque building, meticulously scrubbed clean and restored to re-create something like the honey-coloured stone basilica that replaced the original tenth-century church in 1173. The double staircase to the chancel is a remarkably harmonious late Baroque addition and now provides a perfect stage for chamber music concerts. The choir vault contains a rare early thirteenth-century painting of the New Jerusalem from Revelations – not to be confused with the very patchy sixteenth-century painting on the apse – while to the right of the chancel, only partially visible, are sixteenth-century frescoes of the **burial chapel of sv Ludmila**, grandmother of St Wenceslas, who was murdered by her own daughter-in-law in 921 (see box on p.44), thus becoming Bohemia's first Christian martyr and saint. There's a replica of the recumbent Ludmila, which you can inspect at close quarters, in the south aisle. Also worth a quick peek is the Romanesque crypt, situated beneath the choir, which contains a macabre sixteenth-century statue of Vanity, whose shrouded, skeletal body is crawling with snakes and lizards.

Jiřský klášter

Next door is Bohemia's first monastery, the **Jiřský klášter** (St George's Convent; Tues–Sun 10am–6pm; 50Kč; ⓦwww.ngprague.cz), founded in 973 by Mlada, sister of the Přemyslid prince Boleslav the Pious, who became its first abbess. Like most of the country's religious institutions, it was closed down and turned into a barracks by Joseph II in 1782, and now houses the Národní galerie's **Rudolfine and Baroque art collection** (Rudolfinské a barokní umění). To be honest, this is a collection of only limited interest to the non-specialist, though it's always blissfully peaceful and crowd-free compared with the rest of the castle. The first room you're ushered into off the cloisters is the chapel containing Mlada's sepulchre, set into the wall behind a seventeenth-century gilded grille. The art collection then begins upstairs with a brief taste of the overtly sensual and erotic **Mannerist paintings** that prevailed during the reign of Rudolf II. The majority of the works that survive from Rudolf's superlative collection, however, are actually displayed in the Obrazárna Pražského hradu (see p41). Of the few that remain here, make sure you check out Bartolomeus Spranger's colourfully erotic works, Hans von Aachen's sexually charged *Suicide of Lucretia* and Josef Heintz's riotous orgy in his *Last Judgement*.

The rest of the gallery is given over to a vast collection of Czech **Baroque art**, as pursued by the likes of Bohemia's Karel Škréta and Petr Brandl, whose paintings and sculptures fill chapels and churches across the Czech Lands. Perhaps the most compelling reason to wade through the gallery is to admire the vigorous, gesticulating sculptures of Matthias Bernhard Braun, and, to a lesser extent, Ferdinand Maximilian Brokof.

Zlatá ulička and the castle towers

Around the corner from the convent is the **Zlatá ulička** (Golden Lane), a seemingly blind alley of miniature cottages in dolly-mixture colours. The contrast in scale with the rest of the Hrad makes this by far the most popular sight in the entire complex, and during the day, at least, the whole street is mobbed, so if you want to try and recapture some of the original atmosphere, you really need to come back in the late evening. Originally built in the sixteenth century for the 24 members of Rudolf II's castle guard, the lane allegedly takes its name from the goldsmiths who followed (and modified the buildings) a century later, though the only house which survives from the sixteenth century is no. 13, the least cute of the lot. By the nineteenth century, the whole street had become a kind of palace slum, attracting artists and crafts-men, its two most famous inhabitants being Jaroslav Seifert, the Czech Nobel prize-winning poet, and Franz Kafka. Kafka's youngest sister, Ottla, rented no. 22, and during a creative period in the winter of 1916 he came here in the evenings to write short stories. Finally, in 1951, the Communists kicked out the last residents and the houses now serve as souvenir shops for tourists.

At no. 24, you can climb a flight of stairs to the **Obranná chodba** (defence corridor), which is lined with wooden shields, suits of armour and period cos-tumes. The **Bílá věž** (White Tower), at the western end of the corridor, was the city's main prison from Rudolf's reign onwards. Edward Kelley, the English alchemist, was locked up here by Rudolf for failing to turn base metal into gold, while the emperor's treasurer hanged himself by his gold cord on the treasury keys, after being accused of embezzlement. There's a reconstructed tor-ture chamber on the first floor, and in the shop on the floor above you can kit yourself out as a medieval knight with replica swords and maces, not to men-tion chastity belts and various torture instruments.

In the opposite direction, the corridor leads to a shooting range, where for a small fee you can have a few shots with a crossbow. The tower which lies beyond is the **Daliborka**, dedicated to its first prisoner, the young Czech noble, Dalibor, accused of supporting a peasants' revolt at the beginning of the fifteenth century. According to Prague legend, he learnt to play the violin while imprisoned here, and his playing could be heard all over the castle until his execution in 1498 – a tale that provided material for Smetana's opera *Dalibor*.

Rudolf II (1576–1612)

In 1583 Emperor **Rudolf II** switched the imperial court from Vienna to Prague. This was to be the first and last occasion in which Prague would hold centre-stage in the Habsburg Empire, and as such is seen as something of a second golden age for the city (the first being under Emperor Charles IV, for more on whom, see p.81). Bad-tempered, paranoid and probably insane, Rudolf had little interest in the affairs of state – instead, he holed up in the Hrad and indulged his own personal passions of alchemy, astrology and art. Thus, Rudolfine Prague played host to an impressive array of international artists, including the idiosyncratic Giuseppe Arcimboldo, whose surrealist portraits were composed entirely of fruit and vegetables. The astrologers, Johannes Kepler and Tycho Brahe, were summoned to Rudolf's court to chart the planetary movements and assuage Rudolf's superstitions, and the English alchemists, Edward Kelley and John Dee, were employed in order to dis-cover the secret of the philosopher's stone, the mythical substance that would transmute base metal into gold.

Accompanied by his pet African lion, Otakar, Rudolf spent less and less time in public, hiding out in the Hrad, where he "loved to paint, weave and dabble in inlay-ing and watchmaking", according to modern novelist Angelo Maria Ripellino. With the Turks rapidly approaching the gates of Vienna, Rudolf spent his days amassing exotic curios for his strange and vast *Kunst- und Wunderkammer*, which contained such items as "two nails from Noah's Ark...a lump of clay out of which God formed Adam...and large mandrake roots in the shape of little men reclining on soft velvet cushions in small cases resembling doll beds". He refused to marry, though he sired numerous bastards, since he had been warned in a horoscope that a legitimate heir would rob him of the throne. He was also especially wary of the numerous religious orders which inhabited Prague at the time, having been warned in another horo-scope that he would be killed by a monk. In the end, he was relieved of his throne by his younger brother, Matthias, in 1611, and died the following year, the day after the death of his beloved pet lion.

To get inside the castle's other tower, the **Prašná věž** (Powder Tower) or Mihulka, which once served as the workshop of gunsmith and bell-founder Tomáš Jaroš, you'll have to backtrack to Vikářská, the street which runs along the north side of the cathedral. The powder tower's name comes from the lam-prey (*mihule*), an eel-like fish supposedly bred here for royal consumption, though it's actually more noteworthy as the place where Rudolf's team of alchemists (including Kelley) were put to work trying to discover the secret of the philosopher's stone (see box above). Despite its colourful history, the exhi-bition currently on display within the tower is dull, with just a pair of furry slippers and hat belonging to Emperor Ferdinand I to get excited about.

Muzeum hraček (Toy Museum)

If you continue east down Jiřská, which runs parallel with Zlatá ulička, you'll come to the courtyard of the former Purkrabství (Burgrave's House) on the left, which hides a café, exhibition space and the **Muzeum hraček** (Toy Museum; daily 9.30am–5.30pm; 40Kč), housing the private toy collection of Ivan Steiger. With brief captions and unimaginative displays, the museum is a disappointing venture, which fails to live up to its potential. The succession of glass cabinets contains everything from toy cars and motorbikes to robots and even Barbie dolls, but there are only a few buttons for younger kids to press, and unless you're really lost for something to do, or have a specialist interest in toys, you could happily skip the whole enterprise.

Lobkovický palác (Lobkowicz Palace)

The hotchpotch historical collection in the **Lobkovický palác** (Lobkowicz Palace; Tues–Sun 9am–5pm; 40Kč; ⓦwww.nm.cz), on the opposite side of Jiřská, is marginally more rewarding, despite the ropey English text provided. The exhibition actually begins on the top floor, though by no means all the objects on display deserve attention; the following is a quick rundown of some of the more memorable exhibits. The first cabinet worth more than a passing nod is in the second room, and contains copies of the Bohemian crown jewels (the originals are hidden away above the Chapel of sv Václav in the cathedral and are very rarely on view). Next door, in the Hussite room, there's an interesting sixteenth-century carving of *The Last Supper*, originally an altarpiece from the Betlémská kaple, while, further on, Petr Vok's splendid funeral shield, constructed out of wood covered with cloth shot through with gold, hangs on the wall.

All things post-1620 and pre-1848 are displayed in the six rooms downstairs, starting with the sword of the famous Prague executioner, Jan Mydlář, who could lop a man's head off with just one chop, a skill he demonstrated on 24 of the 27 Protestant leaders who were executed on Staroměstské náměstí in 1621; Mydlář's invoice covering labour and expenses is displayed beside the sword. Several rooms on are some more unusual exhibits – three contemporary scaled-down models of eighteenth-century altars, and further on still, three carved marionettes from later that century, among the oldest surviving in Bohemia.

The Castle Gardens

The Hrad boasts some of the city's loveliest **gardens** (open April–Oct only), particularly in terms of views. The Jižní zahrady (South Gardens) enjoy wonderful vistas over the city and link up the terraced gardens of Malá Strana (see p.68), while the Královska zahrada (Royal Gardens) allow a better view of the cathedral and the Vltava's many bridges.

Jižní zahrady (South Gardens)

For recuperation and a superlative view over the rest of Prague – not to mention a chance to inspect some of Plečnik's quirky additions to the castle – head for the **Jižní zahrady** (April–Oct daily 9am–5pm), accessible via Plečnik's copper-canopied Bull Staircase on the south side of the third courtyard. Originally laid out in the sixteenth century, but thoroughly remodelled in the 1920s by Josip Plečnik, the first garden you come to from the Bull Staircase, the **Zahrada na valech** (Garden on the Ramparts), features an observation terrace and colonnaded pavilion, below which is an earlier eighteenth-century **Hudební pavilón** (Music Pavilion). Two sandstone obelisks further east record the arrival of Slavata and Martinic after their defenestration from the royal palace above (see p.48); beyond them lies yet another of Plečnik's observation pavilions. In the opposite direction, beyond the Baroque fountain lies the smaller **Rajská zahrada** (Paradise Garden), on whose lawn Plečnik plonked a forty-ton granite basin suspended on two small blocks. From here, a quick slog up the monumental staircase will bring you out onto Hradčanské náměstí.

Královská zahrada (Royal Gardens) and Belvedér

Before exploring the rest of Hradčany, it's worth taking a stroll through the north gate of the second courtyard and across the **Prašný most** (Powder

Bridge), erected in the sixteenth century to connect the newly established royal gardens (see below) with the Hrad (the original wooden structure has long since been replaced). Below lies the wooded **Jelení příkop** (Stag Ditch; April–Oct daily 10am–6pm), once used by the Habsburgs for growing figs and lemons, and storing game for the royal hunts, but now populated only by bored castle guards.

Beyond the bridge, opposite the former riding school or **Jízdárna** (Tues–Sun 10am–6pm), now used for temporary art exhibitions, is the entrance to the most verdant of all the castle's gardens, the **Královská zahrada** (April–Oct daily 10am–6pm), founded by Emperor Ferdinand I in the 1530s on the site of a former vineyard. Burned down by the Saxons and Swedes during the Thirty Years' War, and blown up by the Prussians, the gardens were only saved from French attack in 1741 by the payment of thirty pineapples. Today, these are some of the best-kept gardens in the capital, with fully functioning fountains and immaculately cropped lawns. Consequently, it's a very popular spot, though more a place for admiring the azaleas and almond trees than lounging around on the grass. It was here that tulips brought from Turkey were first acclimatized to Europe, before being exported to the Netherlands, and every spring there's an impressive, disciplined crop.

At the entrance to the gardens is the **Lví dvůr** (Lion's Court), now a restaurant but originally built by Rudolf II to house his private zoo, which included leopards, lynxes, bears, wolves and lions, all of whom lived in heated cages to protect them from the Prague winter. Rudolf was also responsible for the Renaissance ball-game court, known as the **Míčovna** (occasionally open to the public for concerts and exhibitions), built into the south terrace and tattooed with sgraffito by his court architect Bonifaz Wolmut. If you look carefully at the top row of allegorical figures on either side of the sandstone half-columns, you can see that the figure of Industry, between Justice and Peace, is holding a hammer and sickle and a copy of the Five-Year Plan, thoughtfully added by restorers in the 1950s. Incidentally, the guarded ochre building to the right of the Míčovna, the **Zahradní dům**, was built as a summerhouse by Dientzenhofer only to be destroyed during the Prussian bombardment of 1757. It was later restored by Pavel Janák who added the building's two modern wings on a postwar whim of the ill-fated President Beneš; it now serves as a presidential hideaway.

At the end of the gardens is Prague's most celebrated Renaissance legacy, Letohrádek královny Anny (Queen Anne's Summer Palace), popularly known as the **Belvedér** (Tues–Sun 10am–6pm), a delicately arcaded summerhouse topped by an inverted copper ship's hull, built by Ferdinand I for his wife, Anne (though she didn't live long enough to see it completed). It was designed by the Genoese architect Paolo della Stella, one of a number of Italian masons who settled in Prague in the sixteenth century, and is decorated by a series of lovely figural reliefs depicting scenes from mythology. Unlike the gardens, the Belvedér is open for most of the year and is mainly used for exhibitions by contemporary artists; if the gardens are closed you'll have to leave the Královská zahrada and head down Mariánské hradby. At the centre of the palace's miniature formal garden is the **Zpívající fontána** (Singing Fountain), built shortly after the palace and named for the musical sound the drops of water used to make when falling in the metal bowls below. From the garden terrace, you also have an unrivalled view of the castle's finest treasure – the cathedral. Note that the Chotkovy sady and the Bílkova vila are both within easy walking distance of the Belvedér (see p.150 for details).

The rest of Hradčany

The monumental scale and appearance of the rest of Hradčany, outside the castle, is a direct result of the **great fire of 1541**, which swept up from Malá Strana and wiped out most of the old dwelling places belonging to the serfs, tradesmen, clergy and masons who had settled here in the Middle Ages. With the Turks at the gates of Vienna, the Habsburg nobility were more inclined to pursue their major building projects in Prague instead, and, following the Battle of Bílá hora in 1620, the palaces of the exiled (or executed) Protestant nobility were up for grabs too. The newly ensconced Catholic aristocrats were keen to spend some of their expropriated wealth, and over the next two centuries they turned Hradčany into a grand architectural showpiece. As the Turkish threat subsided, the political focus of the empire gradually shifted back to Vienna and the building spree stopped. For the last two hundred years, Hradčany has been frozen in time, and, two world wars on, its buildings have survived better than those of any other central European capital.

Hradčanské náměstí

Hradčanské náměstí fans out from the castle gates, surrounded by the oversized palaces of the old Catholic nobility. For the most part, it's a tranquil space that's overlooked by the tour groups marching through, intent on the Hrad. The one spot everyone heads for is the ramparts in the southeastern corner, by the top of the Zámecké schody, which allow an unrivalled view over the red rooftops of Malá Strana, past the famous green dome and tower of the church of sv Mikuláš and beyond, to the Charles Bridge and the spires of Staré Město. Few people make use of the square's central green patch, which is heralded by a giant green wrought-iron lamppost decked with eight separate lamps – one of the few that have survived from the 1860s – and, behind it, a Baroque plague column, with saintly statues by Ferdinand Maximilian Brokof.

Until the great fire of 1541, the square was the hub of Hradčany, lined with medieval shops and stalls but with no real market as such. After the fire, the developers moved in; the **Martinický palác**, at no. 8 in the far northwestern corner of the square, was one of the more modest newcomers, built in 1620 by one of the councillors who survived the second defenestration. Its rich sgraffito decoration, which continues in the inner courtyard, was only discovered during restoration work in the 1970s, and was part of the reason it was featured as Mozart's house in the film *Amadeus*. Close by, Mathey's rather cold, formal **Toskánský palác** was built on a more ambitious scale, replacing the row of butchers' shops that once filled the west end of the square.

The powerful Lobkowicz family replaced seven houses on the south side of the square with the over-the-top sgraffitoed pile at no. 2, known as the **Schwarzenberský palác** after its last aristocratic owners (the present-day Count Schwarzenberg is one of the republic's leading capitalists). For a brief period, it belonged to the Rožmberk family, whose last in line, Petr Vok, held the infamous banquet which proved fatal to the Danish astronomer Tycho Brahe. So as not to offend his host, Tycho refrained from leaving the table before Vok, only to burst his bladder, after which he staggered off to his house in Nový Svět, where he died five days later.

All of which makes the **Vojenské historické muzeum** (Museum of Military History; May–Oct Tues–Sun 10am–5.30pm), which now occupies the palace, seem considerably less gruesome. Predictably enough, it was the Nazis who founded the museum, though the Czechs themselves have a long history of manufacturing top-class weaponry to world powers (Semtex is probably their best-known export). It's no coincidence that of the two Czech words to have made it into the English language, one is pistol (from *pišťale*, a Hussite weapon); the other is robot (from Karel Čapek's play *R.U.R.*). The museum is currently desperately underfunded, yet, somewhat surprisingly, many of the captions are in English. Among the ostentatious Habsburg uniforms and finely crafted instruments of death, all of which are pre-1914, you'll find the first Colt 45 produced outside the USA, manufactured in 1849 for the Austrian Navy, a field altar donated by Prince Eugène of Savoy, and a mannekin of General Windischgrätz surveying Prague, as he did before bombing it into submission in 1848.

The adjacent **Salmovský palác**, at no. 1, was another Schwarzenberg pile, which served as the Swedish Embassy until the 1970s when the dissident writer Pavel Kohout took refuge there. Frustrated in their attempts to force him out, the Communists closed the embassy down and left it to rot, though it looks likely, eventually, to be turned into a hotel. Beside the hotel stands a new statue of the country's founder, T.G. Masaryk, unveiled at the millennium. On the opposite side of the square, just outside the castle gates, stands the sumptuous vanilla-coloured **Arcibiskupský palác** (Archbishop's Palace), seat of the archbishop of Prague since the beginning of the Roman Catholic church's suzerainty over the Czechs, following the Battle of Bílá hora. The Rococo exterior only hints at the even more extravagant furnishings inside, though the interior is open to the public only on Maundy Thursday (the Thursday before Easter).

Šternberský palác – the old European art collection

A passage down the side of the archbishop's palace leads to the early eighteenth-century **Šternberský palác** (Tues–Sun 10am–6pm; 70Kč; Ⓦ www.ngprague.cz), which houses the Národní galerie's **old European art collection** (Staré evropské umění), mostly ranging from the fourteenth to the eighteenth century, but excluding works by Czech artists of the period (you'll find them in the Jiřský klášter in the Hrad – see p.49 – and in the Anežský klášter in Staré Město – see p.91). It would be fair to say that the collection is relatively modest in comparison with those of other major European capitals, though the handful of masterpieces makes a visit here worthwhile, and there's an elegant café in the courtyard. To see the Národní galerie's nineteenth- and twentieth-century European art collection, you need to pay a visit to the Veletržní palác (see p.152).

The **first floor** kicks off with Florentine religious art, most notably a series of exquisite miniature triptychs by Bernardo Daddi, plus several gilded polyptychs by the Venetian artist Antonio Vivarini. Moving swiftly into the gallery's large Flemish contingent, it's worth checking out Dieric Bouts' *Lamentation*, a complex composition crowded with figures in medieval garb, and the bizarre *Well of Life*, painted around 1500 by an unknown artist. The latter features a squatting Christ depicted as a Gothic fountain issuing forth blood which angels in turn serve in goblets to passing punters. One of the most eye-catching works is Jan Gossaert's *St Luke Drawing the Virgin*, an exercise in architectural geometry and perspective which used to hang in the cathedral. The section ends with a series of canvases by the Brueghel family; before you head upstairs, though, don't miss the side rooms containing Orthodox icons from Venice, the Balkans and Russia.

The **second floor** contains one of the most prized paintings in the whole collection, the *Feast of the Rosary* by Albrecht Dürer, depicting, among others, the Virgin Mary, the Pope, the Holy Roman Emperor, and even a self-portrait of Dürer himself (top right). This was one of Rudolf II's most prized aquisitions (he was an avid Dürer fan), and was transported on foot across the Alps to Prague (he didn't trust wheeled transport with such a precious object). There are other outstanding works here, too: two richly coloured Bronzino portraits, a Rembrandt, a Canaletto of the Thames, a whole series by the Saxon master, Lucas Cranach – including the striking, almost minimalist *Portrait of an Old Man* – and a mesmerizing *Praying Christ* by El Greco. Rubens' colossal *Murder of St Thomas* is difficult to miss, with its pink-buttocked cherubs hovering over the bloody scene. Nearby, in the hugely expanded (and uneven) Dutch section, there's a wonderful portrait of an arrogant "young gun" named Jasper by Frans Hals. A few of the rooms in the gallery have preserved their original decor, the best of which is the chinoiserie of the Činský kabinet.

Nový Svět, the Černínský palác and Loreta

At the northwestern corner of Hradčanské náměstí, Kanovnická heads off towards the northwest corner of Hradčany. Nestling in this shallow dip, **Nový Svět** (meaning "New World", though not Dvořák's) provides a glimpse of life on a totally different scale from Hradčanské náměstí. Similar in many ways to the Zlatá ulička in the Hrad, this cluster of brightly coloured cottages, which curls around the corner into Černínská, is all that's left of Hradčany's medieval slums, painted up and sanitized in the eighteenth and nineteenth centuries. Despite having all the same ingredients for mass tourist appeal as Zlatá ulička, it remains remarkably undisturbed, save for a few swish wine bars, and Gambra, a surrealist art gallery at Černínská 5 (March–Oct Wed–Sun noon–6pm; Nov–Feb Sat & Sun noon–6pm), which sells works by, among others, the renowned Czech animator, Jan Švankmajer, and his wife Eva, who live nearby.

Černínský palác

Up the hill from Nový Svět, Loretánské náměstí is dominated by the phenomenal 135-metre-long facade of the **Černínský palác** (not open to the public), decorated with thirty Palladian half-columns and supported by a swathe of diamond-pointed rustication. For all its grandeur – it's the largest palace in Prague, for the sake of which two whole streets were demolished – it's a pretty brutal building, commissioned in the 1660s by Count Humprecht Jan Černín, one-time imperial ambassador to Venice and a man of monumental self-importance. After quarrelling with the master of Italian Baroque, Giovanni Bernini, and disagreeing with Prague's own Carlo Lurago, Count Černín settled on Francesco Caratti as his architect, only to have the finished building panned by critics as a tasteless mass of stone. The grandiose plans, which were nowhere near completion when the count died, nearly bankrupted future generations of Černíns, who were eventually forced to sell the palace in 1851 to the Austrian state, which converted it into military barracks.

Since the First Republic, the palace has housed the Ministry of Foreign Affairs, and during the war it was, for a while, the Nazi *Reichsprotektor*'s residence. On March 10, 1948, it was the scene of Prague's third – and most widely mourned – defenestration. Only days after the Communist coup, **Jan**

Masaryk, the only son of the founder of the Republic, and the last non-Communist in Gottwald's cabinet, plunged 45 feet to his death from the top-floor bathroom window of the palace. Whether it was suicide (he had been suffering from bouts of depression, partly induced by the country's political path) or murder will probably never be satisfactorily resolved, but for most people Masaryk's death cast a dark shadow over the newly established regime.

Loreta

The facade of the **Loreta** (Tues–Sun 9am–12.15pm & 1–4.30pm; 80Kč), immediately opposite the Černínský palác, was built by the Dientzenhofers, a Bavarian family of architects, in the early part of the eighteenth century, and is the perfect antidote to Caratti's humourless monster. It's all hot flourishes and twirls, topped by a tower which lights up like a Chinese lantern at night, and by day clanks out the hymn *We Greet Thee a Thousand Times* on its 27 Dutch bells (it also does special performances of other tunes from time to time).

The facade and the cloisters, which were provided a century earlier to shelter pilgrims from the elements, are, in fact, just the outer casing for the focus of the complex, the **Santa Casa**, founded by Kateřina Lobkowicz in 1626 and smothered in a rich mantle of stucco depicting the building's miraculous transportation from the Holy Land. Legend has it that the Santa Casa (Mary's home in Nazareth), under threat from the heathen Turks, was transported by a host of angels to a small village in Dalmatia and from there, via a number of brief stopoffs, to a small laurel grove (*lauretum* in Latin, hence Loreta) in northern Italy. News of the miracle spread across the Catholic lands, prompting a spate of copycat shrines, and during the Counter-Reformation the cult was actively encouraged in an attempt to broaden the popular appeal of Catholicism. The Prague Loreta is one of fifty to be built in the Czech Lands, each of the shrines following an identical design, with pride of place given to a lime-wood statue of the *Black Madonna and Child*, encased in silver.

Behind the Santa Casa, the Dientzenhofers built the much larger **Church of Narození Páně** (Church of the Nativity), which is like a mini version of sv Mikuláš, down in Malá Strana. There's a high cherub count, plenty of gilding and a lovely organ replete with music-making angels and putti. On either side of the main altar are glass cabinets containing the fully clothed and wax-headed standing skeletons of St Felicissimus and St Marcia, and next to them, paintings of St Apolena – who had her teeth smashed in during her martyrdom and is now invoked for toothache – and St Agatha, carrying her severed breasts on a dish. As in the church, most of the saints honoured in the cloisters are women. Without doubt, the weirdest of the lot is St Wilgefortis (aka Starosta), whose statue stands in the final chapel of the cloisters. Daughter of the king of Portugal, she was due to marry the king of Sicily, despite having taken a vow of virginity. God intervened and she grew a beard, whereupon the king of Sicily broke off the marriage and her father had her crucified. Wilgefortis thus became the patron saint of unhappily married women, and is depicted bearded on the cross (and easily mistaken for Christ in drag).

You can get some idea of the Santa Casa's serious financial backing in the **treasury** (situated on the first floor of the west wing), much ransacked over the years but still stuffed full of gold. The light fittings are a Communist period piece, but most folk come here to gawp at the master exhibit, a tasteless Viennese silver monstrance designed by Fischer von Erlach in 1699, and studded with diamonds taken from the wedding dress of Countess Kolovrat, who had made the Loreta sole heir to her fortune.

Strahovský klášter

Continuing westwards from Loretánské náměstí, Pohořelec, an arcaded street-cum-square, leads to the chunky remnants of the zigzag eighteenth-century fortifications that mark the edge of the old city, as defined by Charles IV back in the fourteenth century. Close by, to the left, is the **Strahovský klášter** (Strahov Monastery; ⑩www.strahovmonastery.cz), founded in 1140 by the Premonstratensian order. Strahov was one of the lucky few to escape Joseph II's 1783 dissolution of the monasteries, a feat it managed by declaring itself a scholarly institution – the monks had, in fact, amassed one of the finest libraries in Bohemia. It continued to function until shortly after the Communists took power, when, along with all other religious establishments, it was closed down and most of its inmates thrown into prison; following the happy events of 1989, the monks have returned.

The Baroque entrance to the monastery is topped by a statue of **St Norbert**, twelfth-century founder of the Premonstratensian order, whose relics were brought here in 1627. Just inside the cobbled outer courtyard is a tiny deconsecrated church built by Rudolf II and dedicated to **sv Roch**, protector against plagues, one of which had very nearly rampaged through Prague in 1599; it's now an art gallery. The other church in this peaceful little courtyard is the still functioning twelfth-century monastery church of **Nanebezvetí Panny Marie**, which was given its last remodelling in Baroque times by Jean-Baptiste Mathey. Now restored to its former glory, it's well worth a peek for its colourful frescoes relating to St Norbert's life.

It's the monastery's two ornate **libraries** (daily 9am–noon & 1–5pm; 50Kč), though, that are the real reason for visiting Strahov; the entrance for both is to the right as you enter the outer courtyard. The first library you come to is the later and larger of the two, the **Filosofický sál** (Philosophical Hall), built in some haste in the 1780s, in order to accommodate the books and bookcases from Louka, a Premonstratensian monastery in Moravia that failed to escape Joseph's decree. The walnut bookcases are so tall they touch the library's lofty ceiling, which is busily decorated with frescoes by the Viennese painter Franz Maulbertsch on the theme of the search for truth. Don't, whatever you do, miss the collection of curios exhibited in the glass cabinets outside the library, which features shells, turtles, crabs, lobsters, dried-up sea monsters, butterflies, beetles, plastic fruit and moths. There's even a pair of whale's penises set amidst a narwhal horn, several harpoons and a model ship. The other main room is the low-ceilinged **Teologický sál** (Theological Hall), studded with ancient globes, its wedding-cake stucco framing frescoes on a similar theme, executed by one of the monks seventy years earlier. Outside the hall the library's oldest book, the ninth-century gem-studded *Strahov Gospel*, is displayed. Look out, too, for the cabinet of books documenting Czech trees, each of which has the bark of the tree on its spine.

An archway on the far side of the church contains the ticket office for the **Strahovská obrazárna** (Strahov Gallery; Tues–Sun 9am–5pm; 50Kč), situated above the cloisters, and accessible from the door on the right, beyond the ticket office. The gallery's collection of religious art, church plate and reliquaries – a mere fraction of the monastery's total – may not be to everyone's taste, but it does contain the odd gem from Rudolf II's collection, including a portrait of the emperor himself by his court painter, Hans von Aachen, plus a superb portrait of Rembrandt's elderly mother by Gerrit Dou. Also housed in this section of the monastery are exhibitions put on by the **Památník národního písemnictví** (National Literary Monument; Tues–Sun 9am–5pm; 30Kč;

@www.pamatniknarodnihopisemnictvi.cz), only of interest to those with some Czech, though the book covers on display are often works of art in themselves.

The monastery's newest attraction is the **Muzeum miniatur** (Museum of Miniatures; daily 9am–5pm; 40Kč), in the northeastern corner of the main courtyard. Displayed in this small museum are forty or so works by Anatoly Konyenko, a Russian who holds the record for constructing the smallest book in the world, a thirty-page edition of Chekhov's *Chameleon*. Among the other miracles of miniature manufacture are a (real, though dead) flea bearing golden horseshoes, scissors and a key and lock, the Lord's Prayer written on a human hair and a caravan of camels passing through the eye of a needle.

If you leave the monastery through the narrow doorway in the eastern wall, you enter the gardens and orchards of the **Strahovská zahrada**, from where you can see the whole city in perspective. The gardens form part of a wooded hill known as Petřín, and the path to the right contours round to the Stations of the Cross that lead up to the miniature Eiffel Tower known as the Rozhledna (see p.72). Alternatively, you can catch tram #22 from outside Strahov's main entrance to Malostranská metro or the centre of town.

Malá Strana

oolishly, many visitors never stray from the well-trodden route that links the Charles Bridge with the castle, thus bypassing most of **MALÁ STRANA**, Prague's picturesque "Little Quarter" that sits below the Hrad. This is easy enough to do given that the whole quarter takes up a mere 600 square metres of land squeezed in between the river and Hradčany, but it means missing out on one of the city's most enjoyable pastimes: exploring Malá Strana's peaceful, often hilly, eighteenth-century backstreets. These streets have changed very little since Mozart walked them during his frequent visits to Prague between 1787 and 1791, and they conceal a whole host of quiet terraced gardens, as well as the wooded Petřín hill, which together provide the perfect inner-city escape in the summer months.

Long before the Přemyslid king, Otakar II, decided to establish a German community here in 1257, a mixture of Jews, merchants and monks had settled on the slopes below the castle. But, as with Hradčany, it was the fire of 1541 – which devastated the entire left bank of the Vltava – and the expulsion of the Protestants after 1620, that together had the greatest impact on the visual and social make-up of the quarter. In place of the old Gothic town, the newly ascendant Catholic nobility built numerous palaces here, though generally without quite the same destructive glee as up in Hradčany.

In 1918, the majority of these buildings became home to the chief foreign embassies of the newly established First Republic, and after 1948 the rest of the real estate was turned into flats to alleviate the postwar housing shortage. The cycle has come full circle again with property in Malá Strana now among the most sought-after in Prague. Yet despite all the changes, the new hotels and the souvenir shops, much of Malá Strana remains remarkably undisturbed and resolutely residential.

Malostranské náměstí and around

The main focus of Malá Strana has always been the sloping, cobbled **Malostranské náměstí**, which is dominated and divided into two by the church of sv Mikuláš (see p.64). Trams and cars hurtle across it, regularly dodged by a procession of people – some heading up the hill to the Hrad, others pausing for coffee and cakes at the numerous bars and restaurants hidden in the square's arcades and Gothic vaults. The most famous (and the most central) of the cafés is the **Malostranská kavárna**, established in 1874, an occasional haunt of Kafka, Brod, Werfel and friends in the 1920s, and under restoration at the time of writing.

On every side, Neoclassical facades line the square, imitating the colour and grandeur of those of Hradčanské and Staroměstské náměstí. The largest Baroque re-development, the **Lichtenštejnský palác**, takes up the square's entire west side and is home to the university music faculty, as well as being a concert venue, art gallery and café. Its pleasing frontage hides a history linked to repression: first as the home of Karl von Liechtenstein, the man who pro-

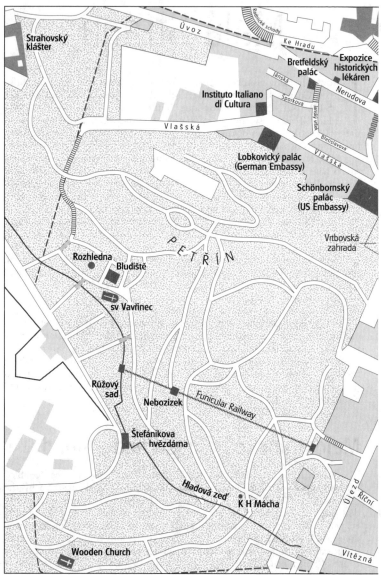

nounced the death sentence on the 27 Protestant leaders in 1621; then as headquarters for the Swedes during the 1648 siege; and later as the base of the
Austrian General Windischgrätz, scourge of the 1848 revolution.

On the north side, distinguished by its two little turrets and rather shocking
pistachio and vanilla colour scheme, is the **dům Smiřických** (no. 18), where
the Protestant posse met up in 1618 to decide how to get rid of Emperor

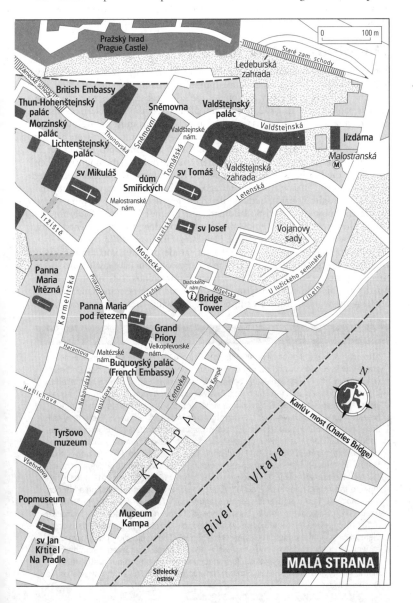

Ferdinand's Catholic governors: whether to attack them with daggers, or, as they eventually attempted to do, kill them by chucking them out of the window (see p.48). Sněmovní, the side street which runs alongside the palace's western facade, takes its name from the **Sněmovna**, the Neoclassical palace at no. 4, which served as the provincial Diet in the nineteenth century, the National Assembly of the First Republic in 1918, the Czech National Council after federalization in 1968, and finally, since 1993, as home to the Chamber of Deputies, the (more important) lower house of the Czech parliament.

The church of sv Mikuláš

Towering above the square, and the whole of Malá Strana, is the church of **sv Mikuláš** or St Nicholas (daily 9am–4pm; 50Kč), easily the most magnificent Baroque building in the city, and one of the last great structures to be built on the left bank, begun in 1702. For Christoph Dientzenhofer, a German immigrant from a dynasty of Bavarian architects, this was his most prestigious commission and is, without doubt, his finest work. For the Jesuits, who were already ensconced in the adjoining college, it was their most ambitious project yet in Bohemia, and the ultimate symbol of their stranglehold on the country. When Christoph died in 1722, it was left to his son Kilian Ignaz Dientzenhofer, along with Kilian's son-in-law, Anselmo Lurago, to finish the project, which they did with a masterful flourish, adding the giant green dome and tower – now among the most characteristic landmarks on Prague's left bank. Sadly for the Jesuits, they were able to enjoy the finished product for just twenty years, before they were banished from the Habsburg Empire in 1773.

Nothing about the relatively plain west facade prepares you for the overwhelming High Baroque **interior**. The vast fresco in the nave, by Johann Lukas Kracker, portrays some of the more fanciful miraculous feats of St Nicholas. Apart from his role as Santa Claus, he is depicted here rescuing sailors in distress, saving women from prostitution by throwing them bags of gold, and

Mozart in Prague

Mozart made the first of several visits to Prague with his wife Constanze in 1787, staying with his friend and patron Count Thun in what is now the British Embassy (Thunovská 14). A year earlier, his opera *The Marriage of Figaro*, which had failed to please the opera snobs in Vienna, had been given a rapturous reception at Prague's Nostitz Theater (now the Stavovské divadlo; see p.94); and on his arrival in 1787 Mozart was already flavour of the month, as he wrote in his diary: "Here they talk about nothing but Figaro. Nothing is played, sung or whistled but Figaro. Nothing, nothing but Figaro. Certainly a great honour for me!" Encouraged by this, he chose to premiere his next opera, *Don Giovanni*, later that year, in Prague rather than Vienna. He arrived with an incomplete score in hand, and wrote the overture at the Dušeks' Bertramka villa in Smíchov, now the Mozart Museum (see p.164), dedicating it to the "good people of Prague". Apart from a brief sojourn whilst on a concert tour, Mozart's fourth and final visit to Prague took place in 1791, the year of his death. The climax of the stay was the premiere of Mozart's final opera, *La Clemenza di Tito*, commissioned for the coronation of Leopold II as king of Bohemia (and completed whilst on the coach from Vienna to Prague). The opera didn't go down quite as well as previous ones – the empress is alleged to have shouted "German hogwash" from her box. Nevertheless, four thousand people turned out for the funeral memorial service, held in Malá Strana's church of sv Mikuláš to the strains of his *Requiem Mass*.

reprieving from death three unjustly condemned men. Even given the over-whelming proportions of the nave, the dome at the far end of the church, built by the younger Dientzenhofer, remains impressive, thanks, more than anything, to its sheer height. Leering over you as you gaze up at the dome are Ignaz Platzer's four terrifyingly oversized and stern Church Fathers, one of whom brandishes a gilded thunderbolt, leaving no doubt as to the gravity of the Jesuit message. Before you leave, check out the church's superb organ, its white case and gilded musical cherubs nicely offsetting the grey pipes. It's also possible to climb the **belfry** (April–Oct daily 10am–6pm; Nov–March Sat & Sun 10am–5pm), for fine views over Malá Strana and the Charles Bridge.

Nerudova

The most important of the various cobbled streets leading up to the Hrad from Malostranské náměstí is **Nerudova**, named after the Czech journalist and writer Jan Neruda (1834–91), who was born at *U dvou sluncü* (The Two Suns), at no. 47, an inn sporting twin Dutch gables at the top of the street; Neruda later lived for ten years at no. 44, now the swish *Hotel Neruda*. His tales of Malá Strana immortalized bohemian life on Prague's left bank, though he's perhaps best-known in the West via the Chilean Nobel prize-winner, Pablo Neruda, who took his pen name from the lesser-known Czech. Historically, this was the city's main quarter for craftsmen, artisans and artists, though the shops and restaurants that line Nerudova now are mostly predictably and shamelessly touristy.

Architecturally, the Baroque houses that line the steep climb up to the Hrad are fairly restrained, many retaining their medieval barn doors, and most adorned with their own peculiar house signs (see box on p.vi). Starting at the bottom of the street, you will shortly pass two of Nerudova's fancier buildings: at no. 5 is the **Morzinský palác**, now the Romanian Embassy, its doorway designed by Giovanni Santini and supported by two Moors (a pun on the owner's name) sculpted by Brokof; diagonally opposite, at no. 20, two giant eagles by Braun hold up the portal of the **Thun-Hohenštejnský palác**, now the Italian Embassy (also by Santini). Further up the street, according to Prague legend, Casanova and Mozart are thought to have met up at a ball given by the aristocrat owners of no. 33, the **Bretfeldský palác**, in 1791, while the latter was in town for the premiere of *La Clemenza di Tito* (see box on p.64). On the opposite side of the street, at no. 32, the former Dittrich pharmacy, dating from 1821, has been restored to its former glory and now houses a small and mild-ly diverting **Expozice historických lékáren** (April–Sept Tues–Fri noon–6pm, Sat & Sun 11am–6pm; Oct–March Sat noon–6pm, Sun 10am–6pm; 20Kč), whose prize exhibits are its leech bottles and a large dried fruit fish.

Halfway up the hill, Nerudova halts at a crossroads where it meets the cob-bled hairpin of Ke Hradu, which the royal coronation procession used to ascend; continuing west along **Úvoz** (The Cutting) takes you to the Strahovský klášter (see p.58). On the south side of Úvoz, the houses come to an end, and a view opens up over the picturesque jumble of Malá Strana's red-tiled roofs, while to the north, narrow stairways squeeze between the towering buildings of Hradčany, emerging on the path to the Loreta.

Tržiště and Vlašská

Running (very) roughly parallel to Nerudova – and linked to it by several side streets and steps – is **Tržiště**, which sets off from the south side of Malostranské náměstí. Halfway up on the left is the **Schönbornský palác**, now the US Embassy. The entrance, and the renowned gardens, are nowadays watched over by closed-circuit TV and twitchy Czech policemen – a far cry from the dilapidated palace in which Kafka rented an apartment in March 1917, and where he suffered his first bout of tuberculosis.

As Tržiště swings to the right, bear left up **Vlašská**, home to yet another **Lobkovický palác**, now the German Embassy. In the summer of 1989, several thousand East Germans climbed over the garden wall and entered the embassy compound to demand West German citizenship, which had been every German's right since partition. The neighbouring streets were soon jam-packed with abandoned Trabants, as the beautiful palace gardens became a muddy home to the refugees. Finally, the Czechoslovak government gave in and organized special trains to take the East Germans – cheered on their way by thousands of Praguers – over the federal border, thus prompting the exodus that eventually brought the Berlin Wall down.

The palace itself is a particularly refined building, best viewed from the rear – you'll have to approach it from Petřín (see p.72). The gardens, laid out in the early nineteenth century by Václav Skalník (who went on to landscape the spa at Mariánské Lázně), are not open to the public, but you should be able to see David Černý's sculpture, *Quo Vadis?*, a gold Trabant on legs, erected in memory of the fleeing East Germans. Opposite the German embassy, at Vlašská 34, is the **Instituto Italiano di Cultura** (Italian Cultural Institute), worth venturing inside if there's an exhibition on, as it contains a lovely Baroque chapel on the ground floor, whose rich plasterwork frames some unusual grisaille frescoes.

Valdštejnský palác and around

To the north of Malostranské náměstí, up Tomášská, lies the **Valdštejnský palác**, which takes up the whole of the eastern side of Valdštejnské náměstí and Valdštejnská. As early as 1621, Albrecht von Waldstein started to build a palace which would reflect his status as commander of the Imperial Catholic armies of the Thirty Years' War. By buying, confiscating, and then destroying 26 houses, three gardens and a brick factory, he succeeded in ripping apart a densely populated area of Malá Strana to make way for one of the first, largest and, quite frankly, most unappealing (at least from the outside) Baroque palaces in the city.

The Czech upper house, or **Senát**, is now housed in the palace, and can be visited on a guided tour at weekends (Sat & Sun 10am–4pm; free). The former stables are also accessible to the public, as they contain the **Pedagogické muzeum** (Tues–Sat 10am–12.30pm & 1–4.30pm; 10Kč; ⓦ www.pmjak.cz), a small and old-fashioned exhibition on Czech education and, in particular, the influential teachings of Jan Amos Komenský (1592–1670) – often anglicized to John Comenius – who was forced to leave his homeland after the victory of Waldstein's Catholic armies, eventually settling in Protestant England. To get to the exhibition, go through the main gateway and continue straight across the first courtyard; the museum is on your right.

If you've no interest in pedagogical matters, the palace's formal gardens, the **Valdštejnská zahrada** (April–Oct daily 10am–6pm; free) – accessible from the palace's main entrance, and also from a doorway in the palace walls along

Waldstein

Albrecht von Waldstein (known to the Czechs as Albrecht z Valdštejna, and to the English as Wallenstein – the name given to him by the German playwright Schiller in his tragic trilogy) was the most notorious warlord of the Thirty Years' War. If the imperial astrologer Johannes Kepler is to be believed, this is all because he was born at four in the afternoon on September 14, 1583. According to Kepler's horoscope, Waldstein was destined to be greedy, deceitful, unloved and unloving. Sure enough, at an early age he tried to kill a servant, for which he was expelled from his Lutheran school. Recuperating in Italy, he converted to Catholicism (an astute career move) and married a wealthy widow who conveniently died shortly after the marriage. Waldstein used his new fortune to cultivate a friendship with Prince Ferdinand, heir to the Habsburg Empire, who in turn thought that a tame Bohemian noble could come in handy.

Within five years of the Battle of Bílá hora in 1620 (see p.162), Waldstein owned a quarter of Bohemia, either by compulsory purchase or in return for money or troops loaned to Ferdinand. By 1630, Waldstein had earned himself the right to keep his hat on in the imperial presence as well as the dubious honour of handing the emperor a napkin after he had used his fingerbowl. However, at this point Waldstein's services became too expensive for Ferdinand, so the duke was relieved of his command.

The following year, the Saxons occupied Prague, and the emperor was forced to reinstate Waldstein. Ferdinand couldn't afford to do without the supplies from Waldstein's estates, but knew he was mortgaging large chunks of the empire to pay for his services. More alarmingly, there were persistent rumours that Waldstein was about to declare himself king of Bohemia and defect to the French enemy. In 1634, Waldstein openly rebelled against Ferdinand, who immediately hatched a plot to murder him, sending a motley posse including English, Irish and Scottish mercenaries to the border town of Cheb (Eger), where they cut the general down in his nightshirt as he tried to rise from his sickbed. Some see him as the first man to unify Germany since Charlemagne, others see him as a wily Czech hero. In reality he was probably just another ambitious, violent man, as his stars had predicted.

Letenská – are a good place to take a breather from the city streets. The focus of the gardens is the gigantic Italianate *sala terrena*, a monumental loggia decorated with frescoes of the Trojan Wars, which stands at the end of an avenue of sculptures by Adriaen de Vries. The originals, which were intended to form a fountain, were taken off as booty by the Swedes in 1648 and now adorn the royal gardens in Drottningholm. In addition, there are a number of peacocks, a pseudo grotto along the south wall, with quasi-stalactites, a door that once led to Waldstein's observatory, and a small aviary.

On the opposite side of the gardens, the palace's former riding school, **Valdštejnská jízdárna** (Tues–Sun 10am–6pm), has been converted into a gallery, which puts on temporary exhibitions of fine art and photography organized by the Národní galerie. The riding school is accessible only from the courtyard of the nearby Malostranská metro station.

Letenská and sv Tomáš

Walking southwest along **Letenská** from the gardens back towards Malostranské náměstí, takes you past **U svatého Tomáše**, the oldest *pivnice* in Prague, established in 1352 by Augustinian monks who brewed their own lethal dark beer on the premises. Unfortunately, the Communists succeeded in kicking out the monks and the surviving pub is now shamelessly touristy and overpriced.

Better preserved is the neighbouring priory church of **sv Tomáš** (St Thomas), rebuilt by Kilian Ignaz Dientzenhofer's in the 1720s. The rich burghers of Malá Strana spared no expense, as is clear from the ornate interior, with its dinky little dome, and fantastically colourful frescoes by Václav Vavřinec Reiner. They also bought a couple of Rubens for the tall main altarpiece (the originals are now in the hands of the Národní galerie) and two dead saints, St Just and St Boniface, whose gruesome clothed skeletons lie in glass coffins on either side of the nave, by the second pillar. A few traces of the church's Gothic origins can be seen in the vaulted chapel at the eastern end of the north aisle.

Malá Strana's terraced gardens

One of the chief joys of Malá Strana is its **terraced gardens**, hidden away behind the Baroque palaces on Valdštejnská, on the slopes below the castle, where the royal vineyards used to be, and commanding superb views over Prague. After lengthy restoration, all the gardens, except the Polish Embassy's Fürstenberská zahrada, are once more open to the public. If you're approaching from below, you enter via the **Ledeburská zahrada** on Valdštejnská (April–Oct daily 10am–6pm; 40Kč), which connect higher up with the Zahrada na valech (see p.52) beneath the Hrad itself.

Another option is to seek out the **Vojanovy sady** (daily: April–Sept 8am–7pm; Oct–March 8am–5pm; free), securely concealed behind a ring of high walls off U lužického semináře. Originally a monastic garden belonging to the Carmelites, it's now an informal public park, with sleeping babies, weeping willows, and lots of grass on which to lounge about; outdoor art exhibitions and occasional concerts also take place here. One final Malá Strana Baroque garden worth exploring is the Vrtbovská zahrada, off Karmelitská (see p.69).

Southern Malá Strana

Karmelitská is the busy cobbled street that runs south from Malostranské náměstí along the base of Petřín towards the industrial suburb of Smíchov, becoming Újezd at roughly its halfway point. Between here and the River Vltava are some of Malá Strana's most picturesque and secluded streets. Although there are no major sights around here, the island of **Kampa**, in particular, makes up one of the most peaceful stretches of riverfront in Prague.

Maltézské náměstí and around

From the trams and traffic fumes of Karmelitská, it's a relief to cut across to the calm restraint of **Maltézské náměstí**, one of a number of delightful little squares between here and the river. At its centre is a plague column, topped by at statue of St John the Baptist, but the square takes its name from the Order of the Knights of St John of Jerusalem (better known by their later title, the Maltese Knights), who in 1160 founded the nearby church of **Panna Maria pod řetězem** (St Mary below-the-chain), so called because it was the Knights' job to guard the Judith Bridge. The original Romanesque church was pulled down by the Knights themselves in the fourteenth century, but only the chancel and towers were successfully rebuilt by the time of the Hussite Wars.

The two bulky Gothic towers are still standing and the apse is now thoroughly Baroque, but the nave remains unfinished and open to the elements.

The Knights have now reclaimed (and restored) not only the church but also the adjacent Grand Priory, which backs onto **Velkopřevorské náměstí**, another pretty little square to the south, which echoes to the sound of music from the nearby Prague conservatoire. Following the violent death of John Lennon in 1980, Prague's youth established an ad hoc shrine smothered in graffiti tributes to the ex-Beatle along the Grand Priory's garden wall. The running battle between police and graffiti artists continued well into the 1990s, with the Maltese Knights taking an equally dim view of the mural, but a compromise has now been reached and the wall's scribblings legalized. On the opposite side of the square from the wall, sitting pretty in pink behind a row of chestnut trees, is the Rococo **Buquoyský palác**, built for a French aristocratic family and appropriately enough now the French Embassy.

Kampa

Heading for **Kampa**, the largest of the Vltava's islands, with its cafés, old mills and serene riverside park, is the perfect way to escape the crowds on the Charles Bridge, from which it can be accessed easily via a staircase. The island is separated from the left bank by Prague's "Little Venice", a thin strip of water called **Čertovka** (Devil's Stream), which used to power several mill-wheels until the last one ceased to function in 1936. In contrast to the rest of the left bank, the fire of 1541 had a positive effect on Kampa, since the flotsam from the blaze effectively stabilized the island's shifting shoreline. Nevertheless, Kampa was still subject to frequent flooding right up until the Vltava was dammed in the 1950s.

For much of its history, the island was the city's main wash house, a fact commemorated by the church of sv Jan Křtitel Na Prádle (St John-the-Baptist at the Cleaners) on Říční, beyond the southernmost tip of the island. It wasn't until the sixteenth and seventeenth centuries that the Nostitz family, who owned Kampa, began to develop the northern half of the island; the southern half was left untouched, and today is laid out as a public park, with riverside views across to Staré Město. To the north, the oval main square, **Na Kampě**, once a pottery market, is studded with slender acacia trees and cut through by the Charles Bridge, to which it is connected by a double flight of steps.

Definitely worth a visit if you're wandering around Kampa is the **Museum Kampa** (Tues–Sun 10am–5pm), a brand new art gallery housed in an old mill by the river in the park. Established in 2001, but only half-completed at the time of going to print, the museum is devoted to the private art collection of Jan and Meda Mládek. As well as short-term exhibitions, there's a permanent display of Czech art by the likes of František Kupka, the father of abstract art, the sculptor Otto Gutfreund and postwar surrealist Jiří Kolář.

Karmelitská and Újezd

On the corner of Karmelitská and Tržiště, at no. 25, is the entrance to one of the most elusive of Malá Strana's many Baroque gardens, the **Vrtbovská zahrada** (April–Oct daily 10am–6pm; 20Kč), founded on the site of the former vineyards of the **Vrtbovský palác**. Laid out on Tuscan-style terraces, dotted with ornamental urns and statues of the gods by Matthias Bernhard Braun, the gardens twist their way up the lower slopes of Petřín Hill to an observation terrace, from where there's a spectacular rooftop perspective on the city.

Panna Maria Vítězná and the Pražské Jezulátko

Further down, on the same side of the street, is the rather plain church of **Panna Maria Vítězná** (Mon–Sat 9.30am–5.30pm, Sun 1–5pm; free; ⓦwww.pragjesu.com), which was begun in early Baroque style by German Lutherans in 1611, and later handed over to the Carmelites after the Battle of Bílá hora. The main reason for coming here is to see the **Pražské Jezulátko** or *Bambino di Praga*, a high-kitsch wax effigy of the infant Jesus as a precocious three-year old, enthroned in a glass case illuminated with strip-lights, which was donated by one of the Lobkowicz family's Spanish brides in 1628. Attributed with miraculous powers, the *pražské Jezulátko* became an object of international pilgrimage equal in stature to the Santa Casa in Loreta (see p.57), similarly inspiring a whole series of replicas. It continues to attract visitors (as the multilingual prayer cards attest) and boasts a vast personal wardrobe of expensive swaddling clothes – approaching a hundred separate outfits at the last count – regularly changed by the Carmelite nuns. If you're keen to see some of the infant's outfits, there's a small museum, up the spiral staircase in the south aisle, which contains his lacy camisoles, as well as a selection of his velvet and satin overgarments sent from all over the world. There are also chalices, monstrances and a Rococo crown studded with diamonds and pearls to admire.

Michnův palác: Tyršovo muzeum

A block or so further south, Karmelitská becomes Újezd, on the east side of which is the **Michnův palác**, at no. 40, built on the site of another former nunnery, this time Dominican. The facade and gateway still incorporate elements of the Renaissance summer palace built by the Kinský family around 1580. From 1787 the building was used as an armoury and fell into disrepair until the Czech nationalist sports movement *Sokol* bought it in 1921. Nowadays, it is home to the little-visited **Tyršovo muzeum**, named after Miroslav Tyrš, one of the founders of *Sokol*, which played an important part in the Czech national revival (*národní obrození*). Set up in 1862, in direct response to the German *Turnverband* physical education movement, *Sokol* (from the Czech for "falcon") organized mass extravaganzas of synchronized gymnastics involving thousands of participants, roughly every six years from 1882 onwards. The Communists outlawed *Sokol* (as the Nazis had also done) and, in its place, established a tradition of similar extravaganzas called *Spartakiáda*, held every five years in the Strahov stadium, behind Petřín. In the 1990s, the *Spartakiáda*, indelibly tainted by their political past, were once more replaced by events organized by the reformed *Sokol*.

Popmuseum

Round the corner from the Tyršovo muzeum, and in its own way equally obscure, is the little-heralded **Popmuseum** (Fri–Sun 2–6pm; 30Kč; ⓦwww.popmuseum.cz), situated in the basement of the Divadlo na prádle, on Besední. Here, you can grab a drink at the conveniently adjacent bar, sit down in the museum's single small room and listen to a whole load of scratchy recordings and bootlegs of Czech bands from the late 1950s' and 1960s' heyday of Czech underground rock (or *bigbít* as it's known in Czech). Against the odds, the locals fought for the right to party, and there's a vast array of memorabilia on display, from old tickets and promo material, to a *Daily Mirror* article on Manfred Mann's 1965 Czech tour, and a display of ancient Czech guitars, including a home-made amp called Samuel, so famous (in Czechoslovakia) it had a band named after it.

△ Pražské Jezulátko

Petřín

The scaled-down version of the Eiffel Tower is the most obvious landmark on the wooded hill of **Petřín**, the largest green space in the city centre. The tower is just one of several exhibits which survive from the 1891 Prague Exhibition, whose modest legacy also includes the **funicular railway** (*lanová dráha*) which climbs up from a station just off Újezd (every 10–15min; daily 9.15am–8.45pm; public transport tickets and travel passes valid). The original funicular was powered by a simple but ingenious system whereby two carriages, one at either end of the steep track, were fitted with large watertanks that were alternately filled at the top and emptied at the bottom; it was replaced in the 1960s by the current electric system. As the carriages pass each other at the halfway station of Nebozízek, you can get out and soak in the view from the restaurant of the same name, or from the nearby *Petřínské terasy* restaurant (see p.201).

Along the Hunger Wall

At the top of the hill, it's possible to trace the southernmost perimeter wall of the old city – popularly known as the **Hladová zeď** (Hunger Wall) – as it creeps eastwards back down to Újezd, and northwestwards to the Strahovský klášter. Instigated in the 1460s by Charles IV, it was much lauded at the time (and later by the Communists) as a great public work which provided employment for the burgeoning ranks of the city's destitute (hence its name); in fact, much of the wall's construction was paid for by the expropriation of Jewish property.

Follow the wall southeast and you come to the aromatic **Růžový sad** (Rose Garden), whose colour-coordinated rose beds are laid out in front of Petřín's observatory, the **Štefánikova hvězdárna** (March & Oct Tues–Sun noon–5pm & 7–9pm; April–Aug Tues–Fri 2–7pm & 9–11pm, Sat & Sun 10am–noon, 2–7pm & 9–11pm; Sept Tues–Sun 1–6pm, & 8–10pm; Nov–Feb Tues–Fri 6–8pm; Sat & Sun 10am–noon & 2–8pm; 20Kč; **W** www.observatory.cz), run by star-gazing enthusiasts. The small astronomical exhibition inside is hardly worth bothering with, but if it's a clear night, a quick peek through either of the observatory's two powerful telescopes is a treat. A little further down the hill, on the other side of the wall from the observatory, stands a bust of the leading Czech nineteenth-century Romantic poet **Karel Hynek Mácha**, who penned the poem *Máj* (May), on the subject of unrequited love. In spring, and in particular on the first of May, the statue remains a popular place of pilgrimage for courting couples.

Another curiosity, hidden in the trees on the southern side of the Hladová zeď, is a **wooden church** that was brought here, log by log, from an Orthodox village in Carpatho-Ruthenia (now part of Ukraine) in 1929. Churches like this are still common in eastern Slovakia, and this is a particularly ornate example from the eighteenth century, with multiple domes like piles of giant acorns.

Back at the Růžový sad, follow the wall northwest and you'll come to Palliardi's twin-towered church of **sv Vavřinec** (St Lawrence), which recalls the German name for Petřín – Laurenziberg. Dotted along the path that leads to Strahov are the Stations of the Cross, culminating in the sgraffitoed Calvary Chapel, just beyond the church. Opposite the church are a series of buildings from the 1891 Exhibition, starting with the diminutive **Rozhledna** (April–Oct daily 10am–7pm; Nov–March Sat & Sun 10am–5pm; 30Kč), an octagonal interpretation – though a mere fifth of the size – of the Eiffel Tower which shocked Paris in 1889, and a tribute to the city's strong cultural and political links with Paris at the time; the view from the public gallery is terrific in fine weather.

The next building along is the **Bludiště** (April–Oct daily 10am–7pm; Nov–March Sat & Sun 10am–5pm; 30Kč), a mini neo-Gothic castle complete with mock drawbridge. The first section of the interior features a **mirror maze**, a stroke of infantile genius by the exhibition organizers. This is followed by an action-packed, life-sized diorama of the victory of Prague's students and Jews over the Swedes on the Charles Bridge in 1648. The humour of the convex and concave mirrors that lie beyond the diorama is so simple, it has both adults and kids giggling away. From the tower and maze, the path with the Stations of the Cross will eventually lead you to the perimeter wall of the Strahovský klášter (see p.58), giving great views over Petřín's palatial orchards and the sea of red tiles below.

Staré Město

S TARÉ MĚSTO, literally the "Old Town", is Prague's most central, vital ingredient. Most of the capital's busiest markets, shops, restaurants and pubs are in this area, and during the day a gaggle of shoppers and tourists fills its complex and utterly confusing web of narrow streets. Yet despite all the commercial activity, there are still plenty of residential streets, giving the area a lived-in feel that is rarely found in European city centres. The district is bounded on one side by the river, on the other by the arc of Národní, Na příkopě and Revoluční, and at its heart is **Staroměstské náměstí**, Prague's showpiece main square, easily the most magnificent in central Europe.

Merchants and craftsmen began settling in what is now Staré Město as early as the tenth century, and in the mid-thirteenth century it was granted town status, with jurisdiction over its own affairs. The fire of 1541, which ripped through the quarters on the other side of the river, never reached Staré Město, though the 1689 conflagration made up for it. Nevertheless, the victorious Catholic nobles built fewer large palaces here than on the left bank, leaving the medieval street plan intact with the exception of the Klementinum (the Jesuits' powerhouse) and the Jewish Quarter, Josefov, which was largely reconstructed in the late nineteenth century (see p.102). Like so much of Prague, however, Staré Město is still, on the surface, overwhelmingly Baroque, built literally on top of its Gothic predecessor to guard against the floods which plagued the town.

From the Karlův most to Malé náměstí

In their explorations of Staré Město, most people unknowingly retrace the **králová cesta**, the traditional route of the coronation procession from the medieval gateway, the Prašná brána (see p.124), to the Hrad. Established by the Přemyslids, the route was followed, with a few minor variations, by every king until the Emperor Ferdinand IV in 1836, the last of the Habsburgs to bother having himself crowned in Prague. It's also the most direct route from the Charles Bridge to Prague's main square, Staroměstské náměstí, and therefore jam-packed with tourists and souvenir shops. However, many of the real treasures of Staré Město lie away from the *králová cesta*, so if you want to escape the crowds, it's worth heading off into the quarter's silent, twisted matrix of streets, then simply following your nose – for details of specific sights to the south of Karlova, see p.93.

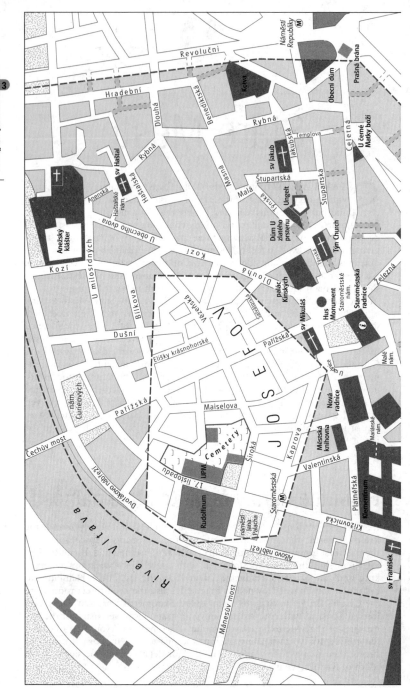

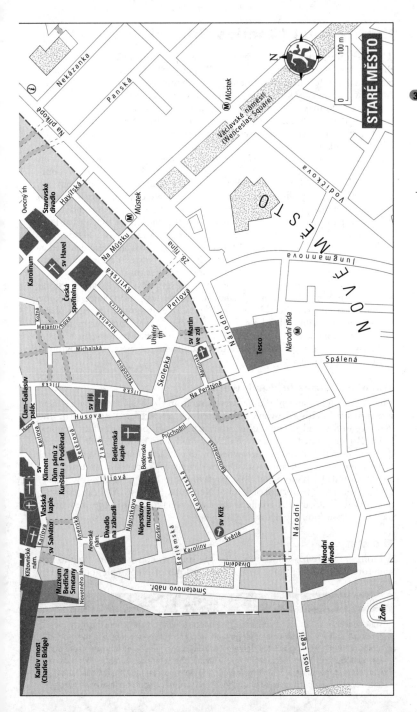

STARÉ MĚSTO

NOVÉ MĚSTO

Václavské náměstí
(Wenceslas Square)

M Můstek

N

0   100 m

Karlův most
(Charles Bridge)

Křížovnické nám.

Muzeum
Bedřicha
Smetany

sv Salvátor

Vlašská
kaple

sv
Kliment

Clam-Gallasův
palác

Dům pánů z
Kunštátu a Poděbrad

Divadlo
na zábradlí

Náprstkovo
muzeum

Betlémská
kaple

sv Jiří

Husova

sv Havel

Karolinum

Stavovské
divadlo

Ovocný trh

Havířská

Na příkopě

i

Nekázanka

Panská

Na Můstku

M Můstek

Rytířská

Česká
spořitelna

Melantrichova

Michalská

Skořepka

Uhelný
trh

sv Martin
ve zdi

Perlová

28. října

Na Perštýně

Průchodní

Konviktská

sv Kříž

Tesco

Národní

Národní třída

M

Spálená

Vodičkova

Jungmannova

Národní
divadlo

Smetanovo nábř.

most Legií

Žofín

Betlémské
nám.

Liliová

Zlatá

Řetězová

Karlova

Anenské
nám.

Náprstkova

Betlémská

Karoliny

Světlé

Divadelní

Novotného lávka

Řetězová

Bartolomějská

Jalovcová

Jilská

Vejvodova

Jilská

Kožná

Havelská

77

Karlův most (Charles Bridge)

The **Karlův most**, or Charles Bridge – which for over four hundred years was the only link between the two halves of Prague – is by far the city's most familiar monument. It's an impressive piece of medieval engineering, aligned slightly askew between two mighty Gothic gateways, but its fame is due almost entirely to the magnificent, mostly Baroque statues, additions to the original structure, that punctuate its length. Individually, only a few of the works are outstanding, but taken collectively, set against the backdrop of the Hrad, the effect is breathtaking.

The bridge was begun in 1357 to replace an earlier structure which had been swept away by one of the Vltava's frequent floods in 1342. Charles IV commissioned his young German court architect, Peter Parler, to carry out the work, which was finally completed in the early fifteenth century. Given its strategic significance, it comes as no surprise that the bridge has played an important part in Prague's history: in 1648, it was the site of the last battle of the Thirty Years' War, fought between the besieging Swedes and an ad hoc army of Prague's students and Jews; in 1744, the invading Prussians were defeated at the same spot; and in 1848, it formed the front line between the revolutionaries on the Staré Město side, and the reactionary forces on the left bank.

For the first four hundred years it was known simply as the Prague or Stone Bridge – only in 1870 was it officially named after its patron. Since 1950, the bridge has been closed to vehicles, and is now one of the most popular places to hang out, day and night: the crush of sightseers never abates during the day, when the niches created by the bridge-piers are occupied by souvenir hawkers and buskers, but at night things calm down a bit, and the views are, if anything, even more spectacular.

The Malá Strana bridge towers

The following account of the statuary starts from the Malá Strana side, where two unequal **bridge towers**, connected by a castellated arch, form the entrance to the bridge. The smaller, stumpy tower was once part of the original Judith Bridge (named after the wife of Vladislav I, who built the twelfth-century bridge); the taller of the two, crowned by one of the pinnacled wedge-spires more commonly associated with Prague's right bank, contains an exhibition (April–Oct daily 10am–6pm; 30Kč) relaying the history of the towers, the bridge itself, and the story of St John of Nepomuk (see p.46). You can also walk out onto the balcony that connects the two towers for a bird's-eye view of the seething masses pouring across the bridge.

The statues

A bronze crucifix has stood on the bridge since its construction, but the first sculpture wasn't added until 1683, when St John of Nepomuk appeared. His

---

Building the bridge

There are countless legends regarding the bridge's initial construction: the most persistent is that the builders mixed eggs (and, in some versions, wine) with the mortar to strengthen it. Having quickly depleted the city's egg supply, orders were sent out for contributions from the surrounding villages: the villagers of Velvary, who were worried that raw eggs wouldn't have quite the right consistency, hard-boiled theirs, and from Unhošt curd, cheese and whey were sent to bond the bricks even harder.

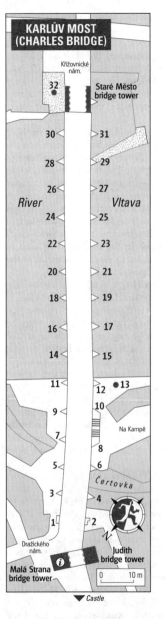

KARLŮV MOST (CHARLES BRIDGE)

Křížovnické nám.

32

Staré Město bridge tower

River

Vltava

Na Kampě

Čertovka

Dražického nám.

Judith bridge tower

Malá Strana bridge tower

0   10 m

▼ Castle

statue was such a propaganda success that the Catholic church authorities ordered another 21 to be erected between 1706 and 1714. These included works by Prague's leading Baroque sculptors, led by Matthias Bernhard Braun and Ferdinand Maximilian Brokof; the Max brothers unimaginatively filled in the remaining piers in the mid-nineteenth century. The sculptures, mostly crafted in sandstone, have weathered badly over the years and are gradually being replaced by copies; to see the originals you can visit the Lapidárium (see p.157).

In the first statue group on the north side, paid for by the university medical faculty, Jesus is flanked by **St Cosmas and St Damian** (1), both dressed in medieval doctors' garb – they were renowned for offering their medical services free of charge to the poor. Opposite stands **St Wenceslas** (2), added by Czech nationalists in the nineteenth century (for more on Wenceslas, see the box on p.44). On the next pier, Brokof's **St Vitus** (3) is depicted as a Roman legionary, his foot being gently nibbled by one of the lions that went on to devour him in a Roman amphitheatre. Facing him is one of the most striking sculptural groups, the founders of the **Trinitarian Order** (4), again by Brokof: saints John of Matha, Felix of Valois and his pet stag (plus, for some unknown reason, St Ivan), whose good works included ransoming persecuted Christians – three petrified souls can be seen through the prison bars below – from the infidels, represented by a bored Turkish jailor and his rabid dog.

Amid all the blackened sandstone, the lightly coloured figure of the (at the time) only recently canonized Servite friar, **St Philip Benizi** (5), stands out as the only marble statue on the bridge. At his feet sits the papal crown, which he refused to accept when it was offered to him in 1268. Opposite stands Prague's second bishop, the youthful **St Adalbert** (6), who was hounded out of the city on more than one occasion by the blissfully pagan citizens of Prague. Another (at the time) recently canonized saint is **Cajetan** (7), founder of the Theatine Order (and of a whole chain of non-profit-making pawnshops in Naples), who stands in front of a column of cherubs sporting a sacred heart.

One of the most successful statues is that of the blind Cistercian nun, **St Lutgard** (**8**), sculpted by Braun when he was just 26 years old. She is depicted here in the middle of her celebrated vision, in which Christ appeared so that she could kiss his wounds. The Augustinians sponsored the next duo, on the other side of the steps leading down to Kampa Island: **St Augustine** (**9**), and one of his later followers, **St Nicholas of Tolentino** (**10**), who is depicted dishing out bread to the poor. On the top-floor balcony of the house immediately behind St Nicholas of Tolentino is a lantern; if it goes out while you're passing by, it means you'll die within the year.

Next pier along, the apostle **St Jude Thaddaeus** (**11**), patron saint of those in dire straits, holds the club with which the pagans beat him to death. On the opposite side, the Dominican friar **St Vincent Ferrer** (**12**) stands over one of his converts to self-flagellation, while the inscription below lists his miraculous achievements, including the conversion of 2500 Jews, some forty resurrections and the exorcism of seventy demons. He is joined on his pedestal, somewhat inexplicably, by Bohemia's best-loved hermit, **St Procopius**. If you look over the side of the bridge at this point, you'll see a nineteenth-century sculpture of **Roland** (**13**) – known as *Bruncvík* in Czech – brandishing his miraculous golden sword (the real thing is said to be embedded in the bridge, to be used in case of municipal emergency). The original, erected to protect the rights of the Staré Město over the full extent of the bridge, was destroyed in 1648.

The Franciscan pier – **St Anthony of Padua** (**14**), and a lifeless nineteenth-century figure of **St Francis of Assisi**, accompanied by two angels (**15**) – is worth passing over to reach the bridge's earliest and most popular sculpture, **St John of Nepomuk** (**16**). The only bronze statue on the bridge, it's now green with age, the gold-leaf halo of stars and palm branch gently blowing in the breeze. St John's appearance in 1683, on the bridge from which he was thrown to his death, was part of the Jesuits' persistent campaign to have him canonized; the statue later inspired hundreds of copies, which adorn bridges throughout central Europe. On the base, there's a bronze relief depicting his martyrdom, the figure of John now extremely worn through years of being touched for good luck (for more on St John's martyrdom, see the box on p.46). Facing St John is Bohemia's first martyr, a rather androgynous version of **St Ludmila** (**17**), holding the veil with which she was strangled and standing alongside her grandson, St Wenceslas, here depicted as a young child; his future martyrdom is recounted in the bas-relief.

With the exception of the Jesuit general **St Francis Borgia** (**19**), the next two piers are glum nineteenth-century space-fillers: a trio of Bohemian saints – **Norbert**, **Sigismund** and, for the third time, **Wenceslas** (**18**) – followed by **John the Baptist** (**20**) and **St Christopher** (**21**). Between the piers (18 & 20), on the north side, a small bronze cross is set into the wall marking the spot where John of Nepomuk was dumped in the river (see above); touch it and, according to the locals, you're guaranteed to return to the city. In 1890, the two Jesuit statues on the next pier were swept away by a flood: the statue of the founder of the order, St Ignatius Loyola, was replaced with the most recent additions to the bridge (completed in 1938), **saints Cyril and Methodius** (**22**), the ninth-century missionaries who first introduced Christianity to the Slavs; the other, the Jesuit missionary **St Francis Xavier** (**23**), survived the order's unpopularity and was replaced by a copy. This is one of the more unusual sculptural groups on the bridge: the saint, who worked in India and the Far East, is held aloft by three Moorish and two "Oriental" converts; Brokof placed himself on the saint's left side.

Next in line are Jesus, Mary, and Mary's mother, **St Ann** (**24**) and, facing them, with a slightly older Jesus at his feet, **Joseph** (**25**), a nineteenth-century replacement for another Brokof, this time destroyed by gunfire during the 1848 revolution. The **Crucifixion** scene (**26**) is where the original fourteenth-century crucifix stood alone on the bridge for two hundred years. The gold-leaf, Hebrew inscription, "Holy, Holy, Holy is Our Lord of the Multitude", from the Book of Isaiah, was added in 1696, paid for by a Prague Jew who was ordered to do so by the city court, having been found guilty of blasphemy before the cross. Somewhat incredibly, the local Jewish community recently succeeded in persuading the local council to erect a plaque below the statue, explaining that the charges were drummed up and the inscription designed to humiliate Prague's Jews. Apart from Christ himself, all the figures, and the **Pietà** opposite (**27**), were added by the Max brothers.

On the penultimate pier, the Dominicans placed their founder, **St Dominic**, and their other leading light, **St Thomas Aquinas**, beside the **Madonna** (**28**); in amongst the cherubs is the order's emblem, a dog with a burning torch in his mouth. Opposite, **St Barbara**, the patron saint of miners, whose beautiful-ly sculpted hands so impressed Kafka, is accompanied by **St Margaret** and **St Elizabeth** (**29**). There's one final **Madonna** (**30**), this time presiding over the kneeling figure of **St Bernard**, and a bubbling mass of cherubs mucking about with the instruments of the Passion – the cock, the dice and the centurion's

Charles IV (1346–78)

There may be more legends and intrigue associated with the reign of Rudolf II (see p.51), but it was under **Emperor Charles IV** (Karel IV to the Czechs) that Prague enjoyed its true golden age. In just over thirty years, Charles transformed Prague into the effective capital of the Holy Roman Empire, establishing the city's archbish-opric, its university, a host of monasteries and churches, an entire new town (Nové Město), plus several monuments which survive to this day, most notably St Vitus Cathedral, and, of course, the Charles Bridge (Karlův most).

Born in 1316 (and christened Václav), Charles was the only son of King John of Luxembourg and Queen Eliška, daughter of Přemyslid King Václav II. Suspecting his wife of plotting to dethrone him, King John imprisoned her and Charles, keeping his three-year-old son in a dungeon with only "a little light coming in from a hole in the ceiling". In 1323, the young Charles was despatched to the fashionable French court to keep him out of any further trouble and complete his education – he never saw his mother again. In France he was given the name Charles (after Charlemagne) by the French king and married off to Blanche de Valois, the first of his four wives.

In 1346, his father (by then totally blind) was killed at the Battle of Crécy, and Charles, who escaped with just a wound, inherited the Czech crown. He immedi-ately busied himself with building up his Bohemian power base, and within two years had got himself elected Holy Roman Emperor. Fluent in Czech, French, German, Latin and Italian, Charles used his international contacts to gather togeth-er a whole host of foreign artists to his new capital, most famously persuading the Italian man of letters, Petrarch, to pay a visit.

Though later chroniclers tried to paint Charles as chaste and pure, even he admit-ted in his autobiography that he had strayed in his youth: "seduced by the pervert-ed people, we were perverted by the perverts", he wrote of his Italian sojourn. And just as Rudolf II created his *Kunst- und Wunderkammer*, Charles also spent much of his spare time amassing a bizarre collection of relics to ensure a smooth passage into the after-life. He cajoled and blackmailed his way into obtaining part of the whip used in the Passion, two thorns from Christ's crown, a few drops of milk from the Virgin Mary and one of Mary Magdalene's breasts, all beautifully encased in reli-quaries designed by Prague's finest goldsmiths.

gauntlet. Lastly, **St Ivo (31)**, patron saint of lawyers, flanked by Justice and a prospective client, stands with an outstretched hand, into which Prague law students traditionally place a glass of beer after their finals.

The Staré Město bridge tower

On the Staré Město side is arguably the finest **bridge tower** (daily: April–Oct 10am–7pm; Nov–March 10am–5pm; 30Kč) of the lot: the western facade was trashed in the battle of 1648 but the eastern facade is still encrusted in Gothic cake-like decorations from Peter Parler's workshop, plus a series of mini-sculptures. The central figures are St Vitus, flanked by Charles IV on the right and his son, Václav IV, on the left; above stand two of Bohemia's patron saints, Adalbert and Sigismund. The severed heads of twelve of the Protestant leaders were suspended from the tower in iron baskets following their execution on Staroměstské náměstí in 1621, and all but one remained there until the Saxons passed through the capital ten years later. The tower now contains a small display of antique musical instruments, and allows you access onto the roof for another aerial perspective on the bridge.

Křižovnické náměstí

Pass under the Staré Město bridge tower and you're in **Křižovnické náměstí**, an awkward space hemmed in by its constituent buildings, and, with traffic hurtling across the square, a dangerous spot for unwary pedestrians. Hard by the bridge tower is a nineteenth-century cast-iron statue of **Charles IV (32)**, erected on the 500th anniversary of his founding of the university, and designed by a German, Ernst Julius Hähnel, in the days before the reawakening of Czech sculpture. To his left is an unusual plaque commemorating a Czech who was shot by mistake by the Red Army during the liberation on May 9, 1945.

The two churches facing onto the square are both quite striking and definitely worth exploring. The half-brick church of **sv František z Assisi** (St Francis of Assisi) was built in the 1680s to a design by Jean-Baptiste Mathey for the Czech Order of Knights of the Cross with a Red Star, the original gatekeepers of the old Judith Bridge. The order was founded by St Anežka (Agnes) in the thirteenth century, and reached the zenith of its power in the seventeenth century, during which its monks supplied most of the archbishops of Prague. The design of the church's interior, dominated by its huge dome, decorated with a fresco of *The Last Judgement* by Václav Vavřinec Reiner, and rich marble furnishings, served as a blueprint for numerous subsequent Baroque churches in Prague.

The **Galerie Křižovníků** (Tues–Sun 10am–1pm & 2–6pm; 40Kč), next door, houses a fairly indifferent Baroque art collection, various robes and mitres relating to the order, and a very bad copy of the altar from the Holy Rood Chapel in Karlštejn (see p.179). Better are the panels from the fifteenth-century altarpiece by Nicholas Puchner depicting the foundation of the order. However, the best section by far is the treasury, which contains a stunning collection of silver and gold chalices, monstrances and reliquaries purporting to harbour, among other things, a thorn from Christ's crown. The gallery also hosts fairly dreadful commercial art exhibitions. On your way out, though, don't miss the subterranean chapel, whose unusual stalactite decor was completed in 1683.

Over the road is the church of **sv Salvátor** (St Saviour), its facade prickling with saintly statues which are lit up enticingly at night. Founded in 1593, but not completed until 1714, sv Salvátor marks the beginning of the Jesuits' rise to power and is part of the Klementinum complex (see below). Like many of their churches, its design copies that of the Gesù church in Rome; it's worth a quick look, if only for the frothy stucco plasterwork and delicate ironwork in its triple-naved interior.

Karlova

Running from Křižovnické náměstí all the way to Malé náměstí is the narrow street of **Karlova**, packed with people winding their way towards Staroměstské náměstí, their attention divided between checking out the souvenir shops, and not losing their way. With Europop blaring from several shops, jesters' hats and puppets in abundance, and a strip club for good measure, the whole atmosphere can be oppressive in the height of summer, and is, in many ways, better savoured at night.

While much of what's on offer in Karlova is eminently missable, there is one sight worth seeking out, and that's the **Muzeum loutkářských kultur** (Puppet Museum; daily 10am–8pm; 100Kč; ⓦwww.puppetart.com), in the cool Gothic cellars of Karlova 12. Despite the appalling lack of information in either Czech or English, the museum, run by the international puppetry organization UNIMA, which has its headquarters here, has an impressive display of historic Czech puppets, both string and rod, mostly dating from the late nineteenth and the early twentieth centuries. Some of the most appealing figures are the wonderfully malevolent devils, and there's a great miniature theatre from 1933, complete with backcloth scenery changes.

At the first wiggle in Karlova, you come to the **Vlašská kaple** (Italian Chapel), which served the community of Italian masons, sculptors and painters who settled in Prague during the Renaissance period, and is still, strictly speaking, the property of the Italian state. The present Vlašská kaple is a tiny oval Baroque chapel completed in 1600, though sadly it's rarely open except for services.

You may have more luck with the adjacent church of **sv Kliment**, accessible from the same portal. It's a minor gem of Prague Baroque by Dientzenhofer with statues by Braun, a spectacular set of frescoes depicting the life of St Clement (whose fate was to be lashed to an anchor and hurled into the Black Sea), and an unusual spiky golden iconostasis added in the 1980s by its new owners, the Greek Catholic church, who observe Orthodox rites but, confusingly, belong to the Roman Catholic church.

On the opposite side of Karlova, at the junction with Liliová, is the former café, **U zlatého hada** (The Golden Serpent), where the Armenian Deomatus Damajan opened the city's first coffee house in 1708. According to legend, the café was always full, not least because Damajan had a red-wine fountain inside. It is now a café-restaurant, though sadly minus the fountain and its original furnishings.

Klementinum

As they stroll down Karlova, few people notice the **Klementinum** (April–Oct Mon–Fri 2–8pm, Sat & Sun 10am–8pm; Nov–March Sat & Sun 10am–8pm; 100Kč), the former Jesuit College on the north side of the street, which covers an area second in size only to the Hrad. In 1556, Ferdinand I summoned the Jesuits to Prague to help bolster the Catholic cause in Bohemia, giving them the church of sv Kliment (see above) which Dientzenhofer later rebuilt for them. Initially, the Jesuits proceeded with caution, but once the Counter-

Reformation set in, they were put in control of the entire university and provincial education system. From their secure base at sv Kliment, they began to establish space for a great Catholic seat of learning in the city by buying up the surrounding land, demolishing more than thirty old town houses, and, over the next two hundred years, gradually building themselves a palatial headquarters. In 1773, not long after the Klementinum was finally completed, the Jesuits were turfed out of the country and the building handed over to the university authorities.

Nowadays the Klementinum houses the National Library's collection of over five million volumes, which include the world's largest collection of works by the early English reformer, Yorkshireman John Wycliffe, whose writings had an enormous impact on the fourteenth-century Czech religious community, inspiring preachers such as Hus to speak out against the social conditions of the time. The **main entrance**, inconspicuously placed just past the church of sv Kliment, lets you into a series of rather plain courtyards. Here and there, however, parts of the original building have been left intact and the best bits are now open to the public. The entrance to the **Zrcadlová kaple** (Mirrored Chapel) is immediately to the left after passing through the archway on the far side of the first courtyard; its interior of fake marble, gilded stucco and mirror panels boasts fine acoustics but is open only for concerts.

Nearby is the visitors' entrance, where you must sign up for a thirty-minute guided tour (in English) in order to see the Klementinum's two most easily accessible attractions. The most spectacular sight is the **Barokní sál** (Baroque Library), a long room lined with leather tomes, whose ceiling is decorated by one continuous illusionistic fresco praising secular wisdom, and whose wrought-iron gallery balustrade is held up by wooden barley-sugar columns. Upstairs, at roughly the centre of the Klementinum complex, is the Jesuits' **Astronomická věž** (Astonomical Tower), from which you can enjoy a superb view over the centre of Prague. The tower is also the only place in the world that has being monitoring and recording meteorological data since 1775. Until 1928, the tower was also used to signal noon to the citizens of Prague: a man would wave a flag from the tower and a cannon would be fired from Petřín Hill.

Incidentally, Prague's most illustrious visiting scientist, **Johannes Kepler**, who succeeded Tycho Brahe as court astronomer to Rudolf II, lived quite close by at Karlova 4 for a number of years. A religious exile from his native Germany, Kepler drew up the first heliocentric laws on the movement of the planets whilst in Prague, though he did his planet-gazing in the Belvedér not in the Klementinum.

Mariánské náměstí and around

Where the Klementinum ends, the Renaissance corner house **U zlaté studně** (The Golden Well), now a wine bar and *pension* (see p.188), stands out like a wedge of cheese; its thick stucco reliefs of assorted saints were commissioned in 1701 by the owner in gratitude for having been spared the plague.

A short diversion here, down Seminářská, brings you out onto **Mariánské náměstí**, generally fairly deserted compared with Karlova. It's hard to believe that the rather severe **Nová radnice** (New Town Hall), on the east side of the square, was built by Osvald Polívka, architect of the exuberant Art-Nouveau Obecní dům (see p.124). Its most striking features are the two gargantuan figures which stand guard at either corner, by the sculptor of the Hus Monument, Ladislav Šaloun. The one on the left, looking like Darth Vader, is the "Iron Knight", mascot of the armourers' guild; to the right is the somewhat grotesquely caricatured sixteenth-century Jewish sage and scholar, Rabbi Löw (see p.101). Löw was visited by Death on several occasions, but escaped his clutches until he reached the ripe old age of 97, when the Grim Reaper hid in a rose innocently given to him by his (in this case, naked) granddaughter.

To get back to Karlova, head down Husova, past the Baroque **Clam-Gallasův palác**, which, despite its size – it takes up a good five or six old houses – is easy to overlook in this narrow space. It's a typically lavish affair by the Viennese architect Fischer von Erlach, with big and burly *Atlantes* supporting the portals. There are regular exhibitions (Tues–Sun 10am–6pm) and evening concerts, which allow you to climb the grandiose staircase and have a peek at the sumptuous Baroque ceremonial rooms.

Malé náměstí

After a couple more shops, boutiques, hole-in-the-wall bars and a final twist in Karlova, you emerge onto **Malé náměstí**, a square originally settled by French merchants in the twelfth century. The square was also home to the first apothecary in Prague, opened by a Florentine in 1353, and the tradition is continued today by the pharmacy **U zlaté koruny** (The Golden Crown), at no. 13, which boasts chandeliers and a restored Baroque interior. The square's best-known building, though, is the russet-red, neo-Renaissance **Rott Haus**, originally an ironmongers' shop founded by V.J. Rott in 1840, whose facade is smothered in agricultural scenes and motifs inspired by the Czech artist Mikuláš Aleš. At the centre of the square stands a fountain dating from 1560, which retains its beautiful, original wrought-iron canopy, though it's no longer functioning.

Staroměstské náměstí

East of Malé náměstí is **Staroměstské náměstí** (Old Town Square), easily the most spectacular square in Prague, and the traditional heart of the city. Most of the brightly coloured houses look solidly eighteenth-century, but their Baroque facades hide considerably older buildings. From the eleventh century onwards, this was the city's main marketplace, known simply as Velké náměstí (Great Square), to which all roads in Bohemia led, and where merchants from all over Europe gathered. When the five towns that made up Prague were united in 1784, it was the Old Town Square's town hall that was made the seat of the new city council, and for the next two hundred years this square (along with Wenceslas Square) witnessed the country's most violent demonstrations and battles. In summer, cafés spread out their tables, in winter there's a Christmas market, and all year round tourists pour in to watch the town hall clock chime, to sit on the steps of the Hus Monument, and to drink in this historic showpiece.

The Hus Monument

The most recent arrival in the square is the colossal **Jan Hus Monument**, a turbulent sea of blackened bodies – the oppressed to his right, the defiant to his left – out of which rises the majestic moral authority of Hus himself, gazing into the horizon (for more on Hus, see box on p.96). For the sculptor

Ladislav Šaloun, a maverick who received no formal training, the monument was his life's work, commissioned in 1900 when the Art-Nouveau style, Viennese Secession, was at its peak, but strangely old-fashioned by the time it was completed in 1915. It would be difficult to claim that it blends in with its Baroque surroundings, yet this has never mattered to the Czechs, for whom its significance goes far beyond aesthetic merit.

The Austrians refused to hold an official unveiling of the statue; in protest, on July 6, 1915, the 500th anniversary of the death of Hus, Praguers smothered the monument in flowers. Since then it has been a powerful symbol of Czech nationalism: in March 1939, it was draped in swastikas by the invading Nazis, and in August 1968, it was shrouded in funereal black by Praguers, protesting at the Soviet invasion. The inscription along the base is a quote from the will of Comenius, one of Hus's later followers, and includes Hus's most famous dictum, *Pravda vítězí* (Truth Prevails), which has been the motto of just about every Czech revolution since then.

Staroměstská radnice

It wasn't until the reign of King John of Luxembourg (1310–46) that Staré Město was allowed to build its own town hall, the **Staroměstská radnice**. Short of funds, the citizens decided against an entirely new structure, buying a corner house on the square instead and simply adding an extra floor; later on, they added the east wing, with its graceful Gothic oriel and obligatory wedge-tower. Gradually, over the centuries, the neighbouring merchants' houses to the west were incorporated into the building, so that now it stretches all the way across to the richly sgraffitoed **Dům U minuty**, which juts out into the square.

On May 8, 1945, on the final day of the Prague Uprising, the Nazis still held on to Staroměstské náměstí, and in a last desperate act set fire to the town hall – one of the few buildings to be irrevocably damaged in the old town. The tower and oriel chapel were rebuilt immediately, but of the neo-Gothic **east wing**, which stretched almost to the church of sv Mikuláš, only a crumbling fragment remains; the rest of it is marked by the stretch of grass to the north. Embedded in the wall of the tower is a plaque marked "Dukla", and a case containing a handful of earth from the Slovak pass where some 80,000 Soviet and Czechoslovak soldiers lost their lives in the first (and most costly) battle to liberate the country in October 1944.

Below, set into the paving, are 27 **white crosses** commemorating the Protestant leaders who were condemned to death on the orders of the Emperor Ferdinand II, following the Battle of Bílá hora. They were publicly executed in the square on June 21, 1621 by the Prague executioner, Jan Mlydář: 24 enjoyed the nobleman's privilege and had their heads lopped off; the three remaining commoners were hung, drawn and quartered. Mlydář also chopped off the right hand of three of the nobles, and hacked off the tongue of the rector of Prague University, Johannes Jessenius, which he then nailed to their respective severed heads for public display on the Charles Bridge.

The Astronomical Clock

Today, the town hall's most popular feature is its *orloj* or **Astronomical Clock** – on the hour (daily 8am–8pm), a crowd of tourists gather in front of the tower to watch a mechanical dumbshow by the clock's assorted figures. The Apostles shuffle past the top two windows, bowing to the audience, while perched on pinnacles below are the four threats to the city as perceived by the medieval mind: Death carrying his hourglass and tolling his bell, the Jew with his moneybags (since 1945 minus his stereotypical beard), Vanity admiring his reflection, and a turbaned Turk shaking his head. Beneath the moving figures, four characters representing Philosophy, Religion, Astronomy and History, stand motionless throughout the performance. Finally, a cockerel pops out and flaps its wings to signal that the show's over; the clock then chimes the hour. The clock itself has been here since the beginning of the fifteenth century; the working figures were added in 1490 by a **Master Hanuš** who, legend has it, was then blinded with a red-hot poker by the town councillors, to make sure he couldn't repeat the job for anyone else. In retaliation, he groped his way around the clock, succeeded in stopping it, and then promptly died of a heart attack – the clock stayed broken for over eighty years.

The complex clock face tells three different sets of time: the golden hand points to a double set of Roman numerals from I to XII, and when the hand points to the top XII, it's noon (Central European Time); it also points to the outer ring of Gothic numbers from 1 to 24, which can rotate independently, and when the hand points to 24 it is sunset (Old Bohemian Time); finally, the numbers from 1 to 12 immediately below the Roman numerals divide the day into twelve hours, however many normal hours of daylight there are, and the golden sun tells you what time of day it is (Babylonian Time). The clock also charts – as the medieval astrologer saw it – the movements of the sun and planets around the earth, and the movement of the sun and moon through the signs of the zodiac; therefore, if you know how, you can determine the date. The revolving dial below the clock face is decorated with bucolic paintings of the "cycle of twelve idylls from the life of the Bohemian peasant", plus the signs of the zodiac, by Josef Mánes, a leading light in the Czech national revival. Around the edge, yet another pointer shows what day of the month and week it is, and, more importantly, what saint's day it is (and therefore when it's a holiday).

The interior of the radnice

The powder-pink facade on the south side of the town hall now forms the **entrance** to the whole complex (Mon 11am–5pm, Tues–Sun 9am–6pm; 30Kč). Apart from getting married, you can also sign up for a twenty-minute guided tour of the few rooms that survived the last war. It was in these rooms that the Bohemian kings were elected until the Habsburgs established hereditary rule, and in 1422 Jan Želivský, the fiery Hussite preacher and inspiration behind Prague's first defenestration (see p.129), was executed here. Despite being steeped in history, there's not much of interest here, apart from a few pretty decorated ceilings, striped with chunky beams, and a couple of Renaissance portals. You'll probably get more enjoyment from climbing the tower (another 30Kč) for the panoramic sweep across Prague's spires. You can also visit the chapel, designed by Peter Parler, which has patches of medieval wall painting, and wonderful grimacing corbels at the foot of the ribbed vaulting. If you get there just before the clock strikes the hour, you can watch the Apostles going out on their parade; the figures all had to be re-carved by a local puppeteer after the war.

The church of sv Mikuláš

The destruction of the east wing of the town hall in 1945 rudely exposed Kilian Ignaz Dientzenhofer's church of **sv Mikuláš**, built in just three years between 1732 and 1735. The original church was founded by German merchants in the thirteenth century, and served as Staré Město's parish church until the Týn church (see p.88) was completed. Later, it was handed over to the

Benedictines, who commissioned Dientzenhofer to replace it with the present building. His hand is obvious: the south front is decidedly luscious – Braun's blackened statuary pop up at every cornice – promising an interior to surpass even its sister church of sv Mikuláš in Malá Strana, which Dientzenhofer built with his father immediately afterwards (see p.64). Inside, however, it's a curious mixture. Although caked in the usual mixture of stucco and fresco and boasting an impressive dome, the church has been stripped over the years of much of its ornament and lacks the sumptuousness of its namesake on the left bank. This is partly due to the fact that Joseph II closed down the monastery and turned the church into a storehouse, and partly because it's now owned by the very "low", modern, Czech Hussite Church.

Palác Kinských and around

The largest secular building on the square is the Rococo **palác Kinských** (Tues–Sun 10am–6pm; Ⓦwww.ngprague.cz), designed by Kilian Ignaz Dientzenhofer and built by his son-in-law Anselmo Lurago. In the nineteenth century it became a German *Gymnasium*, which was attended by, among others, Franz Kafka (whose father ran a haberdashery shop on the ground floor). The palace is perhaps most notorious, however, as the venue for the fateful speech by the Communist prime minister, Klement Gottwald, who walked out onto the grey stone balcony one snowy February morning in 1948, flanked by his Party henchmen, to address the thousands of enthusiastic supporters who packed the square below. It was the beginning of *Vítězná února* (Victorious February), the bloodless coup which brought the Communists to power and sealed the fate of the country for the next 41 years. Gottwald's appearance forms the memorable opening to Milan Kundera's novel *The Book of Laughter and Forgetting* (see "Books", p.266). The top floor now hosts top-flight exhibitions of graphic art put on by the Národní galerie.

Until relatively recently, the adjacent **Dům U kamenného zvonu** (House at the Stone Bell; Tues–Sun 10am–6pm; 80Kč; Ⓦwww.citygalleryprague.cz) was much like any other of the merchant houses that line Staroměstské náměstí – covered in a thick icing of Baroque plasterwork and topped by an undistinguished roof gable. In the process of restoration in the 1970s, however, it was controversially stripped down to its Gothic core, uncovering the original honey-coloured stonework and simple wedge roof, and it now serves as a central venue for cutting-edge modern art exhibitions, lectures and concerts, organized by the City of Prague Gallery.

The south side of the square boasts a fine array of facades, mostly Baroque, with the notable exception of the neo-Renaissance **Štorchův dům**, adorned with a late nineteenth-century sgraffito painting of St Wenceslas by Mikuláš Aleš. Next door, **U bílého jednorožce** (The White Unicorn) – the sixteenth-century house sign actually depicts a one-horned ram – was Prague's one and only *salon*, run by Berta Fanta. An illustrious membership, including Kafka, Max Brod and Franz Werfel, came here to attend talks given by, among others, Albert Einstein and Rudolf Steiner.

The Týn church

Staré Město's most impressive Gothic structure, the mighty **Týn church** (Matka boží před Týnem), is a far more imposing building than the square's church of sv Mikuláš. Its two irregular towers, bristling with baubles, spires and pinnacles, rise like giant antennae above the arcaded houses which otherwise obscure its facade, and are spectacularly lit up at night. Like the nearby Hus Monument, the Týn church, begun in the fourteenth century under Charles IV, is a source of Czech national pride. In an act of defiance, George of Poděbrady, the last Czech and the only Hussite king of Bohemia, adorned the high stone gable with a statue of himself and a giant gilded *kalich* (chalice), the mascot of all Hussite sects. The church remained a hotbed of Hussitism until the Protestants' crushing defeat at the Battle of Bílá hora, after which the chalice was melted down to provide the newly ensconced statue of the Virgin Mary with a golden halo, sceptre and crown.

Despite being one of the main landmarks of Staré Město, it's well-nigh impossible to appreciate the church from anything but a considerable distance, since it's boxed in by the houses around it, some of which are actually built right against the walls. To reach the entrance, take the third arch on the left, which passes under the Venetian gables of the former Týn School. The church's **interior** has recently been restored and the rather appealing gloom of the place has been swept away. Instead, the lofty, narrow nave is now bright white, and punctuated at ground level by black and gold Baroque altarpieces. One or two original Gothic furnishings survive, most notably the fifteenth-century baldachin, housing a winged altar in the north aisle, and, opposite, the pulpit, whose panels are enhanced by some sensitive nineteenth-century icons. Behind the pulpit, you'll find a superb, winged altar depicting John the Baptist, dating from 1520, and executed by the artist known as Master I. P. To view the north portal and canopy, which bears the hallmark of Peter Parler's workshop, you must go back outside and head down Týnská.

The pillar on the right of the chancel steps contains the red marble **tomb of Tycho Brahe**, the famous Danish astronomer who arrived in Prague wearing a silver and gold false nose, having lost his own in a duel over a woman in Rostock. Court astronomer to Rudolf II for just two years, Brahe laid much of the groundwork for Johannes Kepler's later discoveries – Kepler getting his chance of employment when Brahe died of a burst bladder after one of Petr Vok's notorious binges in 1601 – hence the colloquial expression *nechci umřít jako Tycho Brahe* ("I don't want to die like Tycho Brahe", in other words, I need to go to the toilet).

Dům U zlatého prstenů

If you head down the alleyway to the north of the Týn church, known as Týnská, you'll come to the handsome Gothic town house of **Dům U zlatého prstenů** (House of the Golden Ring; Tues–Sun 10am–6pm; 60Kč; ⓦwww .citygalleryprague.cz), now used by the City of Prague Gallery to show some of its twentieth-century Czech art. If you're not heading out to the modern art museum in the Veletržní palác (see p.152), then this is a good taster. The permanent collection is spread out over three floors, and arranged thematically rather than chronologically, while the cellars provide space for contemporary exhibitions; there's also a nice café across the courtyard.

On the first floor, symbolism looms large, with *Destitute Land*, Max Švabinský's none-too-subtle view of life under the Habsburg yoke, and a smattering of works by two of Bohemia's best-loved eccentrics, Josef Váchal and František Bílek. There's a decent selection of dour 1920s paintings, too, typified by *Slagheaps in the Evening II* by Jan Zrzavý, plus the usual Czech Surrealist suspects, Josef Síma, Toyen and Jiří Štyrský. More refreshing is the sight of Eduard Stavinoha's cartoon-like *Striking Demonstrators 24.2.1948*, an ideological painting from 1948 that appears almost like Pop Art.

Antonín Slavíček's easy-on-the-eye Impressionist views of Prague kick off proceedings on the second floor, along with works by Cubist Emil Filla, and less well-known wartime Surrealist Václav Chad, who died in his early twenties. Also on this floor, you'll find Zbyšek Sion's absinthe nightmare, the strange perforated metal sheets of Alena Kučerova and the mechanical relief sculptures of *Blind Men* by Vladimír Janoušek. Very few works have overt political messages – Michael Rittstein's political allegory *Slumber beneath a Large Hand* and Eva Kmentová's plaster-cast *Hands* peppered with bullet holes in response to 1968, being two of the most obvious exceptions.

Highlights on the third floor include an excellent collection of mad collages by Jiří Kolář, made up of cut-up pieces of reproductions of other artists' works; abstract Vorticist works by Zdeněk Sýkora; and studies for kinetic-light sculptures by Zdeněk Pešanek. Don't be surprised, however, if some of the works mentioned above are nowhere to be seen, as the pictures on display do change quite frequently.

Týn (Ungelt)

Just off Týnská, directly behind the Týn church, lies the picturesque cobbled courtyard of **Týn**, better known by its German name, **Ungelt** (meaning "No Money", a pseudonym used to deter marauding invaders), which, as the trading base of German merchants, was one of the first settlements on the Vltava. A hospice, church and hostel were built for the use of the merchants, and by the fourteenth century the area had become an extremely successful international marketplace; soon afterwards the traders moved up to the Hrad, and the court was transformed into a palace. The whole complex has now been fairly recently restored, and is now a great place in which to stroll: the Dominicans have reclaimed one section, while the rest houses various upmarket shops, cafés, pubs, restaurants and a hotel.

From Celetná to the Anežský klášter

Celetná, whose name comes from the bakers who used to bake a particular type of small loaf (*calty*) here in the Middle Ages, leads east from Staroměstské náměstí direct to the Prašná brána, one of the original gateways of the old town. It's one of the oldest streets in Prague, lying along the former trade route from the old town market square, as well as on the *králová cesta*. Its buildings were smartly re-faced in the Baroque period, and their pastel shades are now crisply maintained. Most of Celetná's shops veer towards the chic end of the Czech market, making it a popular place for a bit of window-shopping. Dive down one of the covered passages to the left and into the backstreets, however, and you'll soon lose the crowds, and eventually end up at the atmospheric ruins of **Anežsky klášter**, now home to the Národní galerie's Gothic Czech art collection.

Dům U černé Matky boží

Two-thirds of the way along Celetná, at the junction with Ovocný trh, is the **Dům U černé Matky boží** (House at the Black Madonna; Tues–Sun 10am–6pm; 70Kč; ⓦ www.ecn.cz/cmvu), built as a department store in 1911–12 by

Josef Gočár and one of the best examples of Czech Cubist architecture in Prague. It was a short-lived style, whose most surprising attribute, in this instance, is its ability to adapt existing Baroque motifs: Gočár's house sits much more happily amongst its eighteenth-century neighbours than, for example, the functionalist shop opposite – one of Gočár's later designs from the 1930s.

Appropriately enough, the building now houses a small, but excellent, permanent exhibition of **Český kubismus** (Czech Cubism), on the top two floors, courtesy of the České muzeum výtvarných umění (Czech Museum of Applied Art). There's a little bit of everything from sofas and sideboards by Gočár himself, Pavel Janák and Josef Chochol, to paintings by Emil Filla and Josef Čapek, plus some wonderful sculptures by Otto Gutfreund. If the above has only whetted your appetite, there are more Czech Cubist exhibits in the Veletržní palác (see p.152), and more Cubist buildings in Vyšehrad (see p.137). In the meantime, the first, second and third floors are currently given over to temporary exhibitions of twentieth-century art, while the basement has been converted into a cheap café/restaurant.

The church of sv Jakub

Celetná ends at the fourteenth-century Prašná brána (see p.124), beyond which is náměstí Republiky, at which point, strictly speaking, you've left Staré Město behind. Back in the old town, head north from Celetná into the backstreets which conceal the Franciscan church of **sv Jakub** or St James (Mon–Sat 9am–12.30pm & 2.30–4pm, Sun 2–4pm), with its distinctive bubbling, stucco portal on Malá Štupartská. The church's massive Gothic proportions – it has the longest nave in Prague after the cathedral – make it a favourite venue for organ recitals, Mozart masses and other concerts. After the great fire of 1689, Prague's Baroque artists remodelled the entire interior, adding huge pilasters, a series of colourful frescoes and over twenty side altars. The most famous of these is the tomb of the count of Mitrovice, in the northern aisle, designed by Fischer von Erlach and Prague's own Maximilian Brokof.

The church has close historical links with the butchers of Prague, who were given a chapel in gratitude for their defence of the city in 1611 and 1648. Hanging high up on the west wall, on the right as you enter, is a thoroughly decomposed human forearm. It has been there for over four hundred years now, ever since a thief tried to steal the jewels of the Madonna from the high altar. As the thief reached out, the Virgin supposedly grabbed his arm and refused to let go. The next day the congregation of butchers had no option but to lop it off, and it has hung there as a warning ever since.

Anežský klášter

Further north through the backstreets, the **Anežský klášter** (Convent of St Agnes), Prague's oldest surviving Gothic building, stands within a stone's throw of the river as it loops around to the east. It was founded in 1233 as a Franciscan convent for the Order of the Poor Clares, and takes its name from Agnes (Anežka), youngest daughter of Přemysl Otakar I, who left her life of regal privilege to become the convent's first abbess. Agnes took her vows seriously, living on a diet of raw onions and fruit with long periods of fasting, and in 1874 she was beatified to try and combat the spread of Hussitism amongst the Czechs. There was much speculation about the wonders that would occur when she was officially canonized, an event which finally took place on November 12, 1989, when Czech Catholics were invited to a special mass at

△ Facade, church of sv Jakub

St Peter's in Rome. Four days later the Velvet Revolution began: a happy coincidence, even for agnostic Czechs.

The convent itself has enjoyed a chequered history. It was turned into an arsenal under the Hussites, and eventually closed down in 1782 by Joseph II, who turned it into a place where the Prague poor could live and set up their own workshops. The whole neighbourhood remained a slum area until well into this century, and its restoration only finally took place in the 1980s. The convent now provides a fittingly atmospheric setting for the Národní galerie's **medieval art collection** (Tues–Sun 10am–6pm; 100Kč; Ⓦ www.ngprague.cz), in particular the Gothic art, which first flourished here under the patronage of Charles IV. For an additional charge (40Kč or 120Kč for a combined ticket), you also get to look around the Gothic church and cloisters at the end (see below).

The exhibition is arranged chronologically, starting with a remarkable silver-gilt casket from 1360 used to house the skull of St Ludmila. The nine panels from the altarpiece of the Cistercian monastery at Vyšší Brod in South Bohemia, from around 1350, are among the finest in central Europe: the *Annunication* panel is particularly rich iconographically. The real gems of the collection, however, are the six panels by **Master Theodoric**, who painted over one hundred such paintings for Charles IV's castle chapel at Karlštejn (see p.179). These larger-than-life, half-length portraits of saints, church fathers and so on are full of intense expression and richly coloured, their depictions spilling onto the embossed frames.

The three late fourteenth-century panels by the **Master of Třeboň** show an ever greater variety of balance and depth, and the increasing influence of Flemish paintings of the period. Since the quality of the works in the gallery's largest room is pretty uneven, it's worth moving fairly swiftly on to the smaller rooms beyond, where you'll find two unusual carved wooden bust reliquaries of saints Adalbert and Wenceslas. For a glimpse of some extraordinary draughtsmanship, check out the woodcuts by Cranach the Elder, Dürer and the lesser-known Hans Burgkmair – the seven-headed beast in Dürer's *Apocalypse* cycle is particularly Harry Potter. One oil painting that stands out from the crowd is Albrecht Altdorfer's evocative *Martyrdom of St Florian*. Finally, don't miss the superb sixteenth-century wood sculptures by **Master I.P.**, including an incredibly detailed scene, *Christ the Saviour and the Last Judgement*, in which Death's entrails are in the process of being devoured by a frog.

If you've paid the extra charge, you also get to see the inside of the Gothic cloisters and the bare church that serves as a resting place for, among others, Václav I (1205–53), and St Agnes herself.

Southern Staré Město

The southern half of Staré Město is bounded by the *králová cesta* (the coronation route; see p.75) to the north, and the curve of Národní and Na příkopě, which follow the course of the old fortifications, to the south. There are no showpiece squares like Staroměstské náměstí here, but the complex web of narrow lanes and hidden passageways, many of which have changed little since medieval times, make this an intriguing quarter to explore, and one where it's easy to lose the worst of the crowds (and yourself).

Ovocný trh

Heading southwest from the Dům U černé Matky boží (see p.90), you enter **Ovocný trh**, site of the old fruit market, its cobbles fanning out towards the back of the lime-green and white **Stavovské divadlo** (Estates Theatre). Built in the early 1780s by Count Nostitz (after whom the theatre was originally named) originally for the entertainment of Prague's large and powerful German community, the theatre is one of the finest Neoclassical buildings in Prague, reflecting the enormous self-confidence of its patrons. The Stavovské divadlo has a place in Czech history, too, for it was here that the Czech national anthem, *Kde domov můj* (Where Is My Home), was first performed, as part of the comic opera *Fidlovačka*, by J.K. Tyl (after whom the theatre was later renamed). It is also something of a mecca for Mozart fans, since it was here, rather than in the hostile climate of Vienna, that the composer chose to premiere both *Don Giovanni* and *La Clemenza di Tito*. This is, in fact, one of the few opera houses in Europe which remains intact from Mozart's time (though it underwent major refurbishment during the nineteenth century), and it was used by Miloš Forman to film the concert scenes for his Oscar-laden *Amadeus*.

On the north side of the Stavovské divadlo is the home base of the **Karolinum** or Charles University, named after its founder Charles IV, who established it in 1348 as the first university in this part of Europe. Although it was open to all nationalities, with instruction in Latin, it wasn't long before disputes between the various "nations" came to a head. In 1408, Václav IV issued the Decree of Kutná Hora, which gave the Bohemian "nation" – both Czech- and German-speaking – a majority vote in the university. In protest, the other "nations" upped and left for Leipzig, the first of many ethnic problems which continued to bubble away throughout the university's six-hundred-year history until the forced and extremely violent expulsion of all German-speakers after World War II.

To begin with, the university had no fixed abode; it wasn't until 1383 that Václav IV bought the present site. All that's left of the original fourteenth-

---

The former Gottwald Museum

One block west of the Stavovské divadlo, at Rytířská 29, is the former Prague Savings Bank, a large, pompous, neo-Renaissance building designed in the 1890s by Osvald Polívka, before he went on to erect some of Prague's most flamboyant Art Nouveau structures. The building currently serves as a branch of Česká spořitelna (Mon–Fri 8am–6pm), and is definitely worth a quick peek inside; go up the monumental staircase and check out the main banking hall on the first floor, which now houses a café.

For over thirty years it housed the museum all Praguers loved to hate – dedicated to Klement Gottwald, the country's first Communist president. A joiner by trade, a notorious drunkard and womanizer by repute, he led the party with unswerving faith from the beginnings of Stalinism in 1929 right through to the show trials of the early 1950s. He died shortly after attending Stalin's funeral in 1953 – either from grief or, more plausibly, from drink.

Remarkably, his reputation survived longer than that of any other East European leader. While those whom he had wrongfully sent to their deaths were posthumously rehabilitated, and the figure of Stalin denigrated, Gottwald remained sacred, his statue gracing every town in the country. As late as October 1989, the Communists were happily issuing brand new 100Kčs notes emblazoned with his bloated face, only to have them withdrawn from circulation a month later, when the regime toppled.

century building is the Gothic oriel window which emerges from the south wall; the rest was trashed by the Nazis in 1945. The new main entrance is a modern red-brick curtain wall building by Jaroslav Fragner, set back from the street and inscribed with the original Latin name *Universitas Karolina*. Only a couple of small departments and the chancellor's office and administration are now housed here, with the rest spread over the length and breadth of the city. The heavily restored Gothic vaults, on the ground floor of the south wing, are now used as a contemporary art gallery.

Sv Havel and around

The junction of Melantrichova and Rytířská is always teeming with people pouring out of Staroměstské náměstí and heading for Wenceslas Square. Clearly visible from Melantrichova is Santini's undulating Baroque facade of the church of **sv Havel**, sadly no relation to the playwright-president but named after the Irish monk, St Gall. It was built in the thirteenth century to serve the local German community who had been invited to Prague partly to replace the Jewish traders killed in the city's 1096 pogrom. After the expulsion of the Protestants, the church was handed over to the Carmelites who redesigned the interior, now only visible through an iron grille.

Straight ahead of you as you leave sv Havel is Prague's last surviving **open-air market** – a poor relation of its Germanic predecessor, which stretched all the way from Ovocný trh to Uhelný trh. Traditionally a flower and vegetable market, it runs the full length of the arcaded Havelská, and sells everything from celery to CDs, with plenty of souvenirs and wooden toys in between.

Uhelný trh, sv Martin ve zdi and Bartolomějská

The market on Havelská runs west into **Uhelný trh**, which gets its name from the *uhlí* (coal) that was sold here in medieval times. Nowadays, however, it's Prague's red-light district – particularly along Perlová and Na Perštýně – and although you'll see little evidence during the day, it can get busy at night, as a result of which the local authorities are constantly trying to move the trade elsewhere.

South of Uhelný trh, down Martinská, the street miraculously opens out to make room for the twelfth-century church of **sv Martin ve zdi** (St Martin-in-the-Walls), originally built to serve the Czech community of the village of sv Martin, until it found itself the wrong side of the Gothic fortifications when they were erected in the fourteenth century. It's still essentially a Romanesque structure, adapted to suit Gothic tastes a century later; it was, however, closed down in 1784 by Joseph II and turned into a warehouse, shops and flats. The city bought the church in 1904 and thoroughly restored it, adding the creamy neo-Renaissance tower, and eventually handing it over to the Czech Brethren. For them, it has a special significance as the place where communion "in both kinds" (bread and wine), one of the fundamental demands of the Hussites, was first administered to the whole congregation, in 1414. To be honest, there's very little to see inside, which is just as well as it's open only for concerts nowadays.

Around the corner from sv Martin ve zdi is the gloomy, lifeless street of **Bartolomějská**, dominated by a tall, grim-looking building on its south side, which served as the main interrogation centre of the universally detested Communist secret police, the *Státní bezpečnost*, or StB. As in the rest of Eastern

Europe, the accusations (often unproven) and revelations of who exactly collaborated with the StB continue to cause the downfall of leading politicians right across the political spectrum. The building is now back in the hands of the Franciscan nuns who occupied the place prior to 1948, and its former police cells now serve as rooms for a small *pension* – it's even possible to stay in Havel's old cell (see p.188).

Betlémské náměstí

After leaving the dark shadows of Bartolomějská, the brighter aspect of **Betlémské náměstí** comes as a welcome relief. The square is named after the **Betlémská kaple** (Bethlehem Chapel; daily: April–Oct 9am–6pm; Nov–March 9am–5.30pm; 30Kč), whose high wooden gables face onto the square. This was founded in 1391 by religious reformists, who, denied the right to build a church, proceeded instead to build the largest chapel in Bohemia, with a total capacity of 3000. Sermons were delivered not in the customary Latin, but in the language of the masses – Czech. From 1402 to 1413, **Jan Hus** preached here (see box below), regularly pulling in more than enough commoners to fill the chapel. Hus was eventually excommunicated for his outspokenness, found guilty of heresy and burnt at the stake at the Council of Constance in 1415.

The chapel continued to attract reformists from all over Europe for another two centuries – the leader of the German Peasants' Revolt, **Thomas Müntzer**, preached here in the sixteenth century – until the advent of the Counter-Reformation in Bohemia. Inevitably, the chapel was handed over to the Jesuits, who completely altered the original building, only for it to be demolished after they were expelled by the Habsburgs in 1773. Of the original building, only the three outer walls remain, with restored patches of the biblical scenes, used to get the message across to the illiterate congregation. The rest is a scrupulous reconstruction of the fourteenth-century building by Jaroslav Fragner, using the original plans and a fair amount of imaginative guesswork. The initial reconstruction work was carried out after the war by the

Jan Hus

The legendary preacher – and Czech national hero – **Jan Hus** (often anglicized to John Huss) was born in the small village of Husinec in South Bohemia around 1372. From a childhood of poverty, he enjoyed a steady rise through the Czech education system, taking his degree at the Karolinum in the 1390s, and eventually being ordained as a deacon and priest around 1400. Although without doubt an admirer of the English religious reformer, John Wycliffe, Hus was by no means as radical as many of his colleagues who preached at the Betlémská kaple. Nor did he actually advocate many of the more famous tenets of the heretical religious movement that took his name: Hussitism. In particular, he never advocated giving communion "in both kinds" (bread and wine) to the general congregation.

In the end, it wasn't his disputes over Wycliffe, whose books were burned on the orders of the archbishop in 1414, that proved Hus's downfall, but an argument over the sale of indulgences to fund the papal wars that prompted his unofficial trial at the Council of Constance. Having been guaranteed safe conduct by Emperor Sigismund himself, Hus naïvely went to Constance to defend his views, and was burnt at the stake as a heretic on July 6, 1415. The Czechs were outraged, and Hus became a national hero overnight, inspiring thousands to rebel against the authorities of the day. In 1965, the Vatican finally overturned the sentence, and the anniversary of his death is now a national holiday.

Communists, who were keen to portray Hus as a Czech nationalist and social critic as much as a religious reformer, and, of course, to dwell on the revolutionary Müntzer's later appearances here.

Náprstkovo muzeum

At the western end of the square stands the **Náprstkovo muzeum** (Tues–Sun 9am–noon & 12.45–5.30pm; 30Kč; ⓦ www.aconet.cz/npm), whose founder, Czech nationalist Vojta Náprstek, was inspired by the great Victorian museums of London while in exile following the 1848 revolution. On his return, he turned the family brewery into a museum, initially intending it to concentrate on the virtues of industrial progress. Náprstek's interests gradually shifted towards anthropology, however, and it is his ethnographic collections that are now displayed in the museum; the original technological exhibits are housed in Prague's Národné technické muzeum (see p.152).

Despite the fact that the museum could clearly do with an injection of cash, it still manages to put on some really excellent temporary ethnographic exhibitions on the ground floor, and also does a useful job of promoting tolerance of different cultures. The permanent collection begins on the first floor, where you'll find the skeleton of a fin-whale over 20m long suspended from the ceiling. Underneath it there's a range of exhibits from the Americas, with everything from Inuit furs and Apache smoking pipes, decorated with porcupine quills and beads, to toy skeletons on bicycles from Mexico and Amazonian shrunken heads. Upstairs, there's a much smaller display of stuff from Australia and Oceania including some remarkable sculptures, but sadly the labelling is pretty minimal.

Husova

Between Betlémské náměstí and Karlova lies a confusing maze of streets, passageways and backyards, containing few sights as such, but nevertheless a joy to explore. One building that might catch your eye is the church of **sv Jiljí** (St Giles), on Husova, whose outward appearance suggests another Gothic masterpiece, but whose interior is decked out in the familiar black excess of the eighteenth century, with huge gilded acanthus leaf capitals and barley-sugar columns galore. The frescoes by Václav Vavřinec Reiner (who is buried in the church) are full of praise for his patrons, the Dominicans, who took over the church after the Protestant defeat of 1620. They were expelled, in turn, after the Communists took power, only to return following the events of 1989.

Reiner's paintings also depict the unhappy story of Giles himself, a ninth-century hermit who is thought to have lived somewhere in Provence. Out one day with his pet deer, Giles and his companion were chased by the hounds of King Wanda of the Visigoths. The hounds were rooted to the spot by an invisible power, while the arrow from the hunters struck Giles in the foot as he defended his pet – the hermit was later looked upon as the patron saint of cripples.

A short step away, just off Husova on Řetězová, is the **Dům pánů z Kunštátu a Poděbrad** (House of the Lords of Kunštát and Poděbrady; May–Sept Tues–Sun 10am–6pm; 20Kč), the home of George of Poděbrady before he became the Czechs' first and last Hussite king in 1458. It's not exactly gripping, but it does give you a clear impression of the antiquity of the houses in this area, and illustrates the way in which the new Gothic town was built on top of the old Romanesque one. Thus the floor on which you enter was originally the first floor of a twelfth-century palace, whose ground floor has been excavated in the cellars. Modern art exhibitions are also held here, and there's a laid-back summer-only café in the courtyard.

Anenské náměstí and the waterfront

Continuing west along Řetězová and Anenská brings you eventually to the waterfront. On Anenské náměstí, just before you reach the river, is the **Divadlo na zábradlí** (Theatre on the Balustrade). This was at the centre of Prague's absurdist theatre scene in the 1960s, with Havel himself working first as a stage-hand and later as resident playwright, and it remains one of Prague's better small theatres.

The gaily decorated neo-Renaissance building at the very end of Novotného lávka, on the riverfront itself, was once the city's waterworks. It now houses, among other things, the **Muzeum Bedřicha Smetany** (daily except Tues 10am–noon & 12.30–5pm; 50Kč), situated on the first floor. Bedřich Smetana (1824–84), despite having German as his mother tongue, was without doubt the most nationalist of all the great Czech composers, taking an active part in the 1848 revolution and the later national revival movement. He enjoyed his greatest success as a composer with *The Bartered Bride*, which marked the birth of Czech opera, but he was forced to give up conducting in 1874 with the onset of deafness, and eventually died of syphilis in a mental asylum. Unfortunately, the museum fails to capture much of the spirit of the man, concentrating instead on items such as his spectacles, and the garnet jewellery of his first wife. Still, the views across to the castle are good, and you get to wave a laser baton around in order to listen to his music. Outside, beneath the large weeping willow that droops over the embankment, the statue of the seated Smetana is rather unfortunately placed, with his back towards one of his most famous sources of inspiration, the River Vltava (Moldau in German).

Josefov

It is crowded with horses; traversed by narrow streets not remarkable for cleanliness, and has altogether an uninviting aspect. Your sanitary reformer would here find a strong case of overcrowding.

Walter White, "A July Holiday in Saxony, Bohemia and Silesia" (1857)

Less than half a century after Walter White's comments, all that was left of the former Jewish ghetto of **JOSEFOV** were six synagogues, the town hall and the medieval cemetery. At the end of the nineteenth century, a period of great economic growth for the Habsburg Empire, it was decided that Prague should be turned into a beautiful bourgeois city, modelled on Paris. The key to this transformation was the "sanitization" of the ghetto, a process, begun in 1893, which reduced the notorious malodorous backstreets and alleyways of Josefov to rubble and replaced them with block after block of luxurious five-storey mansions. The Jews, the poor, the gypsies and the prostitutes were cleared out so that the area could become a desirable residential quarter, rich in Art-Nouveau buildings festooned with decorative murals, doorways and sculpturing. This building frenzy marked the beginning of the end for a community which had existed in Prague for almost a millennium.

In any other European city occupied by the Nazis in World War II, what little was left of the old ghetto would have been demolished. But although Prague's Jews were transported to the new ghetto in Terezín, by a grotesque twist of fate the ghetto itself was preserved by Hitler himself in order to provide a site for his planned "Exotic Museum of an Extinct Race". With this in mind, Jewish artefacts from all over central Europe were gathered here, and now make up one of the richest collections of Judaica in Europe, and one of the most fascinating sights in Prague.

Also included in this chapter are the sights around náměstí Jana Palacha, adjacent to, but strictly speaking outside, the Jewish quarter, most notably the city's excellent Museum of Decorative Arts (or UPM).

A brief history of Jewish settlement in Prague

Jews probably settled in Prague as early as the tenth century and, initially at least, are thought to have settled on both sides of the river. In 1096, at the time of the first crusade, the first recorded pogrom took place, an event which may have hastened the formation of a much more closely knit "Jewish town" within Staré Město during the twelfth century. It wasn't until much later that Jews were actually herded into a **walled ghetto** (and several centuries before the

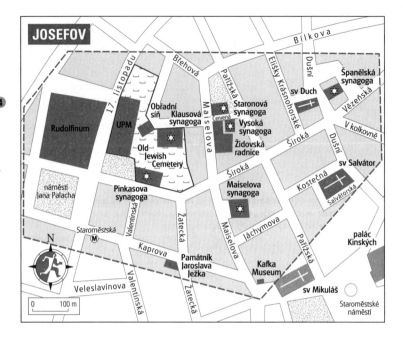

word "ghetto" was actually first coined in Venice), sealed off from the rest of the town and subject to a curfew. Jews were also subject to laws restricting their choice of profession to usury and the rag trade; in addition, some form of visible identification, a cap or badge, remained a more or less constant feature of Jewish life until the Enlightenment.

In 1262, Přemysl King Otakar II issued a *Statuta Judaeorum*, which granted the Jews their own religious and civil self-administration. In effect, however, the Jews were little more than the personal property of the king, and though Otakar himself appears to have been genuine in his motives, later rulers used the *Statuta* as a form of blackmail, extorting money whenever they saw fit. In 1389, during one of the worst pogroms, 3000 Jews were massacred over Easter, some while sheltering in the Old-New Synagogue – an event commemorated every year thereafter on Yom Kippur. In 1541, a fire ripped through Hradčany and Malá Strana and a Jew was tortured into "confessing" the crime. The Bohemian Estates immediately persuaded the Emperor Ferdinand I to expel the Jews from Prague. In the end, however, a small number of families were allowed to remain.

By contrast, the reign of Rudolf II (1576–1612) was a time of economic and cultural prosperity for the community, which is thought to have numbered up to 10,000, making it by far the largest Jewish community in the Diaspora. The Jewish mayor, **Mordecai Maisel**, Rudolf's minister of finance, became one of the richest men in Bohemia and the success symbol of a generation; his money bought and built the Jewish quarter, its town hall, a bath house, pavements and several synagogues. This was the "golden age" of the ghetto: the time of **Rabbi Löw**, the severe and conservative chief rabbi of Prague, who is now best known as the legendary creator of the Jewish Frankenstein's monster or "golem", though, in fact, the story of Rabbi Löw and the golem first appeared only in the nineteenth century (see box on p.101).

Amidst the violence of the Thirty Years' War, the Jews enjoyed an unusual degree of protection from the emperor, who was heavily dependent on their financial acumen. In 1648, Prague's Jews, along with the city's students, repaid their imperial bosses by repelling the marauding Swedes on the Charles Bridge, for which they won the lasting respect of Ferdinand III (1637–57). Things went into reverse again during the eighteenth century, until in 1744 Empress Maria Theresa used the community as a scapegoat for her disastrous war against the Prussians, and ordered the expulsion of all Jews from Prague. She allowed them to return in 1748, though only after much pressure from the guilds, who were missing Jewish custom. It was the enlightened **Emperor Joseph II** (1780–90) who did most to lift the restrictions on Jews. His 1781 Toleration Edict ended the dress codes, opened up education to all non-Catholics, and removed the gates from the ghetto. In 1850, the community paid him homage by officially naming the ghetto Josefov, or Josefstadt.

The downside to Joseph's reforms was that he was hellbent on assimilating the Jews into the rest of the population. The use of Hebrew or Yiddish in business transactions was banned, and Jews were ordered to Germanize their names (the list of permitted names comprised 109 male ones and 35 female). However, it wasn't until the social upheavals of 1848 that Jews were given equal status within the Empire and allowed officially to settle outside the confines of the ghetto – concessions which were accompanied by a number of violent anti-Semitic protests on the part of the Czechs.

The Golem

Legends concerning the animation of unformed matter (which is what the Hebrew word **golem** means), using the mystical texts of the Kabbala, were around long before Frankenstein started playing around with corpses. Two hungry fifth-century rabbis may have made the most practical golem when they sculpted a clay calf, brought it to life and then ate it; but the most famous is undoubtedly **Rabbi Löw's** giant servant made from the mud of the Vltava, who was brought to life when the rabbi placed a *shem* in its mouth, a tablet with a magic Hebrew inscription.

There are numerous versions of the tale, though the earliest invoking Rabbi Löw appeared only in the nineteenth century. In some, Yossel, the golem, is a figure of fun, flooding the rabbi's kitchen rather in the manner of Disney's *Sorcerer's Apprentice*; others portray him as the guardian of the ghetto, helping Rabbi Löw in his struggle with the anti-Semites at Rudolf II's court. In almost all versions, however, the golem finally runs amok. One particularly appealing tale is that the golem's rebellion was because Löw forgot to allow his creature to rest on the Sabbath. He was conducting the service when news of its frenzy arrived, and he immediately ran out to deal with it. The congregation, reluctant to continue without him, merely repeated the verse in the psalm the rabbi had been reciting until Löw returned. This explains the peculiarity at the Staronová synagoga where a line in the Sabbath service is repeated even today. In all the stories, the end finally comes when Löw removes the *shem* once and for all, and carries the remains of his creature to the attic of the Old-New Synagogue, where they have supposedly resided ever since (a fact disputed by the pedantic journalist Egon Erwin Kisch, who climbed in to check).

The legends are amended at each telling, and have proved an enduringly popular theme for generations of artists and writers. Paul Wegener's German expressionist film version and the dark psychological novel of Gustav Meyrink are probably two of the most powerful treatments. Meyrink's golem lives in a room which has no windows and no doors, emerging to haunt the streets of Prague every 33 years – by which reckoning, it's slightly overdue to make a reappearance.

From 1848 to the present day

From 1848, the ghetto went into terminal decline. The more prosperous Jewish families began to move to other districts of Prague, leaving behind only the poorest Jews and strictly Orthodox families, who were rapidly joined by the underprivileged ranks of Prague society: gypsies, beggars, prostitutes and alcoholics. By 1890, only twenty percent of Josefov's population were Jewish, yet it was still the most densely populated area in Prague, with a staggering 186,000 people crammed into its streets. The ghetto had become a carbuncle in the centre of bourgeois Prague, a source of disease and vice: in the words of Gustav Meyrink, a "demonic underworld, a place of anguish, a beggarly and phantasmagorical quarter whose eeriness seemed to have spread and led to paralysis".

The ending of restrictions, and the destruction of most of the old ghetto, increased the pressure on Jews to assimilate, a process which brought with it its own set of problems. Prague's Jews were split roughly half and half between predominantly German- or Yiddish-speakers and Czech-speakers. Yet since some two-thirds of Prague's German population were Jewish, and all Jews had been forced to take German names by Josef II, all Jews were seen by Czech nationalists as a Germanizing influence. Tensions between the country's German-speaking minority and the Czechs grew steadily worse in the run-up to World War I, and the Jewish community found itself caught in the firing line – "like powerless stowaways attempting to steer a course through the storms of embattled nationalities", as one Prague Jew put it.

Despite several anti-Semitic riots in the first few years following the war, the foundation of the new republic in 1918, and, in particular, its founder and first president, T.G. Masaryk, whose liberal credentials were impeccable, were welcomed by most Jews. For the first time in their history, Jews were given equal rights as a recognized ethnic minority, though only a small number opted to be registered as Jewish. The interwar period was probably the nearest Prague's Jewish community came to a second "golden age", a time most clearly expressed in the now famous flowering of its *Deutsche Prager Literatur*, led by German-Jewish writers such as Franz Werfel, Franz Kafka, Max Brod and Egon Erwin Kisch.

After Nazi troops occupied Prague on March 15, 1939, the city's Jews were subject to an increasingly harsh set of regulations, which saw them barred from most professions, placed under curfew, and compelled to wear a yellow Star of David. In November 1941, the first transport of Prague Jews set off for the new ghetto in Terezín, 60km northwest of Prague. Of the estimated 55,000 Jews in Prague at the time of the Nazi invasion, over 36,000 died in the camps. Many survivors emigrated to Israel and the USA. Of the 8000 who registered as Jewish in the Prague census of 1947, a significant number joined the Communist Party, only to find themselves victims of Stalinist anti-Semitic wrath during the 1950s.

It's difficult to calculate exactly how many Jews now live in Prague – around a thousand were officially registered as such prior to 1989 – though their numbers have undoubtedly been bolstered by those Czech Jews who have rediscovered their roots, and, more significantly, by the new influx of Jewish Americans and Israelis. The controversy over Jewish property – most of which was seized by the Nazis, and therefore not covered by the original restitution law – has mostly been resolved, allowing the community to reclaim, among other things, the six synagogues, the town hall and the cemetery of Josefov itself.

The former ghetto

Geographically, Josefov lies within the Staré Město, to the northwest of Staroměstské náměstí, between the main square and the River Vltava. The warren-like street plan of the old ghetto has long since disappeared, and through the heart of Josefov the ultimate bourgeois avenue, **Pařížská**, now runs, a riot of turn-of-the-century sculpturing, spikes and turrets, its ground floor premises home to swanky boutiques and cafés. If Josefov can still be said to have a main street, it is really the parallel street of **Maiselova**, named after the community's sixteenth-century leader. The sheer volume of tourists – over a million a year – that visit Josefov has brought with it the inevitable rash of souvenir stalls, flogging dubious "Jewish" souvenirs, and, it has to be said, the whole area is now something of a tourist trap. Yet to skip this part of the old town is to miss out on a whole slice of the city's cultural history.

Staronová synagoga

Walking down Maiselova, it's impossible to miss the steep, sawtooth brick gables of the **Staronová synagoga** or Altneuschul (Old-New Synagogue), so called because when it was built it was indeed very new, though it eventually became the oldest synagogue in Josefov. Begun in the second half of the thirteenth century, it is, in fact, the oldest functioning synagogue in Europe, one of the earliest Gothic buildings in Prague and still the religious centre for Prague's Orthodox Jews. Since Jews were prevented by law from becoming architects, the synagogue is thought to have been constructed by the Franciscan builders working on the convent of sv Anežka. Its five-ribbed vaulting is unique for Bohemia; the extra, purely decorative rib was added to avoid any hint of a cross.

To enter the synagogue, you need a separate **ticket** (200Kč), which you can buy from the ticket office opposite the synagogue's entrance on Červená; the ticket also covers entry to the Jubilejní synagoga in Nové Město (see p.125). Men are asked to cover their heads out of respect – paper *kippahs* are handed out at the ticket office, though a handkerchief will do. Note, too, that the synagogue closes around 2pm on Fridays, and all day during Jewish holidays.

To get to the **main hall**, you must pass through one of the two low vestibules from which women watch the proceedings through narrow slits. Above the entrance is an elaborate tympanum covered in the twisting branches of a vine tree, its twelve bunches of grapes representing the tribes of Israel. The low glow from the chandeliers is the only light in the hall, which is mostly taken up with the elaborate wrought-iron cage enclosing the *bimah* in the centre. In 1357, Charles IV allowed the Jews to fly their own municipal standard, a moth-eaten remnant of which is still on show, bearing the Star of David (Prague's Jewish

---

Visiting Josefov

All the "sights" of Josefov (Ⓦ www.jewishmuseum.cz), bar the Staronová synagoga, are covered by an all-in-one 280Kč ticket, available from the quarter's numerous ticket offices. Opening hours vary but are basically daily except Saturday April–October 9am–6pm, November–March 9am–4.30pm. In order to try and regulate the flow of visitors, at peak times, a timed entry system comes into operation, giving you around twenty minutes at each sight, though don't worry too much if you don't adhere rigidly to your timetable.

community were the first to adopt the Star as their official symbol). The other flag – a tattered red banner – was a gift to the community from Emperor Ferdinand III for helping fend off the Swedes in 1648. On the west wall a glass cabinet, shaped like Moses' two tablets of stone, is filled with tiny personalized light bulbs, which are paid for by grieving relatives and light up on the anniversary of the person's death (there's even one for Kafka).

To the north of the synagogue is one of the many statues in Prague that were hidden from the Nazis for the duration of the war: an anguished statue of Moses by František Bílek, himself a committed Protestant.

Židovská radnice and Maiselova synagoga

Just south of the Staronová synagoga stands the **Židovská radnice** (Jewish Town Hall), one of the few such buildings to survive the Holocaust. Founded and funded by Maisel in the sixteenth century, it was later rebuilt as the creamy-pink Baroque house you now see, housing, among other things, a kosher restaurant. The belfry, permission for which was granted by Ferdinand III, has a clock on each of its four sides, plus a Hebrew one stuck on the north gable which, like the Hebrew script, goes "backwards". Adjacent to the town hall is the **Vysoká synagoga** (High Synagogue), whose dour, grey facade belies its rich interior, now used for religious services and closed to the general public.

On Kafka's trail

Prague never lets go of you... this little mother has claws. We ought to set fire to it at both ends, on Vyšehrad and Hradčany, and maybe then it might be possible to escape.

Franz Kafka, "Letter to Oskar Polak" (December 2, 1902)

Franz Kafka was born on July 3, 1883, above the *Batalion* Schnapps bar on the corner of Maiselova and Kaprova (the original building has long since been torn down, but a gaunt-looking modern bust now commemorates the site). He spent most of his life in and around Josefov. His father was an upwardly mobile small businessman from a Czech-Jewish family of kosher butchers (Kafka himself eventually became a vegetarian), his mother from a wealthy German-Jewish family of merchants. The family owned a haberdashery shop, located at various premises on or near Staroměstské náměstí. In 1889, they moved out of Josefov and lived for the next seven years in the beautiful Renaissance Dům U minuty, next door to the Staroměstská radnice, during which time Kafka attended the *Volksschule* on Masná (now a Czech primary school), followed by a spell at an exceptionally strict German *Gymnasium*, located on the third floor of the palác Kinských.

At 18, he began a law degree at the German half of the Karolinum, which was where he met his lifelong friend and posthumous biographer and editor, Max Brod. Kafka spent most of his working life as an accident insurance clerk, until he was forced to retire through ill health in 1922. Illness plagued him throughout his life and he spent many months as a patient at the innumerable spas in *Mitteleuropa*. He was engaged three times, twice to the same woman, but never married, finally leaving home at the age of 31 for bachelor digs on the corner of Dlouhá and Masná, where he wrote the bulk of his most famous work, *The Trial*. He died of tuberculosis at the age of 40 in a sanatorium just outside Vienna, on June 3, 1924, and is buried in the Nový židovský hřbitov in Žižkov (see p.147).

As a German among Czechs, a Jew among Germans, and an agnostic among

Founded and paid for entirely by Mordecai Maisel, the neo-Gothic **Maiselova synagoga**, set back from the neighbouring houses south down Maiselova, was, in its day, one of the most ornate synagogues in Josefov. Nowadays, its bare whitewashed turn-of-the-century interior houses an exhibition on the history of the Jewish community up until the 1848 emancipation, as well as glass cabinets filled with gold and silverwork, *hanukkah* candlesticks, *torah* scrolls and other religious artefacts.

Pinkasova synagoga

Jutting out at an angle on the south side of the cemetery, with its entrance on Široká, the **Pinkasova synagoga** was built in the 1530s for the powerful Horovitz family, and has undergone countless restorations over the centuries. In 1958, the synagogue was transformed into a chilling memorial to the 77,297 Czech Jews killed during the Holocaust. The memorial was closed shortly after the 1967 Six Day War – due to damp, according to the Communists – and remained so, allegedly due to problems with the masonry, until it was finally, painstakingly restored in the 1990s. All that remains of the synagogue's original decor today is the ornate *bimah* surrounded by a beautiful wrought-iron grille, supported by barley-sugar columns.

Of all the sights of the Jewish quarter, the Holocaust memorial is perhaps the most moving, with every bit of wall space taken up with the carved stone list

believers, Kafka had good reason to live in a constant state of fear, or *Angst*. Life was precarious for Prague's Jews, and the destruction of the Jewish quarter throughout his childhood – the so-called "sanitization" – had a profound effect on his psyche, as he himself admitted. It comes as a surprise to many Kafka readers that anyone immersed in so beautiful a city could write such claustrophobic and paranoid texts; and that as a member of the café society of the time, he could write in a style so completely at odds with his verbose, artistic friends. It's also hard to accept that Kafka could find no publisher for *The Castle* or *The Trial* during his lifetime.

After his death, Kafka's works were published in Czech and German and enjoyed brief critical acclaim, before the Nazis banned them, first within Germany, then across Nazi-occupied Europe. Even after the war, Kafka, along with most German-Czech authors, was deliberately overlooked in his native country, since he belonged to a community and a culture which had been exiled. In addition, his account of the terrifying brutality and power of bureaucracy over the individual, though not in fact directed at totalitarian systems as such, was too close to the bone for the Communists. The 1962 Writers' Union conference at Liblice finally broke the official silence on Kafka, and, for many people, marked the beginning of the Prague Spring. In the immediate aftermath of the 1968 Soviet invasion, the Kafka bust was removed from Josefov, and his books remained unpublished in Czechoslovakia until 1990.

Having been *persona non grata* in his homeland for most of the last century, Kafka now suffers from over-exposure, due to his popularity with western tourists. The term "Kafkaesque", denoting some unfathomable, bureaucratic nightmare, has now entered the English language, and his image is plastered across T-shirts, mugs and postcards all over the city centre. The small **museum** on the site of Kafka's birthplace (Tues–Sat 10am–6pm; 40Kč), next door to the church of sv Mikuláš, retells Kafka's life simply but effectively with pictures and quotes (in Czech, German and English), and flogs souvenirs.

of victims, stating simply their name, date of birth and date of death or transportation to the camps. It is the longest epitaph in the world, yet it represents a mere fraction of those who died in the Nazi concentration camps. Upstairs in a room beside the women's gallery, there's also a harrowing exhibition of drawings by children from the Jewish ghetto in Terezín (see p.169), most of whom later perished in the camps.

Starý židovský hřbitov (Old Jewish Cemetery)

At the heart of Josefov is the **Starý židovský hřbitov** (Old Jewish Cemetery), known as *beit hayyim* in Hebrew, meaning "House of Life". Established in the fifteenth century, it was in use until 1787, by which time there were an estimated 100,000 buried here, one on top of the other, six palms apart, and as many as twelve layers deep. The enormous numbers of visitors has meant that the graves themselves have been roped off to protect them, and a one-way system introduced: you enter from the Pinkasova synagoga, on Široká, and leave by the Klausová synagoga. The oldest grave, dating from 1439, belongs to the poet Avigdor Karo, who lived to tell the tale of the 1389 pogrom. Get there before the crowds – a difficult task for much of the year – and the cemetery can be a poignant reminder of the ghetto, its inhabitants subjected to inhuman overcrowding even in death. The rest of Prague recedes beyond the sombre lime trees and cramped perimeter walls, the haphazard headstones and Hebrew inscriptions casting a powerful spell.

Each headstone bears a symbol denoting the profession or tribe of the deceased: a pair of hands for the Cohens; a pitcher and basin for the Levites;

scissors for a tailor; a violin for a musician. On many graves you'll see pebbles, some holding down *kvittleh* or small messages of supplication. The greatest number of these sits on the grave of Rabbi Löw, creator of the "golem" (see box on p.101), who is buried by the wall directly opposite the entrance; followed closely by the rich Renaissance tomb of Mordecai Maisel, some ten metres to the southeast.

Obřadní síň and Klausová synagoga

Immediately on your left as you leave the cemetery is the **Obřadní síň**, a lugubrious neo-Renaissance house built in 1906 as a ceremonial hall by the Jewish Burial Society. Appropriately enough, it's now devoted to an exhibition on Jewish traditions of burial and death, though it would probably be more useful if you could visit it before heading off into the cemetery rather than after.

Close to the entrance to the cemetery is the **Klausová synagoga**, a late seventeenth-century building, founded in the 1690s by Mordecai Maisel on the site of several small buildings (*klausen*), in what was then a notorious red-light district of Josefov. The ornate Baroque interior contains a rich display of religious objects from embroidered *kippah* to *Kiddush* cups, and explains the very basics of Jewish religious practice, and the chief festivals or High Holidays.

Španělská synagoga

East of Pařížská, up Široká, stands the **Španělská synagoga** (Spanish Synagogue), built on the spot once occupied by Prague's Alt Schul or Old Synagogue. The current building, begun in 1868, is by far the most ornate synagogue in Josefov, its stunning, gilded Moorish interior deliberately imitating the Alhambra (hence its name). Every available surface is smothered with a profusion of floral motifs and geometric patterns, in vibrant reds, greens and blues, which are repeated in the synagogue's huge stained-glass windows. The synagogue now houses an interesting exhibition on the history of Prague's Jews from the time of the 1848 emancipation to the Holocaust. Lovely, slender, painted cast-iron columns hold up the women's gallery, where the displays include a fascinating set of photos depicting the old ghetto at the time of its demolition. There's a section on Prague's German-Jewish writers, including Kafka, and information on the planned Nazi museum and the Holocaust. Also worth a peek are the changing art exhibitions at the **Galerie Roberta Guttmanna** (hours as for the synagogue), round the back of the synagogue at U staré školy 3.

Around náměstí Jana Palacha

If you happen to be in the Josefov area on a Tuesday afternoon, it's worth taking the opportunity to visit the **Památník Jaroslava Ježeka** (Tues 1–6pm; 10Kč), which occupies one room of the first-floor flat of the avant-garde composer Jaroslav Ježek (1906–42), at Kaprova 10. It's a great way to escape the crowds, hear some of Ježek's music, and admire the Modrý pokoj (Blue Room), with its functionalist furniture and grand piano, in which he did his composing.

· Kaprova and Široká emerge from Josefov at **náměstí Jana Palacha**, previously called náměstí Krasnoarmejců (Red Army Square) and embellished with a flowerbed in the shape of a red star (now replaced by the circular vent of an underground car park), in memory of the Soviet dead who were temporarily buried here in May 1945. It was probably this, as much as the fact that the building on the east side of the square is the Faculty of Philosophy, where Jan Palach (see p.255) was a student, that prompted the new authorities to make the first of the street name changes here in 1989 (there's a bust of Palach on the corner of the building). By a happy coincidence, the road which intersects the square from the north is called 17 listopadu (17 November), originally commemorating the day in 1939 when the Nazis closed down all Czech institutions of higher education, but now equally good for the 1989 march (see p.257).

The north side of the square is taken up by the **Rudolfinum** or Dům umělců (House of Artists), designed by Josef Zítek and Josef Schulz. One of the proud civic buildings of the nineteenth-century Czech national revival, it was originally built to house an art gallery, museum and concert hall for the Czech-speaking community. In 1918, however, it became the seat of the new Czechoslovak parliament, until 1938 when it was closed down by the Nazis. According to Jiří Weil, the Germans were keen to rid the building's balustrade of its statue of the Jewish composer Mendelssohn. However, since none of the statues was actually named, they decided to remove the one with the largest nose; unfortunately for the Nazis, this turned out to be Wagner, Hitler's favourite composer. In 1946, the building returned to its original artistic purpose and it's since been sandblasted back to its original woody-brown hue. Now one of the capital's main concert venues (home to the Czech Philharmonic) and exhibition spaces (Tues–Sun 10am–6pm), it also boasts a wonderfully grand café (see p.197), open to the general public on the first floor.

UPM (Museum of Decorative Arts)

A short way down 17 listopadu from the square is the **UPM** or Uměleckoprůmyslové muzeum (Tues–Sun 10am–6pm; 80Kč), installed in another of Schulz's worthy late nineteenth-century creations, richly decorated in mosaics, stained glass and sculptures. Literally translated, this is a "Museum of Decorative Arts", though the translation hardly does justice to what is one of the most fascinating museums in the capital. From its foundation in 1885 through to the end of the First Republic, the UPM received the best that the Czech modern movement had to offer – from Art Nouveau to the avant-garde – and its collection consequently is unrivalled.

The museum's consistently excellent temporary exhibitions are staged on the ground floor, with the permanent collections on the floor above. Audioguides to the collections are available, at no extra cost, though they're by no means essential, as there's lots of information and labelling in English. The displays start with the **Votivní sál** (Votive Hall), which is ornately decorated with trompe l'oeil wall hangings, lunette paintings and a bewhiskered bust of Emperor Franz-Josef I. Next door is the **Story of a Fibre**, which displays textile exhibits, ranging from a sixteenth-century Brussels tapestry of Samson bringing down the temple to some 1930s curtains by the Surrealist artist Toyen. In the pull-out drawers you can admire numerous examples of intricate lacework through the ages. The room is dominated, however, by a double-decker costume display: above, it's richly embroidered religious vestments from the fifteenth to eighteenth century; below, fashionable attire from the eighteenth century to modern catwalk concoctions, via knock-out outfits such as a pink Charleston dress from the 1920s.

More rooms are planned to open on this side of the Votive Hall, but at the time of going to press, it is necessary to backtrack to reach the **Arts of Fire**, home to the museum's impressive glass, ceramic and pottery displays. The breadth of the stuff on show here means there's bound to be something to please everyone, whether you're into eighteenth-century Meissen figures, Slovak Haban folk faience or Art-Nouveau vases by Bohemian glassmakers such as Lötz. To catch the best examples of Cubist works on display, head for the room's Gočár-designed Cubist bookcase, and look out, too, for Jan Zrzavý's three-piece glass mosaic from the 1930s.

The **print and images** room is devoted mainly to Czech photography, and includes numerous prints from the art form's interwar heyday, including several of František Drtikol's remarkable 1920s geometric nudes, Jaromír Funke's superb still lifes and Josef Sudek's contemplative studio shots. In addition, there are pull-out drawers of early Czech photos from the second half of the nineteenth century, as well as examples of avant-garde graphics by Karel Teige, book designs by Josef Váchal and some of Alfons Mucha's famous turn-of-the-century Parisian advertising posters.

Finally, in the **treasure hall**, there's a kind of modern-day *Kunstkammer* or cabinet of curiosities: everything from ivory objets d'art and seventeenth-century Italian *pietro dure* or hardstone mosaics, to miniature silver furniture and a goblet made from rhino horn. One or two exhibits stand out from this eclectic crowd, in particular the garnet jewellery that has long been a Bohemian speciality, and the glass cabinet stuffed full of Art-Nouveau, Cubist and Rondo-Cubist metalwork.

The UPM also houses a **public library** (Mon noon–6pm, Tues 10am–8pm, Wed–Fri 10am–6pm; ⓦ www.knihovna.upm.cz), specializing in catalogues and material from previous exhibitions, and an excellent café on the ground floor (Mon–Fri 10am–7pm, Sat & Sun 10.30am–7pm).

Nové Město

N OVÉ MĚSTO is the city's main commercial and business district, housing most of its big hotels, cinemas, nightclubs, fast-food outlets and department stores. Architecturally, it comes over as big, bourgeois and predominantly late nineteenth century, yet Nové Město was actually founded way back in 1348 by Emperor Charles IV as an entirely new town – three times as big as Staré Město – intended to link the southern fortress of Vyšehrad with Staré Město to the north. Large market squares, wide streets, and a level of town-planning far ahead of its time were employed to transform Prague into the new capital city of the Holy Roman Empire. Instead, however, Nové Město remained incomplete when Charles died, and quickly became the city's poorest quarter after Josefov, fertile ground for Hussites and radicals throughout the centuries. In the second half of the nineteenth century, the authorities set about a campaign of slum clearance similar to that inflicted on the Jewish quarter; only the churches and a few important historical buildings were left standing, but Charles' street layout survives pretty much intact. The leading architects of the day began to line the wide boulevards with ostenta-tious examples of their work, which were eagerly snapped up by the new class of status-conscious businessman – a process that has continued into this centu-ry, making Nové Město the most architecturally varied part of Prague.

The obvious starting point, and probably the only place in Prague most vis-itors can put a name to, is Wenceslas Square or **Václavské náměstí**, hub of the modern city, and somewhere you're bound to find yourself passing through again and again. The two principal partially pedestrianized streets which lead off it are **Národní třída** and **Na příkopě**, which together form the *zlatý kříž* or "golden cross", Prague's commercial axis and for over a century the most expensive slice of real estate in the capital. The *zlatý kříž* and the surrounding streets also contain some of Prague's finest late nineteenth-century, Art Nouveau and early twentieth-century architecture.

An Art Nouveau hit list

Prague's Art Nouveau (the term is *secesní* in Czech) ranges from the vivacious floral motifs of the Paris metro to the more restrained style of the Viennese Secession. The following are some of the more striking examples covered in this chapter:

Café Imperial	p.126	Pojišťovna Praha	p.122
Grand Hotel Evropa	p.116	Praha hlavní nádraží	p.118
Hlahol	p.131	Topičův dům	p.122
Hotel Central	p.125	U Dörflerů	p.123
Obecní dům	p.124	U Nováků	p.128

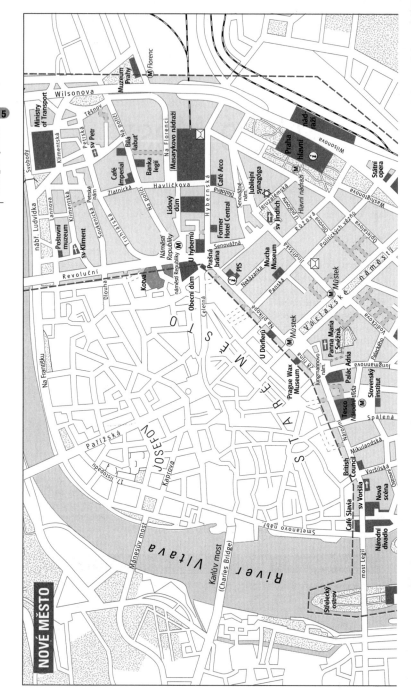

NOVÉ MĚSTO

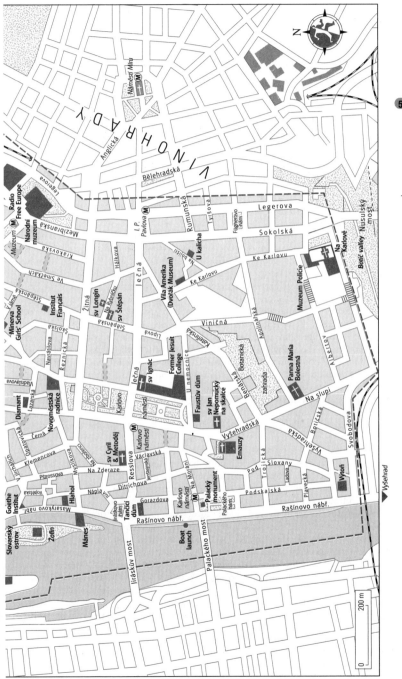

N

VINOHRADY

Náměstí Míru M

Legerova

Anglická

Bělehradská

Radio
Free Europe M
Národní muzeum
Muzeum M

Mezibranská

Krakovská

Ve Smečkách

Rumunská

I. P.
Pavlova M

Tyršova

Legerova

Sokolská

Ke Karlovu

Na
Karlově

Na bolši

U kalicha

Ke Karlovu

Figarovo
Hřbitovů

Bartoňová valley
Nusulsky
most

Žitná

Hálkova

 Ječná

Vila Amerika
(Dvořák Museum)

Muzeum Policie

Minerva
Girls' School

Štěpánská

sv Longin

Na Kokonku

Institut
Français

Navrátilova

Řeznická

Štěpánská

sv Štěpán

Lipová

Viničná

Kateřinská

Apolinářská

Albertov

Školská

Vladislavova

Lazarská

Diamant

Karlovo

Novoměstská
radnice

ječná

sv Ignác

Former Jesuit
College

U nemocnice

Faustův dům

sv Jan
Nepomucký
na skalce

Benátská

Botanická

zahrada

Panna Maria
Bolestná

Na slupi

Vlašská

Opatovická

Černá

Křemencova

Pštrossova

sv Cyril
& Metoděj M

Karlovo
náměstí

Václavská

Resslova

Vyšehradská

Emauzy

Vyšehradská

Boticská

Svobodova

Goethe
Institut

Voršilská

Hlahol

Na Zderaze

Dítřichova

Spálená

Jiráskovo
nám.

Tančící
dům

Karlovo
náměstí
M
Na Moráni

Na Moráni

Palackého
monument

Palackého
nábř.

Pod Slovany

Trojická

Ladová

Plavecká

Vyton

Slovanský
ostrov

Masarykovo nábř.

Zofín

Mánes

Náplavní

Gorazdova

Rašínovo nábř.

Palackého most

Rašínovo nábř.

Podskalská

Boat
launch

Jiráskův most

Vyšehrad

200 m

0

113

The rest of Nové Město, which spreads out northeast and southwest of Wenceslas Square, is much less explored, and for the most part still heavily residential; unusually for Prague, using the tram and metro systems to get around here will save some unnecessary legwork. A few specific sights are worth singling out for attention – the museum devoted to **Dvořák** on Ke Karlovu, the **Mánes** art gallery on the waterfront, and the memorial to the Czechoslovak parachutists off Karlovo náměstí, for example – but the rest is decidedly less exciting than all that's gone before. However, if your ultimate destination is Vyšehrad (see p.137), you can easily take in some of the more enjoyable bits of southern Nové Město en route.

Václavské náměstí (Wenceslas Square) and around

The natural pivot around which modern Prague revolves, **Václavské náměstí** (Wenceslas Square) is more of a wide, gently sloping boulevard than a square as such. It's scarcely a conventional – or even convenient – space in which to hold mass demonstrations, yet for the last hundred and fifty years or more it has been the focus of political protest in Prague. Most memorably, it was here, in late November 1989, that more than 250,000 people crammed into the square night after night, often enduring subzero temperatures, to call for the resignation of the Communist Party leaders and demand free elections. On November 27, the whole of Prague came to a standstill, a bigger crowd than ever converging on the square to show their support for the two-hour nationwide general strike called by the opposition umbrella group, Občanské fórum (Civic Forum), who led the revolution. It was this last mass mobilization that proved decisive – by noon the next day, the Communist old guard had thrown in the towel.

The square's **history of protest** goes back to the 1848 revolution, whose violent denouement began here on June 12 with a peaceful open-air mass organized by the Prague students. On the crest of the nationalist disturbances, the square – which had been known as Koňský trh (Horse Market) since its foundation as such by Charles IV – was given its present name. Naturally enough, it was one of the rallying points for the jubilant crowds on October 28, 1918, when Czechoslovakia's independence was declared. Thirty years later, in 1948, the square was filled to capacity once more, this time with Communist demonstrators enthusiastically supporting the February coup. Then in August 1968, it was the scene of some of the most violent confrontations between the Soviet invaders and the local Czechs, during which the Národní muzeum came under fire – according to the Czechs, the Soviet officer in charge mistook it for the Parliament building, though they were most probably aiming for the nearby Radio Prague building, which was transmitting news of the Soviet invasion out to the West. And, of course, it was at the top of the square, on January 16, 1969, that Jan Palach set fire to himself in protest at the continuing occupation of the country by Russian troops.

Despite the square's medieval origins, its oldest building dates only from the eighteenth century, and the vast majority are much younger. As the city's money moved south of Staré Město during the Industrial Revolution, so the square became the architectural showpiece of the nation, and it is now lined with self-important six- or seven-storey buildings, representing every artistic trend of the last hundred years, from neo-Renaissance to Socialist Realism. In addition, the square has a very good selection of period-piece arcades or *pasáže*, preserved from the commercial boom of the First Republic.

If you've no interest in modern architecture, there's less reason to stroll up the square, which has yet to shake off entirely the seedy reputation it acquired during the 1990s. Prostitution has waned and the discos have mostly closed down, but the petty criminals, dodgy cab drivers and overpriced hotels remain, while the shops and restaurants tend to reflect the familiar roll call of multinational chains.

Around Můstek

The busiest part of Wenceslas Square and a popular place to meet up before hitting town is around **Můstek**, the city's most central metro station, at the northern end of the square. The area is dominated by the **Palác Koruna**, a hulking wedge of sculptured concrete and gold, built for an insurance company in 1914 by Antonín Pfeiffer, one of Jan Kotěra's many pupils. The building is a rare mixture of heavy constructivism and gilded Secession-style ornamentation, but the *pièce de résistance* is the palace's bejewelled crown which lights up at night.

Opposite Palác Koruna, adjacent to one another, are two functionalist buildings designed by Ludvík Kysela in the late 1920s, billed at the time as the first glass curtain-wall buildings. Along with the *Hotel Juliš* (see below), they represent the perfect expression of the optimistic mood of progress and modernism that permeated the interwar republic. The building on the right as you face them, built for the chocolate firm, Lindt, was the first to be erected; the **Baťa** store, on the left, followed a few years later. The latter was one of a chain of functionalist shops built for the Czech shoe magnate, Tomáš Baťa, one of the greatest patrons of avant-garde Czech art. Baťa fled the country in 1948, when the Communists nationalized the shoe industry, only to have several of his old stores returned to the family after 1989. Even if you've no intention of buying a pair of Baťa boots, it's worth taking the lift to the top floor for a bird's-eye view onto the square.

Twenty-five years earlier, Czech architecture was in the throes of its own version of Art Nouveau, one of whose earliest practitioners was Jan Kotěra. The **Peterkův dům**, a slender essay in the new style, was

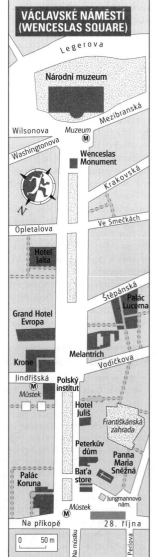

VÁCLAVSKÉ NÁMĚSTÍ (WENCESLAS SQUARE)

Legerova

Národní muzeum

Mezibranská

Wilsonova   Muzeum Ⓜ

Washingtonova

Wenceslas Monument

Krakovská

Ve Smečkách

Opletalova

Hotel Jalta

Štěpánská

Palác Lucerna

Grand Hotel Evropa

Melantrich

Vodičkova

Krone

Jindřišská Ⓜ

Polský institut

Můstek

Hotel Juliš

Františkánská zahrada

Peterkův dům

Panna Maria Sněžná

Palác Koruna

Baťa store

Jungmannovo nám.

Můstek Ⓜ

Na příkopě

28. října

0   50 m

Na můstku

Perlova

his first work, undertaken at the tender age of 28. Kotěra, a pupil of the great architect of the Viennese Secession, Otto Wagner, eventually moved on to a much more brutal modernism. Another supreme example of Czech functionalism, a few doors further up at no. 22, is the former **Hotel Juliš**, designed by Pavel Janák, who had already made his name as one of the leading lights of the short-lived Czech Cubist (and later Rondo-Cubist) movement (see p.143). Another point of interest, on the corner of Jindřišská, is the neo-Baroque **Polský institut** or Polish Institute (Ⓦwww.polskyinstitut.cz). Designed by Osvald Polívka and Bedřich Ohmann, the building once served as the offices of the *Assicurazione Generali* where the young Kafka worked for a couple of years as an insurance clerk.

Beyond Jindřišská

One of the Communists' most miserable attempts to continue the square's tradition of grand architecture was the Družba (Friendship), now **Krone**, department store, which stands like a 1970s reject on the other side of Jindřišská, its only redeeming feature the view from its rooftop disco *Fromin*. Diagonally opposite is the **Melantrich** publishing house, whose first floor is occupied by the offices of the former Socialist Party newspaper, *Svobodné slovo* (The Free Word). For forty years, the Socialist Party was a loyal puppet of the Communist government, but on the second night of the November 1989 demonstrations, the newspaper handed over its well-placed balcony to the opposition speakers of Občanské fórum (Civic Forum), and later witnessed the historic appearance of Havel and Dubček.

Melantrich House faces probably the most famous and the two most ornate buildings on the entire square, the Art Nouveau **Grand Hotel Evropa**, and its slim neighbour, the *Hotel Meran*, both with decor dating from 1903–05, designed by two of Ohmann's disciples, Bendelmayer and Dryák. The *Evropa*, in particular, has kept many of its original fittings intact, and its café retains a sumptuous interior, complete with symbolist art and elaborate brass fittings and light fixtures, all unchanged since the hotel first opened. Unfortunately, at the time of writing, the whole place was at a particularly low ebb in terms of service and, consequently, popularity.

Opposite the hotel is the vast **Palác Lucerna**, one of the more appealing of

Prague's pasáže

Prague has an impressive array of old **shopping arcades** or *pasáže*, as they're known in Czech, the majority of which are located in and around Wenceslas Square and date from the first half of this century. Compared with the chic *passages* off the Champs-Élysées, Prague's *pasáže* offer more modest pleasures: a few shops, the odd café and, more often than not, a cinema. The king of the lot is the lavishly decorated Lucerna *pasáž*, which stretches all the way from Štěpánská to Vodičkova and contains an equally ornate cinema, café and vast concert hall. You can continue your indoor stroll on the other side of Vodičkova through the Světozor *pasáž*, which boasts another cinema, and a wonderful stained-glass mosaic advertising the old Communist electronics company Tesla. The first of the *pasáže* to receive a 1990s facelift was the marble-clad Koruna *pasáž*, on the corner of Na příkopě, now lined with upmarket shops including Prague's largest music store, Bonton Megastore. There have also been renewed attempts to continue the tradition, but judging by the limply modern Myslbek *pasáž*, fronted by a Marks & Spencer store and situated on the other side of Na příkopě, the glory days are over.

the square's numerous dimly lit shopping arcades (see box on p.116). Designed in the early part of this century in Moorish style by, among others, Havel's own grandfather, it was returned to Havel and his brother after 1989, and was subsequently the focus of much public family squabbling. Apart from a brief glance at the **Hotel Jalta**, built in the Stalinist aesthetic of the 1950s, there's nothing more to stop for, architecturally speaking, until you get to the Wenceslas Monument. However, you might, by this point, have noticed the two vintage tram cars stationed in the central reservation, reminders of the days when trams trundled down the square, now converted into a summer café.

The Wenceslas Monument

A statue of St Wenceslas or Václav (see p.44) has stood at the top of the square since 1680, but the present **Wenceslas Monument**, by the father of Czech sculpture, Josef Václav Myslbek, was only unveiled in 1912, after thirty years on the drawing board. It's worthy and heroic but pretty unexciting, with the Czech patron saint sitting resolutely astride his mighty steed, surrounded by smaller-scale representations of four other Bohemian saints – his mother Ludmila, Procopius, Adalbert and Agnes – added in the 1920s. In 1918, 1948, 1968, and again in 1989, the monument was used as a national political notice board, festooned in posters, flags and slogans, and even now it remains the city's favourite soapbox venue.

Two of Prague's most famous martyrs were fatally wounded close by. On October 28, 1939, during the demonstrations against the Nazi occupation, the medical student Jan Opletal was fatally wounded when troops opened fire on protesters. And on January 16, 1969, the 21-year-old philosophy student Jan Palach set himself alight in protest against the continuing occupation of his country by the Soviets; he died from his wounds three days later. Several others followed Palach's example, including Jan Zajíc, who set fire to himself on the same spot on February 25, the anniversary of the Communist coup. Attempts to lay flowers on this spot on the anniversary of Palach's protest provided an annual source of confrontation; Václav Havel received the last of his many prison sentences for just such an action in January 1989. An impromptu martyrs' shrine of candles and messages, set up in the aftermath of the November 1989 revolution, has now been formalized as a simple memorial to *obětem komunismu* (the victims of Communism), adorned with flowers and photos of Palach and Zajíc.

Národní muzeum (National Museum)

At the top, southern, end of Wenceslas Square sits the broad, brooding hulk of the **Národní muzeum** (daily: May–Sept 10am–6pm; Oct–April 9am–5pm; 70Kč; ℗ www.nm.cz), built by Josef Schulz in 1890. Deliberately modelled on the great European museums of Paris and Vienna, it dominates the view up the square like a giant golden eagle with outstretched wings. Along with the National Theatre (see p.122), this is one of the great landmarks of the nineteenth-century Czech *národní obrození*, sporting a monumental gilt-framed glass cupola, worthy clumps of sculptural decoration and narrative frescoes from Czech history.

The museum is old-fashioned and underfunded, but it's worth taking at least a quick look at the ornate marble entrance hall and splendid monumental staircase leading to the glass-domed **Pantheon** at the top of the main staircase, which is decorated with lunette murals depicting key moments in Czech history. Meanwhile at floor level are 48 busts and statues of distinguished bewhiskered Czech men (plus a couple of token women and Czechophile Slovaks), including the universally adored T.G. Masaryk, the country's founding president, whose statue was removed by the Communists from every other public place.

The rest of the museum is dowdy and poorly labelled, though numismatists will enjoy the exhibition of medals and orders belonging to Václav Měřička, from the Order of the Bath to the French Légion d'Honneur. Geologists can admire rocks and minerals in tasteful mahogany cases, while non-specialists should head for the Kabinet drahých kamenů, at the far end, where cut and polished sapphires, rubies, emeralds and other precious stones are displayed. Those with children might like to head upstairs for the fossils and stuffed animals, where you can also view the smallest and the largest butterfly in the world, a range of lovely shells and some frighteningly large and lethal-looking beetles. The museum's temporary exhibitions, displayed on the ground floor, can be very good indeed, so it's always worth checking to see what's on.

Wilsonova

At the southern end of Wenceslas Square is some of the worst blight that Communist planners inflicted on Prague; above all, the six-lane highway that now separates Nové Město from the residential suburb of Vinohrady to the east and south, and effectively cuts off the Národní muzeum from Wenceslas Square. Previously known as Vítězného února (Victorious February) after the 1948 Communist coup, the road was renamed **Wilsonova** in honour of US President Woodrow Wilson (a personal friend of the Masaryk family), who effectively gave the country its independence from Austria-Hungary in 1918 by backing the proposal for a separate Czechoslovak state.

The Prague stock exchange building alongside the Národní muzeum, only completed in the 1930s but rendered entirely redundant by the 1948 Communist coup, was another victim of postwar "reconstruction". The architect Karel Prager was given the task of designing a new "socialist" Federal Assembly building on the same site, without destroying the old bourse: he opted for a supremely unappealing bronze-tinted plate-glass structure, supported by concrete stilts and sitting uncomfortably on top of its diminutive predecessor. Since the break-up of the country, the building has lost its *raison d'être* once more, and now provides a home for, among other things, **Radio Free Europe**'s headquarters. Terrorist threats in 2001 saw the building surrounded by tanks and armoured vehicles, adding a certain frisson to a visit to the excellent *Zahrada v opeře* restaurant within (see p.204).

Next to the old Parliament building, the grandiose **Státní opera** (ⓦ www.opera.cz), built by the Viennese duo Helmer and Fellner, looks stunted and deeply affronted by the traffic which now tears past its front entrance. It was opened in 1888 as the *Neues Deutsches Theater*, shortly after the Czechs had built their own national theatre on the waterfront. Always second fiddle to the Stavovské divadlo, though equally ornate inside, it was one of the last great building projects of Prague's once all-powerful German minority. The velvet and gold interior is still as fresh as it was when the Bohemian-born composer Gustav Mahler brought the traffic to a standstill, conducting the premiere of his *Seventh Symphony*.

The last building on this deafening freeway is **Praha hlavní nádraží**, Prague's main railway station, and one of the final architectural glories of the dying Empire, designed by Josef Fanta and officially opened in 1909 as the

△ Praha hlavní nádraží

Franz-Josefs Bahnhof. Arriving by metro, or buying tickets in the over-polished subterranean modern section, it's easy to miss the station's surviving Art Nouveau parts. The original entrance on Wilsonova still exudes imperial confidence, with its wrought-iron canopy and naked figurines clinging to the sides of the towers; on the other side of the road, two great glass protrusions signal the new entrance that opens out into the seedy green space of the Vrchlického sady. You can sit and admire the main foyer from the *Fantová kavárna* (daily 6am–11pm) – it's also worth heading north from the foyer to take a peek at the ceramic pillars in the former station restaurant.

Národní třída and Na příkopě

Národní třída and **Na příkopě** trace the course of the old Staré Město moat, which was finally filled in in 1760. Their boomerang curve still marks the border between Staré Město and Nové Město, though strictly speaking the dividing line runs down the middle of the street. At the turn of the century, these two partly pedestrianized streets formed the chief venue for the weekend *passeggiata*, and even today they are among the most crowded expanses of pavement in Prague. Along with a variety of chain stores, banks, restaurants and clubs, you'll also discover some of the city's most flamboyant Art Nouveau buildings.

Jungmannovo náměstí and around

Heading west from Můstek, before you hit Národní třída proper, you must pass through **Jungmannovo náměstí**, named for Josef Jungmann (1772–1847), a prolific writer, translator and leading light of the Czech national revival, whose pensive, seated statue was erected here in 1878. This small, ill-proportioned square boasts an unrivalled panoply of Czech architectural curiosities, ranging from Emil Králíček and Matěj Blecha's unique **Cubist streetlamp** (and seat) from 1912, crumbling away beyond the Jungmann statue in the far eastern corner of the square to the gleaming, functionalist facade of the former ARA department store (now the ČSOB), built in the late 1920s on the corner of Perlova and ulica 28 října (October 28 Street, commemorating the foundation of the First Republic).

Palác Adria

Diagonally opposite the ARA department store is the square's most imposing building, the chunky, vigorously sculptured **Palác Adria**, on the south side of the square. It was designed in the early 1920s by Pavel Janák and Josef Zasche, with sculptural extras by Otto Gutfreund and a central *Seafaring* group by Jan Štursa. Janák was a pioneering figure in the short-lived, prewar Czech Cubist movement; after the war, he and Josef Gočár attempted to create a national style of architecture appropriate for the newly founded republic. The style was dubbed "Rondo-Cubism" – semicircular motifs are a recurrent theme – though the Palác Adria owes as much to the Italian Renaissance as it does to the new national style.

Originally constructed for the Italian insurance company Reunione Adriatica di Sicurità – hence its current name – the building's *pasáž* still retains its wonderful original portal featuring sculptures by Bohumil Kafka, depicting the twelve signs of the zodiac. The theatre in the basement of the building was once a studio for the multimedia **Laterna magika** (Magic Lantern) company. In 1989, it became the underground nerve centre of the Velvet Revolution, when Civic Forum found temporary shelter here shortly after their inaugural meeting on the Sunday following the November 17 demonstration. Against a stage backdrop for Dürenmatt's *Minotaurus*, the Forum thrashed out tactics in the dressing rooms and gave daily press conferences in the auditorium during the crucial fortnight before the Communists relinquished power.

The church of Panna Maria Sněžná

Right beside the Cubist streetlamp is the medieval gateway of the church of **Panna Maria Sněžná** (St Mary-of-the-Snows), once one of the great landmarks of Wenceslas Square, but now barely visible from any of the surrounding streets. To enter the church, go through the archway beside the Austrian Cultural Institute, behind the statue of Jungmann, and across the courtyard beyond. Like most of Nové Město's churches, the Panna Maria Sněžná was founded by Charles IV, who envisaged a vast coronation church on a scale comparable with the St Vitus Cathedral, on which work had just begun. Unfortunately, the money ran out shortly after completion of the chancel; the result is curious – a church which is short in length, but equal to the cathedral in height. The 100ft-high, prettily painted vaulting – which collapsed on the Franciscans who inherited the half-completed building in the seventeenth century – is awesome, as is the gold and black Baroque main altar which touches the ceiling. To get an idea of the intended scale of the finished structure, take a stroll through the **Františkánská zahrada**, to the south of the church; these gardens make a lovely hideaway from Nové Mesto's bustle, marred only by the intrusive modern garden furniture.

Wax Museum Prague

A short walk down ulica 28 října, which connects Jungmannovo náměstí with Wenceslas Square, is one of Prague's new commercial museums, the **Wax Museum Prague** (Muzeum voskových figurín; daily 9am–8pm; 120Kč; ⓦwww.waxmuseum.cz), laid out on the ground floor of the Art Nouveau palác Rapid at no. 13. The entrance fee is steep for many Czechs, yet the museum is aimed primarily at a domestic audience. For anyone familiar with London's Madame Tussaud's, the formula is predictable enough, but unless your grasp of Czech history is pretty good, many of the wax tableaux will remain slightly baffling. The most popular section with the locals is the podium of Commie stooges ranging from Lenin to the Czechs' home-grown Stalinist, Klement Gottwald, followed by today's generation of Czech politicians dressed in bad suits, sat amidst naff office furniture.

Národní třída

The eastern end of **Národní** is taken up with shops, galleries and clubs, all of which begin to peter out as you near the river. At the last crossroads before the waterfront is the new **British Council** (Britská rada; ⓦwww.britishcouncil .org/czechrepublic) building, which used to belong to the East German cultural institute. On the outside, the original constructivist facade, designed in the 1930s by Osvald Polívka, has been kept intact, while the light interior has been thoroughly and imaginatively modernized in an interesting synthesis of central European and British architectural styles, using ample helpings of the country's

The masakr – November 17, 1989

On the night of Friday, November 17, 1989, a 50,000-strong, officially sanctioned student demonstration, organized by the students' union, SSM (League of Young Socialists), worked its way down Národní with the intention of reaching Wenceslas Square. Halfway down the street they were confronted by the *bílé přílby* (white helmets) and *červené barety* (red berets) of the hated riot-police. For what must have seemed like hours, there was a stalemate as the students sat down and refused to disperse, some of them handing flowers out to the police. Suddenly, without any warning, the police attacked and what became known as the **masakr** (massacre) began. In the end, no one was actually killed, though it wasn't for want of trying by the police. Under the arches of the Kaňkův dům, Národní 16, there's a small symbolic bronze relief of eight hands reaching out for help, a permanent shrine in memory of the hundreds who were hospitalized in the violence.

surplus glass. There's a window gallery on the ground floor overlooking Národní, which is run by the British Council, and you're free to walk in and take a peek at the lobby – the entrance is up Voršilská – where you can pick up information on the latest cultural offerings sponsored by the BC.

Further down Národní, on the right-hand side, is an eye-catching duo of much earlier Art-Nouveau buildings, designed by Polívka in 1907–08. The first, at no. 7, was built for the **pojišťovna Praha** (Prague Savings Bank), hence the beautiful mosaic lettering above the windows advertizing *život* (life insurance) and *kapital* (loans), as well as help with your *důchod* (pension) and *věno* (dowry). Next door, the slightly more ostentatious **Topičův dům**, headquarters of Československý spisovatel, the official state publishers, provides the perfect accompaniment, with a similarly ornate wrought-iron and glass canopy.

Opposite, the convent and church of **sv Voršila** (St Ursula) are distinguished by the rare sight (in this part of town) of a tree sticking out of its white facade. When it was completed in 1678, this was one of the first truly flamboyant Baroque buildings in Prague, and its white stucco and frescoed interior have recently been restored to their original state. The Ursuline nuns were booted out by the Communists, but returned post-1989 to found one of the first ecclesiastical schools in the country.

Národní divadlo and Café Slavia

At the western end of Národní, overlooking the Vltava, is the gold-crested **Národní divadlo** (National Theatre; Ⓦ www.narodni-divadlo.cz), proud symbol of the Czech nation. Refused money from the Habsburg state coffers, Czechs of all classes dug deep into their pockets to raise funds for the venture themselves. The foundation stones, gathered from various historically significant sites in Bohemia and Moravia, were laid in 1868 by the historian and politician, František Palacký, and the composer, Bedřich Smetana; the architect, Josef Zítek, spent the next thirteen years on the project. In June 1881, the theatre opened with a première of Smetana's opera *Libuše*. In August of the same year, fire ripped through the building, destroying everything except the outer walls. Within two years the whole thing was rebuilt – even the emperor contributed this time – under the supervision of Josef Schulz (who went on to design the National Museum), and it opened once more to the strains of Smetana's *Libuše*. Smetana attended both of the theatre's opening nights, even though the organisers failed to send him any tickets, and he had to blag his way in on each occasion. The grand portal on the north side of the theatre is embellished with suitably triumphant allegorical figures, and, inside, every square inch is taken up with paintings and sculptures by leading artists of the Czech national revival. Tickets are relatively cheap but most productions are in Czech, so unless there's an opera or ballet on, content yourself with a quick peek at the decor prior to a performance.

Standing behind the Národní divadlo, and in dramatic contrast with it, is the theatre's state-of-the-art extension, the ultra-modern glass box of the **Nová scéna**, designed by Karel Prager, the leading architect of the Communist era, and completed in 1983. It's one of those buildings most Praguers love to hate – it was described by one Czech as looking like "frozen piss" – though compared to much of Prague's Communist-era architecture, it's not that bad. Just for the record, the lump of molten rock in the courtyard is a symbolic evocation of *My Socialist Country*, by Malejovský.

The **Café Slavia**, opposite the theatre, has been a favourite haunt of the city's writers, dissidents and artists (and, inevitably, actors) since the days of the First Republic. The Czech avant-garde movement, *Devětsil*, led by Karel Teige, used to hold its meetings here in the 1920s; the meetings are recorded for posterity by another of its members, the Nobel prize-winner Jaroslav Seifert, in his *Slavia Poems*. The café has been carelessly modernized since those arcadian days, but it still has a great riverside view and Manet's famous *Absinthe Drinker* canvas on the wall.

Na příkopě

Heading northeastwards from Můstek at the bottom end of Wenceslas Square, you can join the crush of bodies ambling down **Na příkopě** (literally "On the moat"). The big multinational franchises have staked their claim on this stretch of Prague with **Pasáž Myslbek**, one of the few contemporary works of architecture in central Prague, fronted by Marks & Spencer. The street has, of course, been an architectural showcase for more than a century. On the opposite side of the street, there are grandiose buildings like the former Haas department store at no. 4, built in 1869–71 by Theophil Hansen, the Danish architect responsible for much of the redevelopment of the Ringstrasse in Vienna. Many of the finest turn-of-the-century buildings, though – like the *Café Corso* and the *Café Français*, once the favourite haunts of Prague's German-Jewish literary set – were torn down and replaced during the enthusiastic construction boom of the interwar republic. The Art Nouveau **U Dörflerů**, at no. 7, from 1905, is one of the few survivors along this stretch, its gilded floral curlicues gleaming in the midday sun.

There are another couple of interesting buildings on the opposite side of the street, at nos. 18 and 20, designed by Polívka over the course of a twenty-year period for the Zemská banka and connected by a kind of Bridge of Sighs suspended over Nekázanka. The style is 1890s neo-Renaissance, though there are Art Nouveau elements, such as Jan Preisler's gilded mosaics and Ladislav Šaloun's attic sculptures. It's worth nipping upstairs to the main banking hall of what is now the **Živnostenka banka**, at no. 20, to appreciate the financial might of the Czech capital in the last decades of the Austro-Hungarian Empire. Yet more financial institutions, this time from the dour 1930s, line the far end of Na příkopě, as it opens up into náměstí Republiky, including the palatial Národní banka (National Bank), which underwent a controversial and very expensive makeover in the 1990s.

Northern Nové Město

Náměstí Republiky is worth pausing at, if only to admire the Obecní dům – Prague's most alluring Art Nouveau structure – but this aside, there's nothing in the northern or eastern part of Nové Město that merits a special trip. Nevertheless, you may find yourself in this part of town by dint of its shops, restaurants and hotels, or perhaps en route to Prague's main domestic train station, Masarykovo nádraží. Tourists rarely venture this far east, and for that reason alone it makes an interesting diversion, revealing a side to central Prague that many visitors don't see.

Náměstí Republiky

Náměstí Republiky is an unruly space, made more so since the construction of its metro station and the ugly brown Kotva department store, built by Swedish architects in the 1970s. The oldest structure on the square is the **Prašná brána** (Powder Gate; April–Oct daily 10am–6pm; 30Kč), one of the eight medieval gate-towers that once guarded Staré Město. The present tower was begun by King Vladislav Jagiello in 1475, shortly after he'd moved into the royal court, which was situated next door at the time. Work stopped when he retreated to the Hrad to avoid the wrath of his subjects; later on, it was used to store gunpowder – hence the name and the reason for the damage incurred in 1757. The small historical exhibition inside traces the tower's architectural metamorphosis over the centuries, up to its present remodelling courtesy of the nineteenth-century restorer, Josef Mocker. Most people, though, ignore the displays, and climb straight up for the modest view from the top.

Obecní dům

Attached to the tower, and built on the ruins of the old royal court, the **Obecní dům** (Municipal House) is by far the most exciting Art Nouveau building in Prague, one of the few places that still manages to conjure up the atmosphere of Prague's turn-of-the-century café society. Conceived as a cultural centre for the Czech community, it's probably the finest architectural achievement of the Czech national revival, designed by Osvald Polívka and Antonín Balšánek, and extravagantly decorated inside and out with the help of almost every artist connected with the Czech Secession. From the lifts to the cloakrooms, just about all the furnishings remain as they were when the building was completed in 1911, and every square inch of the interior and exterior has been lovingly renovated. Appropriately enough, it was here that Czechoslovakia's independence was declared on October 28, 1918.

The simplest way of soaking up the interior – peppered with mosaics and pendulous brass chandeliers – is to have a coffee in the cavernous café, or a full meal in the equally spacious *Francouzská restaurace*; there's also the cheaper *Plzeňská restaurace* in the cellar, along with the original 1910 *American Bar*. For a more detailed inspection of the building's spectacular interior (which includes paintings by Alfons Mucha, Jan Preisler and Max Švabinský, among others), you can sign up for a **guided tour** (150Kč); tickets are available from the new information centre (daily 10am–6pm; Ⓦ www.obecni-dum.cz) on the ground floor, beyond the main foyer. Several rooms on the second floor are given over to temporary art exhibitions, while the building's **Smetanova síň**, Prague's largest concert hall, stages numerous concerts, including the opening salvo of the *Pražské jaro* (Prague Spring Festival) – traditionally a rendition of Smetana's *Má vlast* (My Country) – which takes place in the presence of the president.

Hybernská and Senovážné náměstí

Directly opposite the Obecní dům stands a haughty Neoclassical building, **U hybernů** (The Hibernians), built as a customs office in the Napoleonic period, on the site of a Baroque church which belonged to an order of Irish Franciscans who fled Tudor England (hence its name). If you walk down **Hybernská** from here, you'll pass the Art Nouveau former **Hotel Central** on the right. Designed by Dryák and Bendelmayer (who built the *Grand Hotel Evropa* on Wenceslas Square) and dating from 1900, its gilded decoration stands out amidst its plainer nineteenth-century neighbours.

Opposite the hotel is the **Lidový dům**, headquarters of the Social Democratic Party (ČSSD), which was forcibly amalgamated with the Communist Party shortly after the 1948 coup. The party regained its independence in 1989, and emerged as the largest party in the 1998 elections, and again in the 2002 elections. In January 1912, a small backroom in the building was given over to a congress of the exiled Russian Social Democratic Labour Party. The party was deeply divided, and the meeting poorly attended, with only fourteen voting delegates present (all but two of them Bolsheviks), and **Lenin** himself in the chair. It was this meeting which pushed through the formal takeover of the party by the Bolsheviks, to the exclusion of the Mensheviks and others, and gave the Czech Communists the perfect excuse for turning the whole place into a vast museum dedicated to Lenin, of which there is now, not surprisingly, absolutely no trace. In a nice twist of fate, however, the building now houses the American Center for Culture and Commerce.

A little further down Hybernská, a wrought-iron canopy held up by slim green pillars marks the entrance to Prague's first railway station, **Masarykovo nádraží**, opened in 1845 and still much as it was then – a modest, almost provincial affair compared to the flamboyant Art Nouveau Praha hlavní nádraží. On the opposite side of Hybernská is the **Café Arco**, once a favourite of Kafka (who worked nearby), and the circle of Prague-German writers known as the "Arconauts". The café has recently been pretty faithfully reconstructed, though it remains to be seen what sort of clientele (if any) it will attract (see p.197).

Around Senovážné náměstí

South of Masarykovo nádraží, down Dlážděná, is the old hay market, **Senovážné náměstí**, packed out with parked cars and a couple of market stalls. Its most distinguished feature is the freestanding fifteenth-century belfry of the church of **sv Jindřich** (St Henry); both have undergone several facelifts, most recently by the ubiquitous nineteenth-century Gothic restorer, Josef Mocker.

A short way up Jeruzalémská, you'll find the **Jubilejní synagoga** (mid-April to mid-Oct daily except Sat 1–5pm; 30Kč), named in honour of the sixtieth year of the Emperor Franz-Josef I's reign in 1908, and built in an incredibly colourful Moorish style similar to that of the Španělská synagoga in Josefov, but with a touch of Art Nouveau. The Hebrew inscription on the facade strikes a note of liberal optimism:"Do we not have one father? Were we not created by the same God?"

Mucha Museum

Dedicated to **Alfons Mucha** (1860–1939), probably the most famous of all Czech artists in the West, the **Mucha Museum** (daily 10am–6pm; 120Kč; ⓦ www .mucha.cz), housed in the Kaunicky palác on Panská, southwest of Senovážné náměstí, has proved very popular. Mucha made his name in *fin-de-siècle* Paris, where he shot to fame after designing the Art Nouveau poster *Gismonda* for the actress Sarah Bernhardt. "Le Style Mucha" became all the rage, but the artist himself came to despise this "commercial" period of his work, and in 1910, Mucha moved back to his homeland and threw himself into the national cause, designing patriotic stamps, banknotes and posters for the new republic.

The whole of Mucha's career is covered in the permanent exhibition, and there's a good selection of informal photos taken by the artist himself of his models, and of Paul Gauguin (with whom he shared a studio) playing the harmonium with his trousers down. The only work not represented here is his massive *Slav Epic*, but the excellent video (in English) covers the decade of his life he devoted to this cycle of nationalist paintings. In the end, Mucha paid for his Czech nationalism with his life; dragged in for questioning by the Gestapo after the 1939 Nazi invasion, he died shortly after being released.

North of Masarykovo nádraží

Running roughly parallel with Hybernská, to the north of Masarykovo nádraží, is the much busier street of **Na poříčí**, an area that, like sv Havel in Staré Město, was originally settled by German merchants. Kafka spent most of his working life as a frustrated and unhappy clerk for the *Arbeiter-Unfall-Versicherungs-Anstalt* (Workers' Accident Insurance Company), in the grand nineteenth-century building at no. 7. A little further along the street at no. 15, you can soak in a bit more faded *fin de siècle* atmosphere in the beautiful surroundings of the **Café Imperial** (see p.199), which has miraculously retained its utterly over-the-top ceramic tiling from 1914.

On the opposite side of the street is a much more unusual piece of corporate architecture, the **Banka legií** (now a branch of the ČSOB; Mon–Fri 8am–5pm), one of Pavel Janák's rare Rondo-Cubist efforts from the early 1920s. Set into the bold smoky-red moulding is a striking white marble frieze by Otto Gutfreund, depicting the epic march across Siberia undertaken by the Czechoslovak Legion and their embroilment in the Russian Revolution. You're free to wander into the main banking hall on the ground floor, which, though marred by the current bank fittings, retains its curved glass roof and distinctive red-and-white marble patterning. The glass curtain-walled **Bílá labuť** (White Swan) department store, opposite, is a good example of the functionalist style which Janák and others went on to embrace in the late 1920s and 1930s.

As a lively shopping street, Na poříčí seems very much out on a limb, as do the cluster of hotels at the end of the street, and around the corner in **Těšnov**. The reason behind this is the now defunct Těšnov train station, which was demolished in the 1960s to make way for the monstrous Wilsonova flyover. On the far side of the flyover, Antonín Balšánek's purpose-built neo-Renaissance mansion, housing the Muzeum hlavního města Prahy (Museum of the city of Prague), better known simply as the **Muzeum Prahy** (Tues–Sun 9am–6pm; ⓦ www.muzeumprahy.cz; 30Kč), is the lone survivor of this redevelopment. Inside, there's an ad hoc collection of the city's art, a number of antique bicycles, and usually an intriguing temporary exhibition on some aspect of the city. The museum's prize possession, though, is Antonín Langweil's paper model of Prague which he completed in the 1830s. It's a fascinating insight into early nineteenth-century Prague – predominantly Baroque, with the cathedral incomplete and the Jewish quarter "unsanitized" – and, consequently, has served as one of the most useful records for the city's restorers. The most surprising thing, of course, is that so little has changed.

Nábřeží Ludvika Svobody and around

North of Na poříčí, close to the river bank, nábřeží Ludvika Svobody, there's another museum which might appeal to some: the **Poštovní muzeum** (Postal Museum; Tues–Sun 9–5pm; 25Kč; ⓦ www.cpost.cz), housed in the Vávrův dům, an old mill on Nové mlýny, near one of Prague's many water towers. The first floor contains a series of jolly nineteenth-century wall paintings of Romantic Austrian landscapes, and a collection of drawings on postman themes. The real philately is on the ground floor – a vast international collection of stamps arranged in vertical pull-out drawers. The Czechoslovak issues are historically and artistically interesting, as well as of appeal to collectors. Stamps became a useful tool in the propaganda wars of this century; even such short-lived ventures as the Hungarian-backed Slovak Soviet Republic of 1918–19 and the Slovak National Uprising of autumn 1944 managed to print special issues. Under the First Republic, the country's leading artists, notably Alfons Mucha and Max Švabinský, were commissioned to design stamps, some of which are exceptionally beautiful.

The distinctive, glass-domed 1920s building – now the **Ministry of Transport** – further east along the embankment, holds a special place in the country's history. Under the Communists, it served the former headquarters of the Party's Central Committee, where Dubček and his fellow reformers were arrested in August 1968, before being spirited away to Moscow for "frank and fraternal" discussions.

Southern Nové Město

The network of cobbled streets immediately south of Národní and Wenceslas Square are fun to explore, as they harbour a whole range of interesting cafés, pubs, restaurants and shops that have steadily colonised the area. Charles IV's town plan survives intact here, but the streets are now lined with grand, late nineteenth- and twentieth-century buildings. Further south, some of these broad boulevards – in particular, Žitná and Ječná – have become the main arteries for Prague's steadily increasing traffic. Together with the large distances involved, this means that if you're thinking of exploring further south than, say, Karlovo náměstí, it's worth hopping on a tram. Three tram routes worth knowing about are: tram #24, which goes along Vodičkova from Wenceslas Square, up the side of Karlovo náměstí and past the Botanická zahrada; tram #3, which follows a similar route but heads off to Palackého náměstí and south along the riverfront; and tram #18, which heads south from Národní down Spálená, up the side of Karlovo náměstí and past the Botanická zahrada.

South to Karlovo náměstí

Of the many roads which head down towards Karlovo náměstí, **Vodičkova** is probably the most impressive, running southwest for half a kilometre from Wenceslas Square. You can catch several trams along this route, though there are

Milena Jesenská

The most famous "Minervan" was **Milena Jesenská**, born in 1896 into a Czech family whose ancestry stretched back to the sixteenth century. Shortly after leaving school, she was confined to a mental asylum by her father when he discovered that she was having an affair with a Jew. On her release, she married the Jew, Ernst Polak, and moved to Vienna, where she took a job as a railway porter to support the two of them. While living in Vienna, she sent a Czech translation of one of Kafka's short stories to his publisher; Kafka wrote back himself, and so began their platonic, mostly epistolary, relationship. Kafka described her later as "the only woman who ever understood me", and with his encouragement she took up writing professionally. Tragically, by the time Milena had extricated herself from her disastrous marriage, Kafka, still smarting from three failed engagements with other women, had decided never to commit himself to anyone else; his letters alone survived the war, as a moving testament to their love.

Milena returned to Prague in 1925, and moved on from writing exclusively fashion articles to critiques of avant-garde architecture, becoming one of the city's leading journalists. She married again, this time to the prominent functionalist architect Jaromír Krejcar, but later, a difficult pregnancy and childbirth left her addicted to morphine. She overcame her dependency only after joining the Communist Party, but was to quit after the first of Stalin's show trials in 1936. She continued to work as a journalist in the late 1930s, and wrote a series of articles condemning the rise of Fascism in the Sudetenland.

When the Nazis rolled into Prague in 1939, Milena's Vinohrady flat had already become a centre for resistance. For a while, she managed to hang on to her job, but her independent intellectual stance and provocative gestures – for instance, wearing a yellow star as a mark of solidarity with her Jewish friends – soon attracted the attentions of the Gestapo, and after a brief spell in the notorious Pankrác prison, she was sent to Ravensbrück, the women's concentration camp near Berlin, where she died of nephritis (inflammation of the kidneys) in May 1944.

a handful of buildings worth checking out on the way, so you may choose to walk. The first, **U Nováků**, is impossible to miss, thanks to Jan Preisler's mosaic of bucolic frolicking (its actual subject, *Trade and Industry*, is confined to the edges of the picture), and Polívka's curvilinear window frames and delicate, ivy-like ironwork – look out for the frog-prince holding up a windowsill. Originally built for the Novák department store in the early 1900s, for the last sixty years it has been a cabaret hall, restaurant and café all rolled into one; however, the original fittings have long since been destroyed.

Halfway down the street, at no. 15, the *McDonald's* "restaurant" – the first to open in the Czech Republic in 1992 – must qualify as a landmark of sorts. It occupies the site of the *Akademická kavárna*, one of the many lost literary cafés of turn-of-the-century Prague. Directly opposite stands the imposing neo-Renaissance **Minerva girls' school**, covered in bright-red sgraffito. Founded in 1866, it was the first such institution in Prague, and was notorious for the antics of its pupils, the "Minervans", who shocked bourgeois Czech society with their experimentations with fashion, drugs and sexual freedom (see box above). As Vodičkova curves left towards Karlovo náměstí, Lazarská, meeting point of the city's night trams, leads off to the right. At the bottom of this street is **Diamant**, completed in 1912 by Emil Králíček, and so called because its prismatic Cubist style is reminiscent of the facets of a diamond. It's grubby with pollution now, but the geometric sculptural reliefs on the facade, the main portal and the frame enclosing a Baroque statue of St John of Nepomuk on Spálená, remain worth viewing nonetheless.

Karlovo náměstí

Once Prague's biggest square, **Karlovo náměstí**'s impressive proportions are no longer so easy to appreciate, obscured by a tree-planted public garden and cut in two by the busy thoroughfare of Ječná. It was created by Charles IV as Nové Město's cattle market (Dobytčí trh) and used by him for the grisly annual public display of his impressive collection of saintly relics (see p.81), though now it actually signals the southern limit of the city's main commercial district and the beginning of predominantly residential Nové Město.

The **Novoměstská radnice** (New Town Hall; April–Sept daily 10am–5.30pm; 20Kč), at the northeastern corner of the square, sports three impressive triangular gables embellished with intricate blind tracery. It was built, like the one on Staroměstské náměstí, during the reign of King John of Luxembourg, though it has survived rather better, and is now one of the finest Gothic buildings in the city. It was here that Prague's **first defenestration** took place on July 30, 1419, when the radical Hussite preacher Jan Želivský and his penniless religious followers stormed the building, mobbed the councillors and burghers and threw twelve or thirteen of them (including the mayor) out of the town hall windows onto the pikes of the Hussite mob below, who clubbed any survivors to death. Václav IV, on hearing the news, suffered a stroke and died just two weeks later. So began the long and bloody Hussite Wars. After the amalgamation of Prague's separate towns in 1784, the building was used solely as a criminal court and prison. Nowadays, you can visit the site of the defenestration, and climb to the top of the **tower** (added shortly afterwards) for a view over central Prague; the town hall also puts on temporary art exhibitions.

Following the defeat of Protestantism two centuries later, the Jesuits were allowed to demolish 23 houses on the east side of the square to make way for their college (now one of the city's main hospitals) and the accompanying church of **sv Ignác** (St Ignatius), begun in 1665 by Carlo Lurago and Paul Ignaz Bayer. The statue of St Ignatius, which sits above the tympanum surrounded by a sunburst, caused controversy at the time, as until then only the Holy Trinity had been depicted in such a way. The church, modelled, like so many Jesuit churches, on the Gesù in Rome, is quite remarkable inside, a pink and white confection, with lots of frothy stucco work and an exuberant pulpit dripping with gold drapery, cherubs and saints.

At no. 40, at the southern end of the square, is the so-called **Faustův dům** (Faust House), an apricot and grey late Baroque building with a long and diabolical history of alchemy. An occult priest from Opava owned the house in the fourteenth century, and, two hundred years later, the English alchemist and international con-man Edward Kelley was summoned here by the eccentric Emperor Rudolf II to turn base metal into gold. The building is also the traditional setting for the Czech version of the Faust legend, with the arrival one rainy night of a penniless and homeless student, Jan Šťastný (meaning lucky, or *Faustus* in German). Finding money in the house, he decides to keep it – only to discover that it was put there by the Devil, who then claims his soul in return. Seemingly unperturbed by the historical fate of the site, a pharmacy (*lekárna*) now plies its trade on the ground floor.

The Orthodox cathedral of sv Cyril and Metoděj

West off Karlovo náměstí, down Resslova, the noisy extension of Ječná, is the Orthodox cathedral of **sv Cyril and Metoděj** (Tues–Sun 10am–4pm; 30Kč), originally constructed for the Roman Catholics by Bayer and Dientzenhofer in the eighteenth century, but since the 1930s the main base of the Orthodox

Church in the Czech Republic. Amid all the traffic, it's extremely difficult to imagine the scene here on June 18, 1942, when seven of the Czechoslovak secret agents involved in the most dramatic assassination of World War II (see box below) were besieged in the church by hundreds of the Waffen SS. Acting on the basis of a tip-off by one of the Czech resistance who turned himself in,

The assassination of Reinhard Heydrich

The assassination of Reinhard Heydrich in 1942 was the only attempt the Allies ever made on the life of a leading Nazi. It's an incident which the Allies have always billed as a great success in the otherwise rather dismal seven-year history of the Czech resistance. But, as with all acts of brave resistance during the war, there was a price to be paid. Given that the reprisals meted out to the Czech population were entirely predictable, it remains a controversial, if not suicidal, decision to have made.

The target, **Reinhard Tristan Eugen Heydrich**, was a talented and upwardly mobile anti-Semite (despite rumours that he was partly Jewish himself), a great organizer and a skilful concert violinist. He was a late recruit to the Nazi Party, signing up in 1931, after having been dismissed from the German Navy for dishonourable conduct towards a woman. However, he swiftly rose through the ranks of the SS to become second in command after Himmler, and in the autumn of 1941 he was appointed *Reichsprotektor* of the puppet state of *Böhmen und Mähren* – effectively, the most powerful man in the Czech Lands. Although his rule began with brutality, it soon settled into the tried and tested policy which Heydrich liked to call *Peitsche und Zucker* (literally, "whip and sugar").

On the morning of May 27, 1942, as Heydrich was being driven by his personal bodyguard, *Oberscharführer* Klein, in his open-top Mercedes from his manor house north of Prague to his office in Hradčany, three Czechoslovak agents (parachuted in from England) were taking up positions in the northeastern suburb of Libeň. The first agent gave the signal as the car pulled into Kirchmayer Boulevard (now V Holešovičkách). Another agent, a Slovak called Gabčík, pulled out a Sten gun and tried to shoot, but the gun jammed. Rather than driving out of the situation, Heydrich ordered Klein to stop the car and attempted to shoot back. At this point, the third agent, Kubiš, threw a bomb at the car. The blast injured Kubiš and Heydrich, who immediately leapt out and began firing at Kubiš. Kubiš, with blood pouring down his face, jumped on his bicycle and fled downhill. Gabčík meanwhile pulled out a second gun and exchanged shots with Heydrich, until the latter collapsed from his wounds. Gabčík fled into a butcher's, shot Klein – who was in hot pursuit – in the legs and escaped down the backstreets.

Meanwhile, back at the Mercedes, a baker's van was flagged down by a passerby, but refused to get involved. Eventually, a small truck carrying floor polish was commandeered and Heydrich taken to the Bulovka hospital. Heydrich died eight days later from shrapnel wounds and was given full Nazi honours at his Prague funeral; the cortege passed down Wenceslas Square, in front of a crowd of thousands. As the home resistance had forewarned, revenge was quick to follow. The day after Heydrich's funeral, the village of **Lidice** (see p.179) was burnt to the ground and its male inhabitants murdered; two weeks later the men and women of Ležáky suffered a similar fate.

The plan to assassinate Heydrich had been formulated in the early months of 1942 by the Czechoslovak government-in-exile in London, without consultation with the Czech Communist leadership in Moscow, and despite fierce opposition from the resistance within Czechoslovakia. Since it was clear that the reprisals would be horrific (thousands were executed in the aftermath), the only logical explanation for the plan is that this was precisely the aim of the government-in-exile's operation – to forge a solid wedge of resentment between the Germans and Czechs. In this respect, if in no other, the operation was ultimately successful.

the Nazis surrounded the church just after 4am and fought a pitched battle for over six hours, trying explosives, flooding and any other method they could think of to drive the men out of their stronghold in the crypt. Eventually, all seven agents committed suicide rather than give themselves up. There's a plaque at street level on the south wall commemorating those who died, and an exhibition on the whole affair situated in the crypt itself, which has been left pretty much as it was; the entrance is underneath the church steps on Na Zderaze.

Along the embankment

Magnificent turn-of-the-century mansions line the Vltava's right bank, almost without interruption, for some two kilometres from the Charles Bridge south to the rocky outcrop of Vyšehrad. It's a long walk, even just along the length of **Masarykovo** and **Rašínovo nábřeží**, though there's no need to do the whole lot in one go: you can hop on a tram (#17 or #21) at various points, drop down from the embankments to the waterfront itself, or escape to one of the two islands connected to them, Střelecký ostrov, or Slovanský ostrov, better known as Žofín.

Access to either of the two islands in the central section of the Vltava is from close to the Národní divadlo. The first, **Střelecký ostrov**, or Shooters' Island, is where the army held their shooting practice, on and off, from the fifteenth until the nineteenth century. Closer to the other bank, and accessible via most Legií (Legion's Bridge), it became a favourite spot for a Sunday promenade, and is still popular, especially in summer. The first *Sokol* festival took place here in 1882 (see p.70), and the first May Day demonstrations in 1890.

The second island, **Slovanský ostrov**, came about as a result of the natural silting of the river in the eighteenth century. It's commonly known as **Žofín**, after the island's very yellow cultural centre, built in 1835 and named for Sophie, the mother of Emperor Franz-Josef I. By the late nineteenth century the island had become one of the city's foremost pleasure gardens, where, as the composer Berlioz remarked, "bad musicians shamelessly make abominable music in the open air and immodest young males and females indulge in brazen dancing, while idlers and wasters … lounge about smoking foul tobacco and drinking beer". On a good day, things seem pretty much unchanged from those heady times. Concerts, balls and other social gatherings take place here in the cultural centre, and there's a good beer garden round the back; rowing boats can be hired in the summer.

At the southern tip of Slovanský ostrov stands the onion-domed Šítek water tower, which provided a convenient lookout post for the Czech secret police, whose job it was to watch over Havel's nearby flat (see p.132). Close by, spanning the narrow channel between the island and the river bank, is the striking white functionalist box of the **Mánes** art gallery (Tues–Sun 10am–6pm; 25Kč). Designed in open-plan style by Otakar Novotný in 1930, the gallery is named after Josef Mánes, a traditional nineteenth-century landscape painter and Czech nationalist, and puts on consistently interesting contemporary exhibitions; in addition there's a café and an upstairs restaurant, suspended above the channel. Most of the ornate buildings along the waterfront itself are private residential apartments, and therefore inaccessible. One exception is the Art Nouveau concert hall, **Hlahol**, at Masarykovo nábřeží 16, built for the Hlahol men's choir in 1903–06, and designed by the architect of the main railway station, Josef Fanta, with a pediment mural by Mucha and statues by Šaloun – check the listings magazines or the posters outside the hall for details of forthcoming concerts.

Tančící dům and Palackého náměstí

If the Mánes gallery seems at odds with the turn-of-the-century architecture along the embankment, it is as nothing to what stands at the beginning of **Rašínovo nábřeží** (named after the interwar Minister of Finance, Alois Rašín, who was assassinated by a non-card-carrying Communist in the 1920s). Designed by the Canadian-born Frank O. Gehry and the Yugoslav-born Vlado Milunič, the building is known as the **Tančící dům** (Dancing House) or "Fred and Ginger", after the shape of building's two towers, which look vaguely like a couple ballroom dancing. The site is all the more controversial as it stands next door to no. 77, an apartment block built at the turn of the century by Havel's grandfather, where, until the early 1990s, Havel and his first wife, Olga, lived in the top-floor flat.

Further along the embankment, at **Palackého náměstí**, the buildings retreat for a moment to reveal an Art Nouveau sculpture to rival Šaloun's monument in Staroměstské náměstí (see p.85): the **Monument to František Palacký**, the great nineteenth-century Czech historian, politician and nationalist, by Stanislav Sucharda. Like the Hus Monument, which was unveiled three years later, this mammoth project – fifteen years in the making – had missed its moment by the time it was finally completed in 1912, and found universal disfavour. The critics have mellowed over the years, and nowadays it's appreciated for what it is – an energetic and inspirational piece of work. Ethereal bronze bodies, representing the world of the imagination, shoot out at all angles, contrasting sharply with the plain stone mass of the plinth, and below, the giant seated figure of Palacký himself, representing the real world.

Vyšehradská and Ke Karlovu

Behind Palackého náměstí, on **Vyšehradská**, the intertwined concrete spires of the **Emauzy monastery** are an unusual modern addition to the Prague skyline. The monastery was one of the few important historical buildings to be damaged in the last war, in this case by a stray Anglo-American bomb. Charles IV founded the monastery for Croatian Benedictines, who used the Old Slavonic liturgy (hence its Czech name, Klášter na Slovanech, or "Monastery at the Slavs"), but after the Battle of Bílá hora it was handed over to the more mainstream Spanish Benedictines, who renamed it after Emmaus. The cloisters contain some extremely valuable Gothic frescoes, but since the return of the monks from their forty-year exile, access has become unpredictable.

Rising up behind Emauzy, is one of Kilian Ignaz Dientzenhofer's little gems, the church of **sv Jan Nepomucký na skalce** (St John of Nepomuk-on-the-rock), perched high above Vyšehradská, with a facade that displays the plasticity of the Bavarian's Baroque style in all its glory. Heading south, Vyšehradská descends to a junction, where you'll find the entrance to the **Botanická zahrada** (daily 10am–5pm; free), the university's botanic garden laid out in 1897 on a series of terraces up the other side of the hill. Though far from spectacular, the garden is one of the few patches of green in this part of town, and the 1930s' greenhouses (*skleníky*) have recently been restored to their former glory.

On the far side of the gardens, Apolinářská runs along the south wall and past a grimly Gothic red-brick maternity hospital with steeply sided stepped gables, before joining up with **Ke Karlovu**. Head left up here and the first street off to the right is Na bojišti, which is usually packed with tour coaches. The reason for this is **U kalicha** (Ⓦ www.ukalicha.cz), on the right, a pub which was immortalized in the opening passages of the consistently popular comic novel

△ Monument to František Palacký

The Good Soldier Švejk, by Jaroslav Hašek. In the story, on the eve of World War I, Švejk (*Schweik* to the Germans) walks into *U kalicha*, where a plain-clothes officer of the Austro-Hungarian constabulary is sitting drinking and, after a brief conversation, finds himself arrested in connection with the assassination of Archduke Ferdinand. Whatever the pub may have been like in Hašek's day (and even then, it wasn't his local), it's now unashamedly oriented towards reaping in the Euros, and about the only authentic thing you'll find inside – albeit at a price – is the beer.

Vila Amerika (Muzeum Antonína Dvořáka)

Further north along Ke Karlovu, set back from the road behind wrought-iron gates, is a more rewarding place of pilgrimage, the russet-coloured **Vila Amerika** (Tues–Sun 10am–5pm; 70Kč), originally named after the local pub, but now a museum devoted to Czech composer, **Antonín Dvořák** (1841–1904), who lived for a time on nearby Žitná. Even if you've no interest in Dvořák, the house itself is a delight, built as a Baroque summer palace around 1720 and one of Kilian Ignaz Dientzenhofer's most successful secular works. Dvořák, easily the most famous of all Czech composers, for many years had to play second fiddle to Smetana in the orchestra at the Národní divadlo, where Smetana was the conductor. In his forties, Dvořák received an honorary degree from Cambridge before leaving for the "New World", and his gown is one of the very few items of memorabilia to have found its way into the museum, along with the programme of a concert given at London's Guildhall in 1891. However, the tasteful period rooms, with the composer's music wafting in and out and the tiny garden dotted with Baroque sculptures, compensate for what the display cabinets may lack.

Muzeum Policie and Na Karlově church

I. P. Pavlova metro station is not far from Vila Amerika, but if you've got a few hundred more metres left in you, head south down Ke Karlovu. At the end of the street, the former Augustinian monastery of Karlov is now the **Muzeum Policie** (Tues–Sun 10am–5pm; 60Kč; Ⓦ www.mvcr.cz), formerly the Museum of the Security Forces – and, in the heyday of "normalization" in the 1970s, one of the most fascinating museums in the city. Works by Trotsky, photos of Bob Dylan, plays by Havel and contraband goods were all displayed in the grand room of dissidence; closed-circuit TV watched over your every move; and the first thing you saw on entry were two hundred pistols confiscated from western secret agents pointing at you from the wall. But the most famous exhibit was undoubtedly a stuffed German shepherd dog called Brek, who saw twelve years' service on border patrols, intercepted sixty "law-breakers", was twice shot in action and eventually retired to an old dogs' home.

With the barbed wire and border patrols all but disappeared, and the police struggling to improve their popularity, the new exhibition concentrates on road and traffic offences, and the force's latest challenges: forgery, drugs and murder. It's not what it used to be, but it's still mildly diverting, with several participatory displays, including a quiz on the Highway Code (in Czech) and a particularly gruesome section on forensic science.

Attached to the museum is **Na Karlově** church, founded by Charles IV (of course), designed in imitation of Charlemagne's tomb in Aachen, and quite unlike any other church in Prague. If it's open, you should take a look at the dark interior, which was remodelled in the sixteenth century by Bonifaz Wohlmut. The stellar vault has no central supporting pillars – a remarkable feat of engineering for its time, and one which gave rise to numerous legends about the architect being in league with the devil.

From outside the church, there's a great view south across the Botič valley, to a small cluster of skyscraper hotels and the low-lying, supremely ugly **Kongresové centrum**, the country's biggest concert venue, formerly known as the Palác kultury and originally used for party congresses; to the right is the fortress of Vyšehrad (see p.137). Vyšehrad metro is on the other side of the Nuselský most, the flyover bridge; alternatively, you can walk down to the bottom of the valley and catch a tram (#7, #18 or #24).

6

Vyšehrad and the eastern suburbs

B y the end of his reign in 1378, Charles IV had laid out his city on such a grand scale that it wasn't until the Industrial Revolution hit Bohemia in the mid-nineteenth century that Prague began to spread beyond the boundaries of the medieval town. The first of the suburbs, industrial Karlín, was rigidly planned, with public parks and grid street plans strictly laid out to the east of the old town; twentieth-century suburbs have tended to grow with less grace, trailing their tenements across the hills, and swallowing up existing villages on the way.

Vinohrady and **Žižkov**, which are covered in this chapter, still retain their individual late nineteenth-century identities, which makes them worth checking out on even a short visit to the city; they also contain one or two specific sights to guide your wandering. The fortress of **Vyšehrad**, which was actually one of the earliest points of settlement in Prague, is something of an exception to all the above, and is by far the most enticing of the outlying areas. Its cemetery contains the remains of Bohemia's artistic elite; the ramparts afford superb views over the river; and below its fortress, there are several examples of Czech Cubist architecture.

Vyšehrad

At the southern tip of Nové Město, around 3km south of the city centre, the rocky red-brick fortress of **VYŠEHRAD** (Ⓦ www.praha-vysehrad.cz) – literally "High Castle" – has more myths attached to it per square inch than any other place in Bohemia. According to Czech legend, this is the place where the Slav tribes first settled in Prague, where the "wise and tireless chieftain" Krok built a castle, and whence his youngest daughter Libuše went on to found *Praha* itself. Alas, the archeological evidence doesn't bear this claim out, but it's clear that Přemsyl Vratislav II (1061–92), the first Bohemian ruler to bear the title "king", built a royal palace here to get away from his younger brother who was lording it in the Hrad. Within half a century the royals had moved back to Hradčany, into a new palace, and from then on Vyšehrad began to lose its political significance.

The fortress enjoyed something of a renaissance under Emperor Charles IV, who wished to associate his own dynasty with that of the early Přemyslids. A system of walls was built to link the fortress to the newly founded Nové Město, and it was decreed that the *králová cesta* (the coronation route) should begin from here. These fortifications were destroyed by the Hussites in 1420, but the hill was settled again over the next two hundred years. In the mid-seventeenth century,

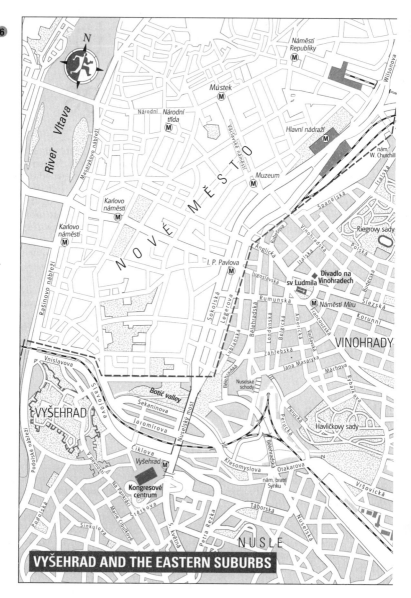

VYŠEHRAD AND THE EASTERN SUBURBS

the Habsburgs turfed everyone out and rebuilt the place as a fortified barracks, only to tear it down in 1866 to create a public park. By the time the Czech national revival movement became interested in Vyšehrad, only the red-brick fortifications were left as a reminder of its former strategic importance; they rediscovered its history and its legends, and gradually transformed it into a symbol of Czech nationhood. Today, Vyšehrad makes for one of the most rewarding

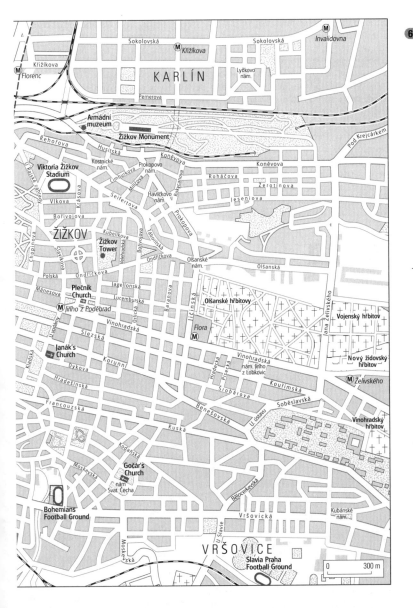

trips away from the human congestion of the city, a perfect afternoon escape and a great place from which to watch the evening sun set behind the Hrad.

The fortress

There are several **approaches to the fortress** (see map on pp.138–139): if you've come by tram #3, #7, #16, #17 or #21, which trundle along the waterfront to stop Výtoň, you can either wind your way up Vratislavova and enter through the Cihelná brána (**a**), or take the steep stairway from Rašínovo nábřeží that leads up through the trees to a small side entrance in the west wall. Alternatively, from Vyšehrad metro station, walk west past the ugly Kongresové centrum, and enter through the Táborská brána (**b**) and Leopoldova brána (**c**), between which there's an **information centre** (daily: April–Oct 9.30am–6pm; Nov–March 9.30am–5pm). Vyšehrad is perfect for a picnic, though food and drink can also be had at the *vinárna* (wine bar) opposite the church of sv Petr and Pavel, or in one of the pubs in the streets below the fortress (see p.209).

The last approach brings you out right in front of the blackened sandstone church of **sv Petr and Pavel** (**d**), rebuilt in the 1880s by Josef Mocker in neo-Gothic style (with further, even more ruthless, additions completed in the 1900s) on the site of an eleventh-century basilica. The twin open-work spires are now the fortress's most familiar landmark, and if luck is on your side, you should be able to view the church's polychrome interior, though opening times can be a bit erratic (March–Nov Tues–Fri 9am–noon & 1–5pm, Sat 9am–noon & Sun 11am–3pm; Dec–Feb Wed–Sun 11am–3pm).

Vyšehrad metro ▼

△ Detail, church of sv Petr and Pavel

Vyšehradský hřbitov (Vyšehrad Cemetery)

One of the first initiatives of the national revival movement was to establish the **Vyšehradský hřbitov** (daily: March, April & Oct 8am–6pm; May–Sept 8am–7pm; Nov–Feb 9am–4pm), which spreads out to the north and east of the church. It's a measure of the part that artists and intellectuals played in the foundation of the nation, and the regard in which they are still held, that the most prestigious graveyard in the city is given over to them: no soldiers, no politicians, not even the Communists managed to muscle their way in here (except on artistic merit). Sheltered from the wind by its high walls, lined on two sides by delicate arcades, it's a tiny cemetery (reflecting, as it were, the size of the nation) filled with well-kept graves, many of them designed by the country's leading sculptors.

To the uninitiated only a handful of figures are well-known, but for the Czechs the place is alive with great names (there's a useful plan of the most notable graves at the entrance nearest the church). Ladislav Šaloun's grave for **Dvořák**, situated under the arches, is one of the more showy ones, with a mosaic inscription, studded with gold stones, glistening behind wrought-iron railings. **Smetana**, who died twenty years earlier, is buried in comparatively modest surroundings near the Slavín monument (see below). The *Pražské jaro* festival begins with a procession from his grave to the Obecní dům, on the anniversary of his death (May 12).

Other graves that attract (mostly Czech) pilgrims are those of the nineteenth-century writer Božena Němcová, by the east end of the church; and playwright Karel Čapek, whose grave faces the arcades – he coined one of the two Czech words to have entered the English language, "robot" (the other is "pistol"). Several graves of lesser-known individuals stand out artistically, too: in particular, František Bílek's towering statue of *Sorrow* on the grave of the writer Václav Beneš Třebízský, which aroused a storm of protest when it was first unveiled; Bohumil Kafka's headstone for Dr Josef Kaizl, with a woman's face peeping out from the grave; and Karel Hladík's modern *Cathedral* sculpture, which sits above his own grave.

The focus of the cemetery, though, is the **Slavín monument** (**e**), a big, bulky stele built in 1893 to a design by Antonín Wiehl, covered in commemorative plaques and topped by a sarcophagus and a statue representing Genius. It's the communal resting place of more than fifty Czech artists, including the painter Alfons Mucha, the sculptors Josef Václav Myslbek and Ladislav Šaloun, the architect Josef Gočár, and the opera singer Ema Destinová.

The grave of the Romantic poet **Karel Hynek Mácha** was the assembly point for the demonstration on November 17, 1989, which triggered the Velvet Revolution. This was organized to commemorate the 50th anniversary of the Nazi attack on Czech higher education institutions in 1939. Student protests against the German occupation reached a peak on October 28, 1939, when violent clashes resulted in the death of medical student, **Jan Opletal**; his funeral, on November 11, was accompanied by more violent disturbances. On November 17, the Nazis took the initiative, executing various student leaders, packing thousands off to the camps and shutting down all Czech higher education institutes. Fifty years later, in 1989, the cemetery was the gathering point for a 50,000-strong crowd who attempted to march from here to Wenceslas Square.

The rest of the fortress

The next best thing to do after a stroll around the cemetery is to head off and explore the **Kasematy** or dungeons (daily: April–Oct 9.30am–6pm; Nov–

March 9.30am–5pm; 20Kč), which you enter via the **Cihelná brána** (**a**). After a short guided tour of a section of the underground passageways underneath the ramparts, you enter a vast storage hall, which shelters several of the original statues from the Charles Bridge, and, when the lights are switched off, reveals a camera obscura image of a tree.

The rest of the deserted fortress makes for a pleasant afternoon meander; you can walk almost the entire length of the ramparts, which give some superb views out across the city. **Galerie Vyšehrad** (daily: April–Oct 9.30am–6pm; Nov–March 9.30am–5pm) is a small art gallery housed in one of the bastions (**f**), which puts on temporary exhibitions. The heavily restored rotunda of **sv Martin** (**g**) – one of a number of Romanesque rotundas scattered across Prague – is the sole survivor of the medieval fortress built by Vratislav II in the eleventh century; it's only open for services. The foundations of the basilica of **sv Vavřinec** (**h**), from the same period, can be seen nearby, and inspected, should you so wish, by obtaining the key from the nearby snack bar (times as for the gallery).

If the weather's good, though, time is probably better spent lounging on the patch of grass to the south of the church, where there are regular outdoor concerts on summer Sundays. Dotted about the grass are the gargantuan statues by Myslbek that used to grace the city's bridge, Palackého most. Four couples are dotted across the green, all taken from Prague legends: *Přemysl and Libuše* (**i**), the husband and wife team who founded Prague and started Bohemia's first royal dynasty, the Přemyslids; *Lumír and Píseň* (**j**), the legendary Czech singer and his muse, Song; *Záboj and Slavoj* (**k**), two mythical Czech warriors; and *Ctirad and Šárka* (**l**), for whose story, see p.161.

Czech Cubism in Vyšehrad

Even if you harbour only a passing interest in modern architecture, it's worth seeking out the cluster of **Cubist villas** below the fortress in Vyšehrad. Whereas Czech Art Nouveau was heavily influenced by the Viennese Secession, it was Paris rather than the imperial capital that provided the stimulus for the short-lived but extremely productive Czech Cubist movement. In

---

Cubist and Rondo-Cubist buildings in Prague

Prague's unique Cubist and Rondo-Cubist buildings, most of which are covered in the text, are scattered right across the city. Here is a checklist of where to find the best examples of the style.

Staré Město
Gočár's Dům U černé Matky boží p.90

Nové Město
Janák & Zasche's Palác Adria p.120   Janák's Banka legií p.126
Blecha & Králíček's lamppost p.120   Králíček's Diamant p.128

Vyšehrad
Chochol's nájemný obytný dům p.144   Chochol's Kovařovicova vila p.144
Belada's nájemný obytný dům p.144   Chochol's Rodinný trojdům p.144

The suburbs
Gočár's Rodinný dvojdům p.150

1911, the *Skupina výtvarných umělců* or SVU (Group of Fine Artists) was founded in Prague, and quickly became the movement's organizing force. **Pavel Janák** was the SVU's chief theorist, **Josef Gočár** its most illustrious exponent, but **Josef Chochol** was the most successful practitioner of the style in Prague.

Cubism is associated mostly with painting, and the unique contribution of its Czech offshoot was to apply the theory to **furniture** (some of which is now on permanent display at the Dům U černé Matky boží; see p.90) and **architecture**. In Vyšehrad alone, Chochol completed three buildings, close to one another below the fortress, using prismatic shapes and angular lines to produce the sharp geometric contrasts of light and dark shadows characteristic of Cubist painting. Outside the Czech Republic, only the preparatory drawings by the French architect Duchamp-Villon for his *Maison Cubiste* (never realized), can be considered remotely similar.

The SVU's plans were cut short by World War I, after which Janák and Gočár attempted to establish a specifically Czechoslovak style of architecture incorporating prewar Cubism. The style was dubbed **Rondo-Cubism** since the prismatic moulding had been replaced by semicircular motifs, but only a few projects got off the ground before Czech architects turned to the functionalist ideals of the international modernist movement.

The buildings

The most impressive example of Czech Cubist architecture, brilliantly exploiting its angular location, is Chochol's **nájemný obytný dům** (m), an apartment block at Neklanova 30, begun in 1913 for František Hodek and now housing a restaurant on its ground floor. Further along Neklanova at no. 2, there's Antonín Belada's **nájemný obytný dům** (n), with its Cubist facade, and around the corner is the most ambitious project of the lot – Chochol's **Kovařovicova vila** (o), which backs onto Libušina. The front, on Rašínovo nábřeží, is presently concealed behind some overenthusiastic shrubs, but it's still possible to appreciate the clever, slightly askew layout of the garden, designed right down to its zigzag garden railings. Further along the embankment is Chochol's largest commission, the **Rodinný trojdům** (p), a large building complex with a heavy mansard roof, a central "Baroque" gable with a pedimental frieze, and room enough for three families.

Vinohrady

Southeast of Nové Město is the predominantly late nineteenth-century district of **VINOHRADY**, Prague's most resolutely bourgeois suburb up until World War II. Under the Communists, the whole area became decidedly run-down, but with the re-emergence of the property market in the 1990s, Vinohrady has once more become a desirable part of town to live in, with two spacious parks – **Riegrovy sady**, to the north, and **Havlíčkovy sady**, to the south – and a fabulous array of turn-of-the-century apartment buildings. In terms of conventional sightseeing, however, the area is definitely low priority, though there are a few places here (and in neighbouring Žižkov) worth a visit, most of them quick and easy to reach by metro.

Náměstí Míru

If Vinohrady has a centre, it's the leafy square of **náměstí Míru**, a good introduction to the aspirations of this confident, bourgeois neighbourhood. At its centre stands the brick-built basilica of **sv Ludmila**, designed by Josef Mocker in the late 1880s in a severe neo-Gothic style, though the interior furnishings have the odd flourish of Art Nouveau. In front of the church is a statue commemorating the **Čapek brothers**, writer Karel and painter Josef, who together symbolized the golden era of the interwar republic. Karel died in 1938, shortly after the Nazi invasion, while Josef perished in Belsen seven years later; their influence was deliberately underplayed by the Communists, and the memorial was erected only in the 1990s. Two more buildings on the square deserve attention, the most flamboyant being the **Divadlo na Vinohradech**, built in 1907, using Art Nouveau and neo-Baroque elements in equal measure. More subdued, but equally ornate inside and out, is the district's former **Národní dům**, a grandiose neo-Renaissance edifice from the 1890s housing a ballroom/concert hall and restaurant.

From náměstí Míru, block after block of alternately decaying and restored tenements, each clothed in its own individual garment of sculptural decoration, form a grid plan of grand bourgeois avenues stretching eastwards to the city's great cemeteries (see p.146). If the weather's nice, you could stroll your way to Plečnik's church (see below). However, distances are deceptive, and you may prefer to take the metro.

Plečnik's church

Vinohrady's other main square, **náměstí Jiřího z Poděbrad**, halfway between náměstí Míru and the cemeteries, contains Prague's most celebrated modern church, **Nejsvětější Srdce Páně** (Most Sacred Heart of Our Lord), built in 1928 by Josip Plečnik, the Slovene architect responsible for much of the remodelling of the Hrad (see box on p.40). It's a marvellously eclectic and individualistic work, employing a sophisticated potpourri of architectural styles: a Neoclassical pediment and a great slab of a clock tower with a giant transparent face in imitation of a Gothic rose window, as well as the bricks and mortar of contemporary constructivism. Plečnik also had a sharp eye for detail; look out for the little gold crosses inset into the brickwork like stars, inside and out, and the celestial orbs of light suspended above the heads of the congregation. If you can collar the priest, it may be possible to climb the clock tower.

Janák and Gočár's functionalist churches

Further afield are two, more uncompromisingly modernist, churches. The first is the **Husův sbor** (Hussite Church), three blocks south of Plečnik's church down U vodárny, on the corner of Dykova. Built in the early 1930s by Pavel Janák, the church's most salient feature is its freestanding hollow tower, which encloses a corkscrew spiral staircase and is topped by a giant copper chalice, symbol of the Hussite faith. A memorial on the wall commemorates the church's pioneering role in the Prague Uprising against the Nazis in May 1945, when it served as a clandestine Czech resistance headquarters.

Josef Gočár's equally severe, functionalist church of **sv Václav**, built around the same time, lies a kilometre or so southeast on náměstí Svatopluka Čecha; take tram #4, #22 or #23 from náměstí Míru or the bottom of U vodárny to the Čechovo náměstí stop. Here it forms the centrepiece of a sloping green square, with a distinctive stepped roof rising up from a slender, smoothly rendered 80m-high tower.

Žižkov

Though they share much the same architectural heritage, **ŽIŽKOV**, unlike Vinohrady, is a traditionally working-class area, and was a Communist Party stronghold even before the war, earning it the nickname "Red Žižkov". Nowadays its peeling turn-of-the-century tenements are home to a large proportion of Prague's Romany community, and it boasts more pubs and brothels per head than any other district in Prague. The main reason for venturing into Žižkov is to visit its two landmarks – ancient (Žižkov hill) and modern (the television tower) – and the city's main cemeteries, at the eastern end of Vinohradská.

Žižkov TV tower

At over 100m in height, the **Žižkov TV tower** (Televizní vysílač; daily 10am–11pm; 120Kč; ⓦ www.tower.cz), is the tallest (and the most unpopular) building in Prague. Close up, it's an intimidating futuristic piece of architecture, made all the more disturbing by the addition of several statues of giant babies crawling up the sides, courtesy of artist David Černý. Begun in the 1970s in a desperate bid to jam West German television transmission, the tower became fully operational only in the 1990s. In the course of its construction, however, the Communists saw fit to demolish part of a nearby Jewish cemetery, that had served the community between 1787 and 1891; a small section survives to the northwest of the tower. From the fifth-floor café or the viewing platform on the eighth floor, you can enjoy a spectacular view across Prague. To get to the tower, take the metro to Jiřího z Poděbrad and walk northeast a couple of blocks – it's difficult to miss.

The cemeteries

Approaching from the west, the first and the largest of Prague's vast cemeteries – each of which is bigger than the entire Jewish quarter – are the **Olšanské**

Jaroslav Seifert of Žižkov

The Czech Nobel prize-winning poet **Jaroslav Seifert** (1901–86) was born and bred in the Žižkov district. He was one of the founding members of the Czechoslovak Communist Party, and in 1920 helped found Devětsil, the most daring and provocative avant-garde movement of the interwar republic. Always accused of harbouring bourgeois sentiments, Seifert and eight other Communist writers were expelled from the Party when Gottwald and the Stalinists hijacked the Party at the Fifth Congress in 1929. After the 1948 coup, he became a *persona non grata*, though he rose to prominence briefly during the 1956 Writers' Union congress, when he attempted to lead a rebellion against the Stalinists. Later on, he became involved in Charter 77, and in 1984, amidst much controversy, he became the one and only Czech to win the Nobel Prize for Literature.

hřbitovy (daily dawn to dusk), originally created for the victims of the great plague epidemic of 1680. The perimeter walls are lined with glass cabinets, stacked like shoe-boxes, containing funereal urns and mementoes, while the graves themselves are a mixed bag of artistic achievements, reflecting the funereal fashions of the day as much as the character of the deceased. The cemeteries are divided into districts and crisscrossed with cobbled streets; at each gate there's a map, and an aged janitor ready to point you in the right direction.

The cemeteries' two most famous incumbents are an ill-fitting couple: Klement Gottwald, the country's first Communist president (see p.94), whose ashes were removed from the mausoleum on Žižkov hill after 1989 and re-interred here, and Jan Palach, the philosophy student who set light to himself in January 1969 in protest at the Soviet occupation. More than 750,000 people attended Palach's funeral in January 1969, and in an attempt to put a stop to the annual vigils at his graveside, the secret police removed his body in 1973 and reburied him in his home town, 60km outside Prague. His place was taken by an unknown woman, Maria Jedličková, who for the next seventeen years had her grave covered in flowers instead. Finally, in 1990, Palach's body was returned to Olšany; you'll find it just to the east of the main entrance on Vinohradská (metro Flora).

To the east of Olšany cemeteries, and usually totally deserted, is the **Vojenský hřbitov** (Military Cemetery); the entrance is 200m up Jana Želivského, on the right (metro Želivského). Its centrepiece is the monument to the 436 Soviet soldiers who lost their lives on May 9, 1945 in the liberation of Prague, surrounded by a small, tufty meadow dotted with simple white crosses. Nearby, the graves of Czechs who died fighting for the Habsburgs on the Italian front in World War I are laid out in a semicircle. There are even Commonwealth war graves here, mostly (though not exclusively) British POWs who died in captivity.

Nový židovský hřbitov (New Jewish Cemetery)

Immediately south of the war cemetery is the **Nový židovský hřbitov** (daily except Sat: April–Aug 8am–5pm; Sept–March 8am–4pm), founded in the 1890s, when the one by the Žižkov TV tower was full (see p.146); it was designed to last for a century, with room for 100,000 graves. It's a melancholy spot, particularly so in the east of the cemetery, where large empty allotments wait in vain to be filled by the generation that perished in the Holocaust. In fact, the community is now so small that it's unlikely the graveyard will ever be full. Most people come here to visit **Franz Kafka**'s grave, 400m east along the south wall and signposted from the entrance. He is buried, along with his mother and father (both of whom outlived him), beneath a plain headstone; the plaque below commemorates his three sisters who died in the camps.

Žižkov hill

Žižkov hill (also known as Vítkov) is the thin green wedge of land that separates Žižkov from Karlín, the grid-plan industrial district to the north. From its westernmost point, which juts out almost to the edge of Nové Město, is the definitive panoramic view over the city centre. It was here, on July 14, 1420, that the Hussites enjoyed their first and finest victory at the **Battle of Vítkov**, under the inspired leadership of the one-eyed general, Jan Žižka (hence the name of the district). Ludicrously outnumbered by more than ten to one, Žižka and his fanatically motivated troops thoroughly trounced Emperor Sigismund and his papal forces.

Despite its overblown totalitarian aesthetics, the giant concrete **Žižkov monument** which graces the crest of the hill was actually built between the wars as a memorial to the Czechoslovak Legion who fought against the Habsburgs – the gargantuan equestrian statue of the mace-wielding Žižka, which fronts the monument, is reputedly the world's largest. The building was later used by the Nazis as an arsenal, and eventually became a Communist mausoleum: presidents Gottwald, Zápotocký and Svoboda were all buried here, along with the obligatory Unknown Soldier and various other Party hacks. Žižkov was an ideal resting place, lying as it does in the heart of "Red Žižkov", from where the Communists drew so much of their pre-1948 working-class support. Gottwald himself was originally pickled and embalmed (à la Lenin), but a fire damaged his corpse so badly that the leader had to be cremated in 1963. In 1990, the remaining bodies were cremated and quietly reinterred in Olšany, and at present there's an ongoing legal battle over what should happen next with the monument.

To get to the monument, take the metro to Florenc, walk under the railway lines, and then up the steep lane U památníku. On the right as you climb the hill is the **Armádní muzeum** (Army Museum; April–Oct Tues–Sun 10am–6pm; Nov–April Mon–Fri 8.30am–5pm; 20Kč; ⓦ www.militarymuseum.cz), guarded by a handful of unmanned tanks, howitzers and armoured vehicles. Before 1989, this museum was a glorification of the Warsaw Pact, pure and simple; its recent overhaul has produced a much more evenly balanced account of both world wars, particularly in its treatment of the previously controversial subjects of the Czechoslovak Legion, the Heydrich assassination (see p.130) and the Prague Uprising. The collection now covers only the period from 1914 to 1945; for the pre-1914 military museum, see p.54.

Holešovice and the western suburbs

The points of interest in Prague's northern and western **suburbs**, on the left bank of the Vltava, are spread over a much larger area than those east of the river. They are also far more varied: some, like Holešovice and parts of Smíchov, date from the late nineteenth century, whereas Dejvice and Střešovice were laid out between the wars as well-to-do garden suburbs. The left bank also boasts a great deal more greenery, including the city's largest public park, Stromovka. All this goes to make up a fascinating patchwork of communities, which few tourists bother to see. It's worth the effort, though, if only to remind yourself that Prague doesn't begin and end at the Charles Bridge.

HOLEŠOVICE & THE WESTERN SUBURBS

There are several specific sights in each suburb that can lend structure to your meandering. The single most important sight is the **Veletržní palác** in **Holešovice**, which houses the country's finest modern art collection. Another popular destination is the **Bertramka** (Mozart Museum) in **Smíchov**. Other sights – for instance the functionalist villas in **Dejvice** and **Střešovice** – are of more specialized interest; and some are simply unknown to most visitors, such as the exquisite Renaissance chateau of **Hvězda**.

Holešovice and Bubeneč

The late nineteenth- and early twentieth-century districts of **HOLEŠOVICE** and **BUBENEČ**, tucked into a huge U-bend in the Vltava, have little in the way of truly magnificent architecture, but they make up for it with two huge splodges of green: to the south, **Letná**, overlooking the city centre, and to the north, **Stromovka**, bordering the Výstaviště funfair and international trade fair grounds. Holešovice also has a couple of excellent museums: the city's **Národní technické muzeum**, which shows off the Czechs' past scientific and industrial achievements, and the aforementioned **Veletržní palác**, Prague's impressive modern art museum.

Chotkovy sady and the Bílkova vila

These first two sights are strictly speaking part of the Hradčany that lies to the northeast of the castle, but, for convenience, they begin this chapter. The easiest way to this part of town is to take tram #22 one stop from Malostranská metro to the Chotkovy sady stop by the Belvedér, or the metro to Hradčanská metro and walk up Tychonova, a street flanked on one side by a series of semidetached houses. These include **Josef Gočár**'s rodinný dvojdům at nos. 4 & 6, built with a traditional mansard roof in a restrained Cubist style, similar to that employed on the Dům U černé Matky boží in Staré Město (see p.90).

Chotkovy sady

At the top of Tychonova, the leafy avenue of Marianské hradby slopes down to the left, past the Belvedér, to the **Chotkovy sady**, Prague's first public park, founded in 1833 by the ecologically minded city governor, Count Chotek. The atmosphere here is a lot more relaxed than in the nearby Královská zahrada (see p.52), and you can happily stretch out on the grass and soak up the sun, or head for the south wall, which enjoys an unrivalled view of the bridges and islands of the Vltava. At the centre of the park there's a bizarre, melodramatic grotto-like memorial to the nineteenth-century Romantic poet Julius Zeyer, an elaborate monument from which life-sized characters from Zeyer's works, carved in white marble, emerge from the blackened rocks amid much drapery.

Bílkova vila

Across the road from the park, hidden behind its overgrown garden at Mieckiewiczova 1, the **Bílkova vila** (mid-May to mid-Oct Tues–Sun 10am–6pm; mid-Oct to mid-May Sat & Sun 10am–5pm; 50Kč) honours one of the most original of all Czech sculptors, František Bílek (1872–1941). Born in a part of South Bohemia steeped in the Hussite tradition, Bílek lived a monkish life, spending years in spiritual contemplation, reading the works of Hus and other Czech reformers. The Bílkova vila was built in 1911 to the artist's own design, intended as both a "cathedral of art" and the family home. At first sight, it appears a strangely mute red-brick building, out of keeping with the extravagant Symbolist style of Bílek's sculptures. It's meant to symbolize a cornfield, with the front porch supported by giant sheaves of corn; only the sculptural group, the fleeing Comenius and his followers, in the garden, gives a clue as to what lies within.

Inside, the brickwork gives way to bare stone walls lined with Bílek's religious sculptures, giving the impression that you've walked into a chapel rather than an artist's studio: "a workshop and temple", in Bílek's own words. In addition to his sculptural and relief work in wood and stone, often wildly expressive and spiritually tortured, there are also ceramics, graphics and a few mementoes of Bílek's life. His work is little known outside his native country, but his contemporary admirers included Franz Kafka, Julius Zeyer and Otakar Březina, whose poems and novels provided the inspiration for much of Bílek's art. Bílek's living quarters have also been restored and opened to the public, with much of the original wooden furniture, designed and carved by Bílek himself, still in place. Check out the dressing table for his wife, shaped like some giant church lectern, and the wardrobe decorated with a border of hearts, a penis, a nose, an ear, an eye plus the sun, stars and moon.

Letná

A high plateau hovering above the city, the flat green expanse of the **Letná** plain has long been the traditional assembly point for invading and besieging armies. It was laid out as a public park in the mid-nineteenth century, but its main post-1948 function was as the site of the May Day parades. For these, thousands of citizens were dragooned into marching past the south side of the city's main football ground, the Sparta stadium, where the old Communist cronies would take the salute from a giant red podium. On November 26, 1989, the park was the scene of a more genuine expression of popular sentiment, when over 750,000 people gathered here to join in the call for a general strike against the Communist regime. The present-day Communists still gather here on May 1 in rather smaller numbers.

Letná's – indeed Prague's – most famous monument is one which no longer exists. The **Stalin monument**, the largest in the world, was once visible from almost every part of the city: a 30m-high granite sculpture portraying a procession of Czechs and Russians being led to Communism by the Pied Piper figure of Stalin, but popularly dubbed *tlačenice* (the crush) because of its resemblance to a Communist-era bread queue. Designed by Jiří Štursa and Otakar Švec, it took 600 workers 500 days to erect the 14,200-tonne monster. Švec, the sculptor, committed suicide shortly before it was unveiled, as his wife had done three years previously, leaving all his money to a school for blind children, since they at least would not have to see his creation. It was eventually revealed to the cheering masses on May 1, 1955 – the first and last popular celebration to take place at the monument. Within a year, Khrushchev had denounced his predecessor and, after pressure from Moscow, the monument was blown to smithereens by a series of explosions spread over a fortnight in 1962.

All that remains above ground is the statue's vast concrete platform and steps, on the southern edge of the Letná plain, now graced with David Černý's symbolic giant red **metronome** (which is lit up at night); it's also a favourite spot for skateboarders and another good viewpoint, with the central stretch of the Vltava glistening in the afternoon sun. Built into the hillside below is Prague's one and only nuclear bunker, intended to preserve the Party elite, post-armageddon. For years, it was actually used to store the city's slowly rotting potato mountain; more recently it has been sporadically squatted and used as a nightclub venue.

Visible to the west of the metronome is the **Hanavský pavilón**, a café-restaurant that looks rather like a Russian Orthodox church. It was devised by Count Hanavský as a showpiece of wrought-ironwork for the 1891 Prague Exhibition, and is executed in a flamboyant style which anticipated the arrival of Art Nouveau a few years later.

Národní technické muzeum

Despite its dull title, the **Národní technické muzeum** (National Technical Museum; Tues–Sun 9am–5pm; 60Kč; ⓦwww.ntm.cz), on Kostelní, is a sur-prisingly interesting museum, with an interactive gallery or two, and even the odd English caption appearing here and there. Its showpiece hanger-like main hall contains an impressive gallery of motorbikes, Czech and foreign, and a wonderful collection of old planes, trains and automobiles from Czechoslovakia's industrial heyday between the wars when the country's Škoda cars and Tatra soft-top stretch limos were really something to brag about. The oldest car in the collection is Laurin & Klement's 1898 *Präsident*, more of a motorized carriage than a car; the museum also boasts the oldest Bugatti in the world. Upstairs, there are interactive displays (a rarity in a Czech museum) trac-ing the development of early photography, and a collection of some of Kepler's and Tycho Brahe's astrological instruments. Below ground, a mock-up of a coal mine offers guided tours (11am, 1pm & 3pm).

Veletržní palác (Trade Fair Palace)

Situated at the corner of Dukelských hrdinů and Veletržní, some distance from the nearest metro station, the **Veletržní palác** (Tues–Sun 10am–6pm; 180Kč; ⓦwww.ngprague.cz) gets nothing like the number of visitors it should. For not only does the building house the Národní galerie's excellent nineteenth- and twentieth-century Czech and international art collection, it is also an architec-tural sight in itself. A seven-storey building constructed in 1928 by Oldřich Tyl and Josef Fuchs, it is Prague's ultimate functionalist masterpiece, not so much from the outside, but inside, where its gleaming white vastness is suitably awe-some. Even the normally hypercritical Le Corbusier, who visited the building the year it was completed, was impressed: "Seeing the Trade Fair Palace, I realised how to make large buildings, having so far built only several relatively small houses on a low budget."

The main exhibition hall is used for its original purpose, trade fairs, with the Národní galerie confined to the north wing. Nevertheless, the gallery is both big and bewildering, and virtually impossible to view in its entirety – you can even pay a reduced fee to visit just part of the collection: 130Kč for two floors or 80Kč for one floor. Special exhibitions occupy the ground, first and fifth floors, while the permanent collection occupies the second, third and fourth floors – the popular French art collection can be found on the third floor. The account below takes a chronological approach, beginning on the fourth floor, with nineteenth-century art. On each floor, there's a side room, with an art stu-dio or library, where you (and your kids, if you have any) can relax and read or draw. From the ground floor you can stare up at the glass-roofed atrium, a glorious space for wacky modern pieces of art, overlooked by six floors of balconies.

To reach the Veletržní palác by public transport, catch tram #5 from náměstí Republiky, tram #12 from Malostranská metro, tram #17 from Staroměstská metro, or tram #5, #12 or #17 from Nádraží Holešovice to the Veletržní stop.

Nineteenth-century art

The **nineteenth-century art** collection kicks off with a series of bronze sculptures from the second half of the century by **Josef Václav Myslbek**, the father of Czech sculpture. The painting collection, however, begins earlier in the century with Antonín Machek's well-crafted portraits of the Czech bourgeoisie, and his 32 naive scenes depicting Bohemian rulers from Krok to Ferdinand IV. Close by are Ludvík Kohl's fantasy paintings: the one of Vienna's Stephansdom shows the cathedral with two complete towers (instead of one); his imaginary completion of Prague's St Vitus Cathedral was eventually fulfilled more or less to the letter by nineteenth-century architects.

In this exhaustive survey of Czech nineteenth-century painting, the influential **Mánes family** have several sections to themselves. Antonín Mánes succeeded in getting the Czech countryside to look like Italy, and thus gave birth to romantic Czech landscape painting. Three of his offspring took up the brush: Quido specialized in idealized peasant genre pictures; Amálie obeyed her father's wishes and restricted herself to a little gentle landscape painting; Josef was the most successful of the trio, much in demand as a portrait artist, and one of the leading exponents of patriotically uplifting depictions of national events (he himself took part in the 1848 disturbances in Prague). The nude portrait by Josef, which intrudes into the otherwise demure nineteenth-century atmosphere, was, not surprisingly, hidden from public view until after his death.

The next few sections can be taken at a steady canter, though make sure you check out the eye-catching paintings of Yugoslavia by **Jaroslav Čermák**, a man who lived life to the full, was decorated for his bravery by the Montenegran prince Nicholas I, and died of a heart attack at the age of just 48. With a dark, treacle-brown palette and an eye for drama, Čermák displays an unhealthy obsession with the depiction of white Slav women being captured by swarthy Ottoman Turks. **Mikuláš Aleš**, whose designs can be seen in the sgraffito on many of the city's nineteenth-century buildings, is underrepresented, though you can admire his wonderfully decorative depiction of the historical meeting between George of Poděbrady and Matthias Corvinus. Difficult to miss is the faintly ludicrous *Judgement of Paris* – a lavishly large canvas in which Paris looks like an underage pixie – by Vojtěch Hynais, who, like Aleš, was involved in decorating the city's National Theatre.

Prize for most striking portrait goes to Václav Brožík's *Lady with a Greyhound*, possibly a portrayal of his wife, the daughter of a wealthy Parisian art dealer. G.C. Max's *Saint Julia*, which features a woman being crucified, is another crowd pleaser. **Antonín Chittussi**'s Corot-esque landscapes proved very popular in the Parisian salons of the 1880s; not so his most influential and uncharacteristic work, *Paris seen from Montmartre*, whose flat colours and precise lines were deemed beyond the pale. Beyond hang several misty, moody streetscapes by Jakub Schikaneder (one of whose ancestors was Mozart's librettist), and a bevy of fantastical Art Nouveau nudes by Maximilián Pirner.

Several wood sculptures by **František Bílek**, one of the country's finest sculptors, offer a taste of his anguished style, but for a more comprehensive insight into his art, you should visit the Bílkova vila (see p.150). **Jan Preisler's** mosaics and murals, which can be found on Art Nouveau buildings all over Prague, tend to be ethereal and slightly detached, whereas his oil paintings, like the cycle of *Black Lake* paintings displayed here, are more typically melancholic, and reveal the influence of the Norwegian painter Edvard Munch, a couple of whose works can be seen further on (see below).

The most successful Czech exponent of moody post-Impressionism was **Antonín Slavíček**, whose depictions of Prague remain perennially popular, as do his landscapes ranging from the Klimt-like *Birch Mood* to paintings such as *In the Rain*, which are full of foreboding. **Gustav Klimt**'s mischievous *Virgins*, a mass of naked bodies and tangled limbs painted over in psychedelic colours, hangs nearby; the gallery also owns one of the square landscapes he used to like painting during his summer holidays in the Salzkammergut.

Egon Schiele's Czech connection is that his mother came from Český Krumlov, the subject of a tiny, gloomy, autumnal canvas, *Dead City*. The gallery also owns one of Schiele's most popular female portraits, wrongly entitled *The Artist's Wife*, an unusually graceful and gentle watercolour of a seated woman in green top and black leggings. In contrast, *Pregnant Woman and Death* is a morbidly bleak painting, in which Schiele depicts himself as both the monk of death and the life-giving mother. Perhaps the most influential non-Czech artist on show is **Edvard Munch**, whose two canvases hardly do justice to the considerable effect he had on a generation of Czech artists after his celebrated 1905 Prague exhibition.

The fourth-floor collection ends in the foyer area, known rather wonderfully as the respirium, where sculptures by **Stanislav Sucharda** and **Jan Štursa**, two of the most important Czech Art Nouveau artists, predominate. On the balcony, there's a mixed bag of applied art from architectural drawings and models to lino patterning and wrought-ironwork. Architects whose work is featured include **Jan Kotěra**, Balšánek, Polívka and Oldřich, and there are several iridescent Lötz vases from Klašterský Mlýn to admire.

Art 1900–30

On entering the **1900 to 1930 art** collection, on the third floor, visitors are greeted by **Otakar Švec**'s life-sized *Motorcyclist* which, along with his much smaller *Racing Car*, is a great three-dimensional depiction of the optimistic speed of the modern age.

These are followed by a whole series of works by **František Kupka**, who was Czech by birth, but lived and worked in Paris from 1895. In international terms, Kupka is by far the most important Czech painter of the last century, having secured his place in the history of art by being (possibly) the first artist in the western world to exhibit abstract paintings. His seminal *Fugue in Two Colours (Amorpha)*, one of two abstract paintings Kupka exhibited at the Salon d'Automne in 1912, is displayed here, along with some earlier, pre-abstract paintings (a couple of self-portraits, a family portrait, a Matisse-like portrait of a Parisian cabaret actress, and *Piano Keys – Lake*, a strange, abstracted, though by no means abstract, work from 1909) and a pretty comprehensive selection of his later abstract and cosmic works.

The aforementioned Edvard Munch retrospective in 1905 prompted the formation in 1907 of the first Czech modern art movement, Osma (The Eight), one of whose leading members was **Emil Filla**, whose *Ace of Hearts* and *Reader of Dostoyevsky* – in which the subject appears to have fallen asleep, though, in fact, he's mind-blown – are both firmly within the Expressionist genre. However, it wasn't long before several of the Osma group were beginning to experiment with Cubism. Filla eventually adopted the style wholesale, helping found the Cubist SVU in 1911. **Bohumil Kubišta**, a member of Osma, refused to follow suit, instead pursuing his own unique blend of Cubo-Expressionism, typified by the wonderful self-portrait, *The Smoker*, and by the distinctly Fauvist *Players*.

To round out the Czech Cubist picture, there's furniture and ceramics (and even a Cubist chandelier) by Gočár, Janák and Chochol, as well as sculptures by **Otto Gutfreund**, a member of SVU, whose works range from the Cubo-Expressionist *Anxiety* (1911–12) to the more purely Cubist *Bust* (1913–14). After World War I, during which he joined the Foreign Legion but was interned for three years for insubordination, Gutfreund switched to depicting everyday folk in technicolour, in a style that prefigures Socialist Realism, examples of which can be seen a little further on in the gallery. His life was cut short in 1927, when he drowned while swimming in the Vltava.

Josef Čapek, brother of the playwright, is another Czech clearly influenced by Cubism, as seen in works such as *Accordion Player*, but like Kubišta, Čapek found Filla's doctrinaire approach difficult to take, and he left SVU in 1912. Another artist who stands apart from the crowd is **Jan Zrzavý**, who joined SVU, but during a long career pursued his own peculiarly individual style typified by paintings such as his 1909 self-portrait, in which he appears Chinese, and *Valley of Sorrow*, his own personal favourite, painted while still a student, and depicting a magical, imaginary and very stylized world.

At this point, signs begin to appear tempting you on to the ever popular **French art** collection, which features anyone of note who hovered around Paris in the fifty years from 1880 onwards. There are few masterpieces here, but it's all high-quality stuff, most of it either purchased for the gallery in 1923, or bequeathed by art dealer Vincenc Kramář in 1960.

The collection kicks off with several works by **Auguste Rodin**, particularly appropriate given the ecstatic reception that greeted the Prague exhibition of his work in 1902. Rodin's sculptures are surrounded by works from the advance guard of Impressionism: Courbet, Delacroix, Corot, Sisley and early Monet and Pissarro. Among the other works here, there's a characteristically sunny, Provençal *Green Wheat* by **Vincent van Gogh**, and *Moulin Rouge* by Toulouse Lautrec, with Oscar Wilde looking on. Beyond, the loose brushwork, cool turquoise and emerald colours of **Auguste Renoir**'s *Lovers* are typical of the period of so-called High Impressionism. *Bonjour Monsieur Gauguin* is a tongue-in-cheek tribute to Courbet's painting of a similar name, with **Paul Gauguin** donning a suitably bohemian beret and overcoat. Also on display is the only known self-portrait by **Henri Rousseau**, at once both confident and comical, the artist depicting himself, palette in hand, against a boat decked with bunting and the recently erected Eiffel Tower.

There's also a surprisingly good collection of works by **Pablo Picasso**, including several paintings and sculptures from his transitional period (1907–08), and lots of examples from the heights of his Cubist period in the 1910s; his *Landscape with Bridge* from 1909 uses precisely the kind of prisms and geometric blocks of shading that influenced the Czech Cubist architects. In addition, there are a couple of late paintings by Paul Cézanne, a classic *pointilliste* canvas by Georges Seurat and Cubist works by Braque. *Joaquine* painted by **Henri Matisse** in 1910–11 is a first-rate portrait, in which both Fauvist and Oriental influences are evident. Look out too for Marc Chagall's *The Circus*, a typically mad work from 1927, and a rare painting by Le Corbusier himself, which clearly shows the influence of Fernand Léger, one of whose works hangs close by.

The respirium features calligraphy and some real, chunky Rondo-Cubist furniture by, among others, Gočár. Meanwhile, out on the balcony, there's a feast of architectural drawings, scenography and industrial design from typewriters and vacuum cleaners to wooden aeroplane propellers. Highlights include Josef Čapek's costume and set designs for Janáček operas, and a model of the Müllerova vila (see p.160).

Art from 1930 to the present day

On the second floor, the section covering **art from 1930 to the present day** has been greatly expanded; it's mostly Czech in origin, and gives a pretty good introduction to the country's artistic peaks and troughs. To be honest, there's too much stuff here – paintings, sculptures and installations – to take in at one go, and the following account aims simply to draw out the works of some of the most significant artists.

First off, there's a wild kinetic-light sculpture by **Zdeněk Pešánek**, a world pioneer in the use of neon in art, who created a stir at the 1937 Paris Expo with a neon fountain. Devětsil, founded back in 1920, was the driving force of the Czech avant-garde between the wars, and is represented here by the movement's two leading artists: **Toyen** (Marie Čermínová) and her life-long companion **Jindřich Štyrský**, whose abstract works – they dubbed them "Artificialism" – reveal the couple's interest in the French Surrealists. Predictably enough, however, there are no examples of Štyrský's pornographic photomontages, or Toyen's sexually charged drawings, which form an important part of their work.

Avant-garde photography featured strongly in Devětsil's portfolio, and there are several fine abstract works on display, as well as some beautiful, abstract "colour tests" and graphics by Vojtěch Preissig, and a few short experimental films from the 1930s to watch. One Czech artist who enthusiastically embraced Surrealism was **Josef Šíma**, who settled permanently in Paris in the 1920s; several of his trademark floating torsos and cosmic eggs can be seen here.

Fans of Communist kitsch should make their way to the excellent **Socialist Realism** section, heralded by Karel Pokorný's monumental *Fraternisation* sculpture, in which a Czechoslovak soldier is engaging in a "kiss of death" with a Soviet comrade. There's a great model and drawing of a Tatra 603, the limo of choice for Party apparatchiks in the 1950s, yet clearly inspired by American car design. Among the paintings on display are works with wildly optimistic titles such as *We Produce More, We Live Better*, and Eduard Stavinoha's cartoon-like *Listening to the Speech of Klement Gottwald, Feb 21, 1948*. Note, too, the model of Otakar Švec's now demolished Stalin statue, which once dominated central Prague (see p.151). Beyond, there's a whole section on the 1958 Brussels Expo, in which Czechoslovakia won several awards, and which, in a sense, signalled the beginning of the slow thaw in censorship.

In the 1960s, **performance art** (*umění akce*) was big in Czechoslovakia, and it, too, has its own section. Inevitably, it's difficult to recapture the original impact of some of the "happenings": the paltry "remants of an installation" by Zdeněk Beran look a bit forlorn, and the photographs of Milan Knížak asking passer-by to crow have lost some of their immediacy. Other photos, such as those of Zorka Ságlová's *Laying out Nappies near Sudoměř*, give you a fair idea of what you missed, and Vladimír Boudník's theory of "explosionalism" would appeal to most small boys. Other works, such as Eva Kmentová's *Footprints*, betray their ephemeral intentions by being reproduced in a gallery: her plastercasts were originally exhibited for one day only in 1970 before being signed and given away.

The gallery owns several works by **Jiří Kolář** – pronounced "collage" – who, coincidentally, specializes in collages of random words and reproductions of other people's paintings. It's at this point in the collection that you get to see one of **Joan Miró**'s characteristically abstract Surrealist works called simply *Composition*, a couple of Henry Moore sculptures and a perforated Lucio Fontana canvas. The rest of the contemporary Czech art collection is interesting enough, if taken at a canter. Ivan Kafka's phallic *Potent Impotency* installation should raise a smile, and there's the occasional overtly political work such as *Great Dialogue* by Karel Nepraš, in which two red figures lambast each other at close quarters with loudspeakers.

If you've any energy left, however, it's definitely worth venturing out on to the balcony, where you'll find, among other things, models of some of the great landmarks of Czechoslovak Communist architecture, a set design by the innovative **Divadlo Drak** (a puppet company from Hradec Králové), and some of **Josef Koudelka**'s famous photographs from the 1968 invasion.

Výstaviště (Exhibition Grounds)

Five minutes' walk north from the Veletržní palác, up Dukelských hrdinů, takes you right to the front gates of the **Výstaviště** (Tues–Fri 2–10pm, Sat & Sun 10am–10pm), a motley assortment of buildings, originally created for the 1891 Prague Exhibition, which have served as the city's main trade fair arena and funfair ever since. From 1948 until the late 1970s, the Communist Party held its rubber-stamp congresses in the flamboyant stained-glass and wrought-iron **Průmyslový palác** at the centre of the complex, and more recently several brand new permanent structures were built for the 1991 Prague Exhibition, including a circular theatre, Divadlo Spirála, and Divadlo Globe, a reconstruction of Shakespeare's Globe Theatre in London, used for summer-only productions of the bard in English and Czech.

The grounds are at their busiest on the weekend, particularly in the summer (during which there's a small entrance charge), when hordes of Prague families descend on the place to down hot dogs, drink beer and listen to traditional brass band music. Apart from the annual trade fairs and special exhibitions, there are a few permanent attractions: the city's **Planetárium** (Mon–Fri 8.30am–noon & 1–8pm, Sat & Sun 9.30am–noon & 1–8pm; 20Kč; ⓦ www.planetarium.cz), which has static displays and shows videos, but doesn't have telescopes (for which you need to go to the Štefánikova hvězdárna – see p.72); the **Maroldovo panorama** (Tues–Fri 2–5pm, Sat & Sun 11am–5pm; 20Kč), a giant diorama of the 1434 Battle of Lipany (see p.243); and the **Lunapark**, a run-down funfair and playground for kids. In the long summer evenings, there's also an open-air cinema (*letní kino*), and regular performances by the **Křižíkova fontána**, dancing fountains devised for the 1891 Exhibition by the Czech inventor František Křižík, which perform a music and light show to packed audiences; for the current schedule, ask at the tourist office, or check the listings magazines or the website ⓦ www.krizikovafontana.cz.

Lapidárium

Lastly, Výstaviště also contains the Národní muzeum's **Lapidárium** (Tues–Fri noon–6pm, Sat & Sun 10am–6pm; 20Kč) – immediately on the right as you enter – official depository for the city's sculptures, which are under threat either from demolition or from the weather. It's actually a much overlooked collection, ranging from the eleventh to the nineteenth century, arranged chronologically over the course of eight rooms.

The first couple of rooms contain a host of salvaged medieval treasures, such as the slender columns decorated with interlacing from the Romanesque basilica that stood on the site of the city's cathedral. Some of the statues saved from the perils of Prague's polluted atmosphere, such as the bronze equestrian statue of **St George**, will be familiar if you've visited Prague Castle (see p.47); others are more difficult to inspect close up in their original sites, for example the figures from the towers of the Charles Bridge; and there are even copies here, too, such as the busts from the triforium of St Vitus' Cathedral.

One of the most outstanding sights is what remains of the **Krocín fountain**, in room 3, a highly ornate Renaissance work in red marble, which used to grace the Staroměstské náměstí, but failed to hold water and was eventually dismantled in 1862. The angels smiting devils, now displayed in room 5, are all that could be rescued from the **Marian Column** which used to stand on Staroměstské náměstí, after it had been attacked as a symbol of oppression by marauding Czech nationalists in 1918. Many of the original statues from the **Charles Bridge** can be seen in room 6, as well as the ones that were fished out of the Vltava after the flood of 1890. The sculptural group commissioned by the Jesuits is particularly good, featuring their founder St Ignatius centre stage, surrounded by figures and animals representing all four known continents.

Several pompous imperial monuments that were bundled off into storage after the demise of the Habsburgs in 1918 round off the museum's collection in room 8. One of the first to be removed was the equestrian bronze statue of **Francis I**, which used to sit under the neo-Gothic baldachin that still stands on Smetanovo nábřeží. By far the most impressive, however, is the bronze statue of **Marshall Radecký**, scourge of the 1848 revolution, carried aloft on a shield by eight Habsburg soldiers, a monument which used to stand on Malostranské náměstí.

Stromovka

To the west of Výstaviště lies the *královská obora* or royal enclosure, more commonly known as **Stromovka**, originally laid out as hunting grounds for the noble occupants of the Hrad, and – again thanks to Count Chotek – now Prague's largest and leafiest public park. If you're heading north for Troja and the city zoo (see p.159), a stroll through the park is by far the most pleasant approach. If you want to explore a little more of the park, head west sticking to the park's southern border and you'll come to a water tunnel, built by the surrealist court painter Giuseppe Arcimboldo as part of Rudolf II's ambitious horticultural scheme to carry water from the Vltava to the lakes he created a little to the north.

Further west still is Stromovka's main sight, the **Místodržitelský letohrádek**, one of the earliest neo-Gothic structures in the city, begun way back in 1805. Originally conceived as a royal hunting chateau, it served as the seat of the Governor of Bohemia until 1918, and now houses the Národní muzeum's periodicals collection (closed to the public). To continue on to Troja and the zoo, head north under the railway, over the canal, and on to the Císařský ostrov (Emperor's Island) – and from there to the right bank of the Vltava.

Troja

Though still well within the municipal boundaries, the suburb of **TROJA**, across the river to the north of Holešovice and Bubeneč, still has a distinctly country feel to it. Its most celebrated sight is Prague's only genuine **chateau** or **zámek**, perfectly situated against a hilly backdrop of vines. Troja's other attraction is the city's slightly dilapidated, but still enormously popular, **zoo**.

To get to Troja, you can either **walk** from Výstaviště (taking the route described above); catch **bus** #112, which runs hourly from metro Nádraží Holešovice; or, from April to September, take a boat from the PPS boat launch between Jiráskův and Palackého most (see map on pp.112–113).

Trojský zámek

The **Trojský zámek** (April–Sept Tues–Sun 10am–6pm; Nov–March Sat & Sun 10am–5pm; 120Kč) was designed by Jean-Baptiste Mathey for the powerful Šternberg family towards the end of the seventeenth century. Despite a recent renovation and rusty red repaint, its plain early Baroque facade is no match for the action-packed, blackened figures of giants and titans who battle it out on the chateau's monumental balustrades. To visit the **interior**, you'll have to join one of the guided tours. The star exhibits are the gushing frescoes depicting the victories of the Habsburg Emperor Leopold I (who reigned from 1657 to 1705) over the Turks, which cover every inch of the walls and ceilings of the grand hall; ask for the *anglický text* when you enter. You also get to wander through the chateau's pristine, trend-setting, French-style formal **gardens**, the first of their kind in Bohemia.

The zoo

On the other side of U trojského zámku, which runs along the west wall of the chateau, is the city's capacious **zoo** (daily: April 9am–5pm; May 9am–6pm; June–Sept 9am–7pm; Oct–March 9am–4pm; 50Kč; ⓦ www.zoopraha.cz), founded in 1931 on the site of one of Troja's numerous hillside vineyards. Despite its rather weary appearance, all the usual animals are on show here, and kids, at least, have few problems enjoying themselves. Thankfully, a programme of modernization is currently under way, though some cramped cages still remain. In the summer, you can take a "ski-lift" (*lanová dráha*) from the duck pond to the top of the hill, where the prize exhibits – a rare breed of miniature horse known as Przewalski – hang out.

Dejvice and beyond

Spread across the hills to the northwest of the city centre are the leafy garden suburbs of **Dejvice** and neighbouring Střešovice, peppered with fashionable modern villas, built between the wars for the upwardly mobile Prague bourgeoisie and commanding magnificent views across the north of the city. Dejvice is short on conventional sights, but interesting to explore all the same; Střešovice has one compelling attraction, the **Müllerova vila**, a perfectly restored functionalist house designed by Adolf Loos. Some distance further west, the valley of **Šárka** is about as far as you can get from an urban environment without leaving the city. To the south of Šárka is the battlefield of **Bílá hora**, and **Hvězda**, a beautiful park containing a pretty star-shaped chateau.

Dejvice

DEJVICE was planned and built in the early 1920s for the First Republic's burgeoning community of civil servants and government and military officials. Its unappealing main square, **Vítězné náměstí** (metro Dejvická), is unavoidable if you're planning to explore any of the western suburbs, since it's a major public transport interchange. There's nothing much of note in this central part of Dejvice, though you can't help but notice the former **Hotel International** (now the *Crowne Plaza*) at the end of Jugoslávských partyzanů, a Stalinist skyscraper that is disturbingly similar to the universally loathed Palace of Culture in Warsaw. For followers of Socialist Realist chic, its workerist motifs merit closer inspection – you can even stay there (see p.189). To get there, take tram #20 or #25 from metro Dejvická two stops to the Podbaba terminal.

Baba

Dejvice's most intriguing villas are located to the north in **Baba** (bus #131 from metro Hradčanská), a model neighbourhood of 33 functionalist houses, each individually commissioned and built under the guidance of one-time Cubist and born-again functionalist, Pavel Janák. A group of leading architects affiliated to the Czech Workers' Alliance, inspired by a similar project in Stuttgart, initiated what was, at the time, a radical housing project to provide simple, single-family villas. The idea was to use space and open-plan techniques rather than expensive materials to create a luxurious living space.

Despite the plans of the builders, the houses were mostly bought up by Prague's artistic and intellectual community. Nevertheless, they have stood the test of time better than most utopian architecture, not least because of the fantastic site – facing south and overlooking the city. Some of them remain exactly as they were when first built, others have been thoughtlessly altered, but as none of them is open to the public you'll have to be content with surreptitious peeping from the following streets: Na ostrohu, Na Babě, Nad Paťankou and Průhledová. To see the inside of an, albeit luxury, functionalist house, you need to head for the Müllerova vila (see below).

Müllerova vila

The most famous of Prague's interwar villas is the **Müllerova vila** (Müller Haus) at Nad hradním vodojemem 14, in Střešovice, to the southwest of Dejvice. Designed by the Brno-born architect, Adolf Loos – regarded by many as one of the founders of modern architecture – and Karel Lhota, and completed in 1930 (after planning permission had been refused ten times), it was one of Loos' few commissions, a typically uncompromising box, wiped smooth with concrete rendering, its window frames picked out in yellow. It's nothing to look at from the outside – Loos believed that "a building should be dumb on the outside and reveal its wealth only on the inside" – but if you've any interest in modernist architecture, then a trip out here is an absolute must. To visit the house, you must phone in advance as each guided tour is limited to seven people (Tues, Thurs, Sat & Sun 10am, noon, 2pm & 4pm; 300Kč; 100Kč more for an English guide; ☎224 312 012, ⊛www.villamuller.cz); to reach the house, take tram #1 or #18 from metro Hradčanská, four stops to Ořechovka.

The Müller family, who had made their money in the building trade, were extremely wealthy, and spared no expense when it came to the interior furnishings. They lived here, with numerous servants, until the 1948 Communist coup, after which they were granted a single room, while the rest of the house was turned into offices. Dr Müller was given a job as a stoker in the house's boiler room, where he died in 1951 in an accident; Mrs Müller continued to live in the boudoir until her death nearly twenty years later. In the 1990s, the City of Prague Museum bought the house back off the Müllers and spent a small fortune restoring it to something like its original state.

Loos' most famous architectural concept was the Raumplan, or open-plan design, at its most apparent in the living room, which is overlooked by the dining room on the mezzanine level, and, even higher up, by the boudoir, itself a Raumplan in miniature. The house is also decorated throughout in the rich materials and minimal furnishings that were Loos' hallmark: green and white Cipolino marble columns, with an inset aquarium in the living room and mahogany panelling for the dining room ceiling. The "American kitchen" was very up to date in the 1930s, as was the use of lino for the floor and walls of the children's room, and there are two lifts in the centre of the house – one for people, one for food. Other highlights include the his and hers dressing rooms off the master bedroom, and the Japanese-style summer dining room, which opens out onto the roof terrace overlooking Prague Castle.

Šárka

If you've had your fill of postcards and crowds, take tram #20 or #26 from metro Dejvice to the last stop and walk north down into the **Šárka valley**, a peaceful limestone gorge that twists eastwards back towards Dejvice. The first section (Divoká Šárka) is particularly dramatic, with grey–white crags rising up on both sides – it was here that Šárka plunged to her death (see box below). Gradually the valley opens up, with a grassy meadow to picnic on, and an open-air swimming pool nearby, both fairly popular with Czechs on summer weekends. There are various points further east from which you can pick up a city bus back into town, depending on how far you want to walk. The full walk to where the Šárka stream flows into the Vltava, just north of Baba, is about 6–7km all told, though none of it is particularly tough going.

Šárka and Ctirad

The Šárka valley takes its name from the Amazonian **Šárka**, who, according to Czech legend, committed suicide here sometime back in the last millennium. The story begins with the death of Libuše, the founder and first ruler of Prague. The women closest to her, who had enjoyed enormous freedom and privilege in her court, refused to submit to the new patriarchy of her husband, Přemysl. Under the leadership of a woman called Vlasta, they left Vyšehrad and set up their own proto-feminist, separatist colony called Děvín, on the opposite bank of the river.

They scored numerous military victories over the men of Vyšehrad, but never managed to finish off the men's leader, a young warrior called **Ctirad**. In the end they decided to ensnare him and tied one of their own warriors naked to a tree, sure in the knowledge that Ctirad would take her to be a maiden in distress and come to her aid. Šárka offered to act as the decoy, luring Ctirad into the ambush, after which he was tortured and killed. However, in her brief meeting with Ctirad, Šárka fell madly in love with him and, overcome with grief at what she had done, threw herself off the aforementioned cliff. And just in case you thought the legend has a feminist ending, it doesn't. Roused by the cruel death of Ctirad, Přemysl and the lads had a final set-to with Vlasta and co, and butchered the lot of them.

Hvězda, Bílá hora and Břevnov

A couple of kilometres southwest of Dejvice, trams #1, #2 and #18 terminate close to the main entrance to the hunting park of **Hvězda** (May–Sept Tues–Sun 9am–5pm; 40Kč), one of Prague's most beautiful and peaceful parks. Wide, soft, green avenues of trees radiate from a bizarre star-shaped building (*hvězda* means "Star") that was designed by Archduke Ferdinand of Tyrol for his wife in 1555. Inside, there's a worthy but dull museum, devoted to the writer Alois Jirásek (1851–1930), who popularized old Czech legends during the national revival, and the artist Mikuláš Aleš (1852–1913), whose drawings were likewise inspired by Czech history. There's also a small exhibition on the Battle of Bílá hora, which took place nearby (see box below). It's the building itself, though – decorated with delicate stucco work and frescoes – that's the real reason for venturing inside; it makes a perfect setting for the chamber music concerts occasionally staged here.

A short distance southwest of Hvězda is the once entirely barren limestone summit of **Bílá hora** (White Mountain), accessible from Hvězda through one of the many holes in the park's southern perimeter wall. It was here in 1620 that the first battle of the Thirty Years' War took place, sealing the fate of the Czech nation for the following three hundred years. In little more than an hour, the Protestant forces of the "Winter King" Frederick of Palatinate were roundly beaten by the Catholic troops of the Habsburg Emperor Ferdinand. As

---

The Battle of Bílá hora

The **Battle of Bílá hora** (White Mountain) may have been a skirmish of minor importance in the Thirty Years' War, but, for the Czechs, it was to have devastating consequences. The victory of the Catholic forces of Habsburg Emperor Ferdinand II in 1620 set the seal on the Czech Lands for the next three hundred years. It prompted an emigration of religious and intellectual figures that relegated the country to a cultural backwater for most of modern history. The defeat also unleashed a decimation of the Bohemian and Moravian aristocracy, which meant that, unlike their immediate neighbours, the Poles and Hungarians, the Czechs had to build their nineteenth-century national revival around writers and composers, rather than counts and warriors.

The 28,000 Catholic soldiers – made up of Bavarians, Spanish, German and French troops (among them the future philosopher, René Descartes) – outnumbered the 21,000-strong Czech, Hungarian and German Protestant army, though the latter occupied the strategic chalky hill to the west of Prague. Shortly after noon on November 8 the imperial troops (under the nominal command of the Virgin Mary) began by attacking the Protestants' left flank, and, after about an hour, prompted a full-scale flight. The Protestant commander, Christian von Anhalt, went hot-foot back to the Hrad, where he met the Czech king, Frederick of Palatinate, who was late for the battle, having been delayed during lunch with the English ambassador.

Frederick, dubbed the "Winter King" for his brief reign, had once tossed silver coins to the crowd, and entertained them by swimming naked in the Vltava, while his wife, Elizabeth, daughter of James I of England, had shocked Prague society with her expensive dresses, her outlandish hairdo, and her plunging décolletage. Now, abandoned by their allies, the royal couple gathered up the crown jewels and left Prague in such a hurry they almost forgot their youngest son – later to become the dashing Prince Rupert of the English Civil War – who was playing in the nursery. The city had no choice but to surrender to the Catholics, who spent a week looting the place, before executing 27 of the rebellion's leaders on Staroměstské náměstí (see p.85).

a more or less direct consequence, the Czechs lost their aristocracy, their religion, their scholars and, most importantly, the remnants of their sovereignty. There's nothing much to see now, apart from the small monument (*mohyla*), and a pilgrims' church, just off Nad višňovkou. This was erected by the Catholics to commemorate the victory, which they ascribed to the timely intercession of the Virgin Mary – hence its name, **Panna Maria Vítězná** (St Mary the Victorious). To get to Bílá hora from the centre of town, take tram #8 from metro Hradčanská or #22 from metro Malostranská to the western terminus, then walk up Nad višňovkou and across the field.

If you've time to spare before heading back into town, it's only five minutes' walk east of the park, down Zeyerova alej, to the idyllic Baroque monastery of **Břevnovský klášter** (guided tours Sat & Sun: Easter to mid-Oct 9am, 11.30am, 1pm, 2.30pm & 4pm; mid-Oct to Easter 10am & 2pm; 50Kč). Founded as a Benedictine abbey by St Adalbert, tenth-century bishop of Prague, it was worked over in the eighteenth century by both Christoph and Kilian Ignaz Dientzenhofer, and bears their characteristic interconnecting ovals, inside and out. The monks have now returned, which has made it easier to gain access to the church. To get back into town, take tram #8 or #22 from the Břevnovský klášter stop just below the monastery.

Smíchov and beyond

SMÍCHOV is for the most part a late nineteenth-century working-class suburb, home to the city's largest brewery, which produces the ubiquitous Staropramen, and a large community of Romanies, its skyline peppered with satanic chimneys dutifully belching out smoke. To the west, as the suburb gains height, the run-down tenements give way to another of Prague's sought-after villa quarters. To the north, Smíchov borders with Malá Strana, and, officially at least, takes in a considerable part of the woods of Petřín, south of the Hladová zeď (see p.72). South of Smíchov, the village of **Zbraslav** is home to the National Gallery's extensive Asian art collection.

Anděl and náměstí 14 října

There's only one important sight in Smíchov – the Bertramka (see p.164) – but a stroll around its busy streets is rewarding in its own way. As you leave Anděl metro station, the modern hub of Smíchov, note the Soviet-designed Socialist Realist marble **mosaic**, a relic from the days when the station was called Moskevská. Downtown Smíchov is now totally dominated by the glasshouse of the Zlatý Anděl shopping centre, which dwarfs the adjacent (disused) **synagogue**, up Plzeňská. Built in 1863 to serve the wealthy Jewish business folk, it was remodelled in the 1930s in functionalist style, and sports unusual crenellations on the roof – only the Hebrew inscription on the ground floor gives any indication of its former use.

The district's traditional heart is **náměstí 14 října**, a short walk from metro Anděl up Štefánikova. The Art Nouveau Národní dům, and the adjacent market hall (now converted into a bland supermarket), both erected around 1906, have seen better days, but the neo-Renaissance **church of sv Václav**, built in the 1880s and overlooking the square, is worth a visit. Inside, the church is a jewel box of rich Byzantine decoration, with gilded mosaics, huge Ionic pillars of red Swedish granite, a coffered ceiling and a wonderfully Turkish-looking gilded pulpit.

Bertramka (Mozart Museum)

Mozart stayed with the Dušeks at their newly acquired villa **Bertramka** (daily: April–Oct 9.30am–6pm; Nov–April 9.30am–5pm; 50Kč; ⓦ www.bertramka.cz) on several occasions – it was here that he put the finishing touches to his *Don Giovanni* overture, the night before the premiere at the Stavovské divadlo (see p.94). It was the sort of household that would have appealed to Mozart, musical

The pink tank

Smíchov's greatest claim to fame is the episode of the **pink tank**. Until 1991, Tank 23 sat proudly on its plinth in náměstí Sovětských tankistů (Soviet tank drivers' square), one of a number of obsolete tanks generously donated by the Soviets after World War II to serve as monuments to the 1945 liberation. Tank 23 was special, however, as it was supposedly the first tank to arrive to liberate Prague, on May 9, hotfoot from Berlin.

The real story of the liberation of Prague was rather different, however. When the Prague uprising began on May 5, the first offer of assistance actually came from a division of the anti-Communist Russian National Liberation Army (KONR), under the overall command of a renegade general, Andrei Vlasov. Vlasov was a high-ranking Red Army officer, who was instrumental in pushing the Germans back from the gates of Moscow, but switched sides after being captured by the Nazis in 1942. The Germans were (rightly, as it turned out) highly suspicious of the KONR, and, for the most part, the renegade Russians were kept well away from the real action. In the war's closing stages, however, the KONR switched sides once more and agreed to fight alongside the Czech resistance, making a crucial intervention against the SS troops who were poised to crush the uprising in Prague. Initially, the Czechs guaranteed Vlasov's men asylum from the advancing Soviets in return for military assistance. In reality, the Czechs were unable to honour their side of the bargain and the KONR finally withdrew from the city late on May 7 and headed west to surrender themselves to the Americans. When the Red Army finally arrived in Prague, many of Vlasov's troops were simply gunned down by the Soviets. Even those in the hands of the Americans were eventually passed over to the Russians and shared the fate of their leader Vlasov who was tried *in camera* in Moscow and hanged with piano wire on August 2, 1946.

The unsolicited reappearance of Soviet tanks on the streets of Prague in 1968 left most Czechs feeling somewhat ambivalent towards the old monument. And in the summer of 1991, situationist artist David Černý painted the tank bubble-gum pink, and placed a large phallic finger on top of it, while another mischievous Czech daubed "Vlasov" on the podium. Since the country was at the time engaged in delicate negotiations to end the Soviet military presence in Czechoslovakia, the new regime, despite its mostly dissident leanings, roundly condemned the act as unlawful. Havel, in his characteristically even-handed way, made it clear that he didn't like tanks anywhere, whether on the battlefield or as monuments.

In the end, the tank was hastily repainted khaki green and Černý was arrested under the familiar "crimes against the state" clause of the penal code, which had been used by the Communists with gay abandon on several members of the then government. In protest at the arrest of Černý, twelve members of the federal parliament turned up the following day in their overalls and, taking advantage of their legal immunity, repainted the tank pink. Finally, the government gave in, released Černý and removed the tank from public view. There's now no trace of tank, podium or plaque, and the square has even been renamed náměstí Kinských.

and slightly rakish: František Dušek was a well-respected pianist in his own right, while his wife, Josefa Dušková, a popular singer seventeen years younger than her husband, was one of Prague's most fashionable hostesses. As long ago as 1838, the villa was turned into a shrine to Mozart, though very little survives of the house he knew, thanks to a fire on New Year's Day, 1871 – not that this has deterred generations of Mozart lovers from flocking here. These days, what the museum lacks in memorabilia, it makes up for with its Rococo ambience, a lovely garden and regular Mozart recitals – the real reason to make a trip out here. To get to Bertramka, take the metro to Anděl, walk a couple of blocks west up Plzeňská, then left up Mozartova.

Zbraslav

One of Prague's more intriguing museums is situated in the little-visited village of **ZBRASLAV**, 10km south of the city centre, though within the municipal boundaries. Přemyslid King Otakar II built a hunting lodge here, which was later turned into a Cistercian monastery – more recently, the buildings housed the National Gallery's modern Czech sculptures, a few of which still pepper the grounds. Now, however, **Zámek Zbraslav** (Tues–Sun 10am–6pm; 70Kč; Ⓦwww.ngprague.cz) shelters the gallery's remarkably extensive Asian art collection.

The collection starts downstairs with Japanese art ranging from late nineteenth-century lacquerwork lunchboxes and exquisite landscapes of birds and flowers on silk, to seventeenth-century travelling altarpieces and cracked glaze porcelain. Upstairs, there's a vast array of Chinese exhibits, from Neolithic axes and ancient funerary art to Ming vases, dishes and even roof tiles. Highlights include an incredibly naturalistic eleventh-century wooden statue of one of the Buddha's aged disciples a large standing Burmese Buddha, and an erotic Yab-Yum, a central icon of Tantric Buddhism.

Appropriately enough, the museum has a teahouse (*čajovna*) in the cloisters, and plenty of grass outside on which to picnic. To reach the gallery, take bus #129, #241, #243, #255 or #360 from metro Smíchovské nádraží or the local train from Smíchovské nádraží to Praha-Zbraslav – there's even the occasional PPS boat (see p.159).

Out from the city

Few capital cities can boast such extensive unspoilt tracts of woodland so near at hand as Prague. Once you leave the half-built high-rise estates of the outer suburbs behind, the traditional provincial feel of **Bohemia** (Čechy) immediately makes itself felt. Many towns and villages still huddle below the grand residences of their former lords, their street layout little changed since medieval times.

To the north, several such chateaux grace the banks of the Vltava, including the wine-producing town of **Mělník**, on the Labe (Elbe) plain. Further north is **Terezín**, the wartime Jewish ghetto that is a living testament to the Holocaust. One of the most obvious day-trip destinations is to the east of Prague: **Kutná Hora**, a medieval silver-mining town with one of the most beautiful Gothic churches in the country, and a macabre gallery of bones in the suburb of Sedlec.

To the south, the **Konopiště** chateau boasts exceptionally beautiful and expansive grounds. Southwest of Prague, a similar mix of woods and rolling hills surrounds the popular castle of **Karlštejn**, a gem of Gothic architecture, dramatically situated above the River Berounka. West of Prague, **Lidice**, razed to the ground by the SS, is another town which recalls the horror of Nazi occupation.

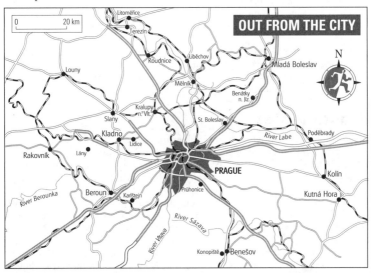

Mělník

Occupying a spectacular, commanding site at the confluence of the Vltava and Labe rivers, **MĚLNÍK**, 33km north of Prague, lies at the heart of Bohemia's tiny wine-growing region. The town's history goes back to the ninth century, when it was handed over to the Přemyslids as part of Ludmila's dowry when she married Prince Bořivoj. It was here, too, that she introduced her heathen grandson Václav (later to become Saint Wenceslas, aka "Good King") to the joys of Christianity. Viticulture became the town's economic mainstay when the Emperor Charles IV, aching for a little of the French wine of his youth, introduced grapes from Burgundy (where he was also king).

The old town

Mělník's greatest monument is its Renaissance **chateau** (March–Dec daily 10am–6pm; ⓦ www.lobkowicz-melnik.cz; guided tours 25Kč–60Kč), perched high above the flat plains and visible for miles around. The present building, its courtyard covered in familiar sgraffito patterns, is now back in the hands of its last aristocratic owners, the Lobkowicz family, who have restored the chateau's magnificently proportioned rooms, which also provide great views out over the plain. Visits are by guided tour only, and you've a choice between exploring seven beautifully painted rooms of the castle interior (60Kč), filled with artefacts and Old Masters returned to the family since 1989, or touring the wine museum in the cellars (25Kč), finishing up with samples of plonk (extra charge). In addition, there's a museum of prams, strollers and baby carriages, which forms part of the local **museum** on the first floor of the chateau.

Below the chateau, vines cling to the south-facing terraces, as the land plunges into the river below. From beneath the great tower of Mělník's onion-domed church of **sv Petr and Pavel**, next door to the chateau, there's an even better view of the rivers' confluence and the subsidiary canal, once so congested with vessels that traffic lights had to be introduced to avoid accidents. The church itself contains a compellingly macabre **ossuary** or *kostnice* (Tues–Sun 10am–12.30pm & 1.15–4pm), filled with more than 10,000 bones of medieval plague victims, fashioned into weird and wonderful skeletal shapes by students in the early part of the last century.

The rest of the old town is pretty small, but it's pleasant enough for a casual stroll. One half of the main square, náměstí Míru, is arcaded Baroque and typical of the region, and there's an old medieval gateway nearby, the Pražská brána, which has been converted into an art gallery.

Practicalities

There's no direct train service to Mělník from Prague, so you'll need to change at Všetaty; connections are pretty good and the journey should take around an hour. There is also a regular **bus service** which leaves from metro Nádraží Holešovice and Florenc, and takes under an hour. On arrival at Mělník bus station, to reach the older part of town, simply head up Krombholcova in the direction of the big church tower. If your next destination is Terezín, you have the choice of either the bus or the train; the **train station** is still further from the old town, a couple of blocks northeast of the bus station, down Jiřího z Poděbrad.

As for **food and drink**, the *Zámecká restaurace* is as good (and cheap) a place as any to sample some of the local wine and enjoy the view: the red Ludmila

is the most famous of Mělník's wines, and there's even a rare Czech rosé produced by the castle vineyards, but if you prefer white, try a bottle of Tramín.
Equally good views can be had from the *Stará škola* restaurant, behind the
church; otherwise, you could try *Na hradbách*, on náměstí Míru, which serves
up big portions of rabbit and game with local wines, plus Guinness and
Kilkenny, in a cosy brick and wood-panelled interior.

Terezín

The old road from Prague to Berlin passes through the fortress town of
TEREZÍN (Theresienstadt; ⓦ www.pamatnik-terezin.cz), just over 60km
northwest of the capital. Purpose-built in the 1780s by the Habsburgs to
defend the northern border against Prussia, it was capable of accommodating
14,500 soldiers and hundreds of prisoners. In 1941, the population was ejected and the whole town turned into a **Jewish ghetto**, and used as a transit
camp for Jews whose final destination was Auschwitz.

A brief history of the ghetto

In October 1941, Reinhard Heydrich and the Nazi high command decided to
turn the whole of Terezín into a Jewish ghetto. It was an obvious choice: fully
fortified, close to the main Prague–Dresden railway line, and with an SS prison
already established in the **Malá pevnost** (Small Fortress) nearby. The original
inhabitants of the town – fewer than 3500 people – were moved out, and transports began arriving at Terezín from many parts of central Europe. Within a
year, nearly 60,000 Jews were interned here in appallingly overcrowded conditions; the monthly death rate rose to 4000. In October 1942, the first transport left for Auschwitz. By the end of the war, 140,000 Jews had passed
through Terezín; fewer than 17,500 remained when the ghetto was finally liberated on May 8, 1945.

One of the perverse ironies of Terezín is that it was used by the Nazis as a
cover for the real purpose of the *Endlösung* or "final solution", devised at the
Wannsee conference in January 1942 (at which Heydrich was present). The
ghetto was made to appear self-governing, with its own council or *Judenrat*, its
own bank printing ghetto money, its own shops selling goods confiscated from
the internees on arrival, and even a café on the main square. For a while, a special "Terezín family camp" was even set up in Auschwitz, to continue the
deception. The deportees were kept in mixed barracks, allowed to wear civilian clothes and – the main purpose of the whole thing – send letters back to
their loved ones in Terezín telling them they were OK. After six months' "quar-
antine", they were sent to the gas chambers.

Despite the fact that Terezín was being used by the Nazis as cynical propaganda, the ghetto population turned their unprecedented freedom to their own
advantage. Since the entire population of the Protectorate (and Jews from many
other parts of Europe) passed through Terezín, the ghetto had an enormous
number of outstanding Jewish artists, musicians, scholars and writers (many of
whom subsequently perished in the camps). Thus, in addition to the officially
sponsored activities, countless clandestine cultural events were organized in the
cellars and attics of the barracks: teachers gave lessons to children, puppet theatre productions were put on, and literary evenings were held.

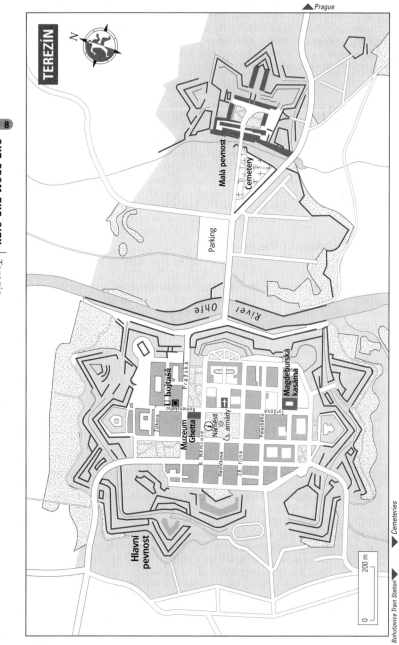

TEREZÍN

N

▲ Prague

Malá pevnost

Cemetery

Parking

River Ohře

U hojtrašů

Pražská

Komenského

Žižkova

Muzeum
Ghetta

ⓘ Náměstí

B. Němcové

Čs. armády

Havlíčkova

Palackého

28. října

Tyršova

Magdeburská
kasárna

Hlavní
pevnost

0   200 m

Bohušovice Train Station ▶   ◀ Cemeteries

Towards the end of 1943, the so-called *Verschönerung* or "beautification" of the ghetto was implemented, in preparation for the arrival of the International Red Cross inspectors. Streets were given names instead of numbers, and the whole place was decked out as if it were a spa town. When the International Red Cross asked to inspect one of the Nazi camps, they were brought here and treated to a week of Jewish cultural events. A circus tent was set up in the main square; a children's pavilion erected in the park; numerous performances of Hans Krása's children's opera, *Brundibár* (Bumble Bee), staged; and a jazz band, called the Ghetto Swingers, performed in the bandstand on the main square. The Red Cross visited Terezín twice, once in June 1944, and again in April 1945; both times the delegates filed positive reports.

Hlavní pevnost (Main Fortress)

Although the **Hlavní pevnost** (Main Fortress) has never been put to the test in battle, Terezín remains intact as a garrison town. Today, it's an eerie, soulless place, built to a dour eighteenth-century grid plan, its bare streets empty apart from the residual civilian population and visitors making their way between the various museums and memorials. As you enter, the red-brick zigzag fortifications are still an awesome sight, though the huge moat has been put to good use by local gardening enthusiasts.

Muzeum Ghetta

The first place to head for is the **Muzeum Ghetta** (Ghetto Museum; daily: April–Sept 9am–6pm; Oct–March 9am–5.30pm; 140Kč, combined ticket with Magdeburská kasárna 160Kč), which was finally opened in 1991, on the fiftieth anniversary of the arrival of the first transports in Terezín. After the war, the Communists had followed the consistent Soviet line by deliberately underplaying the Jewish perspective on Terezín. Instead, the emphasis was on the Malá pevnost (see p.172), where the majority of victims were not Jewish, and on the war as an anti-fascist struggle, in which good (Communism and the Soviet Union) had triumphed over evil (Fascism and Nazi Germany). It wasn't until the Prague Spring of 1968 that the idea of a museum dedicated specifically to the history of the Jewish ghetto first emerged. In the 1970s, however, the intended building was turned into a Museum of the Ministry of the Interior instead.

Now that it's finally open, this extremely informative and well-laid-out exhibition at last attempts to do some justice to the extraordinary and tragic events which took place here between 1941 and 1945, including background displays on the measures which led inexorably to the *Endlösung*. There's also a fascinating video (with English subtitles) showing clips of the Nazi propaganda film shot in Terezín – *Hitler Gives the Jews a Town* – intercut with harrowing interviews with survivors.

Magdeburská kasárna

To the south of the ghetto, the **Magdeburská kasárna** (Magdeburg Barracks; times and entry as for Muzeum Ghetta), former seat of the Jewish self-governing council or *Freizeitgestaltung*, has been turned into a fascinating museum concentrating on the remarkable artistic life of Terezín. First off, however, there's a reconstructed women's dormitory with three-tier bunks, full of luggage and belongings, to give an idea of the cramped living conditions endured by the ghetto inhabitants. The first exhibition room has displays on the various Jewish musicians who passed through Terezín, including Pavel Haas, a pupil of

Janáček; Hans Krása, a pupil of Zemlinsky, who wrote the score for *Brundibár*; and Karel Ančerl, who survived the Holocaust to become conductor of the Czech Philharmonic. The final exhibition room concentrates on the writers who contributed to the ghetto's underground magazines. The rooms in between, however, are given over to the work of Terezín's numerous artists, many of whom were put to work by the SS, who set up a graphics department here; headed by cartoonist Bedřich Fritta, it produced visual propaganda showing how smoothly the ghetto ran. In addition, there are many clandestine works, ranging from portraits of inmates to harrowing depictions of the cramped dormitories, and the transports. These provide some of the most vivid and deeply affecting insights into the reality of ghetto life in the whole of Terezín, and it was for this "propaganda of horror" that several artists, including Fritta, were eventually deported to Auschwitz.

Malá pevnost (Small Fortress)

On the other side of the River Ohře, east down Pražská, lies the **Malá pevnost** (Small Fortress; daily: April–Sept 8am–6pm; Oct–March 8am–4.30pm; 140Kč, combined ticket with Muzeum Ghetta 160Kč), built as a military prison in the 1780s, at the same time as the main fortress. The prison's most famous inmate was the young Bosnian Serb, Gavrilo Princip, who succeeded in assassinating Archduke Ferdinand in Sarajevo in 1914, and was interned and died here during World War I. In 1940 it was turned into an SS prison by Heydrich and, after the war, it became the official memorial and museum of Terezín. The majority of the 32,000 inmates who passed through the prison were active in the resistance (and, more often than not, Communists). Some 2500 inmates perished here, while another 8000 died subsequently in the concentration camps. The vast cemetery laid out by the entrance contains the graves of over 2300 individuals, plus numerous other corpses of unidentified victims, and is rather insensitively dominated by a large Christian cross, plus a smaller Star of David.

There are guides (occasionally survivors of Terezín) to show you around, or else you can simply use the brief guide to the prison in English, and walk around yourself. The infamous Nazi refrain *Arbeit Macht Frei* (Work Brings Freedom) is daubed across the entrance on the left, which leads to the exemplary washrooms, still as they were when built for the Red Cross tour of inspection. The rest of the camp has been left empty but intact, and graphically evokes the cramped conditions under which the prisoners were kept, half-starved and badly clothed, subject to indiscriminate cruelty and execution. The prison's main **exhibition** is housed in the SS barracks opposite the luxurious home of the camp *Kommandant* and his family. A short documentary, intelligible in any language, is regularly shown in the cinema that was set up in 1942 to entertain the SS guards.

Practicalities

Terezín is about an hour's **bus** ride from Prague's Florenc terminal and therefore easy to visit on a day-trip. The nearest train station is at Bohušovice nad Ohří (on the main Prague–Děčín line), 2km south of the fortress. If you can stomach a **meal**, the only acceptable restaurant in town is *U hojtašů*, on Komenského, just north of the museum.

Kutná Hora

For 250 years or so, **KUTNÁ HORA** (Kuttenberg) was one of the most important towns in Bohemia, second only to Prague. At the end of the fourteenth century its population was equal to that of London, its shantytown suburbs straggled across what are now green fields, and its ambitious building projects set out to rival those of the capital itself. Today, Kutná Hora is a small provincial town with a population of just over 20,000, but the monuments dotted around it, its superb Gothic cathedral, and the remarkable monastery and ossuary in the suburb of **Sedlec**, make it one of the most enjoyable of all possible day-trips from Prague. In addition to the new influx of tourists, Kutná Hora has also benefited from a large injection of cash from the American tobacco giant Philip Morris, which now runs the local tobacco factory as a joint venture.

A brief history

Kutná Hora's road to prosperity began in the late thirteenth century with the discovery of **silver deposits** in the surrounding area. German miners were invited to settle and work the seams, and around 1300 Václav II founded the royal mint here and sent for Italian craftsmen to run it. Much of the town's wealth was used to fund the beautification of Prague, but it also allowed for the construction of one of the most magnificent churches in central Europe and a number of other prestigious Gothic monuments in Kutná Hora itself.

At the time of the Hussite Wars, the town was mostly German-speaking, and

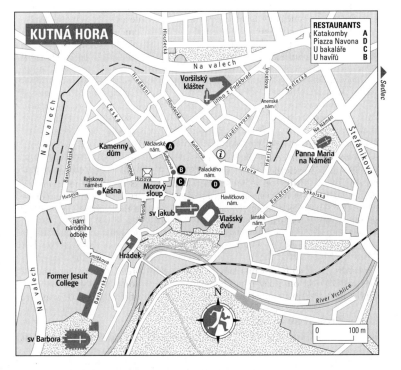

staunchly Catholic; local miners used to throw captured Hussites into the deep mine shafts and leave them to die of starvation. Word got out, and the town was besieged and eventually taken by Žižka's fanatical Táborites in 1421, only to be recaptured by Sigismund and his papal forces shortly afterwards, and again by Žižka, the following year.

While the silver stocks remained high the town was able to recover its former prosperity, but at the end of the sixteenth century the mines dried up and Kutná Hora's wealth and importance came to an abrupt end – when the Swedes marched on the town during the Thirty Years' War, they had to be bought off with beer rather than silver. The town has never fully recovered, shrivelling to less than a third of its former size, its fate emphatically sealed by a devastating fire in 1770.

The Town

The small, unassuming houses that line the town's medieval lanes and main square, **Palackého náměstí**, give little idea of Kutná Hora's former glories. A narrow alleyway on the south side of the square, however, leads to leafy Havlíčkovo náměstí, on which stands the **Vlašský dvůr** (Italian Court), originally conceived as a palace by Václav II, and for three centuries the town's bottomless purse. It was here that Florentine minters produced the Prague Groschen (*pražské groše*), a silver coin widely used throughout central Europe until the nineteenth century. The building itself has been mucked about with over the years, most recently – and most brutally – by nineteenth-century restorers, who left only the chestnut trees, a fourteenth-century oriel window (capped by an unlikely looking wooden onion dome) and the miner's fountain unmolested. The original workshops of the minters have been bricked in, but the outlines of their little doors and windows are still visible in the courtyard. The short **guided tour** (daily: April & Oct 9am–5pm; May, June & Sept 9am–6pm; July & Aug 10am–6pm; 50Kč) of the old chapel, treasury and royal palace gives you a fair idea of the building's former importance.

Outside the court is a statue of the country's founder and first president, T.G. Masaryk, twice removed – once by the Nazis and once by the Communists – but now returned to its pride of place. Before you leave, take a quick turn in the court gardens, which climb down in steps to the River Vrchlice below. This is undoubtedly Kutná Hora's best profile, with a splendid view over to the cathedral of sv Barbora (see below).

Behind the Vlašský dvůr is **sv Jakub** (St James), the town's oldest church, begun a generation or so after the discovery of the silver deposits. Its grand scale is a clear indication of the town's quite considerable wealth by the fourteenth century, though in terms of artistry it pales in comparison with Kutná Hora's other ecclesiastical buildings. The leaning tower is a reminder of the precarious position of the town, the church's foundations being prone to subsidence from the disused mines below. If you want to see some of these, head for the **Hrádek**, an old fort which was used as a second mint and now serves as a **Mining Museum** (Muzeum a středověké důlní dílo; April–Oct Tues–Sun 9am–5pm; 110Kč). Here you can pick up a white coat, miner's helmet and torch, and visit some of the medieval mines that were discovered beneath the fort in the 1960s.

Cathedral of sv Barbora

Kutná Hora's **Cathedral of sv Barbora** (Tues–Sun: April & Oct 9am–noon & 1–4.30pm; May–Sept 9am–6pm; Nov–March 9am–noon & 2–3.30pm;

30Kč) is arguably the most spectacular and moving ecclesiastical building in central Europe. Not to be outdone by the great monastery at Sedlec (see below) or the St Vitus Cathedral in Prague, the miners of Kutná Hora began financing the construction of a great Gothic cathedral of their own, dedicated to St Barbara, the patron saint of miners and gunners. The foundations were probably laid by Peter Parler in the 1380s, but work was interrupted by the Hussite Wars, and the church remains unfinished, despite being worked on in the intervening centuries by numerous architects, including Master Hanuš, Matouš Rejsek and Benedikt Ried.

The approach road to the cathedral, Barborská, is lined with a parade of gesticulating Baroque saints and cherubs that rival the sculptures on the Charles Bridge; on the right-hand side is the palatial former Jesuit College. The cathedral itself bristles with pinnacles, finials and flying buttresses which support its most striking feature, a roof of three tent-like towers, culminating in unequal needle-sharp spires. Inside, cold light streams through the plain glass windows, illuminating a playful vaulted nave whose ribs form branches and petals stamped with coats of arms belonging to Václav II and the local miners' guilds. The wide spread of the five-aisled nave is remarkably uncluttered: a Gothic pulpit – half wood, half stone – creeps tastefully up a central pillar, and black and gold Renaissance confessionals hide discreetly in the north aisle. On the south wall is the Minters' Chapel, decorated with fifteenth-century wall frescoes showing the Florentines at work, while in the ambulatory chapels some fascinating paintings – unique for their period – depict local miners at work.

The rest of the town

There are a few minor sights worth seeking out in the rest of the town. On Rejskovo náměstí, the squat, many-sided **Kašna** (fountain) by Matouš Rejsek strikes a very odd pose – anything less like a fountain would be hard to imagine. At the bottom of the sloping Nultysova is a particularly fine **Morový sloup** (Plague Column), giving thanks for the end of the plague of 1713, while just around the corner, at the top of Lierova, is one of the few Gothic buildings to survive the 1770 fire, the **Kamenný dům**. Built around 1480, with an oriel window and a steep gable covered in an ornate sculptural icing, this now contains an unexceptional local museum (Tues–Sun: April & Oct 10am–4pm; May, June & Sept 9am–6pm; July & Aug 10am–6pm; 30Kč). A couple of blocks down Poděbradova stands Kilian Ignaz Dientzenhofer's unfinished **Voršilský klášter** (**Ursuline convent**). Only three sides of the convent's ambitious pentagonal plan were actually completed, its neo-Baroque church being added in the late nineteenth century while sv Barbora was being restored.

Sedlec

From Kutná Hora's inner ring road, buses #1 and #4 run 3km northeast to **SEDLEC**, once a separate village but now a suburb of Kutná Hora. Adjoining Sedlec's defunct eighteenth-century Cistercian monastery (now the largest tobacco factory in Europe, owned by Philip Morris) is the fourteenth-century church of **Panna Maria** (St Mary), imaginatively redesigned in the eighteenth century by Giovanni Santini, who specialized in melding Gothic with Baroque. Here, given a plain French Gothic church gutted during the Hussite Wars, Santini set to work on the vaulting, adding his characteristic sweeping stucco rib patterns, relieved only by the occasional Baroque splash of colour above the chancel steps.

Cross the main road, following the signs, and you come to the monks' grave-yard, where an ancient Gothic chapel leans heavily over the entrance to the macabre subterranean **ossuary** or *kostnice* (daily: April–Sept 8am–6pm; Oct 9am–noon & 1–5pm; Nov–March 9am–noon & 1–4pm; 30Kč), full to over-flowing with human bones. When holy earth from Golgotha was scattered over the graveyard in the twelfth century, all of Bohemia's nobility wanted to be buried here and the bones mounted up until there were more than 40,000 complete sets. In 1870, worried about the ever-growing piles, the authorities commissioned František Rint to do something creative with them. He rose to the challenge and moulded out of bones four giant bells, one in each corner of the crypt, designed wall-to-ceiling skeletal decorations, including the Schwarzenberg coat of arms, and, as the centrepiece, put together a chandelier made out of every bone in the human body. Rint's signature (in bones) is at the bottom of the steps.

Practicalities

The simplest way to get to Kutná Hora is to take a **bus** from outside metro Želivského (1hr 15min). Fast **trains** from Prague's Masarykovo nádraží take around an hour (there's only one in the morning); slow ones take two hours; trains from Praha hlavní nádraží involve a change at Kolín. The main **train sta-tion** (Kutná Hora hlavní nádraží) is a long way out of town, near Sedlec; bus #1 or #4 will take you into town, or there's usually a shuttle train service ready to leave for Kutná Hora město train station, near the centre of town.

The town has a highly efficient system of orientation signs, and, at almost every street corner, a pictorial list of the chief places of interest (beware, though, that the train station signposted is not the main one). The town's **tourist office** is on Palackého náměstí (April–Oct Mon–Fri 9am–6.30pm, Sat & Sun 9am–5pm; Nov–March Mon–Fri 9am–5pm; ☎327 512 378, Ⓦ www.khora.cz). On the **eating and drinking** front, you're spoilt for choice: *U bakaláře*, at the junction of Husova and Šultysova, is one of the bet-ter restaurants in town, with a reasonable choice for vegetarians; *Katakomby*, just up the street on Václavské náměstí, is a deep gothic cellar, with slightly upmarket Czech cuisine; while *Piazza Navona*, on Palackého náměstí, is an excellent pizzeria, run by an Italian. There are plenty of good pubs, too, where you can get more simple fare: try *U havířu* on Šultysova (closed Mon), which offers a variety of brews and has a quiet back patio.

Konopiště

The popularity of **Konopiště** (daily: April & Nov 9am–3pm; May, June & Oct 9am–4pm; July–Sept 9am–5pm; guided tours 130Kč–260Kč; Ⓦ www .zamek-konopiste.cz), with a quarter of a million visitors passing through its portcullis every year, is surpassed only by the likes of Karlštejn (see p.177). Though Karlštejn looks more dramatic from the outside, Konopiště is the more interesting of the two. Coach parties from all over the world home in on this Gothic chateau, which is stuffed with dead animals, weaponry and hunting trophies. Most interesting are its historical associations: King Václav IV was imprisoned by his own nobles in the chateau's distinctive round tower, and the Archduke Franz Ferdinand, heir to the Habsburg throne, lived here with his wife, Sophie Chotek, until their assassination in Sarajevo in 1914. In addition to remodelling the chateau into its current appearance, the archduke shared his generation's voracious appetite for hunting, eliminating all living creatures foolish enough to venture into the grounds. However, he surpassed all his contemporaries by recording, stuffing and displaying a significant number of the 171,537 birds and animals he shot between the years 1880 and 1906, the details of which are recorded in his *Schuss Liste* displayed inside.

There's a choice of three **guided tours**. The first tour, *I okruh*, explores the period interiors, which contain some splendid Renaissance cabinets and lots of Meissen porcelain, while the *II okruh* takes you through the chapel, past the stuffed bears and deer teeth, to the assorted lethal weapons of one of the finest armouries in Europe. Both the above tours cost 130Kč each, take 45 minutes, and, you'll be relieved to know, include the hunting trophies. The *III okruh* – which takes an hour, costs 260Kč and is restricted to just eight people per tour – concentrates on the personal apartments of the archduke and his wife. Due to the fact that Sophie was a mere countess, and not an archduchess, the couple were shunned by the Habsburg court in Vienna, and hid themselves away in Konopiště. Occasionally there are tours in English, French and German, too, so ask at the box office before you sign up or phone ahead and book one (☏301 721 366).

Even if you don't fancy a guided tour, there are plenty of other things to do in Konopiště. In the main courtyard of the chateau, you can pop into the purpose-built **Střelnice** (Shooting Range; 25Kč), where the archduke used to hone his skills as a marksman against moving mechanical targets, all of which have been lovingly restored. Tucked underneath the south terrace is the **Galerie sv Jiří**, which is stuffed to the gunwales with artefacts from Franz Ferdinand's collection – from paintings to statuettes and trinkets relating to Saint George, the fictional father of medieval chivalry, with whom the archduke was obsessed. Much the best reason to come to Konopiště, though, is to explore its 555-acre **park** (no entrance charge), which boasts several lakes, sundry statuary, an unrivalled rose garden (with café by the greenhouses) and a deer park. There are also regular hour-long displays of **falconry** in the chateau's grounds (April & Oct Sat & Sun 10am–noon & 2–4pm; May–Sept Tues–Sun same times).

Practicalities

To get to Konopiště take a fast (50min) or slow (1hr 5min) **train** from Praha hlavní nádraží to Benešov u Prahy; the chateau is a pleasant two-kilometre walk west of the railway station along the red- or yellow-marked path (buses are relatively infrequent). If the weather's fine take a picnic; otherwise, there are numerous food stalls by the main car park, and decent Czech fare in the nineteenth-century *Stará Myslivna*, on the path to the chateau, and in the bistro in the main courtyard. Back in Benešov, it's possible to while away some time before your train departs at the *Galerijní čajovna* teahouse on Malé náměstí.

Karlštejn

KARLŠTEJN is a small ribbon village, strung out along one of the tributaries of the Berounka. No doubt once pretty, today it boasts a pricey golf course and is jam-packed with tacky souvenir stands and tourists – over a quarter of a million a year – visiting its superbly positioned **castle** (Tues–Sun: Jan–March

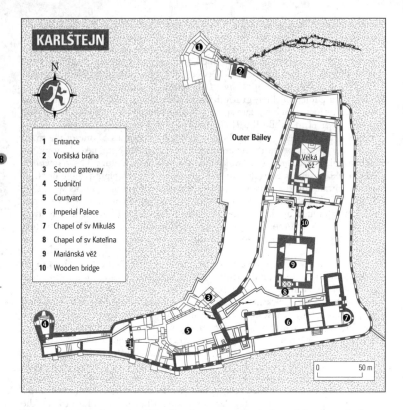

KARLŠTEJN

N

1 Entrance
2 Voršilská brána
3 Second gateway
4 Studniční
5 Courtyard
6 Imperial Palace
7 Chapel of sv Mikuláš
8 Chapel of sv Kateřina
9 Mariánská věž
10 Wooden bridge

Outer Bailey

Velká věž

0   50 m

9am–noon & 1–3pm; April & Oct 9am–noon & 1–4pm; May, June & Sept 9am–5pm; July–August 9am–noon & 1–6pm; guided tours 200Kč–300Kč; cameras forbidden inside the castle; ☎274 008 154, ⓦwww.hradkarlstejn.cz), which occupies a defiantly unassailable position above the village. Designed in the fourteenth century by Matthias of Arras for Emperor Charles IV as a giant safe-box for the imperial crown jewels and his large personal collection of precious relics, it quickly became Charles' favourite retreat from the vast city he himself had masterminded. Women were strictly forbidden to enter the castle, and the story of his third wife Anna's successful break-in (in drag) became one of the most popular Czech comedies of the nineteenth century.

The village of Karlštejn has been transformed over the last decade, with every other house offering rooms to rent or selling souvenirs. Most of what you see, including the decidedly naff **Wax Museum** (daily 9am–6pm; 90Kč), at no. 173, is eminently missable, with the exception of the **Muzeum Betlémů** (Tues–Sun 9am–6pm; 40Kč), which occupies a fourteenth-century house towards the top of the village at no. 11. Inside the museum, you can admire an impressive array of nativity scenes dating back to the early nineteenth century, which range in size from complex mechanical set-ups to miniature affairs that can fit into small sea shells – there are even some in gingerbread.

If only the castle itself – a stunning sight from a distance – had such memorable treats in store. Sadly, centuries of neglect and generations of over-zealous restorers have taken their toll on the interior. Most of the rooms visited on the overpriced Route I guided tour (50min; 200Kč) contain only the barest of furnishings, the empty spaces taken up by uninspiring displays on the history of the castle. Theoretically, the top two chambers would make the whole trip worthwhile: unfortunately, on the basic guided tour, you can only look into (but not enter) the emperor's residential **Mariánská věž**. It was here that Charles shut himself off from the rest of the world, with any urgent business passed to him through a hole in the wall of the tiny ornate chapel of **sv Kateřina**.

The castle's finest treasure, the **Holy Rood Chapel** (*Kaple svatého kříže*), connected by a wooden bridge that leads on from here to the highest point of the castle, the **Velká věž**, is only open to those who book the Route II tour in advance (1hr 10min; 300Kč). Traditionally, only the emperor, the archbishop and the electoral princes could enter this gilded treasure-house, whose six-metre-thick walls contain 2200 semiprecious stones and 128 breathtakingly beautiful painted panels, the work of Master Theodoric, Bohemia's greatest fourteenth-century painter (a small selection of his panels are exhibited in Prague's Anežský klášter – see p.91). The imperial crown jewels, once secured here behind nineteen separate locks, were removed to Hungary after an abortive attack by the Hussites, while the Bohemian jewels are now stashed away in the cathedral in Prague.

Practicalities

Trains for Karlštejn leave Prague's Smíchovské nádraží roughly every hour, and take about 35 minutes to cover the 28km. The village is ten minutes' walk across the river from the station, and it's a further fifteen- to twenty-minute climb up to the castle entrance. If you're looking for somewhere to grab a beer and a bite to **eat**, try hunting-lodge style *U Janů*, which has an outdoor terrace, or the *Koruna*, both on the main street. Alternatively, bring a picnic with you and eat by the banks of the river.

If you're feeling energetic, or have your own wheels, you could go to the popular flooded quarry, **Malá Amerika**, 1km away, a nice spot for a swim. Getting there is tricky, however: either take the red-marked path from near the castle, and head off northwest through the woods at *U dubu* (you may need to ask a Czech to point you in the right direction), or head west down the track, which comes off the road between Mořina and Bubovice.

Lidice

The small mining village of **LIDICE**, 18km northwest of Prague, hit world headlines on June 10, 1942, at the moment when it ceased to exist. On the flimsiest pretext, it was chosen as scapegoat for the assassination of the Nazi leader Reinhard Heydrich. All 173 men from the village were rounded up and shot by the SS, the 198 women were sent to Ravensbrück concentration camp, and the 89 children either went to the camps, or, if they were Aryan enough, were packed off to "good" German homes, while the village itself was burnt to the ground.

Knowing all this as you approach Lidice makes the modern village seem almost perversely unexceptional. At the end of the straight, tree-lined main street, 10 Bervna 1942 (June 10, 1942), there's a dour concrete memorial with a small but horrific **museum** where you can watch a short film about Lidice, including footage shot by the SS themselves as the village was burning. The spot where the old village used to lie is just south of the memorial, now merely smooth green pasture punctuated with a few simple reminders and a new bronze memorial to the 82 local children who were gassed in the camps.

After the massacre, the "Lidice shall live" campaign was launched and villages all over the world began to change their name to Lidice. The first was Stern Park Gardens, Illinois, soon followed by villages in Mexico and other Latin American countries. From Coventry to Montevideo, towns twinned themselves with Lidice, so that rather than "wiping a Czech village off the face of the earth" as Hitler had hoped, the Nazis created an international symbol of anti-fascist resistance.

To reach Lidice, catch one of the regular buses from outside metro Dejvická in Prague, opposite the *Hotel Diplomat*, getting off at the turn-off to the village on the main road.

Listings

Listings

Accommodation

Accommodation is likely to be by far the largest chunk of your daily expenditure, with most half-decent hotels happily charging 5000Kč and upwards for a double room. The problem is that there's a chronic shortage of decent, inexpensive to middle-range places in Prague. At the bottom end of the scale, there are plenty of hostel beds, starting at a mere 200Kč per person, but the number of private rooms available has dwindled since the early 1990s.

Prague is pretty busy for much of the year, so if you're going to visit anytime from Easter to September, or over the Christmas and New Year period, it's sensible to arrange accommodation before you arrive, either directly with the hotels or through one of the specialist agencies listed on p.10. Prices are at their highest over the public holidays, but drop by as much as a third in the low season (Nov–March excluding New Year), and sometimes come down a bit in July and August when business custom is low.

If you arrive in Prague without having booked a room, there are several **accommodation agencies** you can turn to (see box below), most of which

---

Accommodation agencies in Prague

AVE ☎257 555 176, ⊛www.avetravel.cz; hours vary but the airport desk is open daily 7am–10pm. AVE is the largest agency in Prague, with offices at the airport, both international train stations, and several points throughout the city, and is therefore an excellent last-minute fall-back. They offer rooms in a selection of hotels, pensions and hostels, plus a few private rooms.

Mary's Travel Services Italská 31, Vinohrady ☎222 254 007, ⊛www.marys.cz; metro Náměstí Míru; daily 9am–7pm. Good-value agency that will book hotels, pensions and private rooms in Prague, and a few other locations in the Czech Republic.

Pragotur Za Poříčskou bránou 7, Karlín ☎221 714 130, ⊛www.prague-info.cz. The main office is situated just across the road from Florenc bus station, but they also operate through the various PIS tourist offices (see p.18). They can book anything from hotels to hostels, but they specialize in private rooms.

Stop City Vinohradská 24, Vinohrady ☎224 231 233, ⊛www.stopcity.com; metro Muzeum or Náměstí Míru; daily: April–Oct 10am–9pm; Nov–March 11am–8pm. Friendly agency that can book you into hotels, pensions and private rooms at very reasonable rates.

Tom's Travel Ostrovní 7, Nové Město ☎224 990 991, ⊛www.travel.cz; metro Národní třída; daily: June–Aug 8am–10pm; Sept–May 8am–8pm. Well-established, upmarket travel agency that can book you into hotels, pensions and apartments in Prague, and help with accommodation outside Prague, too.

will book you into either a hotel or pension, and some of which can also help
you find a hostel bed or a private room in an apartment. Before agreeing to
part with any money, be sure you know exactly where you're staying and
check about transport to the centre – some places can be a long way out of
town.

Hotels and pensions

Prague now boasts a huge variety of **hotels** and **pensions**, from big multinational chain hotels to places with real character in the old town. The vast
majority of rooms have en-suite bathrooms and TVs, with continental breakfast
either included in the price or offered as an optional extra. There's no hard and
fast rule as to what constitutes a hotel and what a pension – though if you
come across a "residence", then there's likely to be some kind of self-catering
facilities – and it's certainly not reflected in the price. Standards overall can still
vary wildly, though "service with a snarl", once commonplace, is now only
occasionally encountered.

With plenty of centrally located hotels, there's really no need to stay out in the
suburbs unless you're on a very tight budget. The quietest central areas to stay in
are on the left bank in Malá Strana and Hradčany, though there's more choice,
and more nightlife, in Staré Město and Nové Město. Rather than trekking
around any of the places listed below on the off chance that they will have vacan-
cies, you're better off making a reservation by email or phone before you leave
for Prague, or using one of the agencies listed in the box on p.183. The area headings used below correspond to the chapter headings in the guide – for an explanation of the price codes, see the box above. All the hotels and pensions are
marked on the colour map "Accommodation" at the back of the book.

Hradčany

Hradčany is obviously a great area to
stay in, right by the castle. However, it
is extremely quiet, is easily accessible
only by tram or on foot, and boasts
just a limited number of places to eat
and drink. The chief problem is that
there are very few places to stay, and
none is cheap.

Savoy Keplerova 6 ☏ 224 302 430,
ⓦ www.hotel-savoy.cz; tram #22 from metro
Malostranská to Pohořelec stop. Super-luxury
hotel on the western edge of Hradčany,
concealed behind a pretty Art Nouveau
facade and famous for its large marble
bathrooms. This is one of Prague's finest,
and as a result is popular with visiting
celebs. Pretty prices too, with doubles
starting at around 9000Kč. ❾
U krále Karla (King Charles) Úvoz 4 ☏ 257 532
869, ⓦ www.romantikhotels.com. Possibly the
most tastefully exquisite of all the small
luxury hotels in the castle district, with
beautiful antique furnishings and stained-

glass windows. It's situated just at the top of Nerudova, on the edge of Malá Strana, and is a fair walk from the nearest tram stop. **⑥**

U raka (The Crayfish) Černínská 10 ☎ 220 511 100, ⊛ www.romantikhotels.com; tram #22 from metro Malostranská to Brusnice stop. The perfect hideaway, six double rooms in a little half-timbered eighteenth-century

cottage in Nový Svět. No children under 12 or dogs and advance reservation a must. **⑦**

Malá Strana

Malá Strana is a beautiful area, and, with the exception of a few key streets, relatively traffic-free and quiet.

Prague postal districts

If you're thinking of booking a room in advance or planning a long-term stay, it's as well to know a little about the merits, or otherwise, of Prague's various areas and **postal districts** (see map on p.27).

Prague 1 Prague 1 covers all of the old city on both sides of the river, and half of Nové Město, and consequently is generally the most expensive part of the capital in which to stay. However, anything in this area will be within easy walking distance of the main sights, and will save you a lot of hassle.

Prague 2 Prague 2 is another prime central area, taking in the southern half of Nové Město and western half of Vinohrady, a nineteenth-century des. res. with good metro connections.

Prague 3 The less salubrious, eastern half of Vinohrady in Prague 3 is nevertheless well served by the metro; Žižkov, on the other hand, is a crumbling, working-class district, connected to the centre only by trams.

Prague 4 Covers a wide area in the southeast of the city, stretching from half-decent, predominantly nineteenth-century suburbs such as Nusle, Podolí and Braník to the grim high-rise *panelák* buildings of Chodov and Háje. If you find yourself in either of the latter two areas, you can at least be sure of quick metro connections to the city centre.

Prague 5 Vast area in the hilly southwest of the city, with clean air and attractive family villas predominating and a metro line running through some of it. The area closest to the city, however, is

Smíchov, a vibrant, polluted, working-class district, with correspondingly cheap rooms.

Prague 6 The perfect, hilly villa district to the north of the centre, a favourite with foreign embassies and their staff (not to mention Havel himself). The metro goes only as far as Dejvická, however, which means that only Dejvice and Bubeneč enjoy really fast connections with the centre.

Prague 7 The nineteenth-century suburb of Holešovice in the northeast is well served by the metro and trams. Troja, home to numerous ad hoc campsites, is almost bucolic and correspondingly difficult to get to.

Prague 8 The grid-plan streets of nineteenth-century Karlín are close to the centre and well served by the metro, which extends as far as Libeň; the rest of the area is neither aesthetically pleasing, nor easy to reach.

Prague 9 Dominated by factories, Prague 9, in the northeast of the city, is something of a last resort; however, with the extension of the metro to Černý most, it's at least easy enough to get into town.

Prague 10 Beware of Prague 10, which extends right into the countryside, though areas like Strašnice and Vršovice in the southeast of the city are closer to the centre of things and served, in part, by the metro.

Pretty much all of the most beautiful and memorable places to stay in Prague are concentrated here, and, as a result, it's a pricey area; however, there are one or two bargains, for which it's worth booking ahead. The nearest metro station for all the places listed below is Malostranská, though some will require a further tram ride on tram #12, #22 or #23.

Blue Key Letenská 14 ☏ 257 327 250, ⓦ www.bluekey.cz. Friendly swish, blue-themed hotel, and despite the busy road outside, it's a good location, just a short stroll from Malostranské náměstí; ask for a room facing into the lovely courtyard. ❻

Dientzenhofer Nosticova 2 ☏ 257 316 830. Birthplace of its namesake, and a very popular pension due to the fact that it's one of the few reasonably priced places (anywhere in Prague) to have wheelchair access. Just seven rooms on offer. ❹

Dům U velké boty (The Big Shoe) Vlašská 30 ☏ 257 311 107, ⓔ rippl@mbox.vol.cz. The sheer anonymity of this pension, in a lovely old building in the quiet backstreets, is one of its main draws. Run by a very friendly couple, who speak good English, it has a series of characterful, tastefully modernized rooms, some with en-suite, some without. Breakfast is extra, but worth it. ❹

Hoffmeister Pod Bruskou 7 ☏ 251 017 111, ⓦ www.hoffmeister.cz. If you're looking for a large air-conditioned luxury hotel, this place, just a step away from Malostranská metro, has got to be a better bet than many of the more modern monstrosities in the outskirts. Breakfast not included. ❽

Lundborg Lužického semináře 3 ☏ 257 011 911, ⓦ www.lundborg.cz. Very stylish Swedish-run apartment suites for around 8500Kč, with Baroque painted ceilings and tasteful furnishings, as well as jacuzzis and internet access in every room. It is in the thick of it, however, right by the Charles Bridge tower. ❾

Na Kampě 15 Na Kampě 15 ☏ 257 531 432, ⓦ www.nakampe15.cz. Situated on a lovely tree-lined square, just off the Charles Bridge, the rooms in this former brewery have real character, despite the modern fittings. ❻

Neruda Nerudova 44 ☏ 257 535 557, ⓦ www.hotelneruda-praha.cz. Stylish hotel a fair walk up Nerudova, with a funky, glass-roofed foyer, lots of natural stone, and smart, minimalist modern decor in the rooms. ❼

Nosticova Nosticova 1 ☏ 257 312 513, ⓦ www.nosticova.com. A Baroque house with ten beautifully restored apartments replete with antique furnishings, sumptuous bathrooms and small kitchens, on a peaceful square not far from the Charles Bridge. ❼

Pod věží (Under the Tower) Mostecká 2 ☏ 257 532 041, ⓦ www.podvezi.com. This tiny luxury hotel has twelve rooms, kitted out with just about every facility you could want. Proximity to the Charles Bridge means it's a busy little spot, however. ❾

U brány (The Gateway) Nerudova 21 ☏ 257 531 227, ⓦ www.ubrany.cz. Despite the tacky lobby and attached restaurant, the ten en-suite rooms upstairs are plain, pleasant and spacious for Malá Strana. Situated at the top end of Nerudova. ❽

U kříže (The Cross) Újezd 20 ☏ 257 313 272. No airs and graces at this modernized hotel on a busy street in the south of Malá Strana; B&B prices reduced in July and August. ❸

U tří pštrosů (The Three Ostriches) Dražického náměstí 12 ☏ 257 532 410, ⓦ www.utripstrosu.cz. Attractive little Renaissance hotel adjacent to the Charles Bridge; the rooms have wooden floorboards and beams, and some have original ceiling frescoes and views across the river. ❾

U zlaté studně U zlaté studně 4 ☏ 257 011 213, ⓦ www.zlatastudna.cz. The location is pretty special: tucked into the terraces below Prague Castle, next to the Ledeburg Gardens, with incredible views across the rooftops. The rooms aren't half bad either, with lots of original ceilings, and there's a good restaurant attached, with a wonderful summer terrace. All this comes at a price of course – around 10,000Kč a double. ❶

Waldstein Valdštejnské náměstí 6 ☏ 257 533 939, ⓦ www.avetravel.cz. A quiet, small, secluded hotel, with just ten rooms, bookable through the AVE travel agency (see box on p.183). The *Waldstein* has a lovely courtyard and several original Renaissance ceilings, and is tastefully decked out. ❼

Staré Město

Staré Město is right in the centre of things, with lots of pubs and restaurants to choose from, all within easy walking distance. Inexpensive places to stay are few and far between, but there are a few moderately priced options – again, it's worthwhile booking ahead if possible.

Apostolic Staroměstské náměstí 25 ⑦ 221 632 206, ⓦ www.prague-residence.cz; metro Staroměstská. If you want a room overlooking the astronomical clock on Old Town Square, then book in here, well in advance. Beautiful antique furnishings, big oak ceilings, but only a few rooms, including a single, as well as a suite for four for over 9000Kč. ❻

Avalon-Tara Havelská 15 ⑦ 224 228 083, ⓔ avalon-tara@volny.cz; metro Můstek. Perfect location right over the market on Havelská, with seven very small, plainly furnished but clean rooms, with or without en-suite facilities. ❷

Betlém Club Betlémské náměstí 9 ⑦ 222 221 574, ⓦ www.betlemclub.cz; metro Národní třída. Small rooms, but acceptable decor, plus a Gothic cellar for breakfast, and a perfect location on a quiet square at the heart of the old town – a rare bargain. ❸

Černá liška (The Black Fox) Mikulášská 2 ⑦ 224 232 250, ⓔ cerna.liska@volny.cz; metro Staroměstská. Well-appointed rooms, all with lovely wooden floors, some with incredible views onto Old Town Square, quieter ones at the back. ❻

Černý slon (Black Elephant) Týnská 1 ⑦ 222 321 521, ⓦ www.hotelcernyslon.cz; metro Náměstí Republiky. Another ancient building tucked away off Old Town Square by the north portal of the Týn church, now tastefully converted into a very comfortable hotel. ❺

Cloister Inn Konviktská 14 ⑦ 224 211 020, ⓦ www.cloister-inn.com; metro Národní třída. Pleasant, well-equipped hotel housed in a nunnery in one of the backstreets; the rooms are basic, but a bargain for the location. There are even cheaper rooms in the *Pension Unitas*, in the same building (see p.188). ❸

Expres Skořepka 5 ⑦ 224 211 801, ⓦ www.hotel -expres.wz.cz; metro Národní třída. Friendly little hotel with few pretensions: cheap and cheerful fittings, low prices and an excellent location right in the centre of Staré Město. ❷

Grand Hotel Bohemia Kralodvorská 4 ⑦ 224 804 111, ⓦ www.austria-hotels.co.uk; metro Náměstí Republiky. Probably the most sumptuously elegant luxury hotel in the old town, just behind the Obecní dům, with some very tasty Art Nouveau decor, and all the amenities you'd expect from an Austrian outfit. ❾

Metamorphis Malá Štupartská 5 ⑦ 221 771 011, ⓦ www.metamorphis.cz; metro Náměstí Republiky. Rooms with real character situated above a café-restaurant in the picturesque Týn courtyard, right in the thick of tourist Prague, and a step away from Old Town Square. ❻

Paříž U Obecního domu 1 ⑦ 222 195 195, ⓦ www.hotel-pariz.cz; metro Náměstí Republiky. Famous for featuring in Hrabal's *I Served the King of England*, the turn-of-the-century decor here is pleasing to the eye and in good condition; the rooms are repro mostly, but in keeping, and cost an astonishing 12,000Kč a double. ❾

Residence Řetězová Řetězová 9 ⑦ 222 221 800, ⓦ www.residenceretezova.com; metro Staroměstská. Apartments of all sizes, each with a kitchenette, wooden floors and repro furnishings throughout – they don't come cheap though. ❾

U klenotníka Rytířská 3 ⑦ 224 211 699, ⓦ www.uklenotnika.cz; metro Můstek. A former jeweller's, with ten small rooms, none of which will win any interior design awards, but which are clean and relatively inexpensive given the location. ❺

U krále Jiřího (The King George) Liliová 10 ⑦ 224 248 797, ⓦ www.kinggeorge.cz; metro Staroměstská. Eight small, cosy, en-suite rooms with repro furnishings above a set of bars, hidden in the network of lanes off Karlova. ❸

U medvídků (The Little Bears) Na Perštýně 7 ⑦ 224 211 916, ⓦ www.umedvidku.cz; metro Národní třída. The rooms above this famous Prague pub are plainly furnished, quiet considering the locale, and therefore something of an old town bargain; booking ahead essential. ❸

U prince Staroměstské náměstí 29 ⑦ 224 213 807, ⓦ www.hoteluprince.cz. Plush hotel, situated right on Old Town Square, with lots of original wooden ceilings, and views across to the astronomical clock. This is not a place for those who want to lose the crowds, as they're standing right outside your door, but if you want to be central, look no further. **❼**

U zlaté studny (The Golden Well) Karlova 3 ☎222 220 130, ⊛www.uzlatestudny.cz; metro **Staroměstská.** Situated right in the thick of it, overlooking the busy tourist thoroughfare of Karlova, this sixteenth-century house has a handful of rooms decked out in repro-Baroque style, some with original vaulted, panelled and painted ceilings. **❺**

Unitas Bartolomějská 9 ☎224 211 020, ⊛www .unitas.cz; metro **Národní třída.** Run by the *Cloister Inn* (see p.187), with hostel rooms, plus bargain rooms in converted secret police prison cells (Havel stayed in P6), now owned by Franciscan nuns. No smoking or drinking, but unbelievably cheap. **❶**

Nové Město

Nové Město covers a large and very varied area of the city. The streets just to the south of Národní, and to the east of náměstí Republiky, are literally in walking distance of the old town. For places in the nether regions, you'll need to hop on a tram or metro to get into the centre of town.

Alcron Štěpánská 40 ☎222 820 000, ⊛www .radisson.com/praguecs; metro **Muzeum/Můstek.** Giant 1930s hotel, just off Wenceslas Square, that has been superbly restored to its former glory by the Radisson SAS chain. Double rooms, at around 10,000Kč, are without doubt the most luxurious and tasteful you'll find in Nové Město. **❾**

Axa Na poříčí 40 ☎224 812 580, ⊛www.vol.cz /axa; metro **Florenc.** Large, plain, modestly refurbished hotel with handy adjacent swimming pool and gym, just ten minutes' walk from náměstí Republiky – make sure you see your room before booking in, however, as standards (view, noise, etc) can vary. **❺**

Elite Ostrovní 32 ☎224 932 250, ⊛www.hotelelite.cz; metro **Národní třída.** An efficient, stylish and very centrally located modern hotel with its own underground car park, but clearly an ancient building at heart, with an enclosed courtyard and the odd Renaissance feature retained. **❻**

Grand Hotel Evropa Václavské náměstí 25 ☎224 228 117, ⊛www.hotelsprague.org/evropa; metro **Můstek/Muzeum.** Without doubt, the most beautiful hotel in Prague, built in the 1900s and sumptuously decorated in Art Nouveau style; the rooms are furnished in repro Louis XIV, and there are some cheaper ones without en-suite facilities. Yet despite its prime location and its incredible decor, this place is run like an old Communist hotel – a blast from the past in every sense. **❺**

Hotel 16 – U sv Kateřiny Kateřinská 16 ☎224 920 636, ⊛www.hotel16.cz; metro **Karlovo náměstí.** Really friendly family-run hotel offering small, plain but clean en-suite rooms with TV in southern Nové Mesto; small terraced garden at back and botanical gardens nearby. **❹**

Imperial Na poříčí 15 ☎222 316 012, ⊛www.hotelimperial.cz; metro **Náměstí Republiky.** The café on the ground floor is a 1914 period piece; the vast hotel above it is much more basic – clean, simply furnished doubles, triples and quads with shared facilities only. **❸**

Jerome House V jirchářích 13 ☎224 911 011, ⊛www.jerome.cz; metro **Národní třída.** Discreetly tucked away in a nice, quiet area just south of Národní, the Jerome offers plain, bright rooms with upbeat, modern design, plus the odd original feature. Very basic, clean rooms. **❺**

Museum Mezibranská 15 ☎296 325 186, ⊛www .pension.museum.cz; metro **Muzeum.** Although situated on one of the busiest roads in Prague, right by the National Museum, the plain, budget-priced rooms in this pension all face onto a quiet courtyard. **❸**

Na zlatém kříži Jungmannovo náměstí 2 ☎224 219 501, ⊛www.goldencross.cz; metro **Můstek.** Small hotel in a very tall narrow building (no lift) just a step away from the bottom of Wenceslas Square. Rooms are spacious – especially the suites – and decked out in tasteful repro furnishings with nice parquet floors. **❻**

Palace Panská 12 ☎224 093 111, ⊛www .palacehotel.cz; metro **Můstek.** While all the other luxury hotels in Prague try their best, the *Palace*, located just off Wenceslas Square, really is a cut above the rest in terms of service – doubles go for around 10000Kč. **❾**

Salvator Truhlářská 10 ☎222 312 234, ⊛www .salvator.cz; metro **Náměstí Republiky.** Very good location for the price, just a minute's walk from namě̌stí Republiky, with small but clean rooms (the cheaper ones without en-

9

ACCOMMODATION | Hotels and pensions

188

suite facilities), and a sports bar on the ground floor; advance booking advisable. **②**
U šuterů Palackého 4 ☎224 948 235, ⓦwww.usuteru.jsc.cz; metro Můstek/Národní třída. Turn-of-the-century furnishings, parquet flooring, vaulted ceilings and a decent location between Národní and Wenceslas Square make this small pension pretty good value. **⑤**

Vyšehrad and the eastern suburbs

Vinohrady is a pleasant nineteenth-century suburb, a few metro or tram stops east of Wenceslas Square. Žižkov is a more run-down area, best-known for its riotous pubs and large Romany population; it has no metro, but several tram routes run through it.

City Belgická 10, Vinohrady ☎222 521 606, ⓦwww.hotelcity.cz; metro Náměstí Míru. Quiet locale, cheap, clean en-suite rooms with TVs and within walking distance of the top of Wenceslas Square. **③**
Corinthia Towers Kongresová 1, Nusle ☎261 191 111, ⓦwww.corinthia.cz; metro Vyšehrad. High-rise eyesore from the outside, but a popular top-of-the-range business hotel nevertheless; out of the centre, but bang next to a metro, the motorway, and the city's largest conference centre. Famous for having been declared a no-go area for US citizens a few years back due to the owners' alleged links with Libya. Doubles from 8000Kč. **⑨**
Luník Londýnská 50, Vinohrady ☎224 253 974, ⓔhotel.lunik@email.cz; metro I. P. Pavlova. Unpretentious modernized hotel in a fairly peaceful location, just a short walk from Wenceslas Square; rooms are spartan but clean and en suite. **④**
Prague Hilton Pobřežní 1, Karlín ☎224 841 111, ⓦwww.hilton.com; metro Florenc. Wickedly ugly titanium-blue glass cube on the edge of Nové Město, but within walking distance – or a couple of metro/tram stops – of the centre. Good place to be pampered, and favoured by visiting nabobs. **⑨**
Teatrino Bořivojova 53, ☎221 422 111, ⓦwww.arcotel.at; tram #5, #9 or #26 from metro Hlavní nádraží to Lipanská stop. Austrian-run hotel housed in a turn-of-the-century building in the quiet backstreets of Žižkov, tastefully renovated with lots of original features in the public rooms and sleek minimalist touches in the bedrooms. **⑥**

Triška Vinohradská 105 ☎222 727 313, ⓦwww .hotel-triska.cz; metro Jiřího z Poděbrad. Large turn-of-the-century hotel with comfortable rooms; they've made an effort with the interior decor, the service is good and it's close to the metro. **③**

Holešovice and the western suburbs

Holešovice is another pleasant late nineteenth-century residential suburb, within easy walking distance of a lot of greenery, and with good metro and tram connections. Dejvice is a pleasant residential interwar suburb, with garden villas on its fringes and a metro. Smíchov, rather like Žižkov, has a reputation as a bit of a rough, industrial suburb, but it's well connected by metro, and, naturally enough, fairly inexpensive.

Crowne Plaza Koulova 15, Dejvice ☎224 393 111, ⓦwww.crowneplaza.cz; tram #20 or #25 from metro Dejvická to Podbaba terminus. Prague's classic 1950s Stalinist wedding-cake hotel, with its dour socialist realist friezes and large helpings of marble, is now run by the Austrians. **⑧**
Expo Za elektrárnou 3 ☎266 712 470, ⓦwww.expoprag.cz; metro Nádraží Holešovice. Bright, clean and modern hotel right by the Výstaviště exhibition grounds and a short walk from Praha-Holešovice train station. **④**
Julián Elišky Peškové 11, Smíchov ☎257 311 150, ⓦwww.julian.cz; tram #6, #9 or #12 from metro Anděl to Arbešovo náměstí stop. Large hotel just a short tram ride from Malá Strana. Slightly dodgy decor in rooms, but all the usual facilities, plus mini-kitchens, and a nice lounge with a real fire. **③**
Petr Drtinova 17, Smíchov ☎257 314 068, ⓦwww .hotelpetr.cz; tram #6, #9 or #12 from metro Anděl to Kinského zahrada stop. Situated on a leafy street at the foot of Petřín Hill, close to Malá Strana; not that promising from the outside, but modern and pleasant inside. **③**
Praha Sušická 20, Dejvice ☎224 341 111, ⓦwww.htlpraha.cz; tram #2, #20 or #26 from metro Dejvická to Hadovka stop. The old party VIP hotel, where the likes of Ceaușescu once stayed. An appropriately grotesque 1970s concrete palace, though each room has a balcony with a wonderful view over to the Hrad. Inconveniently placed for public transport, so most guests take a taxi. **⑦**

Hostels

There are a fair few **hostels** in Prague which cater for the large number of backpackers who hit the city all year round – and these are supplemented further by a whole host of more transient, high-season-only hostels. Prices in hostels range from 200Kč to 600Kč for a bed, usually in a dormitory. A few operate curfews – it's worth asking before you commit yourself – and, although many rent out blankets and sheets, it's as well to bring your own sleeping bag. Note that some of the accommodation agencies in Prague also deal with hostels; see the box on p.183 for details.

Some Prague hostels give discounts to HI (Hostelling International; Ⓦ www.iyhf.org), and a few can be booked via the HI's online booking service, but, for the most part, you're better off contacting a centrally located organization like the **Traveller's Hostels**, whose chain of hostels are very popular with US students. Their main booking office is at Dlouhá 33, Staré Město (☏ 224 826 662, Ⓦ www.travellers.cz), where there is also a hostel (see below); dorm beds go for 350Kč and upwards per person.

Prague's university, the Karolinum, rents out over a thousand very basic **student rooms** from June to mid-September, starting at around 220Kč for a bed. Go to the central booking office at Voršilská 1, Nové Město (Mon–Fri only; ☏ 224 913 692; metro Národní třída).

The hostels below are marked on the colour map "Accommodation" at the back of the book.

Clown and Bard Bořivojova 102, Žižkov ☏ 222 716 453, Ⓦ www.crownandbard.com; tram #5, #9 or #26 from metro Hlavní nádraží to Husinecká stop. So laid-back it's horizontal, and not a place to go if you don't like hippies, but it's clean, undeniably cheap, stages events, has laundry facilties and rents out doubles (❶) as well as dorm beds for 250Kč per person.

Domov mládeže Dykova 20, Vinohrady ☏ 222 511 777, Ⓦ www.hotel.cz/domov-mladeze-penzion; tram #10, 16 from metro Náměstí Míru to Perunova stop. Nice clean hostel in the villa quarter of Vinohrady; singles, doubles and dorm beds from around 600Kč per person, depending on the season.

ESTEC Hostel Vaníčkova 5, Strahov ☏ 257 210 410, Ⓔ estec@jrc.cz; bus #217, #149 or #143 to the Strahov stadión from metro Dejvická. This is a chaotic, but cheap, hostel in the midst of noisy high-rise student land, but only a fifteen-minute walk from Hradčany through Petřín. To find the hostel, head for block 5, opposite the east stand of the Strahov stadium. Less than 200Kč for a dorm bed; more like 400Kč per person for a double.

Hostel Sokol Újezd 40, Malá Strana ☏ 257 007 397; tram #12, #22 or #23 from metro Malostranská to Hellichova stop. Shambolic student hostel with basic dorm beds for 300Kč, plus a communal kitchen, in a great location in Malá Strana; the entrance is on Všehrdova.

Hostel Týn Týnská 19, Staré Město ☏ 224 828 519, Ⓦ www.hostel-tyn.web2001.cz; metro Náměstí Republiky. The most centrally located hostel, just metres from Old Town Square. Simple doubles for 1100Kč, and six-bed dorms at 400Kč a bed.

Klub Habitat Na Zderaze 10, Nové Město ☏ 224 921 706, Ⓔ hostel@iol.cz; metro Karlovo náměstí. The best of Prague's hostels, offering a discount to HI members, located a short walk from Karlovo náměstí. Dorm beds for 400Kč per person, with breakfast. Book ahead.

Travellers Hostel Dlouhá 33, Staré Město ☏ 224 826 662, Ⓦ www.travellers.cz; metro Náměstí Republiky. Very centrally located hostel and booking office above the *Roxy* nightclub – if there's not enough room here, they'll find you a bed somewhere for 350Kč per person and upwards.

Vesta Wilsonova 8, Nové Město ☏ 224 617 118, Ⓦ www.vestack.cz; metro Hlavní nádraží. Vesta, an accommodation agency with several offices in the main train station (Praha hlavní nádraží), can book you into various places including their very own hostel in the station itself; beds cost 300Kč, and you can ask for sole occupancy.

Campsites

Prague abounds in **campsites** – there's a whole rash of them in Troja (see below) – and most are relatively easy to get to by public transport. Facilities, on the whole, are rudimentary and badly maintained, but the prices reflect this, starting at around 300Kč for a tent and two people.

Džbán Nad lávkou 5, Vokovice ☎ 235 359 006; tram #20 or #26 from metro Dejvická to Nad Džbánem stop. Large field with tent pitches, bungalows and basic facilities, 4km west of the centre, near the Šárka valley. Open all year.

Kotva U ledáren 55, Braník ☎ 244 461 712. The oldest, and nicest, site, with a riverside location 6km south of the city. Tram #3 or #17 from metro Karlovo náměstí to Nádraží Braník stop. Open April–Oct

Trojská Trojská 375, Troja ☎ 283 850 487; bus #112 from metro Nádraží Holešovice. Good location, one of several along the road to Troja chateau, situated in someone's large back garden, 3km north of the centre. Open all year.

Eating and drinking

The good news is that you can eat and drink very cheaply in Prague: the food is filling and the beer is divine. The bad news is that the kindest thing you can say about Czech food is that it is hearty. Forty years of culinary isolation and centralization under the Communists introduced few innovations to Czech cuisine, with its predilection for pork, gravy, dumplings and pickled cabbage. Fresh vegetables (other than potatoes) remain a rare sight on traditional Czech menus, and salads are still waiting for their day.

That said, the choice of places where you can eat has improved enormously over the last decade. You can spend a whole week eating out and never go near a dumpling, should you so wish. Czechs themselves are very keen on pizzas, and there are now some very good pizzerias in the capital – there are even some passably authentic ethnic restaurants ranging from Japanese and Lebanese to Balkan and French.

In addition, there's also a whole range of new, slightly more expensive restaurants aimed at the palates (and wallets) of the passing tourist, the expat community, wealthy Czechs and the diplomatic crowd. So while it's fun to sample authentic Czech food, and experience Czech eating habits, many visitors are happy to pay a bit more for food that is tastier and more imaginative, albeit not always very Czech.

Where to eat

The division between cafés, bars, pubs and restaurants is difficult to draw in Prague. All the places listed below as a **restaurant** (*restaurace* in Czech) are primarily there to serve you food, but some will also have a bar area where you can simply have a drink. Equally, while many **cafés** realize most of their customers want only a drink and maybe a slice of cake, others serve up cheap, hot snacks and even full meals. Czech **pubs** (*pivnice* in Czech) are on the whole the cheapest places to eat, and almost exclusively serve standard Czech food.

More and more Praguers are opting for sandwiches and fast food at lunchtimes, although traditionally Czechs eat their main meal of the day at lunchtime, between noon and 2pm. In pubs, you'll still get the widest choice of dishes around this time of day; in the city's restaurants, the evening sitting is by far the most popular.

Not surprisingly, the places in the main tourist areas along Mostecká and Karlova, on either side of the Charles Bridge, and on Staroměstské náměstí and Wenceslas Square, tend to be overpriced, relying on their location rather than the quality of their food, to bring in custom. Venture instead into the backstreets, such as those north of Celetná, south of Karlova, or south of Národní, and you're more likely to find better service, better value and perhaps even better food.

Czech cuisine

Most Czechs start a meal with **soup** (*polévka*), one of the country's culinary strong points. Some places will have a selection of cold **starters** such as *uzený jazyk* (smoked tongue) or *tresčí játra* (cod's liver). *Šunková rolka* is another favourite, consisting of ham topped with whipped cream and horseradish, but most Czechs skip the starters, which are often little more than a selection of cold meats.

Main courses tend to be divided into several separate sections. *Hotová jídla* (ready-made meals), which should arrive swiftly, and *jídla na objednávku* or *minutky* (meals made to order), for which you'll have to wait. In either case, dishes are overwhelmingly based on **meat** (*maso*), usually pork, sometimes beef. The Czechs are experts on these meats, and although the quality could often be better, the variety of sauces and preparative techniques is usually good. The difficulty lies in decoding names such as *klašterny tajemství* ("mystery of the monastery") or even a common dish like *Moravský vrabec* (literally "Moravian sparrow", but actually just roast pork).

Fish (*ryby*) is generally listed separately, or along with chicken (*drůbez*) and other fowl like duck (*kachna*). River trout (*pstruh*) and carp (*kapr*) – the traditional dish at Christmas – are the cheapest and most widely available fish, and, although their freshness may be questionable, they are usually served, grilled or roasted, in delicious buttery sauces or breadcrumbs.

Side dishes (*přílohy*), most commonly served with fish and fowl, generally consist of potatoes (*brambory*), though with meat dishes you'll more often be served **dumplings** (*knedlíky*), one of the mainstays of Bohemian cooking. The term itself is misleading for English-speakers, since they resemble nothing like the English dumpling – more like a heavy white bread. *Houskové knedlíky* are made from flour and come in large slices (four or five to a dish), while *bramborové knedlíky* are smaller and made from potato and flour. Occasionally, you may be treated to *ovocné knedlíky* (fruit dumplings), the king of *knedlíky*.

Fresh salads rarely rise above the ubiquitous *obloha*, usually a bit of tomato, cucumber and lettuce, or cabbage (*zelí*), often swimming in a slightly sweet, watery dressing.

With the exception of *palačinky* (pancakes) filled with chocolate or fruit and cream, **desserts** (*moučníky*), where they exist at all, can be pretty unexciting. Often the ice cream and cakes on offer in restaurants aren't really up to the standards of the stuff sold on the street, so go to a café or cake shop (*cukrárna* in Czech) if you want a dose of sugar, for more on which, see p.196.

Breakfast, snack and fast-food places

Many Czechs get up so early in the morning (often around 5 or 6am) that they don't have time to start the day with anything more than a quick cup of coffee. As a result, the whole concept of **breakfast** (*snídaně*) as such is alien to the Czechs. Most hotels will serve the "continental" basics of tea, coffee, rolls and cold cheese and meat, but for a real hearty breakfast, you need to go to one of the many places in the city that cater for expats in search of an American-style **brunch**.

Pastries (*pečivo*) are available from Prague's bakeries (*pekářství* or *pekárna*), but rarely in bars and cafés, so you'll most likely have to eat them on the go. Traditional Czech pastry (*koláč*) is more like sweet bread, dry and fairly dense with only a little condiment to flavour it, such as almonds (*oříškový*), poppy seed jam (*mákový*), plum jam (*povidlový*) or a kind of sour-sweet curd cheese (*tvarohový*). Recently, French, American and Viennese bakeries have started to appear in Prague, selling a huge variety of pastries, including croissants (*loupáky*), muffins and lighter cream cakes.

With breakfast, Czechs tend to have white **rolls**, which come in two basic varieties: *rohlík*, a plain finger roll, and *houska*, a rougher, tastier round bun. Czech **bread** (*chléb*) is some of the tastiest around when fresh. The standard loaf is *domácí* or *šumava*, a dense mixture of wheat and rye, which you can buy whole, in halves (*půl*) or quarters (*čtvrtina*). *Český chléb* is a mixture of rye, wheat and whey, with distinctive slashes across the top; *kmínový chléb* is the same loaf packed full of caraway seeds. *Moskva* remains popular, despite the name – a moist, heavy, sour-dough loaf that lasts for days.

Prague's stand-up **bufets** or *jídelna* are open from as early as 6am and offer everything from light snacks to full meals. A cross between a British greasy spoon and an American diner, they're usually self-service (*samoobsluha*) and non-smoking, and occasionally have rudimentary seats. The cheapest of the tired-looking meat sausages on offer is *sekaná*, bits of old meat and bread squashed together to form a meat loaf (for connoisseurs only). *Guláš* (goulash) is popular, usually *Szegedinský* (pork with sauerkraut) after the Hungarian town. Less substantial fare boils down to *chlebíčky* – artistically presented **open sandwiches** with combinations of gherkins, cheese, salami, ham and aspic – and mountains of mayonnaise-type **salad**, bought by weight (200 grammes is a medium-sized portion).

The ubiquitous Czech street **takeaway** is the hot dog or *párek*, a dubious-looking frankfurter (traditionally two – *párek* means a pair), dipped in mustard and served in a white roll (*v rohlíku*). A greasier option is *bramborák*, a thin potato pancake with little flecks of bacon or salami in it; *felafal* or kebabs (known as *gyros*) form another popular takeaway choice, usually with pitta bread and salad. And, of course, there are now numerous Western-style fast-food joints (most notably *McDonald's*) all over Prague. Whatever the season, Czechs also have to have their daily fix of **ice cream** (*zmrzlina*), dispensed from window kiosks in the sides of buildings, or from more substantial outlets, some with seating.

Hradčany

Saté Pohořelec 3. One of the few places you can fill your belly for very little in the vicinity of the Hrad. Simple veggie and non-veggie noodle dishes with a vaguely Indonesian bent. Daily 11am–10pm.

Malá Strana

Bohemia Bagel Újezd 16 ⓦ www.bohemiabagel .cz; tram#12, #22 or #23 from metro Malostranská to Újezd stop. Self-service café at the south end of Újezd, serving filled bagels, all-day breakfasts, soup and chilli, with an internet café attached. Branch at Masná 2 (metro Staroměstská). Mon–Fri 7am–midnight, Sat & Sun 8am–midnight.
Pekařství v Karmelitské Karmelitská 20; tram #12, #22 or #23 from metro Malostranská to Hellichova stop. Local Czech bakery, just south of Malostranské náměstí, with a café attached where you wash down your cakes and pastries with coffee. Bakery: Mon–Fri 7am–7pm, Sun noon–6pm. Café: Mon–Fri 10am–8pm, Sat & Sun 10am–8pm.

Staré Město

Au Gourmand Dlouhá 10; metro Náměstí Republiky. Beautifully tiled French boulangerie, patisserie and traiteur selling wickedly delicious pastries; most folk take away, but there are a few tables and a daily soup on offer. Daily 7.30am–7pm.
Bakeshop Praha V Kolkovně 2; metro Náměstí Republiky. Top-class expat bakery serving excellent bread, sandwiches, quiches, wraps and cakes, which you can either take away or wash down with coffee, whilst reading the news. Daily 7am–7pm.

Country Life Melantrichova 15; metro Můstek.
The sandwiches, salads and soups are the
thing at this healthy, veggie franchise: takeaway or sit-down self-service buffet for
veggie slop in the courtyard behind.
Mon–Thurs 8.30am–7pm, Fri 8.30am–4pm,
Sun 11am–8pm. Branch at Jungmannova
1, Nové Město (Mon–Fri only).

Havelská Koruna Havelská 21; metro Můstek.
Popular no-frills, self-service Czech *jídelna*
serving comfort food classics such as
sekaná, goulash and *zelí*, all for under
50Kč; you pay at the exit – not for the faint-
hearted. Daily 9am–8pm.

Paneria pekařství Kaprova 3 ⓦ www.paneria.cz;
metro Staroměstská. A large chain of Czech
bakeries specializing in providing
sandwiches, toasted panini and pastries for
Prague's hungry office workers. Other
branches at Maiselova 4 (metro
Staroměstská), Francouzská 20 (metro
Náměstí Míru) and Vítězná 15 (tram #6, #9,
#22 or #23 from metro Národní třída to
Újezd stop). Daily 7am–10pm.

Safir Havelská 12 ⓦ www.safirgrill.czrb.cz;
metro Můstek. Inexpensive and centrally
located Middle Eastern kebab and *felafal*
outlet, with eat-in or takeaway. Mon–Sat
10am–8pm.

U Bakaláře Celetná 13; metro Staroměstská/
Náměstí Republiky. Very central, cheap self-
service veggie hole-filler, serving typical
Czech fry-up food to hungry tourists.
Mon–Fri 9am–7pm, Sat & Sun 11am–7pm.

Nové Město

Anis-Adonis Jungmannova 21; metro Národní
třída. Arabic fast food – stuffed vine leaves,
felafal, *taboule* and a salad bar – self-

service sit-in or takeaway, a stone's throw
from Wenceslas Square and Národní třída.
Mon–Fri 10.30am–7pm, Sat 11am–5pm.

Jarmark Vodičkova 30 ⓦ www.jarmark.com;
metro Můstek. Popular, inexpensive self-
service place in the Lucerna pasáž, where
the chef prepares your food in front of you.
Daily 8.30am–8.30pm.

Java Kava Královdvorská 11; metro Náměstí
Republiky. Seats are at a premium at this
tiny café by the side of the Kotva
department store, but takeaway
sandwiches are equally popular. Mon–Fri
8am–8pm, Sat & Sun 11am–5pm.

Juice House Na příkopě 3–5; metro Můstek.
Prague's first juice bar, situated above the
Clockhouse clothes store, with a whole
wild range of juices and smoothies in
Prague's prime shopping district. Daily
10am–10pm.

Le Gourmand Václavské náměstí 18; metro
Můstek. Neither French nor gourmet (and
not to be confused with the superlative *Au
Gourmand*), but a large, cheap, convenient
self-service salad bar with a few standard
hot Czech dishes on offer, too. Daily
8am–11pm.

Na zlatém kříži Jungmannova 34; metro
Můstek. Stand-up *bufet* specializing in
chlebíčky (open sandwiches), which you
can wash down with a small beer. Mon–Fri
6.30am–7pm, Sat 9am–6pm.

Holešovice

Delicatesse Kostelní 16 ⓦ www.delicatesse.cz;
metro Vltavská. French bakery hidden away
in Holešovice serving hot and cold
sandwiches, quiche and pastries; they also
deliver. Daily 9am–9pm.

Cafés

At the beginning of the twentieth century, Prague boasted a café society to
rival that of Vienna or Paris. A handful of these classic Habsburg-era haunts
have survived, or been resurrected, and should definitely be sampled. Like most
metropolitans, Praguers seem to spend a large part of the day smoking and
drinking in cafés, and in the summer, the tables spill out onto the streets and
squares. The cafés listed below are a mixed bunch. The majority serve just coffee and cakes, and more often than not, alcohol; others also serve up cheap and
filling (though rarely gourmet) meals. If you have any Czech, you can find out
the latest on the Czech café scene, and any up-and-coming events, by visiting
ⓦ www.kavarny.cz.

Like the Austrians who once ruled over them, the Czechs have a grotesquely sweet tooth, and the coffee-and-cake hit is part of the daily ritual. The more traditional cafés offer a wide range of **cakes**: *dort*, like the German *Torte*, consist of a series of custard cream, chocolate and sponge layers, while *řez* are lighter, square cakes, usually containing a bit of fruit. A *věneček*, filled with "cream", is the nearest you'll get to an éclair; a *větrník* is simply a larger version with a bit of fresh cream added. One speciality to look out for is *rakvička*, which literally means "little coffin", an extended piece of sugar with cream, moulded vaguely into the shape of a coffin.

Coffee is drunk black and is usually available in espresso (*presso*) form: small, black and strong, though by no means as diminutive as in Italy. Occasionally, you may still come across the original pre-1989 Czech coffee, called somewhat hopefully *turecká* (Turkish) – it's really just hot water poured over coffee grains. Downmarket *bufet*s sell *ledová káva*, a weak, cold black coffee, while at the other

Prague's tea-houses

According to local legend, the Russian anarchist Mikhail Bakunin entered a Prague café in 1848 and ordered tea. When the owner said that he'd never heard of the drink, Bakunin marched into the kitchen and made the city's first cup of tea. Eighty years later, there were an estimated 150 **tea-houses** (*cajovny* in Czech) in Prague, but the culture died out under the Communists. Today's tea-houses are a post-1989 phenomenon, though they have their historical roots in the First Republic. Partly a reaction to the smoke-filled, alcohol-driven atmosphere of the ubiquitous Czech pub, and partly a reaction against the multinational, fast-food culture that has now arrived in Prague, tea-houses tend to be non-smoking, slightly hippified places to enjoy a quiet cuppa and chill out. The tea-drinking is taken very seriously and there's usually a staggering array of leaves on offer, some commanding pretty high prices.

Dahab Dlouhá 33, Staré Město ⓦwww.dahab.cz; metro Náměstí Republiky. The mother of all Prague teahouses, a vast Bedouin tent of a place serving tasty Middle Eastern snacks, couscous and hookahs to a background of funky world music. Daily noon–midnight.

Dobrá čajovna Boršov 2, Staré Město ⓦwww.cajovna.com; metro Staroměstská. The original, slightly precious, mellow, rarefied teahouse, with an astonishing variety of teas (and a few Middle Eastern snacks) served by waiters who slip by silently in their sandals. This place is off Karoliny Světlé and you'll need to ring the bell. Small branch at Václavské náměstí 14, Nové Město; metro Můstek/Muzeum. Mon–Fri 10am–9.30pm, Sun 3–9.30pm.

Malý Buddha Úvoz 46, Malá Strana; tram #12, #22 or #23 one stop from metro Malostranská. Typical Prague tea-house decor, with a Buddhist altar in one corner and vegetarian

Vietnamese snacks on the menu. A very useful haven just down from the Hrad. Tues–Sun 1–10.30pm.

Růžová čajovna Růžová 8, Nové Město ⓦwww.pangea-tea.cz; metro Můstek/Muzeum. The "pink tea-house" is a lighter, more modern version that caters for a less hippified clientele, and doesn't play exclusively non-Western music. Mon–Fri 10am–9pm, Sat & Sun 11am–9pm.

U zeleného čaje Nerudova 19, Malá Strana; tram #12, #22 or #23 one stop from from metro Malostranská. The "green tea" is a great little stop-off for a pot of tea a veggie snack en route to or from the Hrad; the only problem is getting a place at one of the four tables. Daily 11am–9.30pm.

U zlatého kohouta Michalská 3, Staré Město; metro Můstek. Hidden away in a courtyard off Michalská, this is another secretive, relaxing *cajovna* worth knowing about, located in the heart of Staré Město. Mon–Fri 10am–9.30pm, Sat & Sun 2–9.30pm.

end of the scale *Vídeňská káva* (Viennese coffee) is a favourite with the older generation, served with a dollop of whipped cream. Another rather rich option is a mix with advocaat, *Alžírská káva*. **Tea** is drunk weak and without milk, although you'll usually be given a glass of boiling water and a tea bag so you can do your own thing – for milk, say "*s mlékem*". If you want really good tea, you should head for one of the city's tea-houses (see box on p.196).

Cafés are marked on the colour maps at the back of the book.

Malá Strana

Chiméra Lázeňská 6; metro Malostranská. Coffee, toast and cigarettes are the defining features of this pleasant art gallery/café, which has a few comfy armchairs to crash out in. Daily noon–midnight.

St Nicholas Café Tržiště 10; tram #12, #22 or #23 one stop from metro Malostranská. Vaulted cellar café/bar that pulls in well-dressed Czechs and the diplomatic crowd in some numbers. Mon–Fri noon–1am, Sat & Sun 4pm–1am.

U zavěšenýho kafe Úvoz 6; tram #12, #22 or #23 one stop from metro Malostranská. A "hanging coffee" is one that has been paid for by the haves for the have-nots who drop in. That apart, this place is a pleasant smoky cross-over café/pub, serving cheap beer and traditional Czech food in a handy spot on the way up or down from the Hrad. Daily 11am–midnight.

Staré Město

Blatouch Vězeňská 4; metro Staroměstská. Smoky, literary café, frequented mostly by Czech students. Olives, jazz, dubious snacks and alcoholic/non-alcoholic cocktails available. Mon–Fri 11am–midnight, Sat 2pm–1am, Sun 2pm–midnight.

Chez Marcel Haštalská 12 ✆ www.chezmoi.cz; metro Náměstí Republiky. Effortlessly chic French café-bistro. A good place to grab a coffee or a *tarte tatin*, read a French mag or eat some moderately priced bistro-style food. Mon–Sat 8am–1am, Sun 9am–1am.

Damúza Řetězová 10; metro Staroměstská. Relaxed café attached to the drama school, DAMU, offering draught beer and cheap student food in the centre of the old town. Mon–Fri noon–midnight, Sat noon–11.30pm, Sun noon–10pm.

Ebel Týn 2 ✆ www.ebelcoffee.cz; metro Náměstí Republiky. Convenient little café serving very good coffee and tasty snacks, hidden away on the south side of the Týn (Ungelt)

courtyard behind the Týn church. Daily 9am–10pm.

Érra Konviktská 11; metro Národní třída. Vaulted cellar café in the backstreets off Betlémské náměstí that's popular with a professional mixed straight/gay crowd. Tasty salads and snacks on offer too. Mon–Fri 10am–midnight, Sat & Sun 11am–midnight.

Montmartre Řetězová 7; metro Staroměstská. Surprisingly small, barrel-vaulted café that was once a famous First Republic dance and cabaret venue. Mon–Fri 9am–11pm, Sat & Sun noon–11pm.

Paris U obecního domu 1 ✆ www.hotel-pariz.cz; metro Náměstí Republiky. The prices are sky-high for Prague, and the service cold, but there's a certain rather formal elegance about the *Hotel Paříž*'s Art Nouveau café. Daily 10am–midnight.

Rudolfinum Alšovo nábřeží 12; metro Staroměstská. Gloriously grand nineteenth-century café on the first floor of the old parliament building (see p.108) – you don't have to visit the exhibition to go to the café. Tues–Sun 10am–6pm.

Terminal Bar Soukenická 6 ✆ www.terminal.cz; metro Náměstí Republiky. Definitely the number one choice in terms of atmosphere when it comes to going online, this is a funky, loud bar, with a groovy chill-out basement littered with kitsch sofas and weird lighting. Daily 10am–2am.

Nové Město

Archa Na poříčí 26, ✆ www.archatheatre.cz; metro Náměstí Republiky/Florenc. Designer café belonging to the avant-garde venue of the same name, with big fishbowl windows for people-watching. Mon–Fri 9am–10.30pm, Sat 10am–10pm, Sun 1–10pm.

Arco Hybernská/Dlažděná; metro Náměstí Republiky. Once the haunt of a clique of Prague-German writers (including Kafka), now approximately reproduced, though a café is more than the sum of its fittings.

△ Obecní dům café

Mon–Fri 3–9.30pm, Sat & Sun 10am–9.30pm.

Break Café Štěpánská 32; metro Muzeum. Stylish, modern café, popular with expats: muffins, toast and croissants for breakfast; salads, burgers and grilled panini for lunch; and everything from *bramborák* to lasagne and oysters for dinner. Mon–Fri 8am–11pm, Sat 9.30am–7pm.

Globe Pštrossova 6 ⊛ www.globebookstore.cz; metro Národní třída/Karlovo náměstí. Large, buzzing café, at the back of the English-language bookstore of the same name, that's a serious expat hang-out, but enjoyable nevertheless. Mon–Thurs & Sun 10am–midnight, Fri & Sat 10am–1am.

Grand Hotel Evropa Václavské náměstí 25; metro Můstek/Muzeum. This sumptuous Art Nouveau café has all its original fittings, but has reached a new low in ambience and service. For architectural curiosity only. Daily 9.30am–11pm.

Imperial Na poříčí 15 ⊛ www.hotelimperial.cz; metro Náměstí Republiky. An endearingly shabby yet grand Habsburg-era *Kaffeehaus* which has retained its original, over-the-top ceramic tiled decor. The locals clearly approve of its unpretentious air, too, and the free doughnuts go down a treat. Mon–Thurs 9am–midnight, Fri & Sat 9am–1am, Sun 9am–11pm.

Institut Français Štěpánská 35 ⊛ www.ifp.cz; metro Muzeum. Housed in the French cultural centre; great coffee and superb French pastries, plus of course the chance to pose with a French newspaper, make this one of Prague's best cafés. Mon–Fri 9am–6pm.

Káva Káva Káva Národní 37 ⊛ www.kava-coffee .cz; metro Národní třída. Pleasant little café in the Platýz pasáž between Národní and Uhelný trh, offering good coffee, bagels and pastries, plus internet access. Mon–Fri 7am–10pm, Sat & Sun 9am–10pm.

Louvre Národní 20 ⊛ www.kavarny.cz/louvre; metro Národní třída. Turn-of-the-century café, closed down in 1948, but now back in business and a very popular refuelling spot for Prague's shoppers. Dodgy colour scheme, but high ceiling, mirrors, daily papers, lots of cakes, a billiard hall and window seats overlooking Národní. Mon–Fri 8am–11.30pm, Sat & Sun 9am–11.30pm.

Marathon Černá 9; metro Národní třída. Self-styled, smoky "library café" in the university's 1920s-style religious faculty, hidden in the backstreets, south of Národní. Mon–Fri 10am–10pm.

Obecní dům náměstí Republiky; metro Náměstí Republiky. The vast *kavárna*, with its famous fountain, is in the more restrained south hall of this huge Art Nouveau complex, and has recently been glitteringly restored – an absolute aesthetic treat. Daily 7.30am–11pm.

Rybka Opatovická 7; metro Národní třída. Cheerful, zany café, art gallery and bookshop. Daily 9am–10pm.

Shabu Palackého 11; metro Národní třída/Můstek. Tiny little café down a passageway at no. 11, serving an interesting selection of Yugoslav snacks such as grilled aubergine, Balkan salad and *burek*. Daily 10am–midnight.

Slavia Národní 1; metro Národní třída. Famous Prague riverside café that has a special place in the city's cultural and political history (see p.123). Despite losing much of its former character, it still pulls in a mixed crowd from shoppers and tourists to older folk and the pre- and post-theatre mob. Daily 9am–11pm.

U sv Vojtěcha (St Adalbert) Vojtěšská 14; metro Karlovo náměstí. Lively coffee place not far from the Národní divadlo and Žofín, with big windows that open out onto the street in summer. Mon–Fri 8am–11pm, Sat 10am–10pm, Sun 10am–8pm.

Velryba (The Whale) Opatovická 24; metro Národní třída. One of the most determinedly cool student cafés in Prague, not intended as an expat joint (and not keen to entice tourists), serving cheap, Czech food (plus several veggie options) and a wide range of malt whiskies. Mon–Thurs, Sat & Sun 11am–midnight, Fri 11am–2am.

Vyšehrad and the eastern suburbs

Blue Velvet Čerchovská 4, Vinohrady ⊛ www.bluevelvet.cz; metro Jiřího z Poděbrad. Czech literary café housed in an arty bookshop, off Polská, with a busy programme of readings, discussions and folk/jazz/blues concerts. Mon–Fri 10am–11pm, Sat & Sun 3–11pm.

Medúza Belgická 17, Vinohrady; metro Náměstí Míru. Trendy young crowd hangout in this deliberately faded, inexpensive café, which serves breakfast all day and gets packed out most evenings. Mon–Fri 11am–1am, Sat & Sun noon–1am.

Café Apostrof Matoušova, Smíchov. Smart café in a pristinely renovated Dientzenhofer palace on náměstí 28 října, with lots of violins and art on the walls. A positive oasis in Smíchov. Daily 11am–11pm.

Café Orange Puškinovo náměstí 13, Bubeneč; metro Dejvická. Trendy, brightly decorated café with seats outside overlooking a quiet residential square, and good pasta dishes, bruschetta snacks, fresh juice and ice cream on the menu. Mon–Fri 9am–11pm, Sat & Sun 10am–11pm.

Restaurants

Prague's **restaurant** scene has greatly improved in the last few years in terms of both choice and quality. The influx of tourists has, of course, pushed the prices in some restaurants out of the reach of many Czechs, who tend more than ever to stick to pubs when eating out. However, even in the city's top restaurants, you can't guarantee faultless food and service, so keep an open mind. Service is gradually becoming more sophisticated, though surly staff are still no rarity, nor are unscrupulous waiters who exercise dubious arithmetics when totting up the bill. Beware of extras in the pricier restaurants, where you will be charged for everything you touch, including the almonds you thought were courtesy of the house. Most restaurants have an English menu, but for help in decifering a Czech menu, see "Language" p.280. All restaurants are marked on the colour maps at the back of the book. If you want food delivered to your door from a selection of places from *Bohemia Bagel* to *Chez Marcel*, phone ☏224 228 538 or visit ⓦwww.delivery.cz.

Hradčany

Moderate

U ševce Matouše (The Cobbler Matouš) Loretánské náměstí 4; tram #22 from metro Malostranská to Pohořelec stop. Large steak and chips is the speciality of this former cobbler's, which is one of the few half-decent places to eat in the castle district. Daily 11am–11pm.

Malá Strana

The nearest metro for the restaurants in this section is Malostranská, followed either by a short walk or a stop or two on tram #12, #22 or #23.

Inexpensive

Bar Bar Všehrdova 17 ☏257 312 246. Arty crêperie with big cheap salads, savoury and sweet crêpes/*palačinky* on offer. Daily noon–11pm.
Petřínské terasy Seminářská zahrada 13 ☏290 000 457. Gay-owned, but with mixed

---

The restaurant listings are divided into geographical areas that correspond to the chapters, and into price categories, too – inexpensive, moderate and expensive. You should be able to get a soup, a main course, a dessert, plus a couple of beers in the price bracket indicated:

Inexpensive under 300Kč a head
Moderate 300–600Kč a head
Expensive 600Kč and upwards

While 500Kč for a meal is hardly extravagant compared with meal prices in the EU or US, it's still pricey for most Czechs. At popular and/or upmarket restaurants, it's advisable to book a table beforehand either by calling in or by telephoning ahead. All restaurants are marked on the colour maps at the back of the book.

clientele, superb views over Prague, beer and barbecues – get off at the Nebozízek stop on the funicular up Petřín, but walk away from the restaurant of the same name. Daily 11am–10pm.

Rybářský klub U sovových mlýnů 1 ☎257 534 200; tram #12, #22 or #23 from metro Malostranská to Hellichova stop. Fresh fish – carp, trout, pike and others – simply prepared at this unpretentious riverside restaurant, situated in the park on Kampa Island. Daily noon–11pm.

Moderate

Faros Šporkova 5 ☎257 533 964, @www.faros.cz. Cosy little Greek restaurant in the backstreets of Malá Strana that makes a nice change from other Prague restaurants and is relatively veggie-friendly. Daily noon–11pm.

Nebozízek (Little Auger) Petřínské sady 411 ☎257 515 329, @www.nebozizek.cz. Situated at the halfway stop on the funicular up Petřín. The view is superb, there's an oudoor terrace and a traditional Czech menu heavy with game dishes. Daily 11am–11pm.

Pálffý palác Valdštejnská 14 ☎257 530 522, @www.czechreality.cz/palffy. Grand candle-lit room on the first floor of the conservatoire, and a wonderful outdoor terrace from which

you can survey the red rooftops of Malá Strana; the international menu doesn't always live up to the setting. Daily 11am–midnight.

Expensive

Circle Line Malostranské náměstí 12 ☎257 530 023. The fresh seafood and sumptuous salads are the main draw at this luxurious restaurant, though the meat and veggie courses are equally good. Mon–Fri noon–11pm, Sat & Sun 11am–11pm.

David Tržiště 21 ☎257 533 109, @www .restaurant-david.cz. Formal, small, family-run restaurant which specializes in doing Bohemian cuisine full justice for around 1000Kč a head. Daily 11.30am–11pm.

Kampa Park Na Kampě 8b ☎257 532 685, @www.kampapark.com. Pink house exquisitely located right by the Vltava on Kampa Island with a superb fish and seafood menu, top-class service and tables outside in summer. Daily 11.30am–1am.

U Maltézských rytířů (The Maltese Knights) Prokopská 10 ☎257 533 666. One of the best Gothic cellars in Prague in which to sample faultless local cuisine (particularly venison) and excellent apple strudel. Daily 11am–11pm.

U patrona Dražického náměstí 4 ☎257 530 725. An excellent, intimate little restaurant

---

Vegetarian eating

Czech meat consumption has dropped dramatically since 1989, but it remains one of the highest in the world. It's hardly suprisingly then that **vegetarianism** is still a minority sport. Nevertheless, you're better off in Prague than anywhere else in the country. For a start, places which cater mostly for expats usually have one or two veggie options, and there are plenty of pizzerias.

Even in traditional Czech places, most menus have a section called *bezmasa* (literally "without meat") – don't take this too literally, though, for it simply means the main ingredient is not dead animal; dishes like *omeleta se sunkou* (ham omelette) regularly appear under these headings, so always check first. The staple of Czech vegetarianism is *smazeny syr*, a slab of melted cheese, deep-fried in breadcrumbs and served with tartar sauce (*tartarská omacka*) – beware, though, as it's sometimes served *se sunkou* (with ham). Other types of cheese can also be deep fried, as can other vegetables: *ené zampiony* (mushrooms) and *smazeny kveták* (cauliflower). Emergency veggie standbys which most Czech pubs will knock up for you without too much fuss include *knedlíky s vejci* (dumplings and scrambled egg) or *omeleta s hráskem* (pea omelette).

The only exclusively veggie places are *Country Life* (see p.195), *Góvinda* (see p.203), *Lotos* (see p.202), *Maly Buddha* (see p.196), *Radost FX* (see p.204), *U Bakaláre* (see p.195) and *U staré synagogy* (see p.202), though the latter also serves fish. Veggie phrases to remember are *"jsem vegeterián/vegeteriánka. Máte nejaké bezmasa?"* (I'm a vegetarian. Is there anything without meat?); for emphasis, you could add *"nejím maso nebo ryby"* (I don't eat meat or fish).

very close to the Charles Bridge, offering beautifully prepared local dishes – in the same stable as *Circle Line* et al. Mon–Sat 6–11.30pm.

Staré Město and Josefov

Inexpensive

Ariana Rámová 6; metro Náměstí Republiky. Welcoming Afghan restaurant (formerly known as *Kabul*) serving up authentic spicey food a stone's throw from the Old Town Square. Daily 11am–11pm.

Jerusalem Břehová 6; metro Staroměstská. One of a rash of kosher places on Břehová, on the edge of the old Jewish quarter; decor is very plain, service relaxed and the menu vast and tasty, ranging from breakfasts and savoury pancakes to full meals. Daily 8am–11pm.

Lotos Platnéřská 13; metro Staroměstská. The decor's an odd mixture of tie-dye and ultra-tidy sterility, and the food's bizarre too, including banana ragout. Some veggie wholefood versions of Czech cuisine, though – this is your chance to have a meat-free pork and dumplings. No smoking but there is alcohol. Daily noon–10pm.

Maestro Křižovnická 10; metro Staroměstská. Very good pizza place close to the metro (and to Charles Bridge); the chicken *cacciatore* is also worth sampling, as are the profiteroles. Mon–Fri 11am–11pm, Sat & Sun 1–11pm.

Pizzeria Rugantino Dušní 4 ☎ 222 318 172; metro Staroměstská. This pizzeria, just off Dlouhá, is the genuine article: an oak-fired oven, gargantuan thin bases, numerous toppings to choose from, and Bernard on tap. Mon–Sat 11am–11pm, Sun 5–11pm.

U staré synagogy Vězeňská 1; metro Staroměstská. Despite its name, this plainly decorated kosher non-meat restaurant is situated in the modernist extension to the Spanish Synagogue. Daily 10am–11pm.

U třech modrých koulí (The Three Blue Balls) Havelská 8 ☎ 224 238 130, ⊛ www.trikoule.cz; metro Můstek. Candlelit cellar restaurant, with good-value lunchtime menu, and refined Czech cuisine. Daily 11.45am–4pm & 5.45pm–midnight.

Moderate

Kogo Havelská 27 ☎ 224 214 543, metro Můstek; and Na příkopě 22 ☎ 221 451 259,

metro Náměstí Republiky; ⊛ www.kogo-prague.cz. The Havelská site is divided into two intimate spaces by a passageway and has a small courtyard; the Na příkopě site is much larger and more showy, with a more spacious courtyard. Either way, you'll get decent pasta, pizza and salads served by courteous and efficient waiters. Daily 9am–midnight.

Le Saint-Jacques Jakubská 4 ☎ 222 322 685, ⊛ www.saint-jacques.cz; metro Náměstí Republiky. Excellent French brasserie cuisine on offer here in the heart of the so-called "French quarter", with tasteful live music nightly. Mon–Fri noon–3pm & 6pm–midnight, Sat 6pm–midnight.

Red, Hot & Blues Jakubská 12 ☎ 222 314 639; metro Náměstí Republiky. Laid-back joint deep in the heart of expat territory serving chilli-hot Tex-Mex – *burritos*, *étouffées* and Creole food – to the sound of jazz and blues. Daily 9am–11pm.

Stoleti Karoliny Světlé 21; metro Národní třída; ☎ 222 220 008, ⊛ www.stoleti.cz. Imaginative Czech cuisine named after stars of film and stage in unstuffy, simply furnished restaurant. Daily noon–midnight.

Tamura Havelská 6 ☎ 224 232 056; metro Můstek. A fair stab at Japanese sashimi and sushi; your bill can climb in the restaurant, but it'll stay much lower at the street-level buffet. Daily 11am–11pm.

Expensive

Barock Pařížská 24 ☎ 223 229 221; metro Staroměstská. Trendy, candle-lit café-restaurant bathed in russet with framed photos of supermodels on the walls, and wannabes at the bar. The breakfasts are top-notch and the main dishes from the East are all good, but pricey. Mon–Wed 8.30am–1am, Thurs & Fri 8.30am–2am, Sat & Sun 10am–2am.

Bellevue Smetanovo nábřeží 18 ☎ 222 221 438, ⊛ www.praguefinedining.cz; metro Národní třída. The view of Charles Bridge and the Hrad is outstanding and they serve imaginative Czech-centred cuisine – hardly surprising then that it's around 1000Kč a head and you need to book ahead to eat here. Mon–Sat noon–3pm & 5.30–11pm, Sun 11am–3pm & 7–11pm.

Le Café Colonial Široká 6 ☎ 224 818 322; metro Staroměstská. Conveniently situated café/restaurant right opposite the Klausová synagoga. The colonial theme isn't overplayed, though the French-based menu has a touch of Chinese and Indian. Daily 8.30am–1am.

Don Giovanni Karoliny Světlé 34 ☎ 222 222 060, ⊛ www.dongiovanni.cz; metro Národní třída. One of the best Italian restaurants in town; straightforward menu, fresh fish and seafood and top-class *tiramisu*. Daily noon–midnight.

Mlýnec Novotného lávka 9 ☎ 221 082 208, ⊛ www.praguefinedining.cz; metro Staroměstská. Michelin-approved international cuisine and a terrace overlooking Charles Bridge and the Hrad don't come cheap. Daily noon–3pm & 5–11pm.

Náprstek (Thimble) Náprstkova 8; metro Národní třída ☎ 222 221 019, ⊛ www.restaurant-naprstek.cz. Award-winning, elegant restaurant serving a mouthwatering international menu. Daily 11am–midnight.

Pravda Pařížská 17 ☎ 222 326 203; metro Staroměstská. Trendy restaurant on Prague's premier chic street pulling in fashionable customers. Service is attentive and the excellent menu ranges from Cajun to Vietnamese. Daily noon–1am.

Rybí trh Týn 5 ☎ 224 895 447, ⊛ www.flambee .cz; metro Náměstí Republiky. Swish fish and seafood restaurant in the Týn (Ungelt) courtyard, where you pick your victim, and tell the chef how to cook it. Daily 11am–midnight.

U modré kachničky II (The Blue Duckling) Michalská 16 ☎ 224 213 418, ⊛ www .umodrekachnicky.cz; metro Národní třída. Intimate little restaurant, decorated with murals and antiques, and offering a mouth-watering selection of dishes, including many Czech favourites – such as roast with pears – given the gourmet treatment. Daily 11.30am–11.30pm.

V zátiší (Still-Life) Liliová 1 ☎ 222 221 155, ⊛ www.praguefinedining.cz; metro Národní třída. Exquisitely prepared international cuisine with fresh vegetables, fresh pasta, and regular non-meat dishes, all served in *nouvelle cuisine*-sized portions by professional waiters in a space the size of a living room. Daily noon–3pm & 5.30–11pm.

Nové Město

Inexpensive

Góvinda Soukenická 27; metro Náměstí Republiky. Hare Krishna (*Haré Kršna* in

Czech) restaurant serving organic Indian veggie slop for knock-down prices. Mon–Sat 11am–5.30pm.

Íver Purkyňova 4 ☎ 224 946 071; metro Národní třída. Prague's only centrally located Slovak restaurant is an unpretentious affair next door to the Slovak cultural centre behind Tesco, serving up the spicy *kapustnica* soup, *bryndzové halušky*, the national dish, and lots of steaks, plus *tiramisu*. Daily 11am–midnight.

Pizzeria Kmotra (Godmother) V jirchářích 12 ☎ 224 915 809, ⊛ www.kmotra.cz; metro Národní třída. This sweaty basement pizza place is one of Prague's most popular, and justifiably so – if possible book a table in advance. Daily 11am–midnight.

U sádlů (The Lard) Klimentská 2 ☎ 224 813 874, ⊛ www.usadlu.cz; metro Náměstí Republiky. Deliberately over-the-top themed medieval banqueting hall serving inexpensive hearty fare and lashings of frothing ale. Daily 11am–1am.

Moderate

Angel Opatovická 3 ☎ 224 930 019, ⊛ www.thecafe.cz; metro Národní třída. Sleek, light, minimalist decor and seriously delicious designer cooking available at this resolutely expat café-restaurant. Mon–Wed & Sun 11am–3pm, Thurs–Sat 11am–3pm & 7–10pm.

Cicala Žitná 43 ☎ 222 210 375; metro I. P. Pavlova. Very good little Italian basement restaurant that does a wide range of pasta and pizza, has an appetizing antipasti selection and specializes (mid-week) in fresh seafood. Mon–Sat 11.30am–10.30pm.

Dynamo Pštrossova 29 ☎ 224 932 020; metro Národní třída. Eye-catching retro 1960s designer decor, competent fish, chicken, steak and pasta dishes and an incredible single malt whisky selection make this place a popular, trendy little spot. Daily 11.30am–midnight.

Millhouse Sushi – Kaitan Na příkopě 22; metro Můstek. Minimalist conveyor-belt sushi has arrived in Prague, at the back of the Slovanský dům; choose as many dishes (60–180Kč) as you wish, or dig into some of the grills or nigiri on offer. Daily 11am–11pm.

Ostroff Střelecký ostrov ☎ 224 919 235, ⊛ www.ostroff.cz; metro Národní třída. Very popular basement Italian restaurant and summer terrace on the first island you come to on the most Legií. Terrace daily 2–11pm; restaurant Mon–Fri noon–2pm & 7–11pm, Sat 7–11pm.

Plzeňská restaurace Obecní dům, náměstí Republiky 5 ☏ 222 002 770, ⓦ www.obecni-dum.cz; metro Náměstí Republiky. Decent Czech pub-restaurant in the cellar of the Obecní dům, cheaper than the French restaurant upstairs, but nothing like the same aesthetic experience. Daily 11am–11pm.

Zahrada v opeře Legerova 75 ☏ 224 239 685, ⓦ www.zahradavopere.cz; metro Muzeum. Striking modern interior and beautifully presented food from around the world at democratic prices. The entrance is around the back of the Radio Free Europe building. Daily 11.30am–1am.

Expensive

Le Bistrot de Marlène Plavecká 4 ☏ 224 921 853; metro Karlovo náměstí. Very good rustic French cuisine in a pleasant little restaurant with excellent service, in the backstreets near Vyšehrad. Mon–Fri noon–2.30pm & 7–10.30pm, Sat 7–10.30pm.

Casablanca Na příkopě 10 ☏ 224 210 519, ⓦ www.casablanca.co.il; metro Můstek. The full Sephardi monty, both in terms of decor, belly dancing and food (500Kč a head for lunch; 1000Kč a head for dinner). Daily 11.30am–midnight.

Francouzská restaurace Obecní dům, náměstí Republiky 5 ☏ 222 002 270, ⓦ www.obecni-dum.cz; metro Náměstí Republiky. The Art Nouveau decor in this cavernous hall is absolutely stunning; the setting is formal and therefore puts a lot of tourists off, though the French-style food's actually very good and not really that expensive. Daily noon–4pm & 6–11pm.

Vyšehrad and the eastern suburbs

Moderate

Il Ritrovo Lublaňská 11, Vinohrady ☏ 224 251 475, ⓦ www.ilritrovo.cz; tram #6 or #11 from metro I. P. Pavlova to Bruselská stop. Excellent Italian-run outfit with a wide range of pasta dishes and good salads, a great antipasti bar and delicious *tiramisu* for dessert. Mon–Fri noon–3pm & 6–11pm.

Modrá řeka (Blue River) Mánesova 13, Vinohrady ☏ 222 251 601; metro Muzeum/Náměstí Míru. Family-run Bosnian Muslim restaurant with attentive service, and good Balkan home cooking. Mon–Fri 11am–11pm, Sat 5–11pm.

Myslivna (The Hunting Lodge) Jagellonská 21, Žižkov ☏ 222 723 252, ⓦ www.myslivna-restaurant.cz; metro Flora. A hearty game restaurant, serving up excellent venison and quail in the suburbs. Mon–Fri noon–4pm & 5–11pm, Sat & Sun 6–11pm.

Radost FX Café Bělehradská 120, Vinohrady; metro I. P. Pavlova. Without doubt the best choice of vegetarian dishes in town (okay, so there's not much competition), drawing in a large expat posse, particularly for the Sunday brunch. Daily 11.30am–4am.

Holešovice and the western suburbs

Inexpensive

La Crêperie Janovského 4, Holešovice; tram #5, #12 or #17 to Strossmayerovo náměstí stop. Stylish French-run crêperie serving sweet and savoury pancakes, French liqueurs and even the rare Nová Paka beer. Mon–Sat noon–11pm, Sun 11am–10pm.

Moderate

Sushi Bar Zborovská 49, Smíchov ☏ 290 001 517, ⓦ www.sushi.cz; tram #6, #9, #12, #22 or #23 to Újezd stop. Minimalist sushi bar in the part of Smíchov just south of Malá Strana. The sushi and sashimi set dishes are delicious, but beware of mounting bills. Daily noon–10pm.

U cedru (The Cedar) Na hutích 13, Dejvice ☏ 233 342 974; metro Dejvická. A very reasonable Lebanese joint in the suburbs, where you can easily assemble a very decent *meze*. Daily 11am–11pm.

Expensive

Hanavský pavilón Letenské sady 173, Letná ☏ 233 323 641; tram #18 or #22 from metro Malostranská to Chotkovy sady stop. Highly ornate Art Nouveau pleasure pavilion high above the Vltava, with stunning views and a gamey Czech menu. Daily 11.30am–1am.

Svatá Klara (Saint Clare) U Trojského zámku, Troja ☏ 2688 0405; taxi or bus #112 from metro Nádraží Holešovice. Romantic setting for this expense-account restaurant situated between the zoo and the chateau in Troja; the game is the business. Daily 7pm–1am.

Pubs and bars

In the last ten years the Prague **pub** scene has diversified enormously, with the establishment of expat American-style bars, "Irish" pubs and smarter, designer places that attract a more mixed crowd of young professionals. Nevertheless, there are still plenty of traditional Czech pubs (*pivnice* in Czech), smoky, male-dominated places, primarily designed for drinking copious quantities of Czech beer by the half-litre. If you're not interested in drinking (and preferably smoking), you're going to have a hard time having a good time in many of them. Still, as with British pubs, whatever their faults, they remain deeply embedded in the local culture, and to sample that, you'll need to sample the amber nectar. Food, where served, is almost always of the traditional Czech variety (for more on Czech cuisine, see p.193) – cheap and filling, but ultimately it could shorten your life by a couple of years.

Pubs and bars are marked on the colour maps at the back of the book.

Alcohol

Alcohol consumption among Czechs has always been high, and in the decade following the events of 1968 it doubled, as a whole generation found solace in drinking, mostly beer. The Czechs have been top of the world league table of beer consumption for some time now, though it's a problem which seldom spills out onto the streets; violence in pubs is uncommon and you won't see that many drunks in public.

Czech **beer** ranks among the best in the world and the country remains the true home of most of the lager drunk around the world today. It was in the Bohemian city of Plzeň (Pilsen) that the first **bottom-fermented** beer was introduced in 1842, after complaints from the citizens about the quality of the top-fermented predecessor. The new brewing style quickly spread to Germany, and is now blamed for the bland rubbish served up in the English-speaking world as lager or Pils.

The distinctive flavour of Czech beer comes from the famous hand-picked Bohemian hops known as Žatec (Saaz) Red, the Moravian barley, and the soft local water; it should then be served with a high content of absorbed carbon dioxide – hence the thick, creamy head. Under the Communists, brewing methods in the Czech Republic remained stuck in the old ways, but the 1990s have seen many breweries opt for modernization: pasteurization, de-oxidization, rapid maturation and carbon dioxide injections – all of which mean less taste, more fizz. It's a development against which the Czech Beer Party and Britain's own Campaign for Real Ale (CAMRA) are fighting hard.

Beer (*pivo*) is served by the half-litre; if you want anything smaller, you must specifically ask for a *malé pivo* (0.3l). The average jar is medium strength, usually about 1050 specific gravity or 4.2 percent alcohol. Somewhat confusingly, the Czechs class their beers using the Balling scale, which measures the original gravity, calculated according to the amount of malt and dissolved sugar present before fermentation. The most common varieties are 10° (*desítka*), which are generally slightly weaker than 12° (*dvanáctka*). Light beer (*světlé*) is the norm, but many pubs also serve a slightly sweeter dark variety (*černé*) – or, if you prefer, you can have a mixture of the two (*řezané*). For more on Czech beer, see p.206.

Czech **wine** will never win over as many people as its beer, but since the import of French and German vines in the fourteenth century a modest selection of medium-quality wines has been produced. The main wine region is South Moravia, though a little is produced around the Bohemian town of

Mělník (see p.168). Suffice to say that most domestic wine is pretty drinkable – Frankovka is a perfectly respectable, though slightly sweet, red; Veltlínské zelené a good, dry white – and rarely much more than 50Kč a bottle in shops, while the best stuff can only be had from a good wine shop, or the private wine cellars, hundreds of which still exist out in the regions. A Czech speciality to look out for is *burčák*, a very young, misty wine of varying (and often very strong) alcoholic content, which appears on the streets in the vine harvest season in September.

All the usual **spirits** are on sale and known by their generic names, with rum and vodka dominating the market. The home production of brandies is a national pastime, which results in some almost terminally strong liquors. The most renowned of the lot is **slivovice**, a plum brandy originally from the border hills between Moravia and Slovakia. You'll probably also come across *borovička*, a popular Slovak firewater, made from pine trees; *myslivec* is a rough brandy with a firm following. There's also a fair selection of intoxicating herbal concoctions: *fernet* is a dark-brown bitter drink, known as *bavorák* (Bavarian beer) when it's mixed with tonic, while *becherovka* is a supposedly healthy herbal spirit from the Bohemian spa town of Karlovy Vary, with a very unusual, almost medicinal taste.

The Czech Republic is also one of the few countries in the world where **absinthe** is still legal. The preferred poison of Parisian painters and poets in the 1920s, absinthe is a nasty green spirit made from fermented wormwood – it even gets a Biblical mention in Revelations: "and the name of the star is called

Czech beers

The most famous Czech beer is **Pilsner Urquell**, known to the Czechs as Plzeňský Prazdroj, the original bottom-fermented Pils from Plzeň (Pilsen), a city 80km southwest of Prague. Plzeň also boasts the **Gambrinus** brewery, whose domestic sales actually exceed those of Pilsner Urquell. The other big Bohemian brewing town is České Budějovice (Budweis), home to the country's biggest selling export beer, **Budvar**, a mildly flavoured brew for Bohemia but still leagues ahead of Budweiser, the German name for Budvar that was adopted by American brewers, Anheuser-Busch, in 1876 (and a cause of litigious grief ever since).

The biggest brewery in the country is Prague breweries (majority-owned by British beer giants, Bass), whose Smíchov brewery produces **Staropramen** (meaning "ancient spring"), a typical Bohemian brew with a mild hoppy flavour. Some Staropramen is also produced at the Holešovice brewery, better known for its popular, dark **Měšťan** beer. The city's other brewery is in the southern suburb of **Braník**; it produces a light, malty brew and was one of the first to opt for modernization. Prague also boasts several **micro-breweries**: U Fleku (see p.209) – which has been brewing **Flek**, a dark caramel concoction, since 1499 – is now sadly a tourist trap; the beer produced at the newly established *Novoměstský pivovar* (see p.209) is vastly inferior, but the place itself is preferable, as is the nearby *Pivovarsky dum* (see p.209).

It's difficult to avoid **Radegast**, a very popular drinkable brew from North Moravia, and the German-owned **Krušovice** beer. Beers worth seeking out include the award-winning, hoppy and slightly bitter **Velkopopovický kozel**, Bohemian brews Bernard and Pelhřimov, both of which are unpasteurised. Rather worryingly urban Czechs have been impressed by the novelty of **Velvet**, a dark, bland, electrically-pumped ale produced by Prague breweries in Ostrava, and its more Guinness-like cousin, **Kelt**. For the definitive selection of (albeit bottled) Czech beers, head for the *Pivní galerie* (see p.230).

Wormwood: and the third part of the waters became wormwood; and many men died of the waters, because they were made bitter." St John wasn't wrong: at 170 degrees proof, it's dangerous stuff and virtually undrinkable neat. To make it vaguely palatable, you need to set light to an absinthe-soaked spoonful of sugar, and then mix the caramelized mess with the absinthe.

There's not much to say about Czech **soft drinks**, with the exception of the high-energy drink Semtex, a can of which will amuse friends back home. Last of all, if you're looking for a decent **mineral water** (*minerální voda*), ask for the ubiquitous Mattoni, a mild and not too fizzy option.

Hradčany

U černého vola (The Black Ox) Loretánské náměstí 1; tram #22 from metro Malostranská to Pohořelec stop. Great traditional Prague pub doing a brisk business providing the popular light beer Velkopopovický kozel in huge quantities to thirsty local workers, plus a few basic pub snacks. Daily 10am–10pm.

Malá Strana

The nearest metro for the pubs in this section is Malostranská, followed either by a short walk or a stop or two on tram #12, #22 or #23.
Baráčnická rychta Na tržiště 23 (down a narrow passageway leading south off Nerudova). A real survivor – a small backstreet *pivnice* squeezed in between the embassies, with a cheap and filling menu. Daily noon–midnight.
Jo's Bar Malostranské náměstí 7. A narrow bar in Malá Strana that is the original expat/backpacker hang-out. Tex-Mex food served all day, bottled beer only and a heaving crowd guaranteed most evenings. Downstairs is *Jo's Garáž* (see p.212). Daily 11am–4am.
Na Kampě Na Kampě 15. Round the corner from the formal restaurant of the same name is this friendly (and even child-friendly) *pivnice* offering tasty pub snacks; you can sit outside or wander down to the riverside with your Pilsner Urquell. Daily noon–midnight.
Scarlett O'Hara's Mostecká 21 ⓦ www.scarlettoharas.cz. One of Prague's many Irish-theme pubs, better than the *James Joyce* (see p.208), not as cosy as *Molly Malone's* (see p.208), but the only place to watch sports on TV on this side of the river. Daily 3pm–2am.
U bílé kuželky (The White Bowling Pin) Míšeňská 12. Not a bad pub considering its touristy location right by the Charles Bridge. Reasonably priced Pilsner Urquell,

Czech pub food and the occasional accordionist. Daily 11am–11pm.
U hrocha (The Hippo) Thunovská 10. A genuine smoky, Czech local in the heart of Malá Strana – difficult to believe but true. Cheap grub and beer. Daily noon–11.30pm.
U kocoura (The Cat) Nerudova 2. One of the few surviving pubs on Nerudova, owned by the Beer Party, but, for the most part, abandoned by its old clientele. Some of the best Budvar in town, plus the obvious Czech stomach-fillers. Daily 11am–11pm.
U malého Glena Karmelitská 23 ⓦ www.malyglen.cz. Smart-looking pub/jazz bar that attracts a fair mixture of Czechs and expats thanks to its better-than-average food and live music in the basement. Daily 10am–2am.

Staré Město

Banana Bar Štupartská 9; metro Náměstí Republiky. Strange kitsch disco bar above *La Provence* restaurant deep in the heart of expat territory. It has table-top dancers (of both sexes) and gets absolutely packed out with Czech thirtysomethings in suits. Worth experiencing once (perhaps). Daily 8pm–2am.
Blatnička Michalská 6; metro Můstek. Wine shop where you can drink straight from the barrel, take away, or head next door to the popular basement *vinárna* for more wine and cheap Czech food. Shop Mon–Fri 10am–6pm; wine bar daily 3pm–midnight.
Chateau Rouge Malá Štupartská; metro Náměstí Republiky. Loud, posey boozer in the heart of the so-called French Quarter or "Bermuda Triangle", that attracts an international crowd in search of sex, drugs and drink. Daily 4pm–4am.
Divadlo na zábradlí Anenské náměstí 5 ⓦ www.nazabradli.cz; metro Staroměstská. Lovely pale pea-green wood fittings in this theatre bar that attracts an intellectual crowd. Braník on tap and lots of spirits to

It's common practice in Prague pubs to share a table with other eaters or drinkers; *je tu volno*? (Is this seat free?) is the standard question. Waiter service is the norm even in pubs, where if you sit tight a beer should come your way. From this point on your beer should hopefully be replenished by a waiter as soon as you near the bottom of your glass. Note that pouring beer from one glass into another is a social no-no. You may have to ask for the menu (*jídelní lístek*) in pubs – and some cafés – to indicate that you wish to eat. When food arrives for your neighbours, it's common practice to wish them *bon appétit* (*dobrou chut*). When you want to leave, simply say *zaplatím, prosím* (literally "I'll pay, please"), and your tab will be totted up. A modest form of **tipping** exists in all establishments, generally done by rounding up the bill to the nearest few crowns, though beware that the waiters haven't already done this for you. On leaving, bid your neighbours farewell (*na shledanou*).

choose from. Mon–Fri 10am–1am, Sat & Sun 3pm–1am.

James Joyce Liliová 10 ⓦ www.jamesjoyce.cz; **metro Staroměstská.** A soulless and expensive re-creation of an Irish pub, with prices that only foreign businessmen think are reasonable – go to *Molly Malone's* instead (see below). Daily 10am–1am.

Legends Týn (Ungelt) ⓦ www.legends.cz; **metro Náměstí Republiky.** Heaving, loud, full-blown expat bar in the Týn courtyard, which shows the big TV sports events and has disco theme nights. Daily 11am–3am.

Konvikt Bartolomějská 11; **metro Národní třída.** Popular, central, smoky Czech local serving Pilsner and Czech food. Mon–Fri 9am–midnight, Sat & Sun 11am–midnight.

Kozička Kozí 4 ⓦ www.kozicka.cz; **metro Staroměstská.** Busy, designer bare-brick cellar bar with cheap Czech food, tucked away just a short walk from Staroměstské náměstí. Mon–Fri noon–4am, Sat & Sun 6pm–4am.

Marquis de Sade Templová 8; **metro Náměstí Republiky.** Great space: huge high ceiling, big comfy sofas, and a mostly expat crowd. Crap beer and limited snacks, but a good place to start the evening (before the live band kicks in) or end it (after they've packed up). Daily noon–2am.

Molly Malone's U Obecního dvora 4 ⓦ www.mollymalones.cz; **metro Staroměstská.** Best of Prague's Irish pubs with real Irish staff (who speak very little Czech), an open fire, draught Kilkenny and Guinness (neither of them very cheap), and decent Irish-themed food. Daily 11am–2am.

Od soumraku do úsvitu (From Dawn 'til Dusk) Týnská 19; **metro Náměstí Republiky.** Atmospheric, low-lit, late-night bar in the backstreets behind the Týn church, serving cocktails to a smart, but not totally posey crowd. Mon–Fri 2pm–4am, Sat 6pm–4am, Sun 6pm–3am.

Radegast Templová 2; **metro Náměstí Republiky.** Typically smoky, boozy pub divided into booths, serving its namesake plus decent Czech food. Attracts Czechs and expats. Daily 11am–12.30pm.

U medvídků (The Little Bears) Na Perštýně 7; **metro Národní třída.** A Prague beer hall going back to the thirteenth century and still much as it ever was (make sure you turn right when you enter, and avoid the new bar to the left). The Budvar comes thick and fast, and the food is absolutely standard. Mon–Sat 11.30am–11pm, Sun 11.30am–10pm.

U milosrdných (The Merciful) Kozí 21; **metro Staroměstská.** Wood-panelled pub far enough away from the tourist crowds to serve as a genuine local, dishing up typical Czech food and Plzeň beers. Mon–Fri 10am–11pm, Sat 11am–11pm.

U mravence (The Ant) U radnice 20; **metro Staroměstská.** Incredibly, given the top tourist location, this is an alright Czech pub, serving typical Czech pub food at reasonable prices. Daily 11am–midnight.

U zlatého tygra (The Golden Tiger) Husova 17; **metro Staroměstská.** Small central *pivnice* serving excellent Plzeňský Prazdroj to a very local following; the late writer and bohemian, Bohumil Hrabal, was a semi-permanent resident. Daily 3–11pm.

Nové Město

American Bar Obecní dům, náměstí Republiky 5; **metro Náměstí Republiky.** The 1910 bar in the basement of the Obecní dům has been restored to its former glamour. Daily 11am–11pm.

Billiard Club Trojická 10, Nove Město; tram #18 or #24 from Karlovo náměstí to Botanická zahrada stop. Theatre converted into a pool and billiard hall with cheap beer and long hours, and a good pub next door. Daily 1pm–2am.

Branický sklípek Vodičkova 26; metro Můstek. Convenient downtown pub decked out like a pine furniture showroom, serving typical Czech fare, and jugs of Prague's Braník beer. The rough and ready *Branická formanka* next door opens and closes earlier. Mon–Fri 9am–11pm, Sat & Sun 11am–11pm.

Jágr Sport Bar Václavské náměstí 56 ⓦwww.jagrsportbar; metro Muzeum. A shrine to the Czech ice hockey player, Jaromír Jágr, famous (until recently) for his mullet. It's difficult to see this place lasting long, but for the moment, it has kitsch curiosity value. Daily 11am–2am.

Novoměstský pivovar Vodičkova 20 ⓦwww.npivovar.cz; metro Národní třída. Micro-brewery which serves its own misty home brew, plus Czech food, in a series of bright, sprawling modern beer halls. Mon–Sat 11.30am–10.30pm, Sun noon–10pm.

Ostroff Střelecký ostrov ⓦwww.ostroff.cz; metro Národní třída. Very popular sleek, long bar and summer terrace overlooking the National Theatre from the first island you come to on the most Legií. The terrace gets packed in summer, as does the Italian restaurant below. Terrace daily 2–11pm.

Pivovarský dům Corner of Lipová/Ječná; metro Karlovo náměstí. Busy micro-brewery dominated by its big shiny copper vats, serving light, mixed and dark unfiltered beer (plus banana, coffee and wheat varieties), and all the standard Czech pub dishes (including *pivný sýr*). Daily 11am–11.30pm.

Potrefená husa (The Wounded Goose) Jiráskovo náměstí 1; metro Karlovo náměstí. Smart, convivial brick cellar pub that attracts a mix of young and middle-aged professionals; Staropramen and decent pub food on offer. Daily 11.30am–1am.

Red Room Křemencova 17; metro Národní třída. Seriously posey cocktail bar with intense blood red decor, superb vodka mixes and good weekend brunch. Daily 11am–3am.

U bubeníčků (The Little Drummer) Myslíkova 8; metro Karlovo náměstí. Good, unpretentious

place to down a few halves of Pilsner Urquell and eat some simple Czech cuisine after visiting the Mánes gallery. Daily 11am–11pm.

U Fleků Křemencova 11; metro Karlovo náměstí. Famous medieval *pivnice* where the unique dark 13° beer, Flek, has been exclusively brewed and consumed since 1499. Seats over 500 German tourists at a go, serves short measures (0.4l), slaps an extra charge on for the music and still you have to queue. This is a tourist trap and the only reason to visit is to sample the beer, which you're best off doing during the day. Daily 9am–11pm.

U havrana (The Crow) Hálkova 8; metro I. P. Pavlova. Surprisingly unseedy, normal pub serving food and Měšťan and Kozel beer throughout the night. Mon–Fri 24hr, Sat & Sun 6pm–6am.

U kotvy (The Anchor) Spalená 11; metro Národní třída. All-night spot that's perfect for a last Staropramen before you attempt to work out how to catch a night tram home. Daily 24hr.

U zpěváčků (The Choir Boy) Na struze 7; metro Národní třída. Loud and smoky workers/musicians' pub just around the corner from the Národní divadlo, with an ironic line in Marxist-Leninist tracts, and the local Staropramen on tap. Mon–Thurs 11am–2am, Fri 11am–5am, Sat 11am–5am & Sun noon–2am.

Zlatá hvězda (The Golden Star) Ve Smečkách 12 ⓦwww.sportbar.cz; metro Muzeum. The main reason to hit this big, loud pub is to watch the match you want on the numerous satellite TV screens. Mon–Thurs 11am–2am, Fri & Sat 11am–4.30am, Sun noon–midnight.

Vyšehrad and the eastern suburbs

Akropolis Kubelíkova 27, Žižkov ⓦwww.akropolis.cz; metro Jiřího z Poděbrad. Prague's very popular smoke-filled world music venue is also a great place just to have a drink or a bite to eat as well as listen to live gigs. Mon–Fri 10am–1am, Sat & Sun 4pm–1am.

Hapu Orkická 8, Žižkov; metro Flora. Chilled out Žižkov cocktail bar without the snooty/ uptight factor; lots of great mixes and comfy sofas in which to sink. Mon–Sat 6pm–2am.

Hostinec pod Vyšehradem Vratislavova 4, Vyšehrad; tram #3, #16 or #21 from metro Karlovo náměstí to Výtoň stop. Neo-Gothic on

In pubs and inexpensive restaurants, the **menu** (*jídelní lístek*), which should be displayed outside, is often in Czech only and deciphering it without a grounding in the language can be quite a feat. Just bear in mind that the general rule is for the right-hand column to list the prices, while the far left column often gives you the estimated weight of every dish in grammes; if what you get weighs more or less, the price alters accordingly.

The menu is usually divided into various sections beginning with *predkrmy* (starters) or *polévky* (soups), followed by the main courses: *jídla na objednávku* (food to order), *hotová jídla* (ready-made food), *drubez a ryby* (fowl and fish) and, if you're lucky, *bezmasa* (vegetarian dishes). Side dishes are listed under *přílohy*; puddings, where available, are listed under the heading *moucníky*.

the outside but perfectly normal inside, serving cheap mugs of Gambrinus and a typical daily menu. Daily 11am–11pm.

U Houdků Bořivojova 110, Žižkov; tram #5 or #26 from metro Náměstí Republiky to Husinecká stop. Friendly pub in the heart of Žižkov with a beer garden, Velkopopvický kozel and cheap Czech food. Daily 10am–11pm.

U růžového sadu (The Rose Garden) Mánesova 89, Vinohrady; metro Jiřího z Poděbrad. Imaginatively decorated for a Czech pub and perfectly situated if you're visiting the Plečnik Church. Mon–Thurs 10am–midnight, Fri 10am–1am, Sat 11am–1am, Sun 11.30am–10pm.

U vystřelenýho oka (The Shot-Out Eye) U božích bojovníků 3, Žižkov; metro Florenc. Big, loud, smoky, heavy-drinking pub just south of Žižkov Hill, off Husitská, with (unusually) good music playing and lashings of Měšťan beer, plus absinthe chasers. Mon–Sat 3.30pm–1am.

Zvonařka (The Bell) Šafaříkova 1, Vinohrady ⓦwww.zvonarka.cz; tram #6 or #11 from metro I. P. Pavlova to Nuselské schody stop. The slick, futuristic interior hosts DJs at the weekend, while the terrace has great views over the Nuselské schody and Botič valley. Mon–Sat 11am–2am, Sun 11am–midnight.

Holešovice and the western suburbs

Hospoda na verandách Nádražní 90, Smíchov; metro Anděl. The new official Staropramen brewery tap, and therefore the place to taste Prague's most popular beer. Daily 11am–11pm.

Letenský zámeček Letenské sady, Holešovice ⓦwww.letenskyzamecek.cz; tram #1 or #25 from metro Vltavská to Letenské náměstí stop.

Convenient beer garden opposite the Národní technické muzeum serving Velkopopovický kozel, and slightly upgraded Czech pub food, including some veggie options, in the *Ullman* restaurant inside. Daily 11am–11.30pm.

Na slamníku (The Straw Bed) Schwaigrova 7, Bubeneč; bus #131 from metro Hradčanská. Useful place to end up after a stroll in Stromovka: a *pivnice* serving good Czech grub and Staropramen beer. Daily 11am–midnight.

Na staré kovárně v Braníku (The Old Blacksmith's in Braník) Kamenická 17, Holešovice; tram #26 from outside Masarykovo nádraží to Kamenická stop. Nicely refurbished pub that's popular with the locals and a crowd of young Czechs. Small menu of meaty daily dishes, Radegast beer and good music. Mon–Sat 11am–1am, Sun 11am–11.30pm.

Práce (Work) Kamenická 9, Holešovice; tram #26 from outside Masarykovo nádraží to Kamenická stop. Small late-night bar with lots of Communist memorabilia, including a portrait of Stalin overlooking the table football. Daily 4pm–5am.

U buldoka (The Bulldog) Preslova 1, Smíchov ⓦwww.ubuldoka.cz; metro Anděl. A half-decent Smíchov pub is hard to find, but this is one, serving Gambrinus and with occasional DJ nights. Mon–Fri 11am–midnight, Sat & Sun noon–midnight.

U houbaře (The Mushroom) Dukelských hrdinů 30; tram #5 from metro Náměstí Republiky to Veletržní stop. Comfortable, perfectly normal pub serving Pilsner Urquell and pub food, perfectly placed directly opposite the Veletržní palác (Museum of Modert Art). Daily 11am–midnight.

Clubs and live venues

W hile most Praguers go to bed pretty early, a dedicated minority, including many of the city's expats and tourists, stay up until the wee small hours. To service this crowd, Prague has a good selection of late-night drinking holes (covered in "Pubs and Bars" starting p.205) and a handful of half-decent **clubs**. Local DJs, and the odd international one, perform at most of these, and there are a few good one-off raves throughout the year (a case of scouring the fly posters around), but many clubs double as **live music venues**. As well as indigenous live acts, spanning the entire range of musical tastes from Czech reggae to thrash, a surprising array of world music bands find their way to Prague, along with a few big names from the USA and UK. Note that, due to Prague's strict music licensing laws, clubs in residential districts (and that includes most of the city centre) are under constant threat of closure, so don't be surprised if some of those listed below have fallen by the wayside.

Drink **prices** in clubs and live venues are inevitably higher than in the pubs, but the hike-up is usually relatively modest and entry to most late-night places is likewise pretty negligible. To find out the latest on the city's up-and-coming events, check the **listings** sections in *Prague Post* (Ⓦ www.praguepost.com), the bilingual bi-weekly free listings handout *Do města/Downtown* (Ⓦ www .downtown.cz), or the Czech listings monthly *Culture in Prague/Česká kultura* (Ⓦ www.ceskakultura.cz), and, once again, keep your eyes peeled for flyers and posters. To buy **tickets** in advance, try one of the agencies such as Ticketpro, which has branches all over the city, with outlets in the Staroměstská radnice (Old Town Hall), Staroměstské náměstí, Staré Město (Mon–Fri 9am–7pm, Sat & Sun 9am–6pm; Ⓦ www.ticketpro.cz), plus at Salvátorská 10, Staré Město and in the Lucerna pasáž, Štěpánská 61, Nové Město.

Rock, pop, dance & world music

Major Western **bands** often include Prague in their European tours and, to be sure of a full house, many offer tickets at below their usual price in the West. There are gigs by Czech bands almost every night in the city's clubs and discos – a selection of the better venues is listed below, though you should always check in the local listings before setting out.

Larger live venues

Kongresové centrum 5 května 65, Nusle ☎ 261 222 062, ⊛ www.kcp.cz; metro Vyšehrad. Revamped (but still very ugly) 1970s concrete monstrosity used for the old Communist Party congresses.

Výstaviště U Výstaviště, Holešovice ☎ 233 378 222, ⊛ www.vystaviste-praha.cz; tram #5, #12 or #17 to Výstaviště stop. The 1891 Exhibition Hall at Výstaviště is an atmospheric aircraft hangar of a place to watch a band, even if the acoustics aren't up to much.

Strahov Stadion Vaníčkova, Břevnov ⊛ www.cstv.cz/strahov.htm; bus #176 from metro Karlovo náměstí. Europe's largest stadium, which can hold an incredible 200,000 spectators.

Smaller live venues and clubs

Futurum Zborovská 7, Smíchov ☎ 257 328 571, ⊛ www.musicbar.cz; metro Anděl. Impressive, futuristic, high-tech club whose DJs take their house and techno seriously. Daily until 3am.

Jo's Garáž Malostranské náměstí 7, Malá Strana; tram #12 or #22 one stop from metro Malostranská. Loud, sweaty and packed backpacker and expat disco in the cellar under *Jo's Bar*. Daily until 4am.

Karlovy lázně Novotného lavka 1, Staré Město ☎ 222 220 502, ⊛ www.karlovylazne.cz; metro Staroměstská. Mega, high-tech club on four floors of an old bathhouse by the Charles Bridge; techno on the top floor, progressively more retro as you descend the ground floor. Daily until 5am.

Lávka Novotného lavka 1, Staré Město ☎ 224 214 797, ⊛ www.lavka.cz; metro Staroměstská. Cheesy disco with a great riverside terrace overlooking the Charles Bridge and the Hrad. Disco daily until 5am.

Lucerna music bar Vodičkova 36, Nové Město ☎ 224 217 108, ⊛ www.musicbar.cz; metro Můstek. Without doubt the best gig venue in Prague, a gilded turn-of-the-century hall with balcony, situated underneath the Lucerna pasáž. Doors open at 7pm.

Malostranská beseda Malostranské náměstí 21, Malá Strana ☎ 257 532 092; tram #12 or #22 one stop from metro Malostranská. Ramshackle, inexpensive venue that attracts lots of Czechs, despite its location. The programme is a mixture of rock, roots and jazz. Gigs start at 8.30pm.

Mánes Masarykovo nábřeží 250, Nové Město ☎ 224 914 899; metro Karlovo náměstí. Occasional riverside disco, often with a Latin influence, above the functionalist art gallery of the same name. Fri & Sat only until 4am.

Mecca U Průhonu 3, Holešovice ☎ 283 870 522, ⊛ www.mecca.cz; tram #12 or #14 from metro Nádraží Holešovice to U Průhonu stop. Despite being out in Prague 7, this converted factory is one of the best, and most popular, clubs in Prague. Daily 7pm–2am.

Palác Akropolis Kubelíkova 27, Žižkov ☎ 222 712 287, ⊛ www.palacakropolis.cz; tram #5, #9 or #26 to Lipanská stop. Two live venue spaces and a whole complex of bars in scruffy Žižkov, this place is the nerve centre of the city's alternative world music and puts on the most eclectic programme of gigs in Prague. Live venue doors open 7pm.

Radost FX Bělehradská 120, Vinohrady ☎ 224 254 776, ⊛ www.radostfx.cz; metro I. P. Pavlova. Still the slickest (and longest-running) all-round dance club venue in Prague, attracting the usual mix of clubbers and despots; good veggie café upstairs (see p.204). Daily until 5am.

Roxy Dlouhá 33, Staré Město ☎ 224 826 296, ⊛ www.roxy.cz; metro náměstí Republiky. The *Roxy* is a great little venue: a laid-back rambling old theatre with an interesting programme of events from arty films and exhibitions to live acts and DJ nights. Daily from 8pm.

Jazz

Prague has a surprisingly long indigenous jazz tradition, and is home to a handful of good jazz clubs. With little money to attract acts from abroad, the artists are almost exclusively Czech and tend to do virtually the entire round of venues each month. The one exception to all this is *AghaRTA*, which attracts a few big names each year. More often than not, it's a good idea to book a table at the jazz clubs listed below – this is particularly true of *AghaRTA* and *Reduta*.

AghaRTA Jazz Centrum Krakovská 5, Nové Město ☏ 222 211 275, ⊛ www.agharta.cz; metro Muzeum. Probably the best jazz club in Prague, with a good mix of Czechs and foreigners and a consistently good programme of gigs; situated in a side street off the top end of Wenceslas Square. Mon–Fri 5pm–1am, Sat & Sun 7pm–1am.

Jazz Club Železná Železná 16, Staré Město ☏ 224 239 697, ⊛ www.jazzclub.cz; metro Můstek. Inexpensive, centrally located cellar venue that puts on a mixed bag of trad and contemporary jazz, blues and fusion, plus the odd comedy night. Daily gigs from 9pm.

Reduta Národní 20, Nové Město ☏ 224 912 246; metro Národní třída. Prague's best-known jazz club – Bill Clinton played his sax here in front of Havel. Gigs daily from 9pm; box office open from 3pm.

U malého Glena Karmelitská 23, Malá Strana ☏ 257 531 717, ⊛ www.malyglen.cz; tram #12 or #22 one stop from metro Malostranská. Tiny downstairs stage worth checking out for its eclectic mix of Latin jazz, be-bop and blues. Daily 7pm–2am.

U staré paní (The Old Woman) Michalská 9, Staré Město ☏ 224 228 090, ⊛ www.ustarepani.cz; metro Můstek. Decent old town jazz restaurant that really gets going when the live contemporary jazz kicks in from 9pm onwards. Daily 7pm–1am.

Gay and lesbian nightlife

Prague does not have a large, nor very upfront **gay and lesbian scene**, but if the scene has a spiritual heart, it's in leafy Vinohrady and neighbouring Žižkov. On the web, you can find out the latest from ⊛ gayguide.net/europe/czech/prague and from the website of *Amigo* magazine (see below). Once here, *Prague Post* does the occasional update on gay and lesbian nightlife; otherwise you'll need to get hold of the bi-monthly gay magazine *Amigo* (⊛ www.amigo.cz), or the lesbian publications *Promluv* and *Alia*. You'll also find useful flyers at the places listed below. Note that the age of consent is fifteen whatever your sexual orientation.

"A" Klub Milíčova 32, Žižkov ☏ 222 781 623; tram #5, #9 or #26 to Lipanská stop. The city's premier lesbian bar with women-only Friday nights. It's small but stylish and definitely worth checking out. Daily 7pm–6am.

Arco Voroněžská 24, Vinohrady ☏ 271 742 908, ⊛ www.arco-guesthouse.cz; tram #4, #22 or #23 from metro Náměstí Míru to Krymská stop. Gay internet café and guesthouse. Mon–Fri 8am–1am, Sat & Sun 9am–1am.

Babylonia Martinská 6, Staré Město; metro Národní třída. Prague's most centrally located gay sauna, with steam baths, pools and massage on offer. Daily 2pm–3am.

Friends Náprstkova 1, Staré Město ☏ 221 635 408, ⊛ www.friends-prague.cz; metro Národní třída. Friendly, laid-back mixed gay/lesbian cellar bar in the centre of the old town. Daily 4pm–3am.

Gejzee...r Vinohradská 40, Vinohrady ☏ 222 516 036, ⊛ www.gejzeer.cz; metro Náměstí Míru. Prague's largest and most popular gay club with dance floor, DJs and the inevitable darkroom. Tues–Thurs 6pm–4am, Fri & Sat 9pm–5am.

Piano Bar Milesovská 10, Žižkov; metro Jiřího z Poděbrad. Popular, relaxed bar with billiards, a piano and a mixture of ages. Daily 5pm–midnight.

Pinocchio Seifertova 3, Žižkov ☏ 222 710 773, ⊛ www.pinocchio-club.cz; metro Hlavní nádraží. Bar, club, internet café and even hotel, all rolled into one, a short stroll into Žižkov.

Stella Lužická 10, Vinohrady ☏ 224 257 869; metro Náměstí Míru. One of the most popular and relaxed mixed gay/lesbian hot spots in the capital – ring the bell to gain entry. Daily 8pm–5am.

Tom's Bar Pernerova 4, Karlín ☏ 224 813 802; metro Florenc. Small but popular bar and downstairs darkroom frequented almost exclusively by Czech gay men. Daily 8pm–4am.

U Rudolfa Mezibranská 3, Nové Město; metro Muzeum. Straightforward Czech gay pub just off Wenceslas Square. Daily 4pm–2am.

The arts and festivals

Alongside the city's numerous cafés, pubs and clubs, there's a rich **cultural life** in Prague. Music is everywhere in the city: especially in the summer, when the streets, churches, palaces, opera houses, concert halls and even the gardens are filled with the strains of classical music. True, there are too many Mozart concerts pandering to the tourist trade, and too many renditions of works by the big four Czech composers, but equally there are also some very high-quality concerts by Prague's three excellent orchestras.

Czech **theatre and film** both struggled to find their way in the 1990s, following the virtual ending of both subsidies and censorship. Even if you don't understand Czech, there are theatre performances worth catching – Prague has a strong tradition of mime, "black theatre" and puppetry, and many cinemas show films in their original language. Rock, pop and jazz gigs are covered in the previous chapter.

Finally, if you're lucky (or you've planned ahead) you might coincide with one of Prague's **festivals** or annual events.

Tickets

You can obtain **tickets** from the box office (*pokladna*) of the venue concerned, but you might find it easier to go to one of the city's numerous **ticket agencies** – it will cost you more, but might save you a lot of hassle. Ticketpro has branches all over the city, including at the Staroměstská radnice (Old Town Hall), Staroměstské náměstí, Staré Město (Mon–Fri 9am–7pm, Sat & Sun 9am–6pm; ☎224 816 020, ⓦwww.ticketpro.cz), plus at Salvátorská 10, Staré Město and in the Lucerna pasáž, Štěpánská 61, Nové Město. Another option is Bohemia Ticket International (ⓦwww.ticketsbti.cz), which has offices at Malé náměstí 13 (Mon–Fri 9am–5pm, Sat 9am–2pm; ☎224 227 832) and Na příkopě 16, Nové Město (Mon–Fri 10am–7pm, Sat 10am–5pm, Sun 10am–3pm; ☎224 215 031). Ticket **prices**, with a few notable exceptions, are still good value, starting at just 250Kč. Lastly, don't despair if everything is officially sold out (*vyprodáno*), as stand-by tickets are often available at the venue's box office on the night, an hour before the start of the performance.

Listings and information

The English-language **listings** in *Prague Post* (Ⓦ www.praguepost.cz) are selective, but they do at least pick out the events which may be of particular interest to the non-Czech speaker, and list all the major venues and their addresses. Also in English is the monthly handout, *Culture In Prague* (Ⓦ www.ceskakultura.cz), available in Czech as *Česká kultura*, which, along with the bilingual fortnightly listings fold-out *Do města/Downtown* (Ⓦ www.downtown.cz) are available from any PIS office. Any additional **information** you might need can usually be obtained from one of the PIS offices around town: at Na příkopě 20, or in the Staroměstská radnice.

Classical music, opera and ballet

Folk songs lie at the heart of Czech music and have found their way into much of the country's traditional repertoire of **classical music**, of which the Czechs are justifiably proud, having produced four composers of international stature – Dvořák, Janáček, Smetana and Martinů – and a fifth, Mahler, who, though German-speaking, was born in Bohemia. If the music of Mozart appears rather too often in the city's monthly concert programme, it's partly because the tourists love him, but also because of his special relationship with Prague (for more on which see p.64).

The city boasts three large-scale theatres where opera is regularly staged, and has several resident orchestras, the most illustrious of which are the Czech Philharmonic (*Česká filharmonie*), which is based at the Rudolfinum and is currently under the baton of Vladimir Ashkenazy, and the Prague Symphony Orchestra (*Symfonický orchestr hl. m. Prahy*), whose home is the Smetanova síň in the Obecní dům. The country continues to produce top-class conductors, a host of singers, and virtuoso violinists.

By far the biggest annual event is the *Pražské jaro* (Prague Spring), the country's most prestigious **international music festival**, for more on which, see p.222. The main venues are listed below, but keep an eye out for concerts in the city's churches and palaces, gardens and courtyards (the main ones are listed separately below); note that evening performances tend to start fairly early, either at 5 or 7pm.

The major venues

Národní divadlo (National Theatre) Národní 2, Nové Město ☎ 224 913 437, Ⓦ www.narodni-divadlo.cz; metro Národní třída. Prague's grandest nineteenth-century theatre is the living embodiment of the Czech national revival movement, and continues to put on a wide variety of mostly, though by no means exclusively, Czech plays, plus the odd opera and ballet. Worth visiting for the decor alone. Box office Mon–Fri 10am–6pm, Sat & Sun 10am–12.30pm & 3–6.30pm. Closed July & Aug.
Obecní dům – Smetanova síň náměstí Republiky 5, Nové Město ☎ 222 002 105; metro

Náměstí Republiky. Fantastically ornate and recently renovated Art Nouveau concert hall which usually kicks off the Prague Spring festival, and is home to the excellent Prague Symphony Orchestra. Box office Mon–Fri 10am–12.30pm & 1.30–6pm.
Rudolfinum Alšovo nábřeží 12, Staré Město ☎ 224 893 352, Ⓦ www.rudolfinum.cz; metro Staroměstská. A truly stunning Neo-Renaissance concert hall from the late nineteenth century, that's home base for the Czech Philharmonic (Ⓦ www.czechphilharmonie.cz). The Dvořákova síň is the large hall; the Sukova síň is the chamber concert hall. Box office Mon–Fri 10am–6pm, plus 1hr before performance.

Státní opera Praha (Prague State Opera)
Wilsonova 4, Nové Město ☎ 224 227 266,
🌐 www.opera.cz; metro Muzeum. A sumptuous
nineteenth-century opera house, built by
the city's German community, which once
attracted star conductors such as Mahler
and Zemlinsky. Now it's the number two
venue for opera, with a repertoire that
tends to focus on Italian pieces. Box office
Mon–Fri 10am–5.30pm, Sat & Sun
10am–noon & 1–5.30pm, plus 1hr before
performance. Closed mid-July to mid-Aug.
Stavovské divadlo (Estates Theatre) Ovocný
trh 1, Staré Město ☎ 224 215 001, 🌐 www
.narodni-divadlo.cz; metro Můstek. Prague's
oldest opera house, which witnessed the
premiere of Mozart's *Don Giovanni*, puts on
a mixture of opera, ballet and straight
theatre (with simultaneous headphone
translation available). Box office Mon–Fri
10am–6pm, Sat & Sun 10am–12.30pm &
3–6pm, plus 30min before performance.
Closed mid-July to mid-Aug.

Concert venues

Anežký klášter (Convent of sv Anežka) U
milosrdných 17, Staré Město ☎ 233 357 332;
metro Náměstí Republiky. Regular Czech
chamber concerts, often of the big four
Czech composers, are given in the convent's
atmospheric Gothic chapel (see p.91).
Bazilika sv Jakub (St James) Malá Štupartská
6, Staré Město; metro Náměstí Republiky. Choral
church music, sung mass and Prague's
finest organ used for regular recitals (see
p.91).
Bertramka Mozartova 169, Smíchov ☎ 257 318
461; metro Anděl. Occasional concerts given
at the Mozart Museum (see p.165),
consistently featuring at least one work by
the composer.
Chrám sv Mikuláše (St Nicholas)
Malostranské náměstí, Mala Strána; metro
Malostranská. Prague's most sumptuous
Baroque church is the perfect setting for
choral concerts and organ recitals (see
p.64).
**Dům U kamenného zvonu (House at the Stone
Bell)** Staroměstské náměstí 13, Staré Město
☎ 224 827 526, 🌐 www.citygalleryprague.cz;
metro Staroměstská. An adventurous

programme of modern and classical
concerts is staged at this contemporary art
gallery, housed in an old building on Old
Town Square (see p.88).
**Kostel sv Martina ve zdi (St Martin-in-the-
Wall)** Martinská, Staré Město; metro Národní
třída. Daily chamber music concerts mostly,
though not exclusively, of eighteenth-
century composers, held in a bare medieval
church.
Kostel sv Šimona a Judy (St Simon & Jude)
Na Františku/Dušní, Staré Město; metro Náměstí
Republiky. Deconsecrated trompe l'oeil
church, where the Prague Symphony
Orchestra puts on chamber concerts.
**Lichtenštejnský palác (Liechtenstein
Palace)** Malostranské náměstí 13, Malá Strana;
metro Malostranská. The Czech Academy of
Music (HAMU) lives here and puts on
mostly Baroque music by chamber
orchestras and string quartets.
Lobkovický palác (Lobkowicz Palace) Jiřská
3, Hradčany; metro Malostranská. Concerts
held in the palace's main be-frescoed hall
at the eastern edge of Prague Castle (see
p.52).
Míčovna U prašného mostu, Hradčany ☎ 224
373 368, 🌐 www.hrad.cz; tram #22 from metro
Malostranská to Pražský hrad stop. Renaissance
ball game court in the Královská zahrada of
Prague Castle (see p.53).
Nostický palác (Nostitz Palace) Maltézské
náměstí 1, Malá Strana ☎ 257 311 590; metro
Malostranská. Chamber concerts here start
at the civilized hour of 8pm, and include a
glass of wine as part of the ticket price.
Španělský sál (Spanish Hall) Pražský hrad,
Hradčany ☎ 224 373 368, 🌐 www.hrad.cz; tram
#22 from metro Malostranská to Pražský hrad
stop. Spectacularly ornate concert hall in
the castle (see p.40), open to the public
only for occasional concerts.
Valdštejnská zahrada (Valdštejn Gardens)
Letenská, Malá Strana; metro Malostranská.
Probably the finest of the summer-only
outdoor venues (see p.66).
Zrcadlová kaple (Mirrored Chapel)
Klementinum, Mariánské náměstí, Staré Město
☎ 221 663 111; metro Staroměstská. Regular
chamber and organ concerts held in the
Klementinum's beautifully atmospheric pink
Baroque chapel of mirrors (see p.84).

Theatre

Theatre has always had a special place in Czech culture, one which the events of 1989 only strengthened. Not only did the country end up with a playwright as president, but it was the capital's theatres that served as information centres during those first few crucial weeks. After the revolution, however, the whole theatre scene, for so long heavily subsidized – and censored – by the authorities, went through a difficult patch. More recently, audience figures have picked up considerably; tourists are also a lucrative source of income and there are several English-language theatre companies now based in Prague. Ticket prices have risen dramatically, though you can still get into most theatres for around 250Kč; tickets are available from the venues themselves, or for considerably more from the ticket agencies listed on p.211.

Prague also has a strong tradition of **mime** and "**černé divaldo**" or "black light theatre" (visual trickery created by "invisible" actors dressed all in black), ranging from the classical style of the late Ladislav Fialka and his troupe to the more experimental work of Boris Polívka. However, along with Prague's long-running multimedia company, Laterna magika, many of these shows are now deliberately geared towards tourists, and can make for disappointing viewing.

Puppet theatre (*loutkové divadlo*) also has a long indigenous tradition, as an art form for both adults and children, and is currently enjoying something of a renaissance, thanks to its accessibility to non-Czech audiences. Unfortunately, this has meant never-ending performances of Mozart's *Don Giovanni* in period costume specifically aimed at passing tourists. At the other end of the spectrum, few companies now maintain the traditional puppets-only set-up, instead featuring live actors in their productions, many of which can be very wordy, making the shows less accessible if you don't speak the language.

Selected theatres: dance, experimental, fringe, mime and musicals

The Stavovské divadlo and the Národní divadlo both put on plays as well as opera and ballet, and are listed on p.215 and p.216. Below is a selection of Prague's other main theatres.

Divadlo Alfred ve dvoře Fr. Křížka 36, Holešovice ☎220 570 237, ⊕www.divadlo.cz/alfredvedvore; metro Vltavská. Experimental theatre run by mime theatre guru, Ctibor Turba, and an occasional student drama venue. Tickets available in advance from Divadlo v Celetné (see below); box office open 1hr before performance.

Divadlo Archa Na poříčí 26, Nové Město ☎221 716 333, ⊕www.archatheatre.cz; metro Florenc. By far the most innovative venue in Prague, with two very versatile spaces, an art gallery and a café. The programming includes music, dance and theatre with an emphasis on the avant-garde. Box office Mon–Fri 10am–6pm, plus 2hr before performance.

Divadlo Globe Výstaviště, Holešovice; ⊕www.divadlo-globe.cz. A reconstruction of Shakespeare's Globe Theatre in London, used for summer-only productions of the bard in English and Czech.

Divadlo na zábradlí Anenské náměstí 5, Staré Město ☎222 222 026, ⊕www.nazabradli.cz; metro Staroměstská. Havel's old haunt and a centre of absurdist theatre back in the 1960s, it's still a provocative rep theatre, with a wide variety of shows (in Czech) and a lively bar. Box office Mon–Fri 2–7pm, Sat & Sun from 5pm.

Divadlo Spirála Výstaviště, Holešovice ☎220 103 624; tram #5, #12 or #17 from Nádraží Holešovice to Výstaviště stop. Spectacular 360-degree theatre that puts on suitably stagey shows (mostly musicals). Box office Mon–Fri 8am–8pm, Sat noon–8pm, Sun noon–4pm.

Divadlo v Celetné Celetná 17, Nové Město ☎224 809 168, ⊕www.divadlovceletne.cz; metro Náměstí Republiky. Home of several fringe companies, and a student drama venue, which puts on tourist-friendly productions (occasionally puppetry and black theatre or *černé divadlo*). Box office in café Mon–Fri 9am–7.30pm, Sat & Sun noon–7.30pm.

Duncan Centre Branická 41, Braník ☎ 244 461 342, ✆ www.osf.cz/dc; tram #3, #16, #17 or #21, stop Přístaviště. Interesting dance pieces by resident and visiting artists at this theatre based in a school for contemporary dance in the southern suburb of Braník.

Laterna magika (Magic Lantern) Nová scéna, Národní 4, Nové Město ☎ 224 914 129, ✆ www .laterna.cz; metro Národní třída. The National Theatre's *Nová scéna*, one of Prague's most modern and versatile stages, is now the main base for Laterna magika, founders of multimedia theatre way back in 1958, now content just to pull in crowds of tourists. Box office Mon–Sat 10am–8pm.

Ponec Husitská 24a, Žižkov ☎ 224 817 886, ✆ www.divadloponec.cz. Former cinema, now innovative dance venue and centre for the annual Tanec Praha dance festival in June/July.

Ta Fantastika Karlova 8, Staré Město ☎ 222 221 369; metro Staroměstská. Probably the best of the "black theatre" venues, albeit strategically located close to the Charles Bridge, offering dialogue-free shows specifically aimed at tourists. Box office daily 11am–9.30pm.

Puppet theatre

Divadlo minor Vodičkova 6, Nové Město ☎ 222 232 530, ✆ www.minor.cz; metro Karlovov

náměstí. The former state puppet theatre puts on children's puppet shows most days, plus adult shows on occasional evenings – sometimes with English subtitles. Box office Mon–Fri 2–5pm, plus 1hr before performance.

Divadlo na královské cestě Karlova 12, Staré Město ☎ 222 220 928; metro Staroměstská. Prague is the international headquarters of UNIMA, the international marionette organization, so the productions staged at their centrally located theatre should, by rights, be brilliant – sadly, that's seldom the case. Box office daily noon–7pm.

Divadlo Spejbla a Hurvínka Dejvická 38, Dejvice ☎ 224 316 784, ✆ www.spejbl-hurvinek .cz; metro Dejvická/Hradčanská. Features the indomitable puppet duo, Spejbl and Hurvínek, created by Josef Skupa earlier this century and still going strong at one of the few puppets-only theatres in the country. Box office Tues, Thurs & Fri 10am–2pm & 3–6pm, Wed 10am–2pm & 3–7pm, Sat & Sun 1–5pm.

Umělecká scéna říše loutek Žatecká 1, Staré Město ☎ 222 324 565, ✆ www.riseloutek.cz; metro Staroměstská. This company's rather dull marionette version of Mozart's *Don Giovanni* has proved extremely popular, as has its version of *Yellow Submarine*, but they also put on regular kids' shows at the weekends. Box office Wed 3.30–6pm, Sat & Sun 1–5pm.

Film

As with the theatre, **cinema** (*kino*) attendances have been steadily decreasing over the last decade. The advent of video machines, more TV stations and steadily rising ticket prices are to blame for the most part. Nevertheless, the cinema remains a relatively cheap (around 100Kč a ticket) and popular form of entertainment, and although Hollywood blockbusters form a large part of the weekly fare, the Czech film industry continues to chug along, bolstered by the odd success story, such as Jan Svěrák's Oscar-winning *Kolja*.

Foreign films are more often than not shown in their original language with subtitles (*titulky*) rather than dubbed (*dabing*). And thanks to Prague's large expat community, some Czech films are occasionally shown with English subtitles – these are all listed in *Prague Post*, but for a comprehensive rundown of the week's films, check out the bilingual *Do města/Downtown*. Film titles are nearly always translated into Czech, so you'll need to have your wits about you to identify films such as *Po čem ženy touží* as *What Women Want*.

The city's main **cinemas** are concentrated around Wenceslas Square, while the list below is confined to the best screens, plus Prague's art-house film clubs, where you may need to buy a membership card (*legitimace*) in order to purchase tickets. Keep a look out, too, for films shown at the various foreign cultural institutions around town (see p.232 for addresses), and for the summeronly open-air *letní kina* which is held on the Střelecký ostrov and in Výstaviště. The city's short-lived international film festival failed to dislodge Karlovy Vary's annual bash as the country's leading film festival. More interesting is the newly established annual **Days of European Film** (ⓦ www.eurofilmfest.cz), which takes place over ten days sometime in March.

Aero Biskupcova 31, Žižkov ☎271 771 349, ⓦ www.kinoaero.cz; tram #1, #9, #16 or #19, stop Biskupcova. Crumbling art-house cinema that shows rolling mini-festivals, interspersed by more popular movies.
Dlabačov Bělohorská 24, Břevnov ☎233 359 058; tram #8, #22 or #23, stop Malovanka. Excellent film club on the ground floor of the ugly *Hotel Pyramid*, showing a discerning selection of new releases and plenty of art-house classics.
Jalta Václavské náměstí 43, Nové Město ☎224 228 814; metro Můstek/Muzeum. Jalta boasts the only *kinokavárna* left in Prague, where you sit round a café table while watching the film.
Lucerna Vodičkova 36, Nové Město ☎224 216 972; metro Můstek. Without doubt the most ornate film theatre in Prague, decked out in Moorish style by Havel's grandfather, in the *pasáž* the family once owned.
MAT Studio Karlovo náměstí 19, Nové Město ☎224 915 765; metro Karlovo náměstí. Café and cinema popular with the film crowd, with an eclectic programme of shorts, documentaries and Czech films with English subtitles. Entrance is on Odborů.
Ponrepo – Bio Konvikt Bartolomějská 11, Staré Město ☎224 237 233; metro Národní třída. Really old classics from the black-and-white era, dug out from the National Film Archives. Membership cards (150Kč) can only be bought Mon–Fri 2–5pm, and you need to bring a photo.

The visual arts

The Národní galerie (National Gallery) or NG runs the city's main **permanent art collections**, in the Anežský klášter, Jiřský klášter, Šternberský palác, Veletržní palác and Zbraslav, each of which is described in detail in the guide section. Most of these galleries also give over space for **temporary exhibitions**, and there are several which only ever stage special exhibitions. *Prague Post* has selective listings, and there's a list of foreign cultural institutes, which also put on regular exhibitions, on p.232, but as ever you'll find the fullest listings in the Czech monthly listings magazine *Culture in Prague/Česká kultura*. Dozens of **commercial galleries** have sprung up in the last ten years or so, only a handful of which can be relied on regularly to show interesting stuff; below is a selection of the best.

Exhibition spaces

Belvedér Mariánské hradby 1, Hradčany ⓦ www.hrad.cz; tram #22 from metro Malostranská to Královský letohrádek stop. One of the most beautiful Renaissance buildings in Prague (see p.53), which usually shows works by contemporary artists. April–Oct Tues–Sun 10am–6pm.
České muzeum výtvarných umění (Czech Museum of Fine Art) Husova 19–21, Staré Město ⓦ www.ecn.cz/cmvu; metro Staroměstská. Showcases retrospectives of twentieth-century Czech and foreign artists. Tues–Sun 10am–6pm.
Císařská konírna (Imperial Stables) druhé nádvoří, Hradčany; tram #22 from Malostranská to Pražský hrad stop. Impressive exhibition space in Rudolf II's stables, situated in the second courtyard of Prague Castle. Tues–Sun 10am–6pm, Sat until 7pm.
Dům U černé Matky boží (House of the Black Madonna) Celetná 34, Staré Město ⓦ www.ecn.cz /cmvu; metro náměstí Republiky. The first two floors are given over to exhibitions of twentieth-century Czech artists; the top

floor has a permanent exhibition on Czech Cubism (see p.90). Tues–Sun 10am–6pm.

Dům U kamenného zvonu Staroměstské náměstí 13, Staré Město ⓦ www.citygalleryprague.cz; metro Staroměstská. The Prague City Gallery puts on a real range from Baroque to avant-garde in the small Gothic rooms and courtyard of this ancient building (see p.88). Tues–Sun 10am–6pm.

Galerie Hollar Smetanovo nábřeží 6, Nové Město; metro Národní třída. The main exhibition space for Czech graphic artists is situated on the noisy river embankment, but there are plenty of old prints for sale. Tues–Sun 10am–1pm & 2–6pm.

Galerie Václava Špály Národní 30; metro Národní třída. Large exhibition space which hosts exhibitions of Czech modern and contemporary artists' works. Tues–Fri 10am–1pm & 2–6pm, Sat & Sun 1–6pm.

Jízdárna pražkého hradu (Prague Castle Riding School) U prašného mostu, Hradčany ⓦ www.ngprague.cz; tram #22 from Malostranská to Pražský hrad stop. One of the Národní galerie's main temporary exhibition spaces, often used to display twentieth-century Czech art. Tues–Sun 10am–6pm.

Karolinum Ovocný trh 3, Staré Město; metro Můstek. Gothic vaulted room in Prague's Charles University, which puts on shows by Czech and foreign artists. Daily 10am–6pm.

Mánes Masarykovo nábřeží 250, Nové Město; metro Karlovo náměstí. White functionalist building spanning a channel in the Vltava, with an open-plan gallery and a tradition of excellent exhibitions. Tues–Sun 10am–6pm.

Městská knihovna (Municipal Library) Mariánské náměstí 1, Staré Město ⓦ www.citygalleryprague.cz; metro Staroměstská. Slightly off the Staré Město beaten track, exhibitions at this Prague City Gallery space are usually devoted to Czech artists and are well worth checking out. Tues–Sun 10am–6pm.

Obecní dům náměstí Republiky 5, Nové Město ⓦ www.obecni-dum.cz; metro Náměstí Republiky. Exhibitions on a turn-of-the-century theme in the luscious surroundings of the Art Nouveau Obecní dům (see p.124). Daily 10am–6pm.

Palác Kinských (Kinsky Palace) Staroměstské náměstí 12, Staré Město ⓦ www.ngprague.cz; metro Staroměstská. Prints and drawings from the Národní galerie's vast graphics collection. Tues–Sun 10am–6pm.

Rudolfinum Alšovo nábřeží 12, Staré Město ⓦ www.rudolfinum.cz; metro Staroměstská. One of the few galleries in Prague which can take large-scale international exhibitions. Tues–Sun 10am–6pm.

UPM 17 listopadu 2, Staré Město; metro Staroměstská. The UPM, the city's museum of applied art (see p.108) owns some of the finest Czech art in the world, and puts on excellent temporary exhibitions. Tues–Sun 10am–6pm.

Valdštejnská jízdárna (Waldstein Stables) Valdštejnská 3, Malá Strana ⓦ www.ngprague.cz; metro Malostranská. The Národní galerie's most provocative exhibitions tend to be housed in these former stables by Malostranská metro station. Tues–Sun 10am–6pm.

Veletržní palác Dukelských hrdinů 47, Holešovice ⓦ www.ngprague.cz; tram #5, #12 or #17, stop Veletržní. Prague's vast modern art museum puts on excellent temporary exhibitions and retrospectives in the ground and first-floor galleries (see p.152). Tues–Sun 10am–6pm, Thurs until 9pm.

Commercial galleries

Galerie Behémot Elišky Krásnohorské 6, Josefov ⓦ www.behemot.cz; metro Staroměstská. Avant-garde installations by up-and-coming Czech and Slovak contemporary artists. Tues–Sat 11am–6pm.

Galerie Jiřího a Běly Kolářových Betlémské náměsti 8, Staré Město. This is the private gallery of Jiří Kolář, one of the best-known living Czech artists, and his wife, Běla Kolářová, who specialize in surrealist collages. Daily 10am–6pm.

Galerie MXM Nosticova 6, Malá Strana; metro Malostranská. Prague's pioneering and highly influential private gallery puts on consistently good shows by contemporary Czech artists in its one, small vaulted room. Tues–Sun noon–6pm.

Galerie na Jánském vršku Jánský vršek 15, Malá Strana; metro Malostranská. Art gallery, situated just off Nerudova, devoted to glass-making, for which the Czechs have an enviable reputation. March–Oct Tues–Sun 10.30am–5.30pm; Nov–Feb Wed–Sat 11am–6pm.

Gambra Černínská 5, Hradčany; tram #22 from metro Malostranská to Brusnice stop. The gallery of Prague's small but persistent surrealist movement, past and present, hidden in the enchanting backstreets of Hradčany, also provides a window for the works of animator extraordinaire, Jan Švankmajer, and his wife, the artist Eva Švankmajerová. March–Oct Wed–Sun noon–6pm; Nov–Feb Sat & Sun noon–6pm.

Photographic galleries

Atelier Josefa Sudka Úvoz 24, Malá Strana ⓦ www.sudek-atelier.cz; metro Malostranská. Named after the father of the modern Czech art form who had his studio here for many years – the only photo space on the left bank. Tues–Sun: April–Oct 10am–6pm; Nov–March 11am–5pm.

České centrum fotografie Náplavní 1, Nové Město ⓦ www.photogallery.cz; metro Karlovo náměstí. Small exhibition space given over to contemporary photographers' works, Czech and foreign; prints often for sale. Daily 11am–6pm.

Pražský dům fotografie U Řečických, Vodičkova 10, Nové Město ⓦ www.php-gallery.cz; metro Můstek/Museum. Puts on consistently good exhibitions drawn from the group's extensive collections, plus visiting photographic shows. Daily 11am–6pm.

Festivals and events

Prague's **annual festive calendar** is light compared to most European capitals, with just a handful of arts events, in addition to the usual religious festivities.

At **Easter** (*Velikonoce*), the age-old sexist ritual of whipping girls' calves with braided birch twigs tied together with ribbons (*pomlázky*) is still practised. To prevent such a fate, the girls are supposed to offer the boys a coloured Easter egg and pour a bucket of cold water over them. What may once have been an innocent bucolic frolic has now become another excuse for Czech men to harass any woman who dares to venture onto the street during this period.

Halloween comes early to the Czech Republic, on April 30, when the **"Burning of the Witches"** (*pálení čarodějnic*) takes place. Bonfires are lit across the country, and old brooms thrown out and burned as everyone celebrates the end of the long winter. On December 4, the feast day of **Saint Barbara**, cherry tree branches are bought as decorations, the aim being to get them to blossom before Christmas.

On the evening of **December 5**, numerous trios, dressed up as *svatý Mikuláš* (St Nicholas), an angel and a devil, tour round the neighbourhoods, the angel handing out sweets and fruit to children who've been good, while the devil dishes out coal and potatoes to those who've been naughty. The Czech St Nicholas has white hair and a beard, and dresses not in red but in a white priest's outfit, with a bishop's mitre.

With a week or so to go, large barrels are set up in the streets from which huge quantities of live carp (*kapr*), the traditional Christmas dish, are sold. **Christmas Eve** (*štědrý večer*) is traditionally a day of fasting, broken only when the evening star appears, signalling the beginning of the Christmas feast of carp, potato salad, schnitzel and sweetbreads. Only after the meal are the children allowed to open their presents, which miraculously appear beneath the tree, thanks not to Santa Claus, but to *Ježíšek* (Baby Jesus).

Birthdays are much less important for the Czechs than **saints' name days**, which fall on the same day each year. Thus popular names like Jan or Anna are practically national celebrations, and an excuse for everyone to get drunk since you're bound to know at least one person with those names.

Since the 1990s, the **ball season**, which apes that of the old imperial capital, Vienna, has returned to Prague. Each ball (*ples*) takes place in one of the city's many wonderful late nineteenth-century municipal halls and concert theatres from January to March. They're open to anyone, though it can be difficult to get hold of tickets.

Prague's **International Book Fair** (Ⓦwww.bookword.cz) takes place each year in early May at the Výstaviště fairgrounds, and attracts an impressive array of international literary talent; the language of the discussions and readings is often English.

By far the biggest annual arts event is the *Pražské jaro* or **Prague Spring Festival**, the country's most prestigious international music festival. Established in 1946, it traditionally begins on May 12, the anniversary of Smetana's death, with a procession from Smetana's grave in Vyšehrad to the Obecní dům where the composer's *Má vlast* (My Country) is performed in the presence of the president, and finishes on June 2 with a rendition of Beethoven's *Ninth Symphony*. Tickets for the festival sell out fast – try your luck by writing, a month before the festival begins, to the Prague Spring Festival box office at Hellichova 18, Malá Strana (Ⓣ257 312 547, Ⓦwww.festival.cz).

A new highlight in the city's cultural calendar is **Tanec Praha** (Dance Prague; Ⓦwww.tanecpha.cz), an international festival of modern dance which takes place throughout the city in June/July.

Sports

For a small nation, the Czechs have a pretty good record when it comes to sporting triumphs: over the last two decades, they have consistently produced world-class tennis players, a strong national football team and several of the world's top ice hockey players. The two sports which pull in the biggest crowds, by far, are soccer and ice hockey. Getting tickets to watch a particular sport is easy (and cheap) enough on the day – only really big matches sell out. If you want to check forthcoming sports events, read the sports pages in *Prague Post*, or ask at a PIS office. Participating in sports activities is also relatively easy, though the Czechs are fairly lacklustre about the health kick.

Soccer

The Czech national soccer (*fotbal*) team have enjoyed mixed fortunes since splitting from the Slovaks in 1993. After losing the Euro '96 final in extra time, they failed even to qualify for the 1998 World Cup, and performed badly in Euro 2000, despite winning all ten of their qualifying matches. On the domestic front, however, things have been much worse. As with most former Eastern Bloc countries, the best home-grown players have, almost without exception, chosen to seek fame and fortune abroad. As a result, domestic teams usually struggle in European competitions, during which it's common to hear Czech fans racially abusing the opposing team's black players.

The most consistent teams in the *Českomoravského liga* (Ⓦ www.fotbal.cz) are arch rivals Sparta Praha and Slavia Praha. The season runs from August to late November and late February to late May, and matches are usually held on Saturdays. Tickets for domestic games are under 100Kč and four-figure crowds remain the norm. For the moment, however, the best thing about Czech football is that, somewhat unbelievably, you can still drink inexpensive and delicious beer on the terraces.

The most successful club in the country is **Sparta Praha** (Ⓦ www.sparta.cz), who won seven out of the first eight league titles after Czechoslovakia divided in 1993. Their traditional working-class fan base is one of the largest in the country and has possibly the worst reputation for racism. Owned by a German publishing group, Sparta have also enjoyed a modicum of success in the Champions' League, reaching the second group stage on more than one occasion. They play in claret and white at the country's finest, and newly renovated, 20,000 all-seater stadium, by the Letná plain (five minutes' walk from metro Hradčanská); international matches are also regularly played there.

Prague's second most successful team, **Slavia Praha** (Ⓦ www.slavia.cz), majority-owned by a British investment firm, won the league title in 1996 for the first time in nearly fifty years. This did not, however, herald a new dawn for Slavia, who have traditionally attracted a smaller, more educated fan base, and are favourites among the expat community. Slavia play in red and white halved shirts and white shorts, and their ground, optimistically called Eden, is currently being massively revamped, and is on Vladivostocká in Vršovice, just off U Slavie (tram #22 or #23 from metro Náměstí Míru or tram #6, #19, stop Slavia).

Viktoria Žižkov (Ⓦ www.fkviktoriazizkov.cz), based in the traditionally working-class district of Prague 3, won the league championship for the first and only time in 1928. However, they did win the Czech cup in 1994 and 2001, so things are looking up. Viktoria play in red and white vertical stripes and their ground is on Seifertova in Žižkov (tram #5, #9 or #26 from metro Hlavní nádraží to Husinecká stop); the team traditionally plays its games on Sunday mornings. Prague's least successful professional side, **Bohemians** (Ⓦ www.fc-bohemians.cz), are currently enjoying one of their better spells in the top league. Nicknamed the "Kangeroos", they play in green and white at a ground just south of Vršovické náměstí (tram #4, #22 or #23 from metro Náměstí Míru to Vršovické náměstí stop).

The old army team, **Dukla Praha** – immortalized in the pop song *All I Want for Christmas is a Dukla Prague Away-Kit* by British band Half Man Half Biscuit – were forced to leave the capital in 1997, and merge with the local team at Příbram, 60km southwest of Prague. Dukla, now called Marila Příbram, have since bounced back into the first division, but are now firmly ensconced in Příbram.

Ice hockey

Ice hockey (*lední hokej*) runs soccer a close second as the nation's most popular sport. It's not unusual to see kids playing their own form of the game in the street, rather than kicking a football around. As with soccer, the fall of Communism prompted an exodus by the country's best players who left to seek fame and fortune in North America's National Hockey League (NHL). In fact, Jaromír Jágr (Ⓦ www.jaromirjagr.cz), by far the most famous Czech player, remains one of the NHL's top scorers, and currently plays for the Washington Capitals. The Czech national team have been the team to beat in the last five years or so, winning the World Championships three years on the trot.

Games take place on Saturdays and can take anything up to three hours; they are fast and physical and make for cold but compelling viewing. The season starts at the end of September and culminates in the annual World Championships the following summer, when the fortunes of the national side are subject to close scrutiny, especially if pitched against the old enemy Russia, not to mention their former bed-mate and new rival, Slovakia. A double victory against the Soviets in 1969 precipitated riots in towns across the country, culminating in the torching of the Soviet airline Aeroflot's offices in Prague, and even now a victory over Russia prompts wild celebration.

Unlike in football, **Sparta Praha** (Ⓣ 266 727 411, Ⓦ www.hcsparta.cz) are only one of a number of successful teams, and the *Extraliga* (Ⓦ www.hokej.cz) is usually hotly contested. Sparta's *zimní stadión* (winter stadium) is at Za elektrárnou, next door to the Výstaviště exhibition grounds in Holešovice (metro Nádraží Holešovice). Prague's only other first division team are **Slavia Praha**

(☎267 311 417, ⓦwww.hc-slavia.cz), who play at the *zimní stadión* near the Slavia football ground on Vladivostocká in Vršovice (tram #22 or #23 from metro Náměstí Míru or tram #6, #19, stop Kubánské náměstí).

Ice skating

Given the nation's penchant for ice hockey, it's not surprising that **ice skating** (*bruslení*) is Prague's most popular winter activity. There's no shortage of rinks (*zimní stadión*) in the city, although public opening hours are limited, and of course there are the city's two reservoirs, Hostivař and Šárka, which regularly freeze over in winter. Most rinks are open from October to April; however, they often don't rent out skates, and those that do have only a limited selection, so your best bet is to buy a pair downtown; men's skates tend to be for ice hockey, women's for figure skating, and either will set you back around £25/$35.

Sparta Praha Za elektrárnou, Holešovice ☎233 379 442; metro Nádraží Holešovice. Public skating takes place in the small rink that sits beside the hockey team's stadium. Sept–March.

Štvanice Štvanice ostrov, Holešovice ☎233 378 327; 5min walk on to the island from metro Florenc. Skate rental is available, but the rink is open to the public for only a very limited period. Sept–March.

Tennis

Tennis has been one of the country's most successful exports, with the likes of Martina Navrátilová and Ivan Lendl among the game's all-time greats. The glory days of Czech tennis may well be over, but the country still provides a smattering of world-class players each year. Contrary to what you might read in the Western press, however, the Swiss player and top seed Martina Hingis is of Slovak, not Czech, descent.

If you fancy a quick game yourself, you'll have to bring your own racket and balls with you, or buy them downtown. The most central tennis courts are listed below.

Český Lawn Tennis Klub ostrov Štvanice ☎224 810 272; metro Florenc/Vltavská. Floodlit outdoor courts next door to the showpiece courts where the Czech Open used to take place. April–Oct daily 6am–11pm.
Slavia Praha Letenské sady, Holešovice ☎233 374 033; tram #1, #8, #25 or #26 from metro Hradčanská to Sparta stop. Indoor and

outdoor floodlit clay courts situated opposite the Národní technické muzeum. Daily 7am–8pm.
Střelecky ostrov Nové Město ☎224 920 136; tram #6, #9, #22 or #23, stop Újezd or Národní divadlo. Outdoor courts on one of the islands in the Vltava, situated opposite the National Theatre. April–Oct daily 8am–9pm.

Horse racing

Prague's main racecourse is at **Velká Chuchle**, 5km or so south of the city centre; bus #129, #172, #241, #244, or *osobní* train from metro Smíchovské nádraží. Steeplechases and hurdles take place on Sunday afternoons from May to October. There are also less frequent races at a smaller trot course on **Cisářský ostrov** (May–Oct only); walk through the Stromovka park and across the river to the island from metro Nádraží Holešovice.

Swimming

The waters of the Vltava, Beroun and Labe are all pretty polluted – the Sázava is marginally better – so for a clean swim it's best to head for one of the city's swimming pools (*koupaliště*), though these, too, can be of varying water quality.

Divoká Šárka Divoká Šárka, Vokovice; tram #20 or #26 from metro Dejvická to the Divoká Šárka terminus. Idyllically located in a craggy valley to the northwest of Prague, with two small oudoor pools filled with cold but fresh and clean water – great for a full, hot day out. Food and drink and plenty of shade available, too. May to mid-Sept daily 9am–7pm.

Podolí Plavecký stadion Podolská 74, Podolí ☎ 241 433 952; tram #3, #17 or #21, stop Kublov. Well-heated 50-metre indoor pool, plus two smaller outdoor ones and a children's wading pool and water slide. Mon–Fri 6am–9.45pm, Sat & Sun 8am–8pm.

Slavia Plavecký stadion Vladivostocká 10, Vršovice ☎ 267 311 060; tram #7 from metro Strašnická to Kubánské náměstí stop. Clean 25-metre indoor pool in winter, and a very popular summer-only 50-metre outdoor pool, plus mini-golf, table tennis and a playground. Mon–Fri 6am–7pm, Sat & Sun 9am–7pm.

YMCA Na poříčí 12, Nové Město ☎ 224 875 811; metro Náměstí Republiky. The YMCA has a new, clean, 25-metre indoor pool, the best in central Prague, though it often closes during the main part of the day for private classes. Mon–Fri 6.30–10pm, Sat & Sun 10am–9pm.

Gyms and saunas

There's no shortage of fitness centres and hotels in Prague with good gyms, saunas and masseurs. Rates are generally very low compared to the West, but hours are erratic so check before you go.

Fitness Club Intercontinental náměstí Curieových, Staré Město ☎ 2248 81 525, ⓦ www.prague.interconti.com; metro Staroměstská. Well-equipped gym and friendly staff in this very central posh hotel. Mon–Fri 6am–11pm, Sat & Sun 8am–11pm.

Hit Fitness Flora Chrudimská 2, Vinohrady ☎ 267 311 447, ⓦ www.hitfitness.net; metro

Flora. Large gym, squash courts, aerobics, sauna, massage and much more – very close to the metro. Daily 7am–11pm.

YMCA Na poříčí 12, Nové Město ☎ 224 875 811, ⓦ www.scymca.cz; metro Náměstí Republiky. Newly revamped, this leisure centre, with gym, aerobics and pool, is the most central facility available. Mon–Fri 6.30–10pm, Sat & Sun 10am–9pm.

Shopping

Communist shop assistants were famously rude, and service in Prague's shops can still be surly. For the passing tourist, the only real bargains are in goods like glass, ceramics, cutlery and wooden toys, though the Czechs also continue to produce CDs, cassettes, LPs and books and, of course, smoked meats, salamis and alcohol, at a fraction of Western prices. The backstreets of Malá Strana and Staré Město are good for finding interesting little shops, as long as you steer clear of Karlova, Mostecká and Nerudova, where it's strictly puppets, jester hats, Kafka T-shirts, Russian army gear, Mucha merchandise and matrioshka dolls. Praguers do most of their shopping in Nové Město, particularly in the *pasáže* or covered shopping malls on and around Wenceslas Square.

Antiques, arts, crafts and glass

Antique shops (*starožitnosti*) and second-hand junk shops (*bazar*) were popular even in Communist times, and bric-a-brac outlets can be found all over Prague. You'll find few bargains in the ones in the main tourist districts, but you may find some inexpensive curios elsewhere. There are shops selling glass (*sklo*) all over Prague; the difficulty is finding anything you actually like the look of. For folk arts and crafts, look no further than the Havelská market (see p.229) or the ubiquitous *Česká lidová řemesla* chain listed below.

Art Deco Michalská 21, Staré Město; metro **Můstek.** Clothes, shoes, coffee sets, lamps and accessories, all dating from the First Republic between the wars (at a price). Mon–Fri 2–7pm.

Arzenal Valentinská 11, Staré Město ⓦ www.arzenal.cz; metro Staroměstská. Lots of fancy kitchen gear and glassware by leading Czech designer, Boris Šípek, inside a Thai/Japanese restaurant. Daily 10am–midnight.

Bric a Brac Týnská 7, Staré Město; metro Náměstí Republiky. One of the best second-hand shops in central Prague, with everything from antiques to clothes. Daily 10am–6pm.

Česká lidová řemesla Jilská 22, Staré Město ⓦ www.czech-tradition.com; metro Staroměstská. It's impossible to miss this

chain of shops as they've got a branch on just about every main tourist thoroughfare in Prague. Each one stocks wooden toys and Czech folk art from painted eggshells and linen to straw and corn dolls and nativity scenes. Branches at Karlova 12 & 26 (plus many more). Daily 10am–6pm.

Cristallino Celetná 12, Staré Město ⓦ www.cristallino.cz; metro Náměstí Republiky. One of the largest and widest selections of glass and crystal in Prague. Daily 9am–7pm.

Fantazie Rytířská 19, Staré Město; metro **Můstek.** Extensive range of top-notch marionettes, rod and glove puppets. Daily 10am–7pm.

Granát Dlouhá 28–30, Staré Město; metro **Muzeum.** Czech garnets are among the best in the world, and this shop has some interesting pendants and brooches. Mon–Fri 10am–6pm, Sat 10am–1pm.

Kůže Rukavice Michalská 14, Staré Město; metro Můstek. Small shop selling inexpensive hats, gloves, coats and rugs all made from sheepskin. Mon–Fri 10am–6pm, Sat & Sun 10am–5pm.

Le Patio Národní 22, Nové Město; metro Národní třída. Arty wrought-ironwork from chairs and chandeliers to bottle-racks and birdcages. Branch in the Týn courtyard. Daily 10am–7pm.

Military Antique Army Shop Křemencova 7, Nové Město; metro Národní třída. Shop packed with military memorabilia, located opposite the bee-keeping shop (see below). Mon–Fri 11am–5pm.

Modernista Konviktská 5, Staré Město @ www.modernista.cz; metro Národní třída. Authentic top-drawer restored Czech furniture and furnishings in the functionalist style popular between the wars and beyond. Mon–Fri 2–6pm, Sat 11am–4pm.

Moser Na příkopě 12, Nové Město @ www.moser.cz; metro Můstek. The most famous glass and crystal manufacturers in the country – however, you won't find many bargains here (or anywhere else in Prague). Branch at Malé náměstí 11. Mon–Fri 9am–8pm, Sat & Sun 10am–6pm.

Tupesy Havelská 21, Staré Město; metro Můstek. All kinds of brightly coloured folksy pottery cups, mugs and bowls at reasonable prices. Daily 10am–6pm.

Books, maps and graphics

Prague is now home to numerous English-language bookstores (*knihkupectví*), which thrive on the large expat community. The city is also replete with second-hand bookstores (*antikvariát*), though these are often pricey antiquarian-type places rather than cheap, rambling shops; however, many also stock a good selection of old prints and posters.

Academia Václavské náměstí 34, Nové Město; metro Muzeum/Můstek. One of the best downtown bookstores for Czech books, with a fair selection of English-language books, too. Mon–Fri 9am–8pm, Sat & Sun 10am–8pm.

Anagram Týn 4, Nové Město @ www.anagram .cz; metro Náměstí Republiky. Well-stocked, central English-language bookstore not far from Staroměstské náměstí, which has lots of books on Czech politics and culture, plus a small second-hand section. Mon–Sat 10am–8pm, Sun 10am–6pm.

Big Ben Book Shop Malá Štupartská 5, Staré Město @ www.bigbenbookshop.cz; metro Náměstí Republiky. Bookstore that specializes in TEFL material, but also stocks cheap paperbacks, kids' books, magazines and papers. Mon–Fri 9am–7pm, Sat & Sun 10am–6pm.

The Globe Pštrossova 6 @ www.globebookstore.cz; metro Národní třída/Karlovo náměstí. The expat bookstore *par excellence* – both a social centre and superbly well-stocked ramshackle store, with an adjacent café and friendly staff. Mon–Thurs & Sun 10am–midnight, Fri & Sat 10am–1am.

Judaica Široká 7, Staré Město; metro Staroměstská. Probably the best-stocked of all the places flogging Jewish books to passing tourists, with books and prints, second-hand and new. Mon–Fri 10am–6pm, Sun 10am–4pm.

Kanzelsberger Václavské náměstí 4, Nové Město @ www.kanzelsberger.cz; metro Můstek. Well-stocked four-storey Czech bookshop at the bottom of Wenceslas Square. Daily 9am–7pm.

Karel Křenek Celetná 31, Staré Město; metro Náměstí Republiky. High-quality second-hand and antiquarian dealer, with a handful of English books, and lots of old maps, graphics and art books. Mon–Fri 10am–noon & 2–6pm, Sat 10am–2pm.

Kant Opatovická 26, Nové Město; metro Národní třída. Lots of old books, including a fair few English-language ones, plus a good display of prints. Mon–Fri 9am–6pm, Sat 10am–3pm.

Makovský-Gregor Kaprova 9, Staré Město; metro Staroměstská. Appealingly chaotic little second-hand bookshop with old prints and English-language books. Mon–Fri 9am–7pm, Sat & Sun 10am–6pm.

Department stores

For most basic goods, you're best off heading for a department store (*obchodní dům*), which will stock most things – including toiletries, stationery and usually an extensive food and drink selection. The prices are low, but so, often, is the quality.

Bílá labuť Na poříčí 23, Nové Město ✪ www.bilalabut.cz; metro Florenc. Built in the 1930s, when its functionalist design turned more than a few heads, but nowadays in need of serious renovation. Mon–Fri 9am–8pm, Sat 9am–6pm, Sun 10am–6pm.

Kotva náměstí Republiky 8, Nové Město ✪ www.ood-kotva.cz; metro Náměstí Republiky. Ugly, Swedish-built store, with lots of goodies spread over five floors, and a food

section in the basement. Mon–Fri 9am–8pm, Sat 9am–6pm, Sun 10am–6pm.

Tesco Národní 26, Nové Město; metro Národní třída. Neo-functionalist store on four floors, selling a good mix of Czech and imported goods, though it bears absolutely no resemblance to its British supermarket namesake, beyond its neon sign. Mon–Fri 8am–8pm, Sat 9am–6pm, Sun (food supermarket only) 10am–6pm.

Markets and food and drink stores

Prague is chronically short of good **markets** (*trhy* or *tržiště*) of all types, despite the introduction of free enterprise. For bread, butter, cheese, wine and beer, you should simply go to the nearest *potraviny* or supermarket. These have changed enormously since 1989 in terms of what they stock, but they're still a long way from the superstores of the Western world. Christmas markets have now been firmly re-established, and exist from late November onwards at Staroměstské náměstí and Václavské náměstí.

Markets

Havelská Staré Město; metro Můstek. Food, flowers and wooden toys are sold in the only open-air fruit and veg market in central Prague. Mon–Fri 8am–6pm, Sat & Sun 9am–6pm.

Specialist food and drink stores

Au Gourmand Dlouhá 10; metro Náměstí Republiky. Beautifully tiled French boulangerie, patisserie and traiteur selling wickedly delicious pastries to take away. Daily 7.30am–7pm.

Bakeshop Praha V Kolkovně 2, Staré Město; metro Náměstí Republiky. Top-class expat bakery where you can take away excellent bread, sandwiches, quiches, wraps and entire cakes. Daily 7am–7pm.

Blatnička Michalská 6, Staré Město; metro Národní třída. One of the most central places in which to taste and take home Czech *sudová vina* (wine from the barrel). Mon–Fri 10am–6pm.

Cellarius Štěpánská 61, Nové Město ✪ www.cellarius.cz; metro Muzeum. Very well-stocked shop in the Lucerna pasáž, where you can taste and take away Czech wines. Mon–Sat 9.30am–9pm, Sun 3–8pm.

Country Life Melantrichova 15; metro Můstek. All the health food staples, from dried bananas to seaweed, plus freshly baked wholemeal bread. Mon–Thurs 8.30am–7pm, Fri 8.30am–4pm, Sun 11am–1pm.

Fruits de France Jindřišská 9, Nové Město ✪ www.fdf.cz; metro Můstek. Unusually good selection of fruit and vegetables, plus various other longer-lasting delights flown in fresh from France. Branch at Bělehradská 94, Vinohrady. Mon–Fri 9.30am–6.30pm, Sat 9.30am–1pm.

La Bretagne Široká 22, Staré Město; metro Staroměstská. Wide array of fresh fish and seafood available at this centrally located fishmonger's, plus takeaway sushi. Mon–Fri & Sun 9.30am–7pm.

Le Delice Belges Pavilon, Vinohradská 50, Vinohrady ✪ www.pavilon.cz; metro Náměstí Míru. Handmade Belgian chocolates,

including Becherovka chocolates. Mon–Sat 9.30am–9pm, Sun noon–8pm.
Pivní galerie U Průhonu 9, Holešovice; tram #12 or #14, stop U Průhonu. The largest selection of bottled Czech beers in the capital, which you can drink in the shop or takeaway. All under 30Kč a throw. Mon–Fri 10am–8pm, Sat 10am–1pm.

Vzpomínky na Afriku (Memories of Africa) Rybná/Jakubská, Staré Město ⓦ www.ebelcoffee .cz; metro Náměstí Republiky. Prague's largest range of fresh coffee beans from Africa. Daily 10am–7pm.

Music

Czech CDs are priced a little lower than in the West; cassettes and LPs are significantly cheaper. Classical buffs will fare best of all, not just with the Czech composers, but with cheap copies of Mozart, Vivaldi and other favourites on sale at just about every street corner.

Bontonland palác Koruna, Václavské náměstí 1 ⓦ www.bontonland.cz; metro Můstek. Prague's biggest record store in the *pasáž* at the bottom of Wenceslas Square, with rock, folk, jazz and classical, and headphones for previews to boot. Classical branch at Jungamnnova 20, Nové Město. Mon–Sat 9am–8pm, Sun 10am–7pm.
Maximum Underground Jilská 22, Staré Město; metro Staroměstská. The best indie record shop in town, very strong on dance music, and also reggae, ragga, punk and world music. Daily 10am–7pm.

Music antikvariát Národní 25, Nové Město; metro Národní třída. The best second-hand record store in Prague, particularly good for jazz and folk, but also rock/pop – not much in the way of classical. Branch at Mostecká 4, Malá Strana. Mon–Sat 10.30am–7pm.
Talacko Rybná 29, Staré Město; metro Náměstí Republiky. Huge collection of classical and pop sheet music, plus books on music. Mon–Fri 10am–6pm, Sat 10am–4pm.

Specialist shops

Botanicus Týn 3, Staré Město ⓦ www.botanicus.cz; metro Náměstí Republiky. Czech take on the Body Shop, with a folksy look to it, dried flowers and fancy honey, as well as soaps and shampoos. Branches at Mostecká 4, Malá Strana, Michalská 2, Staré Město and many more. Daily 10am–8pm.
Fototechnika a video Vodičkova 36, Nové Město; metro Můstek. New photographic gear, plus an excellent selection of second-hand East German and Soviet equipment.

Mon–Fri 9am–7pm, Sat 9am–2pm.
Sparta Praha Betlémské náměstí 7, Staré Město; metro Národní třída. Centrally located Sparta Praha fan shop stocking everything from shirts to ashtrays, and even the odd Slavia souvenir, too. Mon–Thurs 10am–5pm, Fri 10am–4pm.
Včelařské potřeby Křemencova 8, Nové Město; metro Karlovo náměstí. A beekeeper's paradise, with all the accoutrements required by an apiarist plus a wide selection of honey. Mon–Fri 9am–5pm.

Toys

MPM Myslíkova 19, Nové Město ⓦ www.mpm.cz; metro Karlovo náměstí. Kits for model planes, tanks, trains, ships and cars, and toy soldiers. Mon–Fri 10am–6pm, Sat 10am–1pm.

Sparkys Na příkopě 22, Nové Město ⓦ www .sparkys.cz. Prague's top *dům hraček* (House of Toys) on four floors, which stocks everything from high-tech to wooden toys. Daily 10am–8pm.

Directory

Airlines Austrian Airlines, Revoluční 15, Nové Město ☎224 826 199, ⓦwww.awa.com; metro Staroměstská. British Airways, Ovocný trh 8, Staré Město ☎222 114 444, ⓦwww.britishairways.cz; metro Můstek. British Midland, Kozí 3, Staré Město ☎224 810 180, ⓦwww.britishmidland.cz; metro Staroměstská. Czech Airlines (ČSA), V celnici 5, Nové Město ☎220 104 310, ⓦwww.csa.cz; metro Náměstí Republiky. Delta, Národní 32, Nové Město ☎224 946 733, ⓦwww.delta.com; metro Národní třída. KLM, Na příkopě 21, Nové Město ☎233 090 933, ⓦwww.klm.cz; metro Můstek.

Airport Ruzyně airport ☎220 111 111, ⓦwww.csl.cz.

American Express Amex, Václavské náměstí 56, Nové Město ☎222 800 111 ⓦwww.americanexpress.cz; metro Muzeum; daily 9am–7pm.

Bike rental Bicycles for hire from City Bike, Králodvorská 5, Staré Město ☎776 180 284; they also organize group rides through Prague.

Bottles The Czech Republic has yet to become a fully paid-up member of the throwaway culture and many drinks still come in glass bottles with a deposit on them. For non-deposit bottles, or if you simply can't be bothered to retrieve the deposit, there are now numerous bottle banks scattered around Prague.

Bus information Domestic ☎900 919 041. International ☎224 210 221.

Car rental See p.23.

Contraceptives Condoms (*kondom* or *prezervativ*) are available in metro stations

Children's Prague

The Czech attitude to kids is generally very positive. That said, you'll see few Czech babies out in the open, unless snuggled up in old-fashioned perambulators, and almost no children in pubs, cafés or even most restaurants. Czechs generally expect children to be unreasonably well-behaved and respectful to their elders, and many of the older generation may frown at over-boisterous behaviour. Prague's museums and galleries are pretty old-fashioned, too, with few interactive, hands-on exhibits. Nevertheless, most kids will enjoy Prague, with its hilly cobbled streets and trams, especially in the summer, when the place is positively alive with buskers and street performers.

The obvious attractions for children are the Petřín Hill, with its funicular and mirror maze (see p.72); the Zoo (see p.159); the Muzeum Miniatur (see p.59); the Národní technické muzeum (see p.152), with its trains, planes and automobiles; and the Muzeum MHD (Městské hromadné dopravy), which houses a collection of historic trams and trolleybuses; it's a short walk west of Hradčany at Patočkova 4 (April–Oct Sat & Sun 9am–5pm) – take tram #1 or #8 from metro Hradčanská to the Vozovna Střešovice stop. A year-round option is to hop aboard the regular tram #22, as it goes round some great hairpins, across the river and past a fair few city landmarks. In the summer a historic tram (#91) also crisscrosses the city; tickets are slightly more expensive than normal, and it runs hourly (daily 2–7pm).

in the centre of Prague from machines and from pharmacies.

Credit cards To cancel lost or stolen credit cards, call the following numbers: Access/ Mastercard ☎261 354 650; American Express ☎222 800 111; Diners Club ☎267 314 485; Visa ☎224 125 353.

Cultural institutes

American Center for Culture and Commerce Hybernská 7A, Nové Město ☎224 231 085, ⊛www.usis.cz; metro Náměstí Republiky. Home to the US information service and the embassy's reading room. Tues–Thurs 10am–4pm.

Austrian Cultural Institute (Rakouský kulturní institut), Jungmannovo náměstí 18, Nové Město ☎224 234 875, ⊛www.austria.cz/kultur; metro Můstek. Very good exhibitions of Austrian art, plus the odd concert, film and talk. Gallery Mon–Fri 8am–4.30pm; library Mon–Fri 10am–1pm & 2–4pm.

British Council (Britská rada), Národní 10, Nové Město ☎221 991 111, ⊛www .britishcouncil.org; metro Národní třída. Temporary exhibitions; newspapers and magazines and a reading room; satellite TV in the auditorium and various films, concerts and events during the year. Mon–Fri 9am–4pm.

Goethe Institut Masarykovo nábřeží 32, Nové Město ☎221 962 111, ⊛www.goethe .de; metro Národní třída. Weekly film showings and more frequent lectures; small exhibition space and café. Mon, Wed & Thurs 2–5pm, Tues 10am–1pm & 2–5pm, Fri 10am–1pm.

Hungarian Cultural Centre (Maďarské kulturní středisko), Rytířská 25–27, Staré Město ☎224 222 424; metro Můstek. Weekly film showings and regular exhibitions and concerts. Mon–Thurs 10am–6pm, Fri 10am–2pm.

Institut Français (Francouzský institut), Štěpánská 35, Nové Město ☎222 230 577, ⊛www.ifp.cz; metro Muzeum. Great exhibitions and a great café, with croissants and *journaux*; also puts on more or less daily screenings of classic French films, plus lectures and even the odd concert. Café: Mon noon–6pm, Tues–Sun 9am–6pm.

Instituta Italiana di Cultura (Italský kulturní institut), Šporkova 14, Malá Strana ☎257 533 600. Exhibitions and events are held in various locations including the wonderful Baroque chapel on Vlašská.

Polish Institute (Polský institut), Václavské náměstí 51, Nové Město ☎224 214 708, ⊛www.polskyinstitut.cz; metro Muzeum. Weekly film showings, occasional concerts and lectures. Mon–Fri 9am–5pm, Sat 9am–noon.

Slovenský institut Purkyňova 4, Nové Město ☎224 948 137; metro Národní třída. Concerts, exhibitions and events to remind the Czechs of their other half. Mon 1–5pm, Tues & Fri 1–4pm, Wed & Thurs 10am–12.30pm.

Customs Customs allowances when taking goods from the Czech Republic into EU countries are 250 cigarettes or 50 cigars, 1 litre of spirits and 2 litres of wine. With the Czechs poised to join the EU, these allowances may change, so if in doubt, check with HM Customs and Excise (⊛www.hmce.gov.uk) before you leave for Prague.

Electricity This is the standard continental 220 volts AC. Most European appliances should work as long as you have an adaptor for continental-style two-pin round plugs. North Americans will need this plus a transformer.

Embassies and consulates

Australia Klimentská 10, Nové Město ☎251 018 350, ⊛www.austrade.gov.au; metro Náměstí Republiky. Mon–Fri 8.30am–1pm & 2–5pm.

Belarus Sádky 626, Troja ☎268 88 217; bus #112 from metro Nádraží Holešovice. Mon–Fri 9am–noon & 1–5pm.

Belgium Valdštejnská 6, Malá Strana ☎257 533 524, ⊛www.belemb.cz; metro Malostranská. Mon–Fri 9am–noon.

Britain Thunovská 14, Malá Strana ☎257 402 111, ⊛www.britain.cz; metro Malostranská. Mon–Fri 9am–noon.

Canada Mickiewiczova 6, Hradčany ☎272 101 800, ⊛www.dfait-maeci.gc.ca; metro Hradčanská. Mon–Fri 8.30–10.30am & 2.30–4pm.

Denmark Maltézské náměstí 5, Malá Strana ☎257 531 600, ⊛www.denmark.cz; metro Malostranská. Mon–Fri 8.30am–4.30pm.

Finland Hellichova 1, Malá Strana ☎257 007 130; tram #12, #22 or #23, stop Hellichova. Mon–Fri 8am–4pm.

France Velkopřevorské náměstí 2, Malá Strana ☎257 532 756, ⊕www.france.cz; metro Malostranská. Mon–Fri 9am–noon.

Germany Vlašská 19, Malá Strana ☎257 113 111, ⊕www.german-embassy.cz; metro Malostranská. Mon–Fri 9am–noon.

Ireland Tržiště 13, Malá Strana ☎257 530 061; metro Malostranská. Mon–Fri 9am–12.30pm & 2.30–4.30pm.

Netherlands Gotthardská 6, Bubeneč ☎224 312 190, ⊕www.netherlandsembassy .cz; metro Hradčanská. Mon–Fri 9am–5pm.

New Zealand Dykova 19, Vinohrady ☎222 514 672; metro Jiřího z Poděbrad. Mon–Fri 9am–noon.

Poland Valdštejnská 8, Malá Strana ☎257 530 388, ⊕www.polamb.cz; metro Malostranská. Mon–Fri 9am–noon.

Russia Pod kaštany 1, Bubeneč ☎233 371 549; metro Dejvická. Mon, Wed & Fri 9am–1pm.

Slovakia Pod hradbami 1, Dejvice ☎233 321 442; metro Dejvická. Mon–Fri 8.30am–noon.

Sweden Úvoz 13, Malá Strana ☎220 313 200; metro Malostranská. Mon–Fri 9am–noon.

USA Tržiště 15, Malá Strana ☎257 530 663, ⊕www.usembassy.cz; metro Malostranská. Mon–Fri 9am–noon.

Exchange 24-hour service, near the bottom of Wenceslas Square at 28 října 13, Nové Město, metro Můstek.

Language schools Angličtina expres, Korunní 2, Nové Město ☎222 513 040; Státní jazyková škola, Školská 15, Nové Město ☎222 232 238.

Laundries Expats tend to head for the following launderettes, which all have internet terminals, TV, service washes and self-service machines: Laundry Kings, Dejvická 16, Dejvice (Mon–Fri 6am–10pm, Sat & Sun 8am–10pm; ☎233 343 743; metro Hradčanská); Laundryland, Na příkopě 12, Nové Město (Mon–Fri 9am–8pm, Sat 9am–7pm & Sun 11am–7pm; ☎221 014 632, ⊕www.laundryland.cz; metro Můstek); and Prague Laundromat, Korunní 14, Vinohrady (daily 8am–8pm; ☎222 510 180, ⊕www .volny.cz/laundromat; metro Náměstí Míru).

Left luggage Prague's main bus and train stations have lockers and/or a 24-hour left-luggage office, with instructions in English.

Metric weights and measures

1 ounce = 28.3 grammes (g)
1 inch = 2.54 centimetres (cm)
1 pound = 454g
1 foot = 0.3 metres (m)
2.2 pounds = 1 kilogramme (kg)
1 yard = 0.91m
1 pint = 0.47 litres (l)
1.09 yards = 1m
1 quart = 0.94l
1 mile = 1.61 kilometres (km)
1 gallon = 3.78l
0.62 miles = 1km

Lost property The main train stations have lost property offices – look for the sign ztráty a nálezy – and there's a central municipal one at Karoliny Světlé 5, Staré Město. If you've lost your passport, then get in touch with your embassy (see above).

Newspapers You can get most foreign dailies and magazines at the kiosks at the bottom of Wenceslas Square, outside metro Můstek.

Religious services Anglican, sv Kilment, Klimentská 5, Nové Město (Sun 11am; metro Náměstí Republiky); Baptist, Vinohradská 68, Vinohrady (Sun 11am; metro Jiřího z Poděbrad); Greek/Russian Orthodox, sv Cyril & Metoděj, Resslova 9, Nové Město (Sun 9.30am); Interdenominational, Peroutkova 57, Smíchov (Sun 10.30am; bus #137 from metro Anděl); Jewish Orthodox, Staronová synagóga, Maiselova, Josefov (Mon–Thurs & Sun 8am, Fri dusk, Sat 9am; metro Staroměstská); Jewish Reform, Jubilejní synagóga, Jeruzalemská 7, Nové Město (Fri dusk, Sat 8.45am; metro Hlavní nádraží); Lutheran, sv Michal, V jirchářích 4, Nové Město (Sun 11am; metro Národní třída); Roman Catholic, sv Tomáš, Josefská 8, Malá Strana (in English, Sun 11am; metro Malostranská).

Smoking Like most continental Europeans, the Czechs are keen smokers, and you'll find very few no-smoking areas in cafés, pubs or restaurants, though there is no smoking on the public transport system. If you're a smoker and need a light, say máte oheň? Matches are zápalky.

Time The Czech Republic is generally one hour ahead of Britain and six hours ahead of EST, with the clocks going forward in spring and back again some time in autumn – the exact date changes from year to year. Generally speaking, Czechs use the 24-hour clock.

Train information ☎224 224 200, ⊛idos.datis.cdrail.cz.

Toilets Apart from the automatic ones in central Prague, toilets (*záchody*, *toalety* or *WC*) are few and far between. In some, you still have to buy toilet paper (by the sheet) from the attendant, whom you will also have to pay as you enter. Standards of hygiene can be low. Gentlemen should head for *muži* or *páni*; ladies should head for *ženy* or *dámy*.

Women The Czech Republic remains a deeply conservative and patriarchal society, though the atmosphere in Prague is slightly more liberated than in the rest of the country. On the whole, street-level sexual harassment is much less prevalent than it is in some Western countries. Pubs are about the only places where men always predominate; the usual common-sense precautions apply here and elsewhere. Feminism and women's issues keep a very low profile in the Czech Republic. The city's main feminist organizations are to be found under one roof at the Ženské centrum, Národní dům, náměstí 14 října 16, Smíchov ☎257 324 604 (metro Anděl). Look out, too, for the bi-lingual feminist review *One Eye Open* (⊛www.feminismus.cz/oneeyeopen).

Contexts

Contexts

A history of Prague

Prague has played a pivotal role in European history – "he who holds Bohemia holds mid-Europe", Bismarck is alleged to have said. As the capital of Bohemia, Prague has been fought over and occupied by German, Austrian, French and even Swedish armies. Consequently, it is virtually impossible to write a historical account of the city without frequent reference to the wider events of European history. The history of Prague as the capital of, first Czechoslovakia, and now the Czech Republic, is, in fact, less than a hundred years old, beginning only with the foundation of the country in 1918. Since then, the country's numerous tragedies, mostly focused on Prague, have been exposed to the world at regular intervals – 1938, 1948, 1968 and, most recently (and most happily), 1989.

Legends

The Czechs have a **legend** for every occasion, and the founding of Bohemia and Prague is no exception. The mythical mound of Říp, the most prominent of the pimply hills in the Labe (Elbe) plain, north of Prague, is where **Čech**, the leader of a band of wandering Slavs, is alleged to have founded his new kingdom, Čechy (Bohemia). His brother Lech, meanwhile, headed further north to found Poland. Some time in the seventh or eighth century AD, **Krok** (aka Pace), a descendant of **Čech**, moved his people south from the plains to the rocky knoll that is now Vyšehrad (literally "High Castle").

Krok was succeeded by his youngest daughter, **Libuše**, the country's first and last female ruler, who, handily enough, was endowed with the gift of prophecy. Falling into a trance one day, she pronounced that the tribe should build a city "whose glory will touch the stars", at the point in the forest where they found an old man constructing the threshold of his house. He was duly discovered on the Hradčany hill, overlooking the Vltava, and the city was named *Praha,* meaning "threshold". However, it wasn't long before Libuše's subjects began to demand that she take a husband. As Cosmas, the twelfth-century chronicler put it, "resting on her elbow like one who is giving birth, she lay there on a high pile of soft and embroidered pillows, as is the lasciviously wanton habit of women when they do not have a man at home whom they fear". Again she fell into a trance, this time pronouncing that they should follow her horse to a ploughman, with two oxen, whose descendants (the ploughman's, that is) would rule over them. Sure enough, a man called **Přemysl** (which means "ploughman") was discovered, and became the mythical founder of the Přemyslid dynasty which ruled Bohemia until the fourteenth century.

Early history

So much for the legend. According to Roman records, the area now covered by Bohemia was inhabited as early as 500 BC by a Celtic tribe, the **Boii**, who gave their name to the region. Very little is known about the Boii except that around 100 BC they were driven from their territory by a Germanic tribe, the

Marcomanni, who occupied Bohemia. The Marcomanni were a semi-nomadic people and later proved awkward opponents for the Roman Empire, which wisely chose to use the River Danube as its natural eastern border, thus leaving Bohemia outside the empire.

The disintegration of the Roman Empire in the fifth century AD corresponded with a series of raids into central Europe by eastern tribes: first the **Huns** and later the **Avars**, around the sixth century, settling a vast area including the Hungarian plains and parts of what is now Slovakia. Around the same time, the Marcomanni disappear from the picture to be replaced by **Slav tribes** who entered Europe from somewhere east of the Carpathian mountains. To begin with, at least, they appear to have been subjugated by the Avars. The first successful Slav rebellion against the Avars seems to have taken place in the seventh century, under the Frankish leadership of **Samo**, though the kingdom he created, which was centred on Bohemia, died with him around 658 AD.

The Great Moravian Empire

The next written record of the Slavs in the region isn't until the eighth century, when East Frankish (Germanic) chroniclers report a people known as the **Moravians** as having established themselves around the River Morava, a tributary of the Danube. It was an alliance of Moravians and Franks (under Charlemagne) which finally expelled the Avars from central Europe in 796 AD. This cleared the way for the establishment of the **Great Moravian Empire**, which at its peak included Slovakia, Bohemia and parts of Hungary and Poland. Its significance in political terms is that it was the first and last time (until the establishment of Czechoslovakia, for which it served as a useful precedent) that the Czechs and Slovaks were united under one ruler.

The first attested ruler of the empire, **Mojmír**, found himself at the political and religious crossroads of Europe under pressure from two sides: from the west, where the Franks and Bavarians (both Germanic tribes) were jostling for position with the Roman papacy; and from the east, where the Patriarch of Byzantium was keen to extend his influence across eastern Europe. Mojmír's successor, **Rastislav** (850–870), plumped for Byzantium, and invited the missionaries Cyril and Methodius to introduce Christianity, using the Slav liturgy and Eastern rites. Rastislav, however, was ousted by his nephew, **Svätopluk** (871–894), who captured and blinded his uncle, allying himself with the Germans instead. With the death of Methodius in 885, the Great Moravian Empire fell decisively under the influence of the Roman Catholic Church.

Svätopluk died shortly before the **Magyar invasion** of 896, an event which heralded the end of the Great Moravian Empire and a significant break in Czecho-Slovak history. The Slavs to the west of the River Morava (the Czechs) swore allegiance to the Frankish Emperor, Arnulf, while those to the east (the Slovaks) found themselves under the yoke of the Magyars. This separation, which continued for the next millennium, is one of the major factors behind the social, cultural and political differences between Czechs and Slovaks, which culminated in the separation of the two nations in 1993.

The Přemyslid Dynasty

There is evidence that Bohemian dukes were forced in 806 to pay a yearly tribute of 500 pieces of silver and 120 oxen to the Carolingian empire (a precedent the Nazis were keen to exploit as proof of German hegemony over Bohemia). These early Bohemian dukes "lived like animals, brutal and without knowledge", according to one chronicler. All that was to change when the earliest recorded Přemyslid duke **Bořivoj** (852/53–888/89), appeared on the scene. The first Christian ruler of Prague, Bořivoj was baptized, along with his wife Ludmila, in the ninth century by the Byzantine missionaries Cyril and

Princes, kings, emperors and presidents

The Přemyslid dynasty

Princes

Bořivoj I d. 895
Spytihněv I 895–905
Vratislav I 905–921
Václav I 921–929
Boleslav I 929–972
Boleslav II 972–999
Boleslav III 999–1002
Vladivoj 1002–1003
Jaromir 1003–1012
Ulrich 1012–1034
Břetislav I 1034–1055
Spytihněv II 1055–1061
Vratislav II (king from 1086) 1061–1092
Břetislav II 1092–1110
Bořivoj II 1110–1120
Vladislav I 1120–1125
Soběslav I 1125–1140
Vladislav II (as king, I) 1140–1173
Soběslav II 1173–1189
Otho 1189–1191
Václav II 1191–1192
Otakar I (king from 1212) 1192–1230

Kings

Václav I 1230–1253
Otakar II 1253–1278
Václav II 1278–1305
Václav III 1305–1306

Habsburgs

Rudolf I 1306–1307
Henry of Carinthia 1307–1310

The Luxembourg dynasty

John 1310–1346
Charles I (as emperor, IV) 1346–1378
Václav IV 1378–1419
Sigismund 1436–1437

Habsburgs

Albert 1437–1439
Ladislav the Posthumous 1439–1457

Czech Hussite

George of Poděbrady 1458–1471

The Jagiellonian dynasty

Vladislav II 1471–1516
Louis I 1516–1526

The Habsburg dynasty

Ferdinand I 1526–1564
Maximilian 1564–1576
Rudolf II 1576–1611
Matthias 1611–1619
Ferdinand II 1619–1637
Ferdinand III 1637–1657
Leopold I 1657–1705
Joseph I 1705–1711
Charles II (as emperor, VI) 1711–1740
Maria Theresa 1740–1780
Joseph II 1780–1790
Leopold II 1790–1792
Franz 1792–1835
Ferdinand IV (I) 1835–1848
Franz Joseph 1848–1916
Charles III 1916–1918

Presidents

Tomáš Garrigue Masaryk 1918–1935
Edvard Beneš 1935–1938 & 1945–1948
Klement Gottwald 1948–1953
Antonín Zápatocký 1953–1957
Antonín Novotný 1957–1968
Ludvík Svoboda 1968–1975
Gustáv Husák 1975–1989
Václav Havel 1989–1992 & 1993–2003

Methodius (see p.238). Other than being the first to build a castle on Hradčany, nothing very certain is known about Bořivoj, nor about any of the other early Přemyslid rulers, although there are numerous legends, most famously that of **Prince Václav** (St Wenceslas), who was martyred by his pagan brother Boleslav the Cruel in 929 (see p.44).

Cut off from Byzantium by the Hungarian kingdom, Bohemia lived under the shadow of the **Holy Roman Empire** from the start. In 950, Emperor Otto I led an expedition against Bohemia, making the dukedom officially subject to the empire and its leader one of the seven electors of the emperor. In 973, under Boleslav the Pious (967–999), a bishopric was founded in Prague, subordinate to the archbishopric of Mainz. Thus, by the end of the first millennium, German influence was already beginning to make itself felt in Bohemian history.

The **thirteenth century** was the high point of Přemyslid rule over Bohemia. With Emperor Frederick II preoccupied with Mediterranean affairs and dynastic problems, and the Hungarians and Poles busy trying to repulse the Mongol invasions from 1220 onwards, the Přemyslids were able to assert their independence. In 1212, Otakar I (1192–1230) managed to extract a **"Golden Bull"** (formal edict) from the emperor, securing the royal title for himself and his descendants (who thereafter became kings of Bohemia). Prague prospered too, benefiting from its position on the central European trade routes. Czechs, Germans, Jews and merchants from all over Europe settled there, and in 1234 the first of Prague's historic five towns, **Staré Město**, was founded to accommodate them.

As a rule, the Přemyslids welcomed **German colonization**, none more so than King Otakar II (1253–78), the most distinguished of the Přemyslid rulers, who systematically encouraged German craftsmen to settle in the kingdom. At the same time, the gradual switch to a monetary economy and the discovery of copper and silver deposits heralded a big shift in population from the countryside to the towns. German immigrants founded whole towns in the interior of the country, where German civic rights were guaranteed them, for example Kutná Hora, Mělník and, in 1257, **Malá Strana** in Prague. Through battles, marriage and diplomacy, Otakar managed to expand his territories so that they stretched (almost) from the Baltic to the Adriatic. In 1278, however, Otakar met his end on the battlefield of Marchfeld, defeated by Rudolf of Habsburg.

The beginning of the fourteenth century saw a series of dynastic disputes – messy even by medieval standards – beginning with the death of Václav II from consumption and excess in 1305. The following year, the murder of his son, the heirless, teenage Václav III, marked the **end of the Přemyslid dynasty** (he had four sisters, but female succession was not recognized in Bohemia). The nobles' first choice of successor, the Habsburg Albert I, was murdered by his own nephew, and when Albert's son, Rudolf I, died of dysentery not long afterwards, Bohemia was once more left without any heirs.

Carolingian Prague

The crisis was finally solved when the Czech nobles offered the throne to **John of Luxembourg** (1310–46), who was married to Václav III's youngest sister. German by birth, but educated in France, King John spent most of his reign participating in foreign wars, with Bohemia footing the bill, and John himself paying for it first with his sight, and finally with his life, on the field at Crécy in 1346.

His son, **Charles IV** (1346–78), was wounded in the same battle, but thankfully for the Czechs lived to tell the tale. It was Charles – Karel to the Czechs – who ushered in Prague's **golden age** (see p.81). Although born and bred in France, Charles was a Bohemian at heart (his mother was Czech and his real name was Václav). In 1344, he had wrangled an archbishopric for Prague, independent of Mainz, and two years later he became not only king of Bohemia, but also, by election, Holy Roman Emperor. In the thirty years of his reign, Charles transformed Prague into the new imperial capital. He established institutions and buildings that still survive today and founded an entire new town, **Nové Město**, to accommodate the influx of students and clergy. He promoted Czech as the official language alongside Latin and German and, perhaps most importantly of all, presided over a period of peace in central Europe while western Europe was tearing itself apart in the Hundred Years' War.

Sadly, Charles' son, **Václav IV** (1378–1419), was no match for such an inheritance. Stories that he roasted an incompetent cook alive on his own spit, shot a monk whilst hunting, and tried his own hand at lopping off people's heads with an axe, are almost certainly myths. Nevertheless, he was a legendary drinker, prone to violent outbursts, and so unpopular with the powers that be that he was imprisoned twice – once by his own nobles, and once by his brother, Sigismund. His reign was also characterized by religious divisions within the Czech Lands and in Europe as a whole, beginning with the **Great Schism** (1378–1417), when rival popes held court in Rome and Avignon. This was a severe blow to Rome's centralizing power, which might otherwise have successfully combated the assault on the Church that was already under way in the Czech Lands towards the end of the fourteenth century.

The Bohemian Reformation

Right from the start, Prague was at the centre of the **Bohemian Reformation**. The increased influence of the Church, and its independence from Mainz established under Charles, led to a sharp increase in debauchery, petty theft and alcoholism among the clergy – a fertile climate for militant reformers like Jan Milič of Kroměříž, whose fiery sermons drew crowds of people to hear him at Prague's Týn church. In Václav's reign, the attack was led by the peasant-born preacher **Jan Hus**, who gave sermons at Prague's Betlémská kaple (see p.96).

Hus's main inspiration was the English reformist theologian John Wycliffe, whose heretical works found their way to Bohemia via Václav's sister, Anne, who married King Richard II. Worse still, as far as Church traditionalists were concerned, Hus began to preach in the language of the masses (ie, Czech) against the wealth, corruption and hierarchical tendencies within the Church at the time. A devout, mild-mannered man himself, he became embroiled in a dispute between the conservative clergy, led by Archbishop Zbyněk and backed by the pope, and the Wycliffian Czechs at the university. When Archbishop Zbyněk gave the order to burn the books of Wycliffe, Václav backed Hus and his followers, for political and personal reasons (Hus was, among other things, the confessor to his wife, Queen Sophie).

There can be little doubt that King Václav used Hus and the Wycliffites to further his own political cause. He had been deposed as Holy Roman Emperor in 1400, and, as a result, bore a grudge against the current emperor, Ruprecht of the Palatinate, and his chief backer, Pope Gregory XII in Rome. His chosen battleground was Prague's university, which was divided into four "nations" with equal voting rights: the Saxons, Poles and Bavarians, who supported Václav's enemies, and the Bohemians, who were mostly Wycliffites. In 1409 Václav issued the **Kutná Hora Decree**, which rigged the voting within the university giving the Bohemian "nation" three votes, and the rest a total of one. The other "nations", who made up the majority of the students and teachers, left Prague in protest.

Three years later the alliance between the king and the Wycliffites broke down. Widening his attacks on the Church, Hus began to preach against the sale of religious indulgences to fund the inter-papal wars, thus incurring the enmity of Václav, who received a percentage of the sales. In 1412 Hus and his followers were expelled from the university, excommunicated and banished from Prague, and spent the next two years as itinerant preachers spreading their reformist gospel throughout Bohemia. In 1414 Hus was summoned to the **Council of Constance** to answer charges of heresy. Despite a guarantee of safe conduct from Emperor Sigismund, Hus was condemned to death and, having refused to renounce his beliefs, was burned at the stake on July 6, 1415.

Hus's martyrdom sparked off **widespread riots** in Prague, initially uniting virtually all Bohemians – clergy and laity, peasant and noble (including many of Hus's former opponents) – against the decision of the council, and, by inference, against the established Church and its conservative clergy. The Hussites immediately set about reforming church practices, most famously by administering communion *sub utraque specie* ("in both kinds", ie bread and wine) to the laity, as opposed to the established practice of reserving the wine for the clergy.

The Hussite Wars: 1419–34

In 1419, Václav inadvertently provoked further large-scale rioting by endorsing the readmission of anti-Hussite priests to their parishes. In the ensuing violence, several councillors (including the mayor) were thrown to their death from the windows of Prague's Novoměstská radnice, in Prague's **first defenestration** (see p.129). Václav himself was so enraged (not to say terrified) by the mob that he suffered a stroke and died, "roaring like a lion", according to a contemporary chronicler. The pope, meanwhile, declared an international crusade against the Czech heretics, under the leadership of Emperor Sigismund, Václav's brother and, since Václav had failed to produce an heir, chief claimant to the Bohemian throne.

Already, though, cracks were appearing in the Hussite camp. The more radical reformers, who became known as the **Táborites** after their south Bohemian base, Tábor, broadened their attacks on the Church hierarchy to include all figures of authority and privilege. Their message found a ready audience among the oppressed classes in Prague and the Bohemian countryside, who went around eagerly destroying church property and massacring Catholics. Such actions were deeply disturbing to the Czech nobility and their supporters who backed the more moderate Hussites – known as the **Utraquists** (from the Latin *sub utraque specie*) – who confined their criticisms to religious matters.

For the moment, however, the common Catholic enemy prevented a serious split developing amongst the Hussites, and under the inspirational military leadership of the Táborite **Jan Žižka**, the Hussites' (mostly peasant) army enjoyed some miraculous early victories over the numerically superior "crusaders", most notably at the Battle of Vítkov in Prague in 1420. The Bohemian Diet quickly drew up the **Four Articles of Prague**, a compromise between the two Hussite camps, outlining the basic tenets about which all Hussites could agree, including communion "in both kinds". The Táborites, meanwhile, continued to burn, loot and pillage ecclesiastical institutions from Prague to the far reaches of the kingdom.

At the **Council of Basel** in 1433, Rome reached a compromise with the Utraquists over the Four Articles, in return for ceasing hostilities. The peasant-based Táborites rightly saw the deal as a victory for the Bohemian nobility and the status quo, and vowed to continue the fight. However, the Utraquists, now in cahoots with the Catholic forces, easily defeated the remaining Táborites at the **Battle of Lipany**, outside Kolín, in 1434. The Táborites were forced to withdraw to the fortress town of Tábor. Poor old Sigismund, who had spent the best part of his life fighting the Hussites, died only three years later.

Compromise

Despite the agreement of the Council of Basel, the pope refused to acknowledge the Utraquist church in Bohemia. The Utraquists nevertheless consolidated their position, electing the gifted **George of Poděbrady** first as regent and then king of Bohemia (1458–71). The first and last Hussite king, George – Jiří to the Czechs – is remembered primarily for his commitment to promoting religious tolerance and for his far-sighted, but ultimately futile, attempts to establish some sort of "Peace Confederation" in Europe.

On George's death, the Bohemian Estates handed the crown over to the **Polish Jagiellonian dynasty**, who ruled *in absentia*, effectively relinquishing the reins of power to the Czech nobility. In 1526, the last of the Jagiellonians, King Louis, was decisively defeated by the Turks at the Battle of Mohács, and died fleeing the battlefield, leaving no heir to the throne. The Roman Catholic Habsburg, Ferdinand I (1526–64), was elected king of Bohemia – and what was left of Hungary – in order to fill the power vacuum, marking the **beginning of Habsburg rule** over what is now the Czech Republic. Ferdinand adroitly secured automatic hereditary succession over the Bohemian throne for his dynasty, in return for which he accepted the agreement laid down at the Council of Basel back in 1433. With the Turks at the gates of Vienna, he had little choice but to compromise at this stage, but in 1545 the international situation eased somewhat with the establishment of an armistice with the Turks.

The following year, the Utraquist Bohemian nobility provocatively joined the powerful Protestant Schmalkaldic League in their (ultimately successful) war against the Holy Roman Emperor, Charles V. After a brief armed skirmish in Prague, however, victory initially fell to Ferdinand, who took the opportunity to extend the influence of Catholicism in the Czech Lands, executing several leading Protestant nobles, persecuting the reformist Unity of Czech Brethren, who had figured prominently in the rebellion, and inviting Jesuit missionaries to establish churches and seminaries in the Czech Lands.

Like Václav IV, **Emperor Rudolf II** (1576–1611), Ferdinand's eventual successor, was moody and wayward, and by the end of his reign Bohemia was again rushing headlong into a major international confrontation. But Rudolf also shared characteristics with Václav's father, Charles, in his genuine love of the arts, and in his passion for Prague, which he re-established as the royal seat of power, in preference to Vienna, which was once more under threat from the Turks. He endowed Prague's galleries with the best Mannerist art in Europe, and, most famously, invited the respected astronomists Tycho Brahe and

Johannes Kepler, and the infamous English alchemists John Dee and Edward Kelley, to Prague (see p.51).

Czechs tend to regard Rudolfine Prague as a second golden age, but as far as the Catholic Church was concerned, Rudolf's religious tolerance and indecision were a disaster. In the early 1600s, Rudolf's melancholy began to veer dangerously close to insanity, a condition he had inherited from his Spanish grandmother, Joanna the Mad. And in 1611, the heirless Rudolf was forced to abdicate by his brother **Matthias**, to save the Habsburg house from ruin. Ardently Catholic, but equally heirless, Matthias proposed his cousin **Ferdinand II** as his successor in 1617. This was the last straw for Bohemia's mostly Protestant nobility, and the following year conflict erupted again.

The Thirty Years' War: 1618–48

On May 23, 1618, two Catholic governors appointed by Ferdinand were thrown out of the windows of Prague Castle (along with their secretary) – the country's **second defenestration** (see p.48) – an event that's now taken as the official beginning of the complex religious and dynastic conflicts collectively known as the **Thirty Years' War**. Following the defenestration, the Bohemian Diet expelled the Jesuits and elected the youthful Protestant "Winter King", Frederick of the Palatinate, to the throne. In the first decisive set-to of the war, on November 8, 1620, the Czech Protestants were utterly defeated at the **Battle of Bílá hora** or Battle of the White Mountain (see p.162) by the imperial Catholic forces under Count Tilly. In the aftermath, 27 Protestant nobles were executed on Prague's Staroměstské náměstí, and the heads of ten of them displayed on the Charles Bridge.

It wasn't until the Protestant Saxons occupied Prague in 1632 that the heads were finally taken down and given a proper burial. The Catholics eventually drove the Saxons out, but for the last ten years of the war Bohemia became the main battleground between the new champions of the Protestant cause – the Swedes – and the imperial Catholic forces. In 1648, the final battle of the war was fought in Prague, when the Swedes seized Malá Strana, but failed to take Staré Město, thanks to the stubborn resistance of Prague's Jewish, and newly Catholicized student populations on the Charles Bridge.

The Counter-Reformation and the Dark Ages

The Thirty Years' War ended with the **Peace of Westphalia**, which, for the Czechs, was as disastrous as the war itself. An estimated five-sixths of the Bohemian nobility went into exile, their properties handed over to loyal Catholic families from Austria, Spain, France and Italy. Bohemia had been devastated, with towns and cities laid waste, and the total population reduced by almost two-thirds; Prague's population halved. On top of all that, Bohemia was now decisively within the Catholic sphere of influence, and the full force of the **Counter-Reformation** was brought to bear on its people. All forms of

Protestantism were outlawed, the education system was handed over to the Jesuits and, in 1651 alone, more than two hundred "witches" were burned at the stake in Bohemia.

The next two centuries of Habsburg rule are known to the Czechs as the **Dark Ages**. The focus of the empire shifted back to Vienna, the Habsburgs' absolutist grip over the Czech Lands catapulted the remaining nobility into intensive Germanization, while fresh waves of German immigrants reduced Czech to a despised dialect spoken only by peasants, artisans and servants. The situation was so bad that Prague and most other urban centres became practically German-speaking cities. By the end of the eighteenth century, the Czech language was on the verge of dying out, with government, scholarship and literature carried out exclusively in German. For the newly ensconced Germanized aristocracy, and for the Catholic Church, of course, the good times rolled and Prague was endowed with numerous Baroque palaces, churches, monasteries and monuments, many of which still grace the city today.

The Enlightenment

After a century of iron-fisted Habsburg rule, dispute arose over the accession of Charles VI's daughter, **Maria Theresa** (1740–80), to the Habsburg throne, and Prague, as usual, found itself at the centre of the battlefield. In November 1741, Prague was easily taken by Bavarian, French and Saxon troops, but the occupation force quickly found itself besieged in turn by a Habsburg army, and in January 1743 was forced to abandon the city. By November 1744, Prague was again besieged, this time by the Prussian army, who bombed the city into submission in a fortnight. After a month of looting, they left the city to escape the advancing Habsburg army. During the Seven Years' War, in 1757, Prague was once more besieged and bombarded by the Prussian army, though this time the city held out, and following their defeat at the Battle of Kolín, the Prussians withdrew.

Maria Theresa's reign also marked the beginning of the **Enlightenment** in the Habsburg Empire. Despite her own personal attachment to the Jesuits, the empress acknowledged the need for reform, and followed the lead of Spain, Portugal and France in expelling the order from the empire in 1773. But it was her son, **Joseph II** (1780–90), who, in the ten short years of his reign, brought about the most radical changes to the social structure of the Habsburg lands. His 1781 Edict of Tolerance allowed a large degree of freedom of worship for the first time in over 150 years, and went a long way towards lifting the restrictions on Jews within the empire. The following year, he ordered the dissolution of the monasteries, and embarked upon the abolition of serfdom. Despite all his reforms, Joseph was not universally popular. Catholics – some ninety percent of the Bohemian population – viewed him with disdain, and even forced him to back down when he decreed that Protestants, Jews, unbaptized children and suicide victims should be buried in consecrated Catholic cemeteries. His centralization and bureaucratization of the empire placed power in the hands of the Habsburg civil service, and thus helped entrench the **Germanization** of Bohemia. He also offended the Czechs by breaking with tradition and not bothering to hold an official coronation ceremony in Prague.

The Czech national revival

The Habsburgs' enlightened rule inadvertently provided the basis for the economic prosperity and social changes of the **Industrial Revolution**, which in turn fuelled the Czech national revival of the nineteenth century. The textile, glass, coal and iron industries began to grow, drawing ever more Czechs from the countryside and swamping the hitherto mostly German-speaking towns and cities, including Prague. A Czech working class, and even an embryonic Czech bourgeoisie emerged, and, thanks to Maria Theresa's reforms, new educational and economic opportunities were given to the Czech lower classes.

For the first half of the century, the Czech **national revival** or *národní obrození* was confined to the new Czech intelligentsia, led by philologists like Josef Dobrovský and Josef Jungmann at the Charles University or Karolinum in Prague. Language disputes (in schools, universities and public offices) remained at the forefront of Czech nationalism throughout the nineteenth century, only later developing into demands for political autonomy from Vienna. The leading figure of the time was the historian **František Palacký**, a Moravian Protestant who wrote the first history of the Czech nation, rehabilitating Hus and the Czech reformists in the process. He was in many ways typical of the early Czech nationalists – pan-Slavist, virulently anti-German, but not yet entirely anti-Habsburg.

1848 and all that

The fall of the French monarchy in February 1848 prompted a crisis in the German states and in the Habsburg Empire. The new Bohemian bourgeoisie, both Czech and German, began to make political demands: freedom of the press, of assembly, of religious creeds. In March, when news of the revolutionary outbreak in Vienna reached Prague, the city's Czechs and Germans began organizing a joint National Guard, while the students formed an Academic Legion, in imitation of the Viennese. Eventually, a National Committee of Czechs and Germans was formed, and Prague itself got its own elected mayor.

However, it wasn't long before cracks began to appear in the Czech-German alliance. Palacký and his followers were against the dissolution of the empire and argued instead for a kind of multinational federation. Since the empire contained a majority of non-Germans, Prague's own Germans were utterly opposed to Palacký's scheme, campaigning for unification with Germany to secure their interests. On April 11, Palacký refused an invitation to attend the Pan-German National Assembly in Frankfurt. The Germans immediately withdrew from the National Committee, and Prague's other revolutionary institutions began to divide along linguistic lines. On June 2, Palacký convened a **Pan-Slav Congress** the following month, which met on Prague's Slovanský ostrov, an island in the Vltava. Czechs and Slovaks made up the majority of the delegates, but there were also Poles, Croats, Slovenes and Serbs in attendance.

On June 12, the congress had to adjourn, as fighting had broken out on the streets the previous day between the troops of the local Habsburg commander, Alfred Prince Windischgrätz, and Czech protesters. The radicals and students took to the streets of Prague, barricades went up overnight, and martial law was declared. During the night of June 14, Windischgrätz withdrew his troops to the left bank and proceeded to bombard the right bank into submission. On the morning of June 17 the city capitulated – the counter-revolution in Bohemia had begun. The upheavals of 1848 left the absolutist Habsburg Empire shaken but fundamentally unchanged and served to highlight the sharp differences between German and Czech aspirations in Bohemia.

Dualism

The Habsburg recovery was, however, short-lived. In 1859, and again in 1866, the new emperor, Franz-Joseph II, suffered humiliating defeats at the hands of the Italians and Prussians respectively, the latter getting their hands on Prague yet again. In order to buy some more time, the compromise or *Ausgleich* of 1867 was drawn up, establishing the so-called **Dual Monarchy** of Austria-Hungary – two independent states united by one ruler.

For the Czechs, the *Ausgleich* came as a bitter disappointment. While the Magyars became the Austrians' equals, the Czechs remained second-class citizens. The Czechs' failure in bending the emperor's ear was no doubt partly due to the absence of a Czech aristocracy that could bring its social weight to bear at the Viennese court. Nevertheless, the *Ausgleich* did mark an end to the absolutism of the immediate post-1848 period, and, compared with the Hungarians, the Austrians were positively enlightened in the wide range of civil liberties they granted, culminating in universal male suffrage in 1907.

The Industrial Revolution continued apace in Bohemia, bringing an ever-increasing number of Czechs into the newly founded suburbs of Prague, such as Smíchov and Žižkov. Thanks to the unfair voting system, however, the German-speaking minority managed to hold onto power in the Prague city council until the 1880s. By the turn of the century, German-speakers made up just five percent of the city's population – fewer than the Czechs in Vienna – and of those more than half were Jewish. Nevertheless, German influence in the city remained considerable, far greater than their numbers alone warranted; this was due in part to economic means, and in part to overall rule from Vienna.

Under Dualism, the Czech *národní obrození* flourished. Towards the end of the century, Prague was endowed with a number of symbolically significant Czech monuments, like the Národní divaldo (National Theatre), the Národní muzeum (National Museum) and the Rudolfinum. Inevitably, the movement also began to splinter, with the liberals and conservatives, known as the **Old Czechs**, advocating working within the existing legislature to achieve their aims, and the more radical **Young Czechs** favouring a policy of non-cooperation. The most famous political figure to emerge from the ranks of the Young Czechs was the Prague university professor **Tomáš Garrigue Masaryk**, who founded his own Realist Party in 1900 and began to put forward the (then rather quirky) concept of closer cooperation between the Czechs and Slovaks.

The Old Czechs, backed by the new Czech industrialists, achieved a number of minor legislative successes, but by the 1890s the Young Czechs had gained the upper hand and conflict between the Czech and German communities became a daily ritual in the boulevards of the capital – a favourite spot for confrontations being the promenade of Na příkopě. Language was also a volatile issue, often fought out on the shop and street signs of Prague. In 1897 the **Badeni Decrees**, which put Czech on an equal footing with German in all dealings with the state, drove the country to the point of civil war, before being withdrawn by the cautious Austrians.

World War I

At the outbreak of **World War I**, the Czechs and Slovaks showed little enthusiasm for fighting alongside their old enemies, the Austrians and Hungarians, against their Slav brothers, the Russians and Serbs. As the war progressed, large numbers defected to form the **Czechoslovak Legion**, which fought on the Eastern Front against the Austrians. Masaryk travelled to the USA to curry favour for a new Czechoslovak state, while his two deputies, the Czech Edvard Beneš and the Slovak Milan Štefánik, did the same in Britain and France.

Meanwhile, the Legion, which by now numbered some 100,000 men, became embroiled in the Russian revolutions of 1917, and, when the Bolsheviks made peace with Germany, found itself cut off from the homeland. The uneasy cooperation between the Reds and the Legion broke down when Trotsky demanded that they hand over their weapons before heading off on their legendary **anabasis**, or march back home, via Vladivostok. The soldiers refused and became further involved in the Civil War, for a while controlling large parts of Siberia and, most importantly, the Trans-Siberian Railway, before arriving back to a tumultuous reception in the new republic.

Meanwhile, during the course of the summer of 1918, the Slovaks finally threw in their lot with the Czechs, and the Allies recognized Masaryk's provisional Czechoslovak government. On October 28, 1918, as the Habsburg Empire began to collapse, the first **Czechoslovak Republic** was declared in Prague. In response, the German-speaking border regions (later to become known as the Sudetenland) declared themselves autonomous provinces of the new republic of *Deutsch-Österreich* (German-Austria), which, it was hoped, would eventually unite with Germany itself. The new Czechoslovak government was having none of it, but it took the intervention of Czechoslovak troops before control of the border regions was rested from the secessionists.

Last to opt in favour of the new republic was **Ruthenia** (known as Sub-Carpatho-Ruthenia), a rural backwater of the old Hungarian Kingdom which became officially part of Czechoslovakia by the Treaty of St Germain in September 1919. Its incorporation was largely due to the campaigning efforts of Ruthenian émigrés in the USA. For the new republic the province was a strategic bonus, but otherwise a huge drain on resources.

The First Republic

The new nation of Czechoslovakia began postwar life in an enviable economic position – **tenth in the world industrial league table** – having inherited seventy to eighty percent of Austria-Hungary's industry intact. Prague regained its position at the centre of the country's political and cultural life, and in the interwar period was embellished with a rich mantle of Bauhaus-style buildings. Less enviable was the diverse make-up of the country's population – a melange of minorities which would in the end prove its downfall. Along with the six million Czechs and two million Slovaks who initially backed the republic, there were more than three million Germans and 600,000 Hungarians, not to mention sundry other Ruthenians (Rusyns), Jews and Poles.

That Czechoslovakia's democracy survived as long as it did is down to the powerful political presence and skill of **Masaryk**, the country's president from

1918 to 1935, who shared executive power with the cabinet. It was his vision of social democracy that was stamped on the nation's new constitution, one of the most liberal of the time (if a little bureaucratic and centralized), aimed at ameliorating any ethnic and class tensions within the republic by means of universal suffrage, land reform and, more specifically, the Language Law, which ensured bilinguality to any area where the minority exceeded twenty percent.

The elections of 1920 reflected the mood of the time, ushering in the left-liberal alliance of the **Pětka** (The Five), a coalition of five parties led by the Agrarian, Antonín Švehla, whose slogan, "we have agreed that we will agree", became the keystone of the republic's consensus politics between the wars. Gradually all the other parties (except the Fascists and the Communists) – including even Andrej Hlinka's Slovak People's Party and most of the Sudeten German parties – began to participate in (or at least not disrupt) parliamentary proceedings. On the eve of the Wall Street Crash, the republic was enjoying an economic boom, a cultural renaissance and a temporary *modus vivendi* among its minorities.

The Thirties

The 1929 Wall Street Crash plunged the whole country into crisis. Economic hardship was quickly followed by **political instability**. In Slovakia, Hlinka's People's Party fed off the anti-Czech resentment that was fuelled by Prague's manic centralization, consistently polling around thirty percent, with an increasingly nationalist/separatist message. In Ruthenia, the elections of 1935 gave only 37 percent of the vote to parties supporting the republic, the rest going to the Communists, pro-Magyars and other autonomist groups.

But without doubt the most intractable of the minority problems was that of the Sudeten Germans, who lived in the heavily industrialized border regions of Bohemia and Moravia. Nationalist sentiment had always run high in the Sudetenland, many of whose German-speakers resented having been included in the new republic, but it was only after the Crash that the extremist parties began to make significant electoral gains. Encouraged by the rise of Fascism in Austria, Italy and Germany, and aided by rocketing Sudeten German unemployment, the far-right **Sudeten German Party** (SdP), led by a bespectacled gym teacher called Konrad Henlein, was able to win just over sixty percent of the German-speaking vote in the 1935 elections.

Although constantly denying any wish to secede from the republic, the activities of Henlein and the SdP were increasingly funded and directed from Nazi Germany. To make matters worse, the Czechs suffered a severe blow to their morale with the death of Masaryk late in 1937, leaving the country in the less capable hands of his Socialist deputy, Edvard Beneš. With the Nazi annexation of Austria (the *Anschluss*) on March 11, 1938, Hitler was free to focus his attention on the Sudetenland, calling Henlein to Berlin on March 28 and instructing him to call for outright autonomy.

The Munich crisis

On April 24, 1938, the SdP launched its final propaganda offensive in the **Karlsbad Decrees**, demanding (without defining) "complete autonomy". As this would clearly have meant surrendering the entire Czechoslovak border defences, not to mention causing economic havoc, Beneš refused to bow to the SdP's demands. Armed conflict was only narrowly avoided and, by the beginning of September, Beneš was forced to acquiesce to some sort of autonomy. On Hitler's orders, Henlein refused Beneš's offer and called openly for the secession of the Sudetenland to the German Reich.

On September 15, as Henlein fled to Germany, the British prime minister, Neville Chamberlain, flew to Berchtesgaden on his own ill-conceived initiative to "appease" the Führer. A week later, Chamberlain flew again to Germany, this time to Bad Godesburg, vowing to the British public that the country would not go to war (in his famous words) "because of a quarrel in a far-away country between people of whom we know nothing". Nevertheless, the French issued draft papers, the British Navy was mobilized, and the whole of Europe fully expected war. Then, in the early hours of September 30, in one of the most treacherous and self-interested acts of modern European diplomacy, prime ministers Chamberlain (for Britain) and Daladier (for France) signed the **Munich Diktat** with Mussolini and Hitler, agreeing – without consulting the Czechoslovak government – to all of Hitler's demands. The British and French public were genuinely relieved, and Chamberlain flew back to cheering home crowds, waving his famous piece of paper that guaranteed "peace in our time".

Ⓒ The Second Republic

Betrayed by his only Western allies and fearing bloodshed, Beneš capitulated, against the wishes of most Czechs. Had Beneš not given in, however, it's doubtful anything would have come of Czech armed resistance, surrounded as they were by vastly superior hostile powers. Beneš resigned on October 5 and left the country. On October 15, **German troops occupied Sudetenland**, to the dismay of the forty percent of Sudeten Germans who hadn't voted for Henlein (not to mention the half a million Czechs and Jews who lived there). The Poles took the opportunity to seize a sizeable chunk of North Moravia, while in the short-lived "rump" **Second Republic** (officially known as Czecho-Slovakia), Emil Hácha became president, Slovakia and Ruthenia electing their own autonomous governments.

The Second Republic was not long in existence before it too collapsed. On March 15, 1939, Hitler informed Hácha of the imminent Nazi occupation of what was left of the Czech Lands, and persuaded him to demobilize the army, again against the wishes of many Czechs. The Germans encountered no resistance (nor any response from the Second Republic's supposed guarantors, Britain and France) and swiftly set up the Nazi **Protectorate of Bohemia and Moravia**. The Hungarians effortlessly crushed Ruthenia's brief independence, while the Slovak People's Party, backed by the Nazis, declared **Slovak independence**, under the leadership of the clerical fascist Jozef Tiso.

World War II

In the first few months of the occupation, left-wing activists were arrested, and Jews were placed under the infamous Nuremberg Laws, but Nazi rule in the Protectorate was not as harsh as it would later become. The relatively benign, conservative aristocrat, **Baron von Neurath**, was appointed *Reichsprotektor*, though his deputy was the rabid Nazi, Karl Hermann Frank. Then, on October 28 (Czechoslovak National Day), during a demonstration against the Nazi occupiers, **Jan Opletal**, a Czech medical student, was fatally wounded; he died in hospital on November 11. Prague's Czech students held a wake in the pub, *U Fleků*, after which there were further disturbances. Frank used these as an excuse to close down all Czech institutions of higher education, on November 17, executing a number of student leaders and sending over a thousand more off to the camps.

In 1941, Himmler's deputy in the SS, **Reinhard Heydrich**, was made *Reichsprotektor*. More arrests and deportations followed, prompting the Czech government-in-exile to organise the most audacious assassination to take place in Nazi-occupied Europe. In June 1942, Heydrich was fatally wounded by Czech parachutists on the streets of Prague (see p.130). The reprisals were swift and brutal, culminating in the destruction of the villages of Lidice (see p.179) and Ležáky. Meanwhile, the "final solution" was meted out on the country's remaining Jews, who were transported first to the ghetto in Terezín (see p.169), and then on to the extermination camps. The rest of the population were frightened into submission – very few acts of active resistance being undertaken in the Czech Lands until the Prague Uprising of May 1945 (see below).

By the end of 1944, Czechoslovak and Russian troops had begun to liberate the country, starting with Ruthenia, which Stalin decided to take as war booty despite having guaranteed to maintain Czechoslovakia's pre-Munich borders. On April 4, 1945, under Beneš's leadership, the provisional National Front or **Národní fronta** government – a coalition of Social Democrats, Socialists and Communists – was set up in Košice. By April 18, the US Third Army, under General Patton, had crossed the border in the west, meeting very little German resistance.

On the morning of May 5, the Prague radio station, behind the National Museum, began broadcasting in Czech only. The **Prague Uprising** had officially begun. Luckily for the Czechs, Vlasov's anti-Bolshevik Russian National Liberation Army were in the vicinity and were persuaded to turn on the Germans, successfully resisting the two crack German armoured divisions, not to mention the extremely fanatical SS troops, in and around the capital. Barriers were erected across the city, and an American OSS jeep patrol arrived from Plzeň, which the Third Army were on the point of taking. The Praguers (and Vlasov's men) were pinning their hopes on the Americans. In the end, however, the US military leadership made the politically disastrous decision not to cross the demarcation line that had been agreed between the Allies at Yalta. On May 7, Vlasov's men fled towards the American lines, leaving the Praguers to hold out against the Germans. The following day, a ceasefire was agreed and the Germans retreated, for the most part, and headed, like Vlasov, in the direction of the Americans. The Russians entered the city on May 9, and overcame the last pockets of Nazi resistance.

The Third Republic

Violent reprisals against suspected collaborators and the German-speaking population in general began as soon as the country was liberated. All Germans were immediately given the same food rations as the Jews had been given during the war. Starvation, summary executions and worse resulted in the deaths of countless thousands of ethnic Germans. With considerable popular backing and the tacit approval of the Red Army, Beneš began to organize the forced **expulsion of the German-speaking population**, referred to euphemistically by the Czechs as the *odsun* (transfer). Only those German-speakers who could prove their anti-Fascist credentials were permitted to stay – the Czech community was not called on to prove the same – and by the summer of 1947, nearly 2.5 million Germans had been expelled from the country or had fled in fear. On this occasion, Sudeten German objections were brushed aside by the Allies, who had given Beneš the go-ahead for the *odsun* at the postwar Potsdam Conference. Attempts by Beneš to expel the Hungarian-speaking minority from Slovakia in similar fashion, however, proved unsuccessful.

On October 28, 1945, in accordance with the leftist programme thrashed out at Košice, sixty percent of the country's industry was nationalized. Confiscated Sudeten German property was handed out by the largely Communist-controlled police force, and in a spirit of optimism and/or opportunism, people began to join the Communist Party (KSČ) in droves; membership more than doubled in less than a year. In the **May 1946 elections**, the Party reaped the rewards of their enthusiastic support for the *odsun*, of Stalin's vocal opposition to Munich, and of the recent Soviet liberation, emerging as the strongest single party in the Czech Lands with up to forty percent of the vote (the largest ever for a European Communist Party in a multi-party election). In Slovakia, however, they achieved just thirty percent, thus failing to push the Democrats into second place. President Beneš appointed the KSČ leader, **Klement Gottwald**, prime minister of another Národní fronta coalition, with several strategically important cabinet portfolios going to Party members, including the ministries of the Interior, Finance, Labour and Social Affairs, Agriculture and Information.

Gottwald assured everyone of the KSČ's commitment to parliamentary democracy, and initially at least even agreed to participate in the Americans' Marshall Plan (the only Eastern Bloc country to do so). Stalin immediately summoned Gottwald to Moscow, and on his return the KSČ denounced the Plan. By the end of 1947, the Communists were beginning to lose support, as the harvest failed, the economy faltered and malpractices within the Communist-controlled Ministry of the Interior were uncovered. In response, the KSČ began to up the ante, constantly warning the nation of imminent "counter-revolutionary plots", and arguing for greater nationalization and land reform as a safeguard.

Then in February 1948 – officially known as **"Victorious February"** – the latest in a series of scandals hit the Ministry of the Interior, prompting the twelve non-Communist cabinet ministers to resign en masse in the hope of forcing Beneš to dismiss Gottwald. No attempt was made, however, to rally popular support against the Communists. Beneš received more than 5000 resolutions supporting the Communists and just 150 opposing them. Stalin sent word to Gottwald to take advantage of the crisis and ask for military assistance – Soviet troops began massing on the Hungarian border. It was the one time in his life when Gottwald disobeyed Stalin; instead, by exploiting the divisions within the Social Democrats, he was able to maintain his majority in parliament. The KSČ took to the streets (and the airwaves), arming "workers' militia" units to defend the country against counter-revolution, calling a general strike and finally, on February 25, organizing the country's biggest ever demonstration in Prague. The same day Gottwald went to an indecisive (and increasingly ill) Beneš with his new cabinet, all Party members or "fellow travellers". Beneš accepted Gottwald's nominees and the most popular Communist coup in Eastern Europe was complete, without bloodshed and without the direct intervention of the Soviets. In the aftermath of the coup, thousands of Czechs and Slovaks fled abroad.

The People's Republic

Following Victorious February, the Party began to consolidate its position, a relatively easy task given its immense popular support and control of the army, police force, workers' militia and trade unions. A **new constitution** confirming the "leading role" of the Communist Party and the "dictatorship of the proletariat" was passed by parliament on May 9, 1948. President Beneš refused to sign it, resigned in favour of Gottwald, and died (of natural causes) shortly afterwards. Those political parties that were not banned or forcibly merged with the KSČ were prescribed fixed-percentage representation within the so-called "multi-party" Národní fronta.

With the Cold War in full swing, the **Stalinization** of Czechoslovak society was quick to follow. In the Party's first Five Year Plan, ninety percent of industry was nationalized, heavy industry (and in particular the country's defence industry) was given a massive boost and compulsory collectivization forced through. Party membership reached an all-time high of 2.5 million, and "class-conscious" Party cadres were given positions of power, while "class enemies" (and their children) were discriminated against. It wasn't long, too, before the Czechoslovak mining "gulags" began to fill up with the regime's political opponents – "kulaks", priests and "bourgeois oppositionists" – numbering more than 100,000 at their peak.

Having incarcerated most of its non-Party opponents, the KSČ, with a little prompting from Stalin, embarked upon a ruthless period of internal blood-letting. As the economy nose-dived, calls for intensified "class struggle", rumours of impending "counter-revolution" and reports of economic sabotage by fifth columnists filled the press. An atmosphere of fear and confusion was created to justify **large-scale arrests of Party members** with an "international" background: those with a wartime connection with the West, Spanish Civil War veterans, Jews and Slovak nationalists.

In the early 1950s, the Party organized a series of Stalinist **show trials** in Prague, the most spectacular of which was the trial of Rudolf Slánský, who had been second only to Gottwald in the KSČ before his arrest. Slánský, Vladimír Clementis, the former KSČ foreign minister, and twelve other leading Party members (eleven of them Jewish, including Slánský) were sentenced to death as "Trotskyist-Titoist-Zionists".

After Stalin

Gottwald died in mysterious circumstances in March 1953, nine days after attending Stalin's funeral in Moscow (some say he drank himself to death). The whole nation heaved a sigh of relief, but the regime seemed as unrepentant as ever. The arrests and show trials continued. Then, on May 30, the new Communist leadership announced a drastic currency devaluation, effectively reducing wages by ten percent, while raising prices. The result was a wave of isolated **workers' demonstrations** and rioting in Plzeň and Prague. Czechoslovak army units called in to suppress the demonstrations proved unreliable, and it was left to the heavily armed workers' militia and police to disperse the crowds and make the predictable arrests and summary executions.

In 1954, in the last of the show trials, Gustáv Husák, the post-1968 president, was given life imprisonment, along with other leading Slovak comrades. So complete were the Party purges of the early 1950s, so sycophantic (and scared) was the surviving leadership, that Khrushchev's 1956 thaw was virtually ignored by the KSČ. An attempted rebellion in the Writers' Union Congress was rebuffed and an enquiry into the show trials made several minor security officials scapegoats for the "malpractices". The genuine mass base of the KSČ remained blindly loyal to the Party for the most part; Prague basked under the largest statue of Stalin in the world; and in 1957, the dull, unreconstructed neo-Stalinist **Antonín Novotný** – alleged to have been a spy for the Gestapo during the war – became First Secretary and President.

Reformism and invasion

The first rumblings of protest against Czechoslovakia's hardline leadership appeared in the official press in 1963. At first, the criticisms were confined to the country's worsening economic stagnation, but soon developed into more generalized protests against the KSČ leadership. Novotný responded by ordering the belated release and rehabilitation of victims of the 1950s purges, permitting a slight cultural thaw and easing travel restrictions to the West. In effect, he was simply buying time. The half-hearted economic reforms announced in the 1965 **New Economic Model** failed to halt the recession, and the minor political reforms instigated by the KSČ only increased the pressure for greater changes within the Party.

In 1967, Novotný attempted a pre-emptive strike against his opponents. Several leading writers were imprisoned, Slovak Party leaders were branded as "bourgeois nationalists" and the economists were called on to produce results or else forego their reform programme. Instead of eliminating the opposition, though, Novotný unwittingly united them. Despite Novotný's plea to the Soviets, Brezhnev refused to back a leader whom he saw as "Khrushchev's man in Prague", and on January 5, 1968, the young Slovak leader **Alexander Dubček** replaced Novotný as First Secretary. On March 22, the war hero Ludvík Svoboda dislodged Novotný from the presidency.

1968: The Prague Spring

By inclination, Dubček was a moderate, cautious reformer – the perfect compromise candidate – but he was continually swept along by the sheer force of the reform movement. The virtual **abolition of censorship** was probably the single most significant step Dubček took. It transformed what had been until then an internal Party debate into a popular mass movement. Civil society, for years muffled by the paranoia and strictures of Stalinism, suddenly sprang into life in the dynamic optimism of the first few months of 1968, the so-called **"Prague Spring"**. In April, the KSČ published their Action Programme, proposing what became popularly known as "socialism with a human face" – federalization, freedom of assembly and expression, and democratization of parliament.

Throughout the spring and summer, the reform movement gathered momentum. The Social Democrat Party (forcibly merged with the KSČ after 1948) re-formed, anti-Soviet polemics appeared in the press and, most famously of all, the writer and lifelong Party member Ludvík Vaculík published his personal manifesto entitled **"Two Thousand Words"**, calling for radical de-Stalinization within the Party. Dubček and the moderates denounced the manifesto and reaffirmed the country's support for the Warsaw Pact military alliance. Meanwhile, the Soviets and their hardline allies – Gomulka in Poland

and Ulbricht in the GDR – viewed the Czechoslovak developments on their doorstep very gravely, and began to call for the suppression of "counter-revolutionary elements" and the reimposition of censorship.

As the summer wore on, it became clear that the Soviets were planning military intervention. Warsaw Pact manoeuvres were held in Czechoslovakia in late June, a Warsaw Pact conference (without Czechoslovak participation) was convened in mid-July and, at the beginning of August, the Soviets and the KSČ leadership met for **emergency bilateral talks** at Čierna nad Tisou on the Czechoslovak–Soviet border. Brezhnev's hardline deputy, Alexei Kosygin, made his less than subtle threat that "your border is our border", but did agree to withdraw Soviet troops (stationed in the country since the June manoeuvres) and gave the go-ahead to the KSČ's special Party Congress scheduled for September 9.

In the early hours of August 21, fearing a defeat for the hardliners at the forthcoming KSČ Congress, and claiming to have been invited to provide "fraternal assistance", the Soviets gave the order for the **invasion of Czechoslovakia** to be carried out by all the Warsaw Pact forces (only Romania refused to take part). Dubček and the KSČ reformists immediately condemned the invasion before being arrested and flown to Moscow for "negotiations". President Svoboda refused to condone the formation of a new government under the hardliner Alois Indra, and the people took to the streets in protest, employing every form of non-violent resistance in the book. Individual acts of martyrdom, with the self-immolation of **Jan Palach** on Prague's Wenceslas Square, hit the headlines, but casualties were light compared with the Hungarian uprising of 1956 – the cost in terms of the following twenty years was much greater.

Normalization

In April 1969, there were anti-Soviet riots during the celebrations of the country's double ice hockey victory over the Soviets. On this pretext, another Slovak, **Gustáv Husák**, replaced the broken Dubček as First Secretary, and instigated his infamous policy of **"normalization"**. More than 150,000 fled the country before the borders closed, around 500,000 were expelled from the Party, and an estimated one million people lost their jobs or were demoted. Inexorably, the KSČ reasserted its absolute control over the state and society. The only part of the reform package to survive the invasion was **federalization**, which gave the Slovaks greater freedom from Prague (on paper at least), though even this was severely watered down in 1971. Dubček, like countless others, was forced to give up his job, working for the next twenty years as a minor official in the Slovak forestry commission.

An unwritten social contract was struck between rulers and ruled during the 1970s, whereby the country was guaranteed a tolerable standard of living (second only to that of the GDR in Eastern Europe) in return for its passive collaboration. Husák's security apparatus quashed all forms of dissent during the early 1970s, and it wasn't until the middle of the decade that an organized opposition was strong enough to show its face. In 1976, the punk rock band The Plastic People of the Universe were arrested and charged with the familiar "crimes against the state" clause of the penal code. The dissidents who rallied to their defence – a motley assortment of people ranging from former KSČ members to right-wing intellectuals – agreed to form **Charter 77**

(*Charta* 77 in Czech), with the purpose of monitoring human rights abuses in the country. One of the organization's prime movers and initial spokespeople was the absurdist Czech playwright **Václav Havel**. Havel, along with many others, endured relentless persecution (including long prison sentences) over the next decade in pursuit of Charter 77's ideals. The initial gathering of 243 signatories had increased to more than 1000 by 1980, and caused panic in the moral vacuum of the Party apparatus, but consistently failed to stir a fearful and cynical populace into action.

The 1980s

In the late 1970s and early 1980s, the inefficiencies of the economy prevented the government from fulfilling its side of the social contract, as living standards began to fall. Cynicism, alcoholism, absenteeism and outright dissent became widespread, especially among the younger (post-1968) generation. The **Jazz Section** of the Musicians' Union, who disseminated "subversive" Western pop music (such as pirate copies of "Live Aid"), highlighted the ludicrously harsh nature of the regime when they were arrested and imprisoned in the mid-1980s. Pop concerts, religious pilgrimages and, of course, the anniversary of the Soviet invasion all caused regular confrontations between the security forces and certain sections of the population. Yet still a mass movement like Poland's Solidarity failed to emerge.

With the advent of **Mikhail Gorbachev**, the KSČ was put in an extremely awkward position, as it tried desperately to separate *perestroika* from comparisons with the reforms of the Prague Spring. Husák and his cronies had prided themselves on being second only to Honecker's GDR as the most stable and orthodox of the Soviet satellites – now the font of orthodoxy, the Soviet Union, was turning against them. In 1987, **Miloš Jakeš**, the hardliner who oversaw Husák's normalization purges, took over from Husák as General (First) Secretary and introduced *přestavba* (restructuring), Czechoslovakia's lukewarm version of *perestroika*.

The Velvet Revolution

Everything appeared to be going swimmingly for the KSČ as it entered 1989. Under the surface, however, things were becoming more and more strained. As the country's economic performance worsened, divisions were developing within the KSČ leadership. The protest movement was gathering momentum: even the Catholic Church had begun to voice dissatisfaction, compiling a staggering 500,000 signatures calling for greater freedom of worship. But the twenty-first anniversary of the Soviet invasion produced a demonstration of only 10,000, which was swiftly and violently dispersed by the regime.

During the summer, however, more serious cracks began to appear in Czechoslovakia's staunch hardline ally, the GDR. The trickle of East Germans fleeing to the West turned into a mass exodus, with thousands besieging the West German embassy in Prague. Honecker, the East German leader, was forced to resign and, by the end of October, nightly mass demonstrations were taking place on the streets of Leipzig and Dresden. The opening of the Berlin Wall on November 9 left Czechoslovakia, Romania and Albania alone on the Eastern European stage still clinging to the old truths.

All eyes were now turned upon Czechoslovakia. Reformists within the KSČ began plotting an internal coup to overthrow Jakeš, in anticipation of a Soviet denunciation of the 1968 invasion. In the end, events overtook whatever plans they may have had. On Friday, **November 17**, a 50,000-strong peaceful demonstration organized by the official Communist youth organization was viciously attacked by the riot police. More than 100 arrests, 500 injuries and one death were reported (the fatality was later retracted) in what became popularly known as the *masakr* (massacre). Prague's students immediately began an occupation strike, joined soon after by the city's actors, who together called for an end to the Communist Party's "leading role" and a general strike to be held for two hours on November 27.

Civic Forum and the VPN

On Sunday, November 19, on Václav Havel's initiative, the established opposition groups, including Charter 77, met and agreed to form *Občanské fórum* or **Civic Forum**. Their demands were simple: the resignation of the present hardline leadership, including Husák and Jakeš; an enquiry into the police actions of November 17; an amnesty for all political prisoners; and support for the general strike. In Bratislava, a parallel organization, *Veřejnosť proti nasiliu* or **People Against Violence** (VPN), was set up to coordinate protest in Slovakia.

On the Monday evening, the first of the really big **nationwide demonstrations** took place – the biggest since the 1968 invasion – with more than 200,000 people pouring into Prague's Wenceslas Square. This time the police held back and rumours of troop deployments proved false. Every night for a week people poured into the main squares in towns and cities across the country, repeating the calls for democracy, freedom and an end to the Party's monopoly of power. As the week dragged on, the Communist media tentatively began to report events, and the KSČ leadership started to splinter under the strain, with the prime minister, **Ladislav Adamec**, alone in sticking his neck out and holding talks with the opposition.

The end of one-party rule

On Friday evening, Dubček, the ousted 1968 leader, appeared alongside Havel, before a crowd of 300,000 in Wenceslas Square, and in a matter of hours the entire Jakeš leadership had resigned. The weekend brought the largest demonstrations the country had ever seen – more than 750,000 people in Prague alone. At the invitation of Civic Forum, Adamec addressed the crowd, only to be booed off the platform. On Monday, November 27, eighty percent of the country's workforce joined the two-hour **general strike**, including many of the Party's previously stalwart allies, such as the miners and engineers. The following day, the Party agreed to an end to one-party rule and the formation of a new "coalition government".

A temporary halt to the nightly demonstrations was called and the country waited expectantly for the "broad coalition" cabinet promised by Prime Minister Adamec. On December 3, another Communist-dominated line-up was announced by the Party and immediately denounced by Civic Forum and the VPN, who called for a fresh wave of demonstrations and another general strike for December 11. Adamec promptly resigned and was replaced by the Slovak Marián Čalfa. On December 10, one day before the second threatened general strike, Čalfa announced his provisional **"Government of National Understanding"**, with Communists in the minority for the first time since 1948 and multi-party elections planned for June 1990. Having sworn in the new government, President Husák, architect of the post-1968 "normalization", finally threw in the towel.

By the time the new Čalfa government was announced, the students and actors had been on strike continuously for over three weeks. The pace of change surprised everyone involved, but there was still one outstanding issue: the election of a new president. Posters shot up all round the capital urging **"HAVEL NA HRAD"** (Havel to the Castle – the seat of the presidency). The students were determined to see his election through, continuing their occupation strike until Havel was officially elected president by a unanimous vote of the Federal Assembly, and sworn in at the Hrad on December 29.

The 1990 elections

Czechoslovakia started the new decade full of optimism for what the future would bring. On the surface, the country had a lot more going for it than its immediate neighbours (with the possible exception of the GDR). The Communist Party had been swept from power without bloodshed, and, unlike the rest of Eastern Europe, Czechoslovakia had a strong interwar democratic tradition with which to identify – Masaryk's First Republic. Despite Communist economic mismanagement, the country still had a relatively high standard of living, a skilled workforce and a manageable foreign debt.

In reality, however, the situation was somewhat different. Not only was the country economically in a worse state than most people had imagined, it was also environmentally devastated, and its people were suffering from what Havel described as "post-prison psychosis" – an inability to think or act for themselves. The country had to go through the painful transition "from being a big fish in a small pond to being a sickly adolescent trout in a hatchery". As a result, it came increasingly to rely on its new-found saviour, the humble playwright-president, Václav Havel.

In most people's eyes, "Saint Václav" could do no wrong, though he himself was not out too woo his electorate. His call for the rapid withdrawal of Soviet troops was popular enough, but his apology for the postwar expulsion of Sudeten Germans was deeply resented, as was his generous amnesty which eased the country's overcrowded prisons. The amnesty was blamed by many for the huge **rise in crime** in 1990. Every vice in the book – from racism to homicide – raised its ugly head in the first year of freedom.

In addition, there was still a lot of talk about the possibility of "counter-revolution", given the thousands of unemployed StB (secret police) at large. Inevitably, accusations of previous StB involvement rocked each political party in turn in the run-up to the first elections. The controversial **lustrace** (literally "lustration" or cleansing) law, which barred all those on StB files from public office for the following five years, ended the career of many public figures, often on the basis of highly unreliable StB reports.

Despite all the inevitable hiccups and the increasingly vocal Slovak nationalists, Civic Forum/VPN remained high in the opinion polls. The **June 1990 elections** produced a record-breaking 99 percent turnout. With around sixty percent of the vote, Civic Forum/VPN were clear victors (the Communists won just 13 percent) and Havel immediately set about forming a broad "Coalition of National Sacrifice", including everyone from Christian Democrats to former Communists.

The main concern of the new government was how to transform an outdated command-system economy into a **market economy**. The argument over the speed and model of economic reform eventually caused Civic Forum to split into two main camps: the centre-left Občánské hnutí or Civic Movement (OH), led by the foreign minister and former dissident Jiří Dienstbier, who favoured a more gradualist approach; and Občánská democratická strana, the right-wing **Civic Democratic Party** (ODS), headed by the finance minister **Václav Klaus**, whose pronouncement that the country should "walk the tightrope to Thatcherism" sent shivers up the spines of those familiar with the UK in the 1980s.

One of the first acts of the new government was to pass a **restitution law**, handing back small businesses and property to those from whom it had been expropriated after the 1948 Communist coup. This proved to be a controversial issue, since it excluded Jewish families driven out in 1938 by the Nazis, and, of course, the millions of Sudeten Germans who were forced to flee the country after the war. A law was later passed to cover the Jewish expropriations, but the Sudeten German issue remains a tricky one, and one which will continue to surface in the run-up to Czech entry to the EU.

The Slovak crisis

One of the most intractable issues facing post-Communist Czechoslovakia turned out to be the **Slovak problem**. Having been the victim of Prague-inspired centralization from Masaryk to Gottwald, the Slovaks were in no mood to suffer second-class citizenship any longer. In the aftermath of 1989, feelings were running high in Slovakia, and more than once the spectre of a "Slovak UDI" was threatened by Slovak politicians, who hoped to boost their popularity by appealing to voters' nationalism. Despite the tireless campaigning and negotiating by both sides, a compromise failed to emerge.

The **June 1992 elections** soon became an unofficial referendum on the future of the federation. Events moved rapidly towards the break-up of the republic after the resounding victory of the Movement for a Democratic Slovakia (HZDS), under the wily, populist politician Vladimir Mečiar, who, in retrospect, was quite clearly seeking Slovak independence, though he never explicitly said so during the campaign. In the Czech Lands, the right-wing ODS emerged as the largest single party, under Václav Klaus, who – ever the economist – was clearly not going to shed tears over losing the economically backward Slovak half of the country.

Talks between the two sides got nowhere, despite the fact of opinion polls in both countries consistently showing majority support for the federation. The HZDS then blocked the re-election of Havel, who had committed himself entirely to the pro-federation cause. Havel promptly resigned, leaving the country president-less and Klaus and Mečiar to talk over the terms of the divorce. On January 1, 1993, after 74 years of troubled existence, Czechoslovakia was officially divided into two new countries: the Czech Republic and Slovakia.

Czech politics under Klaus

Generally speaking, life was much kinder to the Czechs than the Slovaks in the immediate period following the break-up of Czechoslovakia. While the Slovaks had the misfortune of being led by the increasingly wayward and isolated

Mečiar, the Czechs enjoyed a long period of political stability under Klaus. Under his guidance, the country jumped to the front of the queue for the EU and NATO, and was held up as a shining example to all other former Eastern Bloc countries. Prague attracted more foreign investment than anywhere else in the country – plus thousands of American expats into the bargain – and was transformed beyond all recognition, its main thoroughfares lined with brand new hotels, shops and restaurants.

Klaus and his party, the ODS, certainly proved themselves the most durable of all the new political forces to emerge in the former Eastern Bloc. Nevertheless, in the **1996 elections**, although the ODS again emerged as the largest single party, they failed to gain an outright majority. They repeated the failure again in November 1996 during the first elections for the Czech Senate, the upper house of the Czech parliament. The electorate was distinctly unenthusiastic about the whole idea of another chamber full of overpaid politicians, and a derisory thirty percent turned out to vote in the second round. In the end, however, it was – predictably enough – a series of allegations of corruption over the country's privatization that eventually prompted **Klaus's resignation** as prime minister in November 1997.

One of the biggest problems to emerge in the 1990s was the issue of **Czech racism towards the Romany minority** within the country. The issue became headline news across the world in late 1997, when a misleading documentary broadcast on Czech TV showed life for the handful of Czech Romanies who had emigrated to Canada as a proverbial bed of roses. At last, the documentary seemed to be suggesting, they had found a life free from the racism and unemployment that is the reality for most of the Czech Republic's estimated quarter of a million gypsies. The programme prompted a minor exodus of up to one thousand Czech Romanies to Canada. Another Nova documentary, this time extolling life for Czech Romanies in Britain, had a similar effect, with several hundred Czech and Slovak Romanies seeking political asylum on arrival at Dover.

Czech politics since 1998

The **1998 elections** proved that the Czechs had grown sick and tired of Klaus's dry, rather arrogant, style of leadership. However, what really did for Klaus was that for the first time since he took power, the economy had begun to falter. The Social Democrats (ČSSD), under Miloš Zeman, emerged as the largest single party, promising to pay more attention to social issues. Unable to form a majority government, Zeman followed the Austrian example, and decided to make an **"opposition agreement"** with the ODS. This Faustian pact was dubbed the "Toleranzpatent" by the press, after the 1781 Edict of Tolerance issued by Joseph II (see p.245). The Czech public were unimpressed, seeing the whole deal as a cosy stitch-up, and in 2000, thousands turned out in Wenceslas Square for the *Díky a odejděte* (Thank you, now leave) protest, asking for the resignation of both Zeman and Klaus.

Havel, Czech president since 1993, has been dogged by ill health, and steps down in 2003 – whoever succeeds him is unlikely to command the same moral respect. That said, Havel's standing is nowhere near as high as it used to be, particularly at home. His marriage to the actress Dagmar Veškrnová, seventeen years his junior, in January 1997, less than a year after his first wife, Olga, died of cancer, was frowned upon by many. And his very public fall-out with his sister-in-law, Olga Havlová, over the family inheritance of the multi-million crown Lucerna complex in Prague, didn't do his reputation any favours either.

Czech Romanies featured large in the European media again in 1999 over the planned building of a wall to separate Romanies and non-Romanies in the north Bohemian city of **Ústí nad Labem**. The central government, under pressure from the EU, condemned the construction of the wall, and eventually the local council rehoused the white Czechs elsewhere. This is an issue that won't go away easily – only a concerted campaign of anti-racism, grass-roots social work and the implementation of equal opportunities policies, will effectively counter the prejudices of the vast majority of Czechs.

Meanwhile, Czechs have become more and more disillusioned with their politicians, with just 58 percent turning out for the **2002 elections**, and 18 percent of them voting for the Communists. The ČSSD, under Vladimír Špidla, again emerged as the single largest party, with ODS in second place – this time, however, Špidla was able to form a government with the newly formed centre party of Coalition 2, giving them the slimmest of majorities. Once more, the new government has put their social policies at the top of their agenda, but with EU entry looming near, the crucial issue is how well the ČSSD can handle the economy.

Books

For books published in English in Prague, you'll need to go to one of the English-language bookstores in Prague (listed on p.228). Publishers are detailed below in the form of British publisher/American publisher, where both exist. Where books are published in one country only, UK or US follows the publisher's name. Out of print books are designated o/p; University Press is abbreviated UP. Books tagged with the ⊡ symbol are particularly recommended.

History, politics and society

Peter Demetz *Prague in Black and Gold: Scenes from the Life of a European City* (Penguin/Hill & Wang). Demetz certainly knows his subject, both academically and at first hand, having been brought up in the city before World War II (when his account ends). His style can be a little dry, but he is determinedly un-partisan, and refreshingly anti-nationalist in his reading of history.

R. J. W. Evans *Rudolf II and his World* (Thames & Hudson, UK). First published in 1973, and still the best account of the alchemy-mad emperor, but not as salacious as one might hope.

Jan Kaplan and Krystyna Nosarzewska *Prague: The Turbulent Century* (Könemann, Prague). This is the first real attempt to cover the twentieth-century history of Prague with all its warts. The text isn't as good as it should be, but the book is worth it just for the incredible range of photographs and images.

Karel Kaplan *The Short March: The Communist Takeover in Czechoslovakia, 1945–48* (o/p); *Report on the Murder of the General Secretary* (o/p). *The Short March* is an excellent account of the electoral rise and rise of the Communists in Czechoslovakia after the war, which culminated in the bloodless coup of February 1948. *Report on the Murder of the General Secretary* is an incredibly detailed

study of the country's brutal Stalinist show trials, and most famously that of Rudolf Slánský, number two in the Party until his arrest.

⊡ **Callum MacDonald** *The Killing of SS Obergruppenführer Reinhard Heydrich* (Macmillan/Da Capo). Gripping account of the build-up to the most successful and controversial act of wartime resistance, which took place in May 1942, and prompted horrific reprisals by the Nazis on the Czechs.

Callum MacDonald and Jan Kaplan *Prague in the Shadow of the Swastika* (Quartet, UK). Excellent account of the city under Nazi occupation, with an incisive, readable text illustrated by copious black-and-white photos.

Jan Musil (ed) *The End of Czechoslovakia* (Central European UP). Academics from both the Czech and Slovak Republics attempt to explain why Czechoslovakia split into two countries just at the point when it seemed so successful.

Derek Sayer *The Coasts of Bohemia* (Princeton UP). A very readable cultural history, concentrating on Bohemia and Prague, which aims to dispel the ignorance shown by the Shakespearean quote of the title, and particularly illuminating on the subject of twentieth-century artists.

R. W. Seton-Watson *The History of the Czechs and Slovaks* (o/p). Seton-Watson's informed and balanced account, written during World War II, is hard to beat. The Seton-Watsons were lifelong Slavophiles but maintained a scholarly distance in their writing, rare amongst émigré historians.

Kieran Williams *The Prague Spring and its Aftermath: Czechoslovak Politics, 1968-70* (CUP). Drawing on declassified archives, this book analyzes the attempted reforms under Dubček and takes a new look at the Prague Spring.

★ **Elizabeth Wiskemann** *Czechs and Germans* (o/p). Researched and written in the build-up towards Munich, this is the most fascinating and fair treatment of the Sudeten problem. Meticulous in her detail, vast in her scope, Wiskemann manages to suffuse the weighty text with enough anecdotes to keep you gripped. Unique.

Essays, memoirs and biographies

Margarete Buber-Neumann *Milena* (Arcade). A moving biography of Milena Jesenská, one of interwar Prague's most beguiling characters, who befriended the author while they were both interned in Ravensbrück concentration camp.

Karel Čapek *Talks with T. G. Masaryk* (Catbird Press). Čapek was a personal (and political) friend of Masaryk, and his diaries, journals, reminiscences and letters give great insights into the man who personified the First Republic.

Jana Cerná *Kafka's Milena* (Souvenir Press/Northwestern UP). Another biography of Milena Jesenská, this time written by her daughter, a surrealist poet, whose own works were banned under the Communists.

Timothy Garton Ash *We The People: The Revolutions of 89* (Penguin/Vintage). A personal, anecdotal, eye-witness account of the Velvet Revolution (and the events in Poland, Berlin and Budapest). By far the most compelling of all the post-1989 books. Published as *The Magic Lantern* in the US.

Patrick Leigh Fermor *A Time of Gifts* (Penguin). The first volume of Leigh Fermor's trilogy based on his epic walk along the Rhine and Danube rivers in 1933–34. In the last quarter of the book he reaches Czechoslovakia, indulging in a quick jaunt to Prague before crossing the border into Hungary. Written forty years later in dense, luscious and highly crafted prose, it's an evocative and poignant insight into the culture of *Mitteleuropa* between the wars.

Patricia Hampl *A Romantic Education* (Norton). The American author goes to Prague in search of her Czech roots and the contrasting cultures of East and West.

Václav Havel *Living in Truth* (Faber); *Letters to Olga* (Faber/Holt); *Open Letters: Selected Prose*; *Disturbing the Peace*; *Summer Meditations* (all Faber/Vintage); *The Art of the Impossible* (Fromm, US). The first essay in *Living in Truth* is "Power of the Powerless", Havel's lucid, damning indictment of the inactivity of the Czechoslovak masses in the face of "normalization". *Letters to Olga* is a collection of Havel's letters written under great duress (and heavy censorship) from prison in the early

1980s to his wife, Olga – by turns philosophizing, nagging, effusing, whingeing. *Disturbing the Peace* is probably Havel's most accessible work yet: a series of autobiographical questions and answers in which he talks interestingly about his childhood, the events of 1968 when he was in Liberec, and the path to Charter 77 and beyond (though not including his reactions to being thrust into the role of president). *Summer Meditations* are post-1989 essays by the playwright-president, while *The Art of the Impossible: Politics as Morality in Practice* is a collection of speeches given since he became the country's president in 1990.

Václav Havel et al *Power of the Powerless* (M. E. Sharpe, US). A collection of essays by leading Chartists, kicking off with Havel's seminal title-piece. Other contributors range from the dissident Marxist Petr Uhl to devout Catholics like Václav Benda.

Miroslav Holub *The Dimension of the Present Moment* (Faber, UK); *Shedding Life: Disease, Politics and Other Human Conditions* (Milkweed, US). Two books of short philosophical musings/essays on life and the universe by this unusual and clever scientist-poet.

John Keane *Václav Havel: A Political Tragedy in Six Acts* (Bloomsbury, UK). The first book to tell both sides of the Havel story: Havel the dissident playwright and civil rights activist who played a key role in the 1989 Velvet Revolution, and Havel the ageing and increasingly ill president, who has, in many people's opinion, simply stayed on the stage too long.

Antonín Klimek and Zbyněk Zeman *The Life of Edvard Beneš: Czechoslovakia in Peace & War* (Clarendon Press). Beneš is a fascinating figure in Czech history, revered as number two to Masaryk

while the latter was alive, only to find himself held responsible firstly for the Munich debacle, and secondly for allowing the Communists into power in 1948.

Heda Margolius Kovaly *Prague Farewell* (Orion/Holmes & Meier). An autobiography that starts in the concentration camps of World War II and ends with the author's flight from Czechoslovakia in 1968. Married to one of the Party officials executed in the 1952 Slánský trial, she tells her story simply and without bitterness. The best account there is of the fear and paranoia whipped up during the Stalinist terror. Published as *Under a Cruel Star* in the US.

Benjamin Kuras *Czechs and Balances*; *Is There Life After Marx?*; *As Golems Go* (all Baronet, Prague). The first two are witty, light, typically Czech takes on national identity and Central European politics; the latter is a more mystical look at Rabbi Löw's philosophy and the Kabbalah.

Ota Pavel *How I Came to Know Fish* (New Directions US). Pavel's childhood innocence shines through particularly when his Jewish father and two brothers are sent to a concentration camp and he and his mother have to scrape a living.

Angelo Maria Ripellino *Magic Prague* (Picador/University of California Press). A wide-ranging look at the bizarre array of historical and literary characters who have lived in Prague, from the mad antics of the court of Rudolf II to the escapades of Jaroslav Hašek. Scholarly, rambling, richly and densely written – unique and recommended.

Josef Škvorecký *Talkin' Moscow Blues* (Faber/Ecco Press). Without doubt the most user-friendly of Škvorecký's works, containing a collection of essays on his wartime childhood, Czech jazz, literature and contemporary politics, all told in his inimitable, irreverent and infuriating way. Published as *Headed for the Blues* in the US.

Ludvík Vaculík *A Cup of Coffee with My Interrogator* (Readers International). A Party member until 1968, and signatory of Charter 77, Vaculík revived the *feuilleton* – a short political critique once much loved in central Europe. This collection dates from 1968 onwards.

Klaus Wagenbach *Kafka's Prague: A Travel Reader* (Overlook Press). Hardback book that takes you through the streets in the footsteps of Kafka.

Zbyněk Zeman *The Masaryks: The Making of Czechoslovakia* (I. B. Tauris, UK). Written in the 1970s while Zeman was in exile, this is a very readable, none-too-sentimental biography of the country's founder Tomáš Garrigue Masaryk, and his son Jan Masaryk, the postwar Foreign Minister who died in mysterious circumstances shortly after the 1948 Communist coup.

Czech fiction

★ **Josef Čapek** *Stories about Doggie and Cat* (Albatros, Prague). Josef Čapek (Karel's older brother) was a Cubist artist of some renown, and also a children's writer. These simple stories about a dog and a cat are wonderfully illustrated, and seriously postmodern.

Karel Čapek *Towards a Radical Centre* (Catbird Press); *The War with the Newts* (Penguin/Catbird Press); *Nine Fairy Tales* (Catbird Press). Karel Čapek was the literary and journalistic spokesperson for Masaryk's First Republic, but he's better known in the West for his plays, some of which feature in the anthology, *Towards a Radical Centre*.

Daniela Fischerová *Fingers Pointing Somewhere Else* (Catbird Press). Subtly nuanced, varied collection of short stories from dissident playwright Fischerová.

Ladislav Fuks *The Cremator* (Marion Boyars); *Mr Theodore Mundstock* (Four Walls Eight Windows, US). Two readable novels – the first about a man who works in a crematorium in

occupied Prague, and is about to throw in his lot with the Nazis when he discovers that his wife is half-Jewish. The second is set in 1942 Prague, as the city's Jews wait to be transported to Terezín.

Jaroslav Hašek *The Good Soldier Švejk* (Penguin/1st Books Library). A rambling, picaresque tale by Bohemia's most bohemian writer, of Czechoslovakia's famous fictional fifth columnist, *Švejk*, who wreaks havoc in the Austro-Hungarian army during World War I.

Václav Havel *Selected Plays 1963–87*; *Selected Plays 1984–87* (Faber, UK); *The Garden Party and Other Plays* (Grove Press, US). Havel's plays are not renowned for being easy to read (or watch). *The Memorandum*, one of his earliest works, is a classic absurdist drama that, in many ways, sets the tone for much of his later work, of which the *Three Vaněk Plays*, featuring Ferdinand Vaněk, Havel's alter ego, are perhaps the most successful. The 1980s collection includes *Largo Desolato, Temptation* and *Redevelopment*;

freedom of thought, Faustian opportunism and town planning as metaphors of life under the Communists.

Bohumil Hrabal *Closely Observed Trains/Closely Watched Trains* (Abacus/Northwestern UP); *I Served the King of England* (Picador/Vintage); *Too Loud a Solitude* (Abacus/Harcourt Brace). Hrabal is a thoroughly mischievous writer, slim but superb *Closely Observed Trains* is a postwar classic, set in the last days of the war and relentlessly unheroic; it was made into an equally brilliant film by Jiří Menzl. *I Served the King of England* follows the antihero Dítě, who works at the *Hotel Paříž*, through the decade after 1938. *Too Loud a Solitude*, about a waste-paper disposer under the Communists, has also been made into a film, again by Menzl.

Alois Jirásek *Old Czech Legends* (Forest Books/Dufour). A major figure in the nineteenth-century Czech *národní obrození*, Jirásek popularized Bohemia's legendary past. This collection includes all the classic texts, as well as the story of the founding of the city by the prophetess Libuše.

Franz Kafka *Kafka: the Complete Novels*; *The Complete Short Stories*; *Letters to Felice*; *Diaries* (all Penguin/Vintage). A German-Jewish Praguer, Kafka has drawn the darker side of central Europe – its claustrophobia, paranoia and unfathomable bureaucracy – better than anyone else, both in a rural setting, as in *The Castle*, and in an urban one, in one of the great novels of the twentieth century, *The Trial*.

Ivan Klíma *My Merry Mornings: Stories from Prague* (Readers International); *Love and Garbage* (Penguin/Vintage); *Judge on Trial* (Vintage); *My Golden Trades* (Granta); *Waiting for the Dark, Waiting for the Light* (Penguin/Picador); *The Spirit of Prague* (Granta); *Ultimate Intimacy* (Granta/Grove-Atlantic). A survivor of Terezín, Klíma is another writer in the Kundera mould as far as sexual politics goes, but his stories are a lot lighter. *Judge on Trial*, written in the 1970s, is one of his best, concerning the moral dilemmas of a Communist judge. *Waiting for the Dark, Waiting for the Light* is a pessimistic novel set before, during and after the Velvet Revolution of 1989. *The Spirit of Prague* is a very readable collection of biographical and more general essays on subjects ranging from Klíma's childhood experiences in Terezín to the current situation in Prague. *Ultimate Intimacy* is his latest novel, set in the cynical post-revolutionary Czech Republic.

Milan Kundera *Laughable Loves*; *The Farewell Party*; *The Joke*; *The Book of Laughter and Forgetting*; *The Unbearable Lightness of Being*; *The Art of the Novel*; *Immortality*; *Slowness*; *Identity*; *Testaments Betrayed* (all Faber/HarperCollins); *Life is Elsewhere* (Faber/Penguin). Milan Kundera is the country's most popular writer – at least with non-Czechs. His early books were very obviously "political", particularly *The Book of Laughter and Forgetting*, which led the Communists to revoke Kundera's citizenship. *The Joke*, written while he was still living in Czechoslovakia and in many ways his best work, is set in the very unfunny era of the 1950s. Its clear, humorous style is far removed from the carefully poised posturing of his most famous novel, *The Unbearable Lightness of Being*, set in and after 1968, and successfully turned into a film some twenty years later. *Slowness* is a slim volume set in France, and his first work written in French; *Identity* is a series of slightly detached musings on the human condition and is typical of his later works. *Testaments Betrayed*, on the other hand, is a fascinating series of essays about a range of subjects from the formation of historical reputation to the problems of translations. His latest novel, *No Saints and Angels* (Granta), is set in bleak, contemporary Prague.

Arnošt Lustig *Diamonds of the Night*; *Night and Hope* (both Quartet/ Northwestern UP); *A Prayer for Kateřina Horovitová* (Quartet/ Overlook Press). A Prague Jew exiled since 1968, Lustig spent World War II in Terezín, Buchenwald and Auschwitz, and his novels and short stories are consistently set in the Terezín camp.

Gustav Meyrink *The Golem* (Dedalus/Ariadne); *The Angel of the West Window* (Dedalus/Ariadne). Meyrink was another of Prague's weird and wonderful characters. He started out as a bank manager but soon became involved in cabalism, alchemy and drug experimentation. His *Golem*, based on Rabbi Löw's monster, is one of the classic versions of the tale. *The Angel of the West Window* is a historical novel about John Dee, an English alchemist invited to Prague in the late sixteenth century by Rudolf II.

Jan Neruda *Prague Tales* (Central European UP). These are short, bittersweet snapshots of life in Malá Strana at the close of the last century. The author is not to be confused with the Chilean Pablo Neruda (who took his name from the Czech writer).

Ivana Pecháčková *The Legend of the Golem* (Meander). The legend of the Golem is the basis of this novel about ambition and chicanery at the end of Rudolf II's reign

Karel Poláček *What Ownership's All About* (Catbird Press/Independent Publishers Group). A darkly comic novel set in a Prague tenement block, dealing with Fascism and appeasement, by a Jewish-Czech

Praguer who died in the camps in 1944.

Rainer Maria Rilke *Two Stories of Prague* (University Press of New England, US). Both tales deal with the artificiality of Prague's now defunct German community, whose claustrophobic parochialism drove the author into self-imposed exile in 1899 (for more on Rilke see "Poetry", p.268).

Peter Sís *The Three Golden Keys* (Frances Foster US). Short, hauntingly illustrated children's book set in Prague, by Czech-born American Sís.

Josef Škvorecký *The Cowards*; *The Miracle Game* (both Faber/Norton); *The Swell Season*; *The Bass Saxophone* (both Vintage/Ecco Press); *Miss Silver's Past*; *Dvořák in Love* (both Vintage/Norton); *The Engineer of Human Souls* (Vintage/Dalkey Archive); *The Republic of Whores* (Faber/Ecco Press). A relentless anti-Communist, Škvorecký is typically Bohemian in his bawdy sense of humour and irreverence for all high moralizing. *The Cowards* (which briefly saw the light of day in 1958) is the tale of a group of irresponsible young men in the last days of the war, an antidote to the lofty prose from official authors at the time, but hampered by its dated Americanized translation.

Josef Škvorecký *The Mournful Demeanour of Lieutenant Boruvka*; *Sins for Father Knox*; *The Return of Lieutenant Boruvka*; *The End of Lieutenant Boruvka* (all Faber/Norton). Less well-known (and understandably so) are Škvorecký's detective stories featuring a podgy, depressive Czech cop, which he wrote in the 1960s at a time when his more serious work was banned. His latest book, written in English, *Two Murders in My Double Life* (Picador), is a murder mystery set partly in

Canada where he now lives and partly in the Czech Republic.

★ **Zdena Tomin** *Stalin's Shoe* (Hutchinson/Dodd Mead); *The Coast of Bohemia* (Everyman/Dent). Although Czech-born, Tomin writes in English (the language of her exile since 1980); she has a style and fluency all her own. *Stalin's Shoe* is the compelling and complex story of a girl coming to terms with her Stalinist childhood, while *The Coast of Bohemia* is based on Tomin's experiences of the late 1970s dissident movement, when she was an active member of Charter 77.

Ludvík Vaculík *The Guinea Pigs* (Northwestern UP, US). Vaculík was expelled from the Party during the 1968 Prague Spring; this novel catalogues the slow dehumanization of Czech society in the aftermath of the Soviet invasion.

Jiří Weil *Life With a Star* (Penguin/ Northwestern UP); *Mendelssohn is on the Roof* (Northwestern UP, US). Two novels written just after the war and based on Weil's experiences as a Czech Jew in hiding during the Nazi-occupation of Prague.

Paul Wilson (ed) *Prague: A Traveler's Literary Companion* (Whereabouts Press, US). A great selection of short stories and snippets on Prague from, among others, Meyrink, Kisch and Čapek, plus contemporary writers like Jáchym Topol.

Poetry

Jaroslav Čejka, Michal Černík and Karel Sýs *The New Czech Poetry* (Bloodaxe/Dufour). Slim but interesting volume by three Czech poets; all in their late forties, all very different. Čejka is of the Holub school, and comes across simply and strongly; Černík is similarly direct; Sýs the least convincing.

Sylva Fischerová *The Tremor of Racehorses: Selected Poems* (Bloodaxe/ Dufour). Poet and novelist Fischerová is one of the new generation of Czech writers, though in many ways she is continuing in the Holub tradition. Her poems are by turns powerful, obtuse and personal, as was necessary to escape censorship during the late 1980s.

Josef Hanzlík *Selected Poems* (Bloodaxe/Dufour). Refreshingly accessible collection of poems written over the last 35 years by a poet of Havel's generation.

Miroslav Holub *Supposed to Fly*; *The Jingle Bell Principle*; *Poems Before and After* (all Bloodaxe/Dufour); *Vanishing Lung Syndrome* (Faber/Field Translations). Holub is a scientist and scholar, and his poetry reflects this unique fusion of master poet and chief immunologist. Regularly banned in his own country, he is the Czech poet *par excellence* – classically trained, erudite, liberal and westward-leaning. *Vanishing Lung Syndrome* is his latest volume; the other two are collections.

Rainer Maria Rilke *Selected Poetry* (Picador/Vintage). Rilke's upbringing was unexceptional, except that his mother brought him up as a girl until the age of six. In his adult life, he became one of Prague's leading authors of the interwar period and probably the best-known poet outside Czechoslovakia.

Jaroslav Seifert *The Poetry of Jaroslav Seifert* (Catbird Press). Czechoslovakia's only author to win the Nobel prize for literature, Seifert was a founder-member of the Communist Party and the avant-garde arts movement *Devětsil*, later falling from grace and signing the Charter in his old age.

His longevity means that his work covers some of the most turbulent times in Czechoslovak history, but his irrepressible lasciviousness has been known to irritate.

Literature by foreign writers

David Brierley *On Leaving a Prague Window* (Warner, UK). A very read-able thriller set in post-Communist Prague, which shows that past con-nection with dissidents can still lead to violence.

Bruce Chatwin *Utz* (Vintage). Chatwin is from the "exotic" school of travel writers, hence this slim, intriguing and mostly true-to-life account of an avid crockery collector from Prague's Jewish quarter.

Lionel Davidson *The Night of Wenceslas* (Arrow/St Martin's Press). A Cold War thriller set in pre-1968 Czechoslovakia that launched Davidson's career as a spy-writer.

Sue Gee *Letters from Prague* (Arrow, UK). The central character in this book falls in love with a Czech stu-dent in England in 1968, but returns home when the Russians invade. Twenty years later, together with her ten-year-old daughter, she goes in search of him.

Martha Gellhorn *A Stricken Field* (o/p). The story of an American journalist who arrives in Prague just as the Nazis march into Sudetenland. Based on the author's own experiences, this is a fascinating, if sentimental, insight into the panic and confusion in "rump" Czecho-Slovakia after the Munich Diktat. First published in 1940.

★ **Jill Paton Walsh** *A Desert in Bohemia* (Black Swan/Plume). A gripping story set against the aftermath of World War II and the subsequent political upheaval in Czechoslovakia.

Philip Roth *Prague Orgy* (Vintage). A novella about a world-famous Jewish novelist (ie, Roth) who goes to Communist Prague to recover some unpublished Jewish stories. Prague "is the city I imagined the Jews would buy when they had accumulated enough money for a homeland", according to Roth. A coda to Roth's Zuckerman trilogy.

Anthony J. Rudel *Imagining Don Giovanni* (Grove/Atlantic). Mozart, Da Ponte and Casanova collaborate on the production of *Don Giovanni* with the Marquis de Sade thrown in.

Art, photography and film

Czech Modernism 1900–1945 (Bullfinch Press/Museum of Fine Arts, Houston). Wide-ranging and superbly illustrated, this American publication records the journey of the Czech modern movement through Cubism and Surrealism to Modernism and the avant-garde. The accompanying essays by leading art and film critics cover fine art, archi-tecture, film, photography and theatre.

Devětsil: Czech Avant-Garde Art, Architecture and Design of the 1920s and 30s (Museum of Modern Art, Oxford, UK). Published to accompany the 1990 Devětsil exhibition at Oxford, this is the definitive account of interwar Czechoslovakia's most famous left-wing art movement, which attracted artists from every discipline.

Disorientations: Eastern Europe in Transition (Thames & Hudson, UK). A self-explanatory book of photos accompanied by Pavel Kohout's text.

Nature Illuminated Lee Hendrix (Thames & Hudson, UK). Exquisite paintings of flora and fauna, commissioned by Rudolf II to illuminate a master calligrapher's manuscript.

Prague: A Guide to Twentieth-century Architecture Ivan Margolius (Ellipsis, London, UK). Dinky little pocket guide to all the major modern landmarks of Prague (including a black-and-white photo of each building), from the Art Nouveau Obecní dům, through functionalism and Cubism, to the Fred & Ginger building.

Prague's leading personalities – past and present

Brahe, Tycho (1546–1601). Ground-breaking Danish astronomer, who was summoned to Prague by Rudolf II in 1597, only to die from over-drinking in 1601.

Beneš, Edvard (1884–1948). Hero to some, traitor to others, Beneš was president from 1935 until 1938 – when he resigned, having refused to lead the country into bloodshed over the Munich Crisis – and again from 1945 until 1948, when he aquiesced to the Communist coup.

Čapek, Josef (1887–1945). Cubist artist and writer and illustrator of children's books, Josef was older brother to the more famous Karel (see below); he died in Belsen concentration camp.

Čapek, Karel (1890–1938). Czech writer, journalist and unofficial spokesperson for the First Republic. His most famous works are *The Insect Play* and *R.U.R.*, which introduced the word *robot* into the English language.

Dobrovský, Josef (1753–1829). Jesuit-taught pioneer in Czech philology. Wrote the seminal text *The History of Czech Language and Literature*.

Dubček, Alexander (1921–92). Slovak Communist who became First Secretary in January 1968, at the beginning of the Prague Spring. Expelled from the Party in 1969, but returned to become speaker in the federal parliament after 1989, before being killed in a car crash in 1992.

Dvořák, Antonín (1841–1904). Perhaps the most famous of all Czech composers. His best-known work is the *New World Symphony*, inspired by an extensive sojourn in the USA.

Fučik, Julius (1903–43). Communist journalist murdered by the Nazis, whose prison writings, *Notes from the Gallows*, were obligatory reading in the 1950s. Hundreds of streets were named after him, but doubts about the authenticity of the work, and general hostility towards the man, have made him *persona non grata*.

Gottwald, Klement (1896–1953). One of the founders of the KSČ, general secretary from 1927, prime minister from 1946 to 1948, and president from 1948 to 1953, Gottwald is universally abhorred for his role in the show trials of the 1950s.

Hašek, Jaroslav (1883–1923). Anarchist, dog-breeder, lab assistant, bigamist, cabaret artist and People's Commissar in the Red Army, Hašek was one of prewar Prague's most colourful characters, who wrote the famous *The Good Soldier Švejk* and died from alcohol abuse in 1923.

Havel, Václav (1936–). Absurdist playwright of the 1960s, who became a leading spokesperson of Charter 77 and, following the Velvet

Revolution, the country's first post-Communist president.

Havlíček-Borovský, Karel (1821–56). Satirical poet, journalist and nationalist, exiled to the Tyrol by the Austrian authorities after 1848.

Hrabal, Bohumil (1936–97). Writer and bohemian, whose novels were banned under the Communists, but revered worldwide.

Hus, Jan (1370–1415). Rector of Prague University and reformist preacher who was burnt at the stake as a heretic by the Council of Constance.

Husák, Gustáv (1913–91). Slovak Communist who was sentenced to life imprisonment in the show trials of the 1950s, released in 1960, and eventually became General Secretary and president following the Soviet invasion. Resigned in favour of Havel in December 1989.

Jirásek, Alois (1851–1930). Writer who popularized Czech legends for both children and adults and became a key figure in the Czech national revival.

Jungmann, Josef (1773–1847). Prolific Czech translator and author of the seminal *History of Czech Literature* and the first Czech dictionary.

Kafka, Franz (1883–1924). German-Jewish Praguer who worked as an insurance clerk in Prague for most of his life, and also wrote some of the most influential novels of the twentieth century, most notably *The Trial*.

Kelley, Edward. English occultist who was summoned to Prague by Rudolf II, but eventually incurred the wrath of the emperor and was imprisoned in Kokořín castle.

Kepler, Johannes (1571–1630). German Protestant forced to leave Linz for Denmark because of the Counter-Reformation. Succeeded Tycho de Brahe as Rudolf II's chief astronomer. His observations of the planets became the basis of the laws of planetary motion.

Kisch, Egon Erwin (1885–1948). German-Jewish Praguer who became one of the city's most famous investigative journalists.

Klaus, Václav (1941–). Known somewhat bitterly as "Santa Klaus". Prime minister (1992–97), confirmed Thatcherite, and driving force behind the country's present economic reforms.

Komenský, Jan Amos (1592–1670). Leader of the Protestant Czech Brethren. Forced to flee the country and settle in England during the Counter-Reformation. Better known to English-speakers as Comenius.

Mácha, Karel Hynek (1810–36). Romantic nationalist poet, great admirer of Byron and Keats and, like them, died young. His most famous poem is *Maj*, published just months before his death.

Masaryk, Jan Garrigue (1886–1958). Son of the founder of the republic (see below), foreign minister in the postwar government and the only non-Communist in Gottwald's cabinet when the Communists took over in February 1948. Died ten days after the coup in suspicious circumstances.

Masaryk, Tomáš Garrigue (1850–1937). Professor of philosophy at Prague University, president of the Republic from 1918 to 1935. His name is synonymous with the First Republic and was removed from all street signs after the 1948 coup. Now back with a vengeance.

Mucha, Alfons (1860–1939). Moravian graphic artist and designer whose Art Nouveau posters and art-work for Sarah Bernhardt brought him international fame. After the founding of Czechoslovakia, he returned to the country to design stamps, bank notes, and complete a cycle of giant canvases on Czech nationalist themes.

Němcová, Božena (1820–62). Highly popular writer who became involved with the nationalist move-ment and shocked many with her unorthodox behaviour. Her most famous book is *Grandmother*.

Neruda, Jan (1834–91). Poet and journalist for the *Národní listy*. Wrote some famous short stories describing Prague's Malá Strana.

Palacký, František (1798–1876). Nationalist historian, Czech MP in Vienna and leading figure in the events of 1848.

Purkyně, Jan Evangelista (1787–1869). Czech doctor, natural scientist and pioneer in experimental physiology who became professor of physiology at Prague and then at Wrocław University.

Rieger, Ladislav (1818–1903). Nineteenth-century Czech politician and one of the leading figures in the events of 1848 and the aftermath.

Rilke, Rainer Maria (1876–1926). Despite having been brought up as a girl for the first six years of his life, Rilke ended up as an officer in the Austrian army, and wrote some of the city's finest German *fin-de-siècle* poetry.

Smetana, Bedřich (1824–84). Popular Czech composer and fervent nationalist whose *Má vlast* (My Homeland) traditionally opens the Prague Spring Music Festival.

Svoboda, Ludvík (1895–1979). Victorious Czech general from World War II, who acquiesced to the 1948 Communist coup and was Communist president from 1968 to 1975.

Tyl, Josef Kajetán (1808–56). Czech playwright and composer of the Czech half of the national anthem, *Where is my Home?*

Werfel, Franz (1890–1945). One of the German-Jewish literary circle, which included Kafka, Kisch and Brod.

Zeman, Miloš (1944–) Social Democrat (ČSSD) prime minister (1998–2002), best known for his dif-ficult relationship with the press.

Žižka, Jan (died 1424). Brilliant, blind military leader of the Táborites, the radical faction of the Hussites.

Language

Language

Language

The official language of the Czech Republic is Czech (český), a highly complex western Slav tongue. Any attempt to speak Czech will be heartily appreciated, though don't be discouraged if people seem not to understand, as most will be unaccustomed to hearing foreigners stumble through their language. If you don't know any Czech, brush up on your German, since, among the older generation at least, this is still the most widely spoken second language. Russian, once the compulsory second language, has been practically wiped off the school curriculum, and the number of English-speakers has been steadily increasing, especially among the younger generation.

Pronunciation

English-speakers often find Czech impossibly difficult to pronounce. In fact, it's not half as daunting as it might first appear from the "traffic jams of consonants", as Patrick Leigh-Fermor put it, which crop up on the page. An illustration of this is the Czech tongue-twister, *strč prst skrz krk* (stick your finger down your neck). Apart from a few special letters, each letter and syllable is pronounced as it's written – the trick is always to **stress the first syllable** of a word, no matter what its length; otherwise you'll render it unintelligible.

Short and long vowels

Czech has both short and long vowels (the latter being denoted by a variety of accents). The trick here is to lengthen the vowel without affecting the principal stress of the word, which is invariably on the first syllable.

a like the u in cup
á as in father
e as in pet
é as in fair
ě like the ye in yes
i or y as in pit

í or ý as in seat
o as in not
ó as in door
u like the oo in book
ů or ú like the oo in fool

Vowel combinations and diphthongs

There are very few diphthongs in Czech, so any combinations of vowels other than those below should be pronounced as two separate syllables.

au like the ou in foul

ou like the oe in foe

A Czech language guide

There are very few **teach-yourself Czech** courses available and each has drawbacks. *Colloquial Czech* by James Naughton is good, but a bit fast and furious for most people; *Teach Yourself Czech* is a bit dry for some. Numerous **Czech phrasebooks** are available, not least the *Czech Rough Guide Phrasebook*, laid out dictionary-style for instant access.

The alphabet

In the Czech alphabet, letters which feature a **háček** (as in the č of the word itself) are considered separate letters and appear in Czech indexes immediately after their more familiar cousins. More confusingly, the consonant combination *ch* is also considered as a separate letter and appears in Czech indexes after the letter *h*. In the index in this book, we use the English system, so words beginning with *c*, *č* and *ch* all appear under *c*.

Consonants and accents

There are no silent consonants, but it's worth remembering that r and l can form a syllable if standing between two other consonants or at the end of a word, as in Brno (Br–no) or Vltava (Vl–ta–va). The consonants listed below are those which differ substantially from the English. Accents look daunting – particularly the háček, which appears above c, d, l, n, r, s, t and z – but the only one which causes a lot of problems is ř, probably the most difficult letter to say in the entire language – even Czech toddlers have to be taught how to say it.

c like the **ts** in boats
č like the **ch** in chicken
ch like the **ch** in the Scottish loch
ď like the **d** in duped
g always as in goat, never as in general
h always as in have, but more energetic
j like the **y** in yoke
kd pronounced as **gd**
ľ like the **lli** in colliery

mě pronounced as mnye
ň like the **n** in nuance
p softer than the English **p**
r as in rip, but often rolled
ř like the sound of r and ž combined
š like the **sh** in shop
ť like the **t** in tutor
ž like the **s** in pleasure; at the end of a word like the **sh** in shop

Words and phrases

Basics

Yes – ano
No – ne
Please/excuse me – prosím vás
Don't mention it – není zač
Sorry – pardon
Thank you – děkuju
Bon appétit – dobrou chuť
Bon voyage – šťastnou cestu
Hello/goodbye (informal) – ahoj
Goodbye (formal) – na shledanou
Good day – dobrý den
Good morning – dobré ráno
Good evening – dobrý večer
Good night (when leaving) – dobrou noc
How are you? – jak se máte?
Today – dnes

Yesterday – včera
Tomorrow – zítra
The day after tomorrow – pozítří
Now – hnet
Later – později
Leave me alone – dej mi pokoj
Go away – jdi pryč
Help! – pomoc!
This one – tento
A little – trochu
Large/small – velký/malý
More/less – více/méně
Good/bad – dobrý/špatný
Hot/cold – horký/studený
With/without – s/bez

Getting around

Over here - tady
Over there - tam
Left - nalevo
Right - napravo
Straight on - rovně
Where is ...? - kde je ...?
How do I get to Prague? - jak se dostanu do Prahy?
How do I get to the university? - jak se dostanu k univerzitě?
By bus - autobusem
By train - vlakem
By car - autem

On foot - pěšky
By taxi - taxíkem
Ticket - jízdenka/lístek
Return ticket - zpateční
Railway station - nádraží
Bus station - autobusové nádraží
Bus stop - autobusová zastávka
When's the next train to Prague? - kdy jede další vlak do Prahy?
Is it going to Prague? - jede to do Prahy?
Do I have to change? - musím přestupovat?
Do I need a reservation? - musím mit místenku?

Questions and answers

Do you speak English? - mluvíte anglicky?
I don't speak German - nemluvím německy
I don't understand - nerozumím
I understand - rozumím
Speak slowly - mluvíte pomalu
How do you say that in Czech? - jak se tohle řekne česky?
Could you write it down for me? - mužete mí to napsat?
What - co
Where - kde
When - kdy
Why - proč
How much is it? - kolík to stojí?

Are there any rooms available? - máte volné pokoje?
I would like a double room - chtěl bych dvou lůžkovy pokoj
For one night - na jednu noc
With shower - se sprchou
Is this seat free? - je tu volna?
May we (sit down)? - můžeme (se sednout)?
The bill please - zaplatím prosím
Do you have ...? - máte ...?
We don't have - nemáme
We do have - máme

Some signs

Entrance - vchod
Exit - východ
Toilets - záchody/toalety
Men - muži
Women - ženy
Ladies - dámy
Gentlemen - pánové
Open - otevřeno
Closed - zavřeno

Danger! - pozor!
Hospital - nemocnice
No smoking - kouření zakázáno
No bathing - koupání zakázáno
No entry - vstup zakázán
Arrival - příjezd
Departure - odjezd
Police - policie

Days of the week

Monday - pondělí
Tuesday - utery
Wednesday - středa
Thursday - čtvrtek

Friday - pátek
Saturday - sobota
Sunday - neděle
Day - den

Week - týden
Month - měsíc
Year - rok

Months of the year

Many Slav languages have their own highly individual systems in which the words for the names of the months are descriptive nouns – sometimes beautifully apt for the month in question.

January - leden – ice
February - únor – hibernation
March - březen – birch
April - duben – oak
May - květen – blossom
June - červen – red

July - červenec – redder
August - srpen – sickle
September - zaří – blazing
October - říjen – rutting
November - listopad – leaves falling
December - prosinec – slaughter of pigs

Numbers

1 - jeden	**11** - jedenáct	**21** - dvacetjedna	**155** - sto padesát pět
2 - dva	**12** - dvanáct	**30** - třicet	**200** - dvě stě
3 - tří	**13** - třináct	**40** - čtyřicet	**300** - tři sta
4 - čtyři	**14** - čtrnáct	**50** - padesát	**400** - čtyři sta
5 - pět	**15** - patnáct	**60** - šedesát	**500** - pět set
6 - šest	**16** - šestnáct	**70** - sedmdesát	**600** - šest set
7 - sedm	**17** - sedmnáct	**80** - osmdesát	**700** - sedm set
8 - osm	**18** - osmnáct	**90** - devadesát	**800** - osm set
9 - devět	**19** - devatenáct	**100** - sto	**900** - devět set
10 - deset	**20** - dvacet	**101** - sto jedna	**1000** - tisíc

Food and drink terms

Basics

chléb - bread
chlebíček - (open) sandwich
cukr - sugar
hořčice - mustard
houska - round roll
knedlíky - dumplings
křen - horseradish
lžíce - spoon
maso - meat
máslo - butter
med - honey
mléko - milk
moučník - dessert

nápoje - drinks
nůž - knife
oběd - lunch
obloha - garnish
ocet - vinegar
ovoce - fruit
pečivo - pastry
pepř - pepper
polévka - soup
předkrmy - starters
přílohy - side dishes
rohlík - finger roll
rybby - fish

rýže - rice
sklenice - glass
snídaně - breakfast
sůl - salt
šálek - cup
talíř - plate
tartarská omáčka - tartare sauce
večeře - supper/dinner
vejce - eggs
vidlička - fork
volské oko - fried egg
zeleniny - vegetables

Soups

boršč - beetroot soup
bramborová - potato soup

čočková - lentil soup
fazolová - bean soup

hovězí vývar - beef broth
hrachová - pea soup

kapustnica – sauerkraut, mushroom and meat soup

kuřecí – thin chicken soup
rajská – tomato soup

zeleninová – vegetable soup

Fish

kapr – carp
losos – salmon
makrela – mackerel
platys – flounder

pstruh – trout
rybí filé – fillet of fish
sardinka – sardine
štika – pike

treska – cod
zavináč – herring/rollmop

Meat dishes

bažant – pheasant
biftek – beef steak
čevapčiči – spicy meat balls
dršťky – tripe
drůbež – poultry
guláš – goulash
hovězí – beef
husa – goose
játra – liver
jazyk – tongue

kachna – duck
klobásy – sausages
kotleta – cutlet
kuře – chicken
kýta – leg
ledvinky – kidneys
řízek – steak
roštěná – sirloin
salám – salami
sekaná – meat loaf

skopové maso – mutton
slanina – bacon
svíčková – fillet of beef
šunka – ham
telecí – veal
vepřový – pork
vepřové řízek – breaded pork cutlet or schnitzel
zajíc – hare
žebírko – ribs

Vegetables

brambory – potatoes
brokolice – broccoli
celer – celery
cibule – onion
česnek – garlic
chřest – asparagus
čočka – lentils
fazole – beans
houby – mushrooms

hranolky – chips, French fries
hrášek – peas
karot – carrot
květák – cauliflower
kyselá okurka – pickled gherkin
kyselé zelí – sauerkraut
lečo – ratatouille

lilek – aubergine
okurka – cucumber
pórek – leek
rajče – tomato
ředkev – adish
řepná bulva – beetroot
špenát – spinach
zelí – cabbage
žampiony – mushrooms

Fruit, cheese and nuts

banán – banana
borůvky – blueberries
broskev – peach
brusinky – cranberries
bryndza – goat's cheese in brine
citrón – lemon
grejp – grapefruit
hermelín – Czech brie
hrozny – grapes
hruška – pear
jablko – apple
jahody – strawberries
kompot – stewed fruit

maliny – raspberries
mandle – almonds
meruňka – apricot
niva – semi-soft, crumbly, blue cheese
oříšky – peanuts
ostružiny – blackberries
oštěpek – heavily smoked, curd cheese
parenica – rolled strips of lightly smoked, curd cheese
pivní sýr – cheese flavoured with beer
pomeranč – orange
rozinky – raisins
švestky – plums

třešně – cherries
tvaroh – fresh curd cheese
urda – soft, fresh, whey cheese

uzený sýr – smoked cheese
vlašské ořechy – walnuts

Common terms

čerstvý – fresh
domácí – home-made
dušený – stew/casserole
grilovaný – roast on the spit
kyselý – sour
na kmíně – with caraway seeds
na roštu – grilled
na zdraví – cheers!
nadívaný – stuffed
nakládaný – pickled
(za)pečený – baked/roast
plněný – stuffed

s.m. (s máslem) – with butter
sladký – sweet
slaný – salted
smažený – fried in breadcrumbs
studený – cold
syrový – raw
sýrový – cheesy
teplý – hot
uzený – smoked
vařený – boiled
znojmský – with gherkins

Drinks

čaj – tea
destiláty – spirits
káva – coffee
koňak – brandy
láhev – bottle
minerální (voda) – mineral (water)
mléko – milk
pivo – beer
presso – espresso

s ledem – with ice
soda – soda
suché víno – dry wine
šumivý – fizzy
svařené víno/svařák – mulled wine
tonic – tonic
vinný střik – white wine with soda
víno – wine

A glossary of Czech words and terms

brána gate
český Bohemian
chata chalet-type bungalow, country cottage
  or mountain hut
chrám large church
divadlo theatre
dóm cathedral
dům house
dům kultury generic term for local arts and
  social centre; literally "House of Culture"
hora mountain
hospoda pub
hostinec pub
hrad castle
hřbitov cemetery
kaple chapel
katedrála cathedral
kavárna coffee house
klášter monastery/convent
kostel church
koupaliště swimming pool
Labe River Elbe
lanovka funicular or cable car
les forest
město town

most bridge
muzeum museum
nábřeží embankment
nádraží train station
náměstí square
ostrov island
palác palace
památník memorial or monument
pasáž indoor shopping mall
pivnice pub
radnice town hall
restaurace restaurant
sad park
sál room or hall (in a chateau or castle)
schody steps
svatý/svatá saint; often abbreviated to sv
třída avenue
ulice street
věž tower
vinárna wine bar or cellar
Vltava River Moldau
vrchy hills
výstava exhibition
zahrada garden
zámek chateau

An architectural glossary

Ambulatory Passage round the back of the altar, in continuation of the aisles.

Art Nouveau French term for the sinuous and stylized form of architecture dating from 1900 to 1910; known as the Secession in the Czech Republic and as *Jugendstil* in Germany.

Baroque Expansive, exuberant architectural style of the seventeenth and mid-eighteenth centuries, characterized by ornate decoration, complex spatial arrangement and grand vistas.

Chancel The part of the church where the altar is placed, usually at the east end.

Empire Highly decorative Neoclassical style of architecture and decorative arts, practised in the early 1800s.

Fresco Mural painting applied to wet plaster, so that the colours immediately soak into the wall.

Functionalism Plain, boxy, modernist architectural style, prevalent in the late 1920s and 1930s in Czechoslovakia, often using plate-glass curtain walls and open-plan interiors.

Gothic Architectural style prevalent from the fourteenth to the sixteenth century, characterized by pointed arches and ribbed vaulting.

Loggia Covered area on the side of a building, often arcaded.

Nave Main body of a church, usually the western end.

Neoclassical Late eighteenth- and early nineteenth-century style of architecture and design returning to classical Greek and Roman models as a reaction against Baroque and Rococo excesses.

Oriel A bay window, usually projecting from an upper floor.

283

Rococo Highly florid, fiddly, though (occasionally) graceful, style of architecture and interior design, forming the last phase of Baroque.

Romanesque Solid architectural style of the late tenth to thirteenth century, characterized by round-headed arches and geometrical precision.

Secession Linear and stylized form of architecture and decorative arts imported from Vienna as a reaction against the academic establishment.

Sgraffito Monochrome plaster decoration effected by means of scraping back the first white layer to reveal the black underneath.

Stucco Plaster used for decorative effects.

Trompe l'oeil Painting designed to fool the onlooker into believing that it is actually three-dimensional.

Index

and small print

Index

Map entries are in colour

W

Y

Z

INDEX

At the time of going to press in August 2002, Prague suffered the worst floods for over 100 years, which inundated a large part of Malá Strana, the river islands and several other areas of the city. By the time you read this, much of the damage will have been cleared up, but it's likely that it may take many months for the metro system to be repaired and for those businesses that have been affected to get back to normal.

Twenty Years of Rough Guides

In the summer of 1981, Mark Ellingham, Rough Guides' founder, knocked out the first guide on a typewriter, with a group of friends. Mark had been travelling in Greece after university, and couldn't find a guidebook that really answered his needs.There were heavyweight cultural guides on the one hand – good on museums and classical sites but not on beaches and tavernas – and on the other hand student manuals that were so caught up with how to save money that they lost sight of the country's significance beyond its role as a place for a cool vacation. None of the guides began to address Greece as a country, with its natural and human environment, its politics and its contemporary life.

Having no urgent reason to return home, Mark decided to write his own guide. It was a guide to Greece that tried to combine some erudition and insight with a thoroughly practical approach to travellers' needs. Scrupulously researched listings of places to stay, eat and drink were matched by careful attention to detail on everything from Homer to Greek music, from classical sites to national parks and from nude beaches to monasteries. Back in London, Mark and his friends got their Rough Guide accepted by a farsighted commissioning editor at the publisher Routledge and it came out in 1982.

The Rough Guide to Greece was a student scheme that became a publishing phenomenon. The immediate success of the book – shortlisted for the Thomas Cook award – spawned a series that rapidly covered dozens of countries. The Rough Guides found a ready market among backpackers and budget travellers, but soon acquired a much broader readership that included older and less impecunious visitors. Readers relished the guides' wit and inquisitiveness as much as the enthusiastic, critical approach that acknowledges everyone wants value for money – but not at any price.

Rough Guides soon began supplementing the "rougher" information – the hostel and low-budget listings – with the kind of detail that independent-minded travellers on any budget might expect. These days, the guides – distributed worldwide by the Penguin group – include recommendations spanning the range from shoestring to luxury, and cover more than 200 destinations around the globe. Our growing team of authors, many of whom come to Rough Guides initially as outstandingly good letter-writers telling us about their travels, are spread all over the world, particularly in Europe, the USA and Australia. As well as the travel guides, Rough Guides publishes a series of dictionary phrasebooks covering two dozen major languages, an acclaimed series of music guides running the gamut from Classical to World Music, a series of music CDs in association with World Music Network, and a range of reference books on topics as diverse as the Internet, Pregnancy and Unexplained Phenomena. Visit **www.roughguides.com** to see what's cooking.

Rough Guide Credits

Text editor: Claire Saunders
Series editor: Mark Ellingham
Editorial: Martin Dunford, Jonathan Buckley, Kate Berens, Ann-Marie Shaw, Helena Smith, Judith Bamber, Olivia Swift, Ruth Blackmore, Geoff Howard, Gavin Thomas, Alexander Mark Rogers, Polly Thomas, Joe Staines, Richard Lim, Duncan Clark, Peter Buckley, Lucy Ratcliffe, Clifton Wilkinson, Alison Murchie, Matthew Teller, Andrew Dickson, Fran Sandham (UK); Andrew Rosenberg, Stephen Timblin, Yuki Takagaki, Richard Koss, Hunter Slaton, Julie Feiner (US)
Production: Susanne Hillen, Andy Hilliard, Link Hall, Helen Prior, Julia Bovis, Michelle Draycott, Katie Pringle, Zoë Nobes, Rachel Holmes, Andy Turner

Cartography: Melissa Baker, Maxine Repath, Ed Wright, Katie Lloyd-Jones
Cover art direction: Louise Boulton
Picture research: Sharon Martins, Mark Thomas
Online: Kelly Cross, Anja Mutic-Blessing, Jennifer Gold, Audra Epstein, Suzanne Welles, Cree Lawson (US)
Finance: John Fisher, Gary Singh, Edward Downey, Mark Hall, Tim Bill
Marketing & Publicity: Richard Trillo, Niki Smith, David Wearn, Chloë Roberts, Demelza Dallow, Claire Southern (UK); Simon Carloss, David Wechsler, Kathleen Rushforth (US)
Administration: Tania Hummel, Julie Sanderson, Karoline Densley

Publishing Information

This fifth edition published September 2002 by **Rough Guides Ltd**, 80 Strand, London WC2R 0RL
345 Hudson St, 4th Floor, New York, NY 10014, USA
Distributed by the Penguin Group
Penguin Books Ltd, 80 Strand, London WC2R ORL
Penguin Putnam, Inc.
375 Hudson Street, NY 10014, USA
Penguin Books Australia Ltd, 487 Maroondah Highway, PO Box 257, Ringwood, Victoria 3134, Australia
Penguin Books Canada Ltd, 10 Alcorn Avenue, Toronto, Ontario, Canada M4V 1E4
Penguin Books (NZ) Ltd, 182–190 Wairau Road, Auckland 10, New Zealand
Typeset in Bembo and Helvetica to an original design by Henry Iles.

Printed in Italy by LegoPrint S.p.A

©Rob Humphreys, 2002

No part of this book may be reproduced in any form without permission from the publisher except for the quotation of brief passages in reviews.

336pp includes index
A catalogue record for this book is available from the British Library

ISBN 1-85828-900-9

The publishers and authors have done their best to ensure the accuracy and currency of all the information in **The Rough Guide to Prague**; however, they can accept no responsibility for any loss, injury or inconvenience sustained by any traveller as a result of information or advice contained in the guide.

Help us update

We've gone to a lot of effort to ensure that the fifth edition of **The Rough Guide to Prague** is accurate and up to date. However, things change – places get "discovered", opening hours are notoriously fickle, restaurants and rooms raise prices or lower standards. If you feel we've got it wrong or left something out, we'd like to know, and if you can remember the address, the price, the time, the phone number, so much the better.

We'll credit all contributions, and send a copy of the next edition (or any other Rough Guide if you prefer) for the best letters. Everyone who writes to us and isn't already a subscriber will receive a copy of our full-colour thrice-yearly newsletter. Please mark letters: **"Rough Guide Prague Update"** and send to: Rough Guides, 80 Strand, London WC2R 0RL, or Rough Guides, 4th Floor, 345 Hudson St, New York, NY 10014. Or send an email to **mail@roughguides.com**
  Have your questions answered and tell others about your trip at
www.roughguides.atinfopop.com

Acknowledgements

Special thanks to Claire for getting her tongue twisted round the Czech, to Kate for enduring a chilly December inversion, to Gordon for hacking round the suburbs in the rain, to Elizabeth for letting us share her Prague penthouse, and to Val for the biblio and other bits of research. Thanks, too, to Ed Wright and Stratigraphics for the maps, Andy Turner for picture layout and typesetting, Michelle Draycott for picture research, Louise Boulton for the jacket and Carole Mansur for proofreading.

Readers' letters

Thanks to all the readers who took the trouble to write in with their comments and suggestions (and apologies to anyone whose name we've misspelt or omitted):

Anne Amison & Michael Albutt, Rich Ballerini, Liana O. Blum, Michael Carlton, Ben Caudell, Mark Ellerby, Karen Fielding, James Foley, Tim Hammond, Paul Heidelberg, Keith Howells, Stephen Hunt, Ciaran Hyde, P. Jares, D. Kushner, Simon Looi, Jason Masala, Trevor Marshall, Alan R. Maxwell, Shaun McFadden, Jake Morgan, Annie Morrison, Janice Murdoch, Richard Ross, Monica Shelley, Bob Smith, Peter F. Smith, Carol Lesley Stockton, S.W. Stopford, Martin Stynes, Michael Wallace, Rachel Welton, Dr. R. D. Marsh, Charlie Walker-Wise, Sylvia Warner, Peter & Lucie Wise, Stephen Worsfold.

Photo Credits

SMALL PRINT

Cover Credits
Front (small top image) Astronomical Clock ©Gregory Wrona
Front (small bottom image) House sign, Nerudova ©Robert Harding
Back (top) Mánesův Bridge ©Robert Harding
Back (lower) The Loreta ©John Wright

Colour introduction
Title page – Bridges and River Vltava ©Robert Harding
Main full page – Malá Strana spires from Charles Bridge ©Robert Harding
Intro small insert – Astronomical Clock ©Peter Wilson
Prague bridges ©John Probert
Statues, Charles Bridge ©Michael Jenner
Three violins house sign, Mála Strana ©John Probert
Puppets ©John Probert
"Fred and Ginger" building ©John Probert
Zeyer Monument ©John Probert
Praha hlavní nádraží ©Robert Harding
Prague buskers ©John Probert

Things not to miss
1.Charles Bridge (detail) ©Greg Evans
2.Café Imperial ©John Probert
3.Veletržní palác ©Rob Humphreys
4. Cobbled backstreets, Staré Město ©Robert Harding
5.Týn church ©John Probert
6.Old Jewish cemetery ©Robert Harding
7.Prague nightlife ©Naki/PYMCA
8.Vyšehrad ©Hans-Horst Skupy
9.Lucerna pasáž ©John Probert
10.Prague Castle ©John Probert
11.Obecni dům ©John Probert
12.Mini Eiffel Tower, Petřín ©John Probert
13.Bílkova vila ©John Probert
14.Dobrá čajovna teahouse ©John Probert
15.Terezín ©John Probert
16.Ledeburská zahrada, Malá Strana ©John Probert
17.Stavovské divadlo ©John Probert
18. Church of sv Mikuláš, Malá Strana ©Robert Harding
19. Astronomická věž ©John Probert
20. Pub ©Trip

Black and white photos
Guard at palace gates ©Peter Wilson (p.45)
Pražské Jezulátko ©Mirek Frank (p.71)
Baroque relief statuary c.Jakuba, Staré Město ©John Probert (p.92)
Old street lamp ©Ellen Rooney/Robert Harding (p.106)
Main train station ©John Probert (p.119)
Palacký Monument ©John Probert (p.133)
Vyšehrad Church of SS Petr and Pavel, detail of main door ©Phil Robinson/Robert Harding (p.141)
Obecni dum café, two men ©M.Maclean/Trip (p.198)

Rough Guides travel

Europe

Algarve
Amsterdam
Andalucia
Austria
Barcelona
Belgium
 & Luxembourg
Berlin
Britain
Brittany
 & Normandy
Bruges & Ghent
Brussels
Budapest
Bulgaria
Copenhagen
Corsica
Costa Brava
Crete
Croatia
Cyprus
Czech & Slovak
 Republics
Devon & Cornwall
Dodecanese
 & East Aegean
Dordogne
 & the Lot
Dublin
Edinburgh
England
Europe
First-Time Europe
Florence
France
French Hotels
 & Restaurants
Germany
Greece
Greek Islands
Holland
Hungary
Ibiza
 & Formentera
Iceland
Ionian Islands
Ireland
Italy
Lake District

Languedoc
 & Roussillon
Lisbon
London
London Mini Guide
London
 Restaurants
Madeira
Madrid
Mallorca
Malta & Gozo
Menorca
Moscow
Norway
Paris
Paris Mini Guide
Poland
Portugal
Prague
Provence & the
 Côte d'Azur
Pyrenees
Romania
Rome
Sardinia
Scandinavia
Scotland
Scottish Highlands
 & Islands
Sicily
Spain
St Petersburg
Sweden
Switzerland
Tenerife & La
 Gomera
Turkey
Tuscany & Umbria
Venice
 & The Veneto
Vienna
Wales

Asia

Bali & Lombok
Bangkok
Beijing
Cambodia
China

First-Time Asia
Goa
Hong Kong
 & Macau
India
Indonesia
Japan
Laos
Malaysia,
 Singapore
 & Brunei
Nepal
Singapore
South India
Southeast Asia
Thailand
Thailand Beaches
 & Islands
Tokyo
Vietnam

Australasia

Australia
Gay & Lesbian
 Australia
Melbourne
New Zealand
Sydney

North America

Alaska
Big Island of
 Hawaii
Boston
California
Canada
Florida
Hawaii
Honolulu
Las Vegas
Los Angeles
Maui
Miami & the
 Florida Keys
Montréal
New England
New Orleans
New York City

New York City
 Mini Guide
New York
 Restaurants
Pacific Northwest
Rocky Mountains
San Francisco
San Francisco
 Restaurants
Seattle
Southwest USA
Toronto
USA
Vancouver
Washington DC
Yosemite

Caribbean & Latin America

Antigua & Barbuda
Argentina
Bahamas
Barbados
Belize
Bolivia
Brazil
Caribbean
Central America
Chile
Costa Rica
Cuba
Dominican
 Republic
Ecuador
Guatemala
Jamaica
Maya World
Mexico
Peru
St Lucia
Trinidad & Tobago

Africa & Middle East

Cape Town
Egypt
Israel & Palestinian
 Territories

Jerusalem
Jordan
Kenya
Morocco
South Africa,
 Lesotho
 & Swaziland
Syria
Tanzania
Tunisia
West Africa
Zanzibar
Zimbabwe

Dictionary Phrasebooks

Czech
Dutch
European
 Languages
French
German
Greek
Hungarian
Italian
Polish
Portuguese
Russian
Spanish
Turkish
Hindi & Urdu
Indonesian
Japanese
Mandarin Chinese
Thai
Vietnamese
Mexican Spanish
Egyptian Arabic
Swahili

Maps

Amsterdam
Dublin
London
Paris
San Francisco
Venice

Rough Guides publishes new books every month

Rough Guides music, reference & CDs

Music

Acoustic Guitar
Blues: 100 Essential CDs
Cello
Clarinet
Classical Music
Classical Music: 100 Essential CDs
Country Music
Country: 100 Essential CDs
Cuban Music
Drum'n'bass
Drums
Electric Guitar & Bass Guitar
Flute
Hip-Hop
House
Irish Music
Jazz
Jazz: 100 Essential CDs
Keyboards & Digital Piano
Latin: 100 Essential CDs
Music USA: a Coast-To-Coast Tour
Opera
Opera: 100 Essential CDs
Piano
Reading Music
Reggae
Reggae: 100 Essential CDs
Rock
Rock: 100 Essential CDs
Saxophone
Soul: 100 Essential CDs
Techno
Trumpet & Trombone
Violin & Viola
World Music: 100 Essential CDs

World Music Vol1
World Music Vol2

Reference

Children's Books, 0–5
Children's Books, 5–11
China Chronicle
Cult Movies
Cult TV
Elvis
England Chronicle
France Chronicle
India Chronicle
The Internet
Internet Radio
James Bond
Liverpool FC
Man Utd
Money Online
Personal Computers
Pregnancy & Birth
Shopping Online
Travel Health
Travel Online
Unexplained Phenomena
Videogaming
Weather
Website Directory
Women Travel
World Cup

Music CDs

Africa
Afrocuba
Afro-Peru
Ali Hussan Kuban
The Alps
Americana
The Andes
The Appalachians
Arabesque
Asian Underground
Australian Aboriginal Music
Bellydance
Bhangra

Bluegrass
Bollywood
Boogaloo
Brazil
Cajun
Cajun and Zydeco
Calypso and Soca
Cape Verde
Central America
Classic Jazz
Congolese Soukous
Cuba
Cuban Music Story
Cuban Son
Cumbia
Delta Blues
Eastern Europe
English Roots Music
Flamenco
Franco
Gospel
Global Dance
Greece
The Gypsies
Haiti
Hawaii
The Himalayas
Hip Hop
Hungary
India
India and Pakistan
Indian Ocean
Indonesia
Irish Folk
Irish Music
Italy
Jamaica
Japan
Kenya and Tanzania
Klezmer
Louisiana
Lucky Dube
Mali and Guinea
Marrabenta Mozambique
Merengue & Bachata
Mexico
Native American Music
Nigeria and Ghana
North Africa

Nusrat Fateh Ali Khan
Okinawa
Paris Café Music
Portugal
Rai
Reggae
Salsa
Salsa Dance
Samba
Scandinavia
Scottish Folk
Scottish Music
Senegal & The Gambia
Ska
Soul Brothers
South Africa
South African Gospel
South African Jazz
Spain
Sufi Music
Tango
Thailand
Tex-Mex
Wales
West African Music
World Music Vol 1: Africa, Europe and the Middle East
World Music Vol 2: Latin & North America, Caribbean, India, Asia and Pacific
World Roots
Youssou N'Dour & Etoile de Dakar
Zimbabwe

Visit us online
roughguides.com

Information on over 25,000 destinations around the world

Music Reference Guides

CD Guides

Mini Guides

www.roughguides.com

Rough Guide Music Guides

NOTES

The ideas expressed in this code were developed by and for independent travellers.

Learn About The Country You're Visiting

Start enjoying your travels before you leave by tapping into as many sources of information as you can.

The Cost Of Your Holiday

Think about where your money goes - be fair and realistic about how cheaply you travel. Try and put money into local peoples' hands; drink local beer or fruit juice rather than imported brands and stay in locally owned accommodation. Haggle with humour and not aggressively. Pay what something is worth to you and remember how wealthy you are compared to local people.

Embrace The Local Culture

Open your mind to new cultures and traditions - it will transform your experience. Think carefully about what's appropriate in terms of your clothes and the way you behave. You'll earn respect and be more readily welcomed by local people. Respect local laws and attitudes towards drugs and alcohol that vary in different countries and communities. Think about the impact you could have on them.

Exploring The World – The Travellers' Code

Being sensitive to these ideas means getting more out of your travels - and giving more back to the people you meet and the places you visit.

Minimise Your Environmental Impact

Think about what happens to your rubbish - take biodegradable products and a water filter bottle. Be sensitive to limited resources like water, fuel and electricity. Help preserve local wildlife and habitats by respecting local rules and regulations, such as sticking to footpaths and not standing on coral.

Don't Rely On Guidebooks

Use your guidebook as a starting point, not the only source of information. Talk to local people, then discover your own adventure!

Be Discreet With Photography

Don't treat people as part of the landscape, they may not want their picture taken. Ask first and respect their wishes.

We work with people the world over to promote tourism that benefits their communities, but we can only carry on our work with the support of people like you. For membership details or to find out how to make your travels work for local people and the environment, visit our website.

www.tourismconcern.org.uk

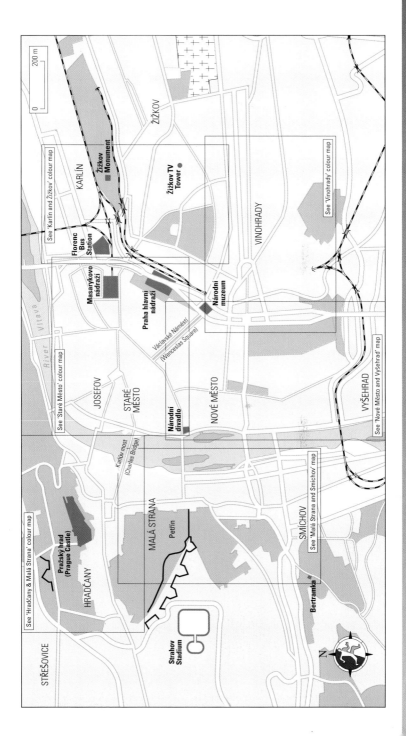

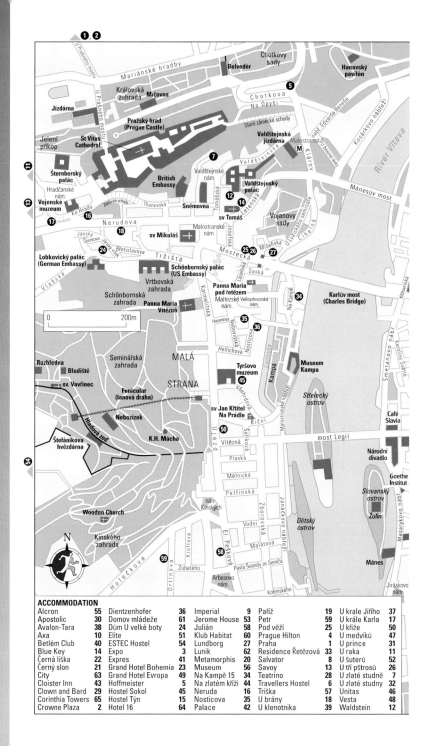

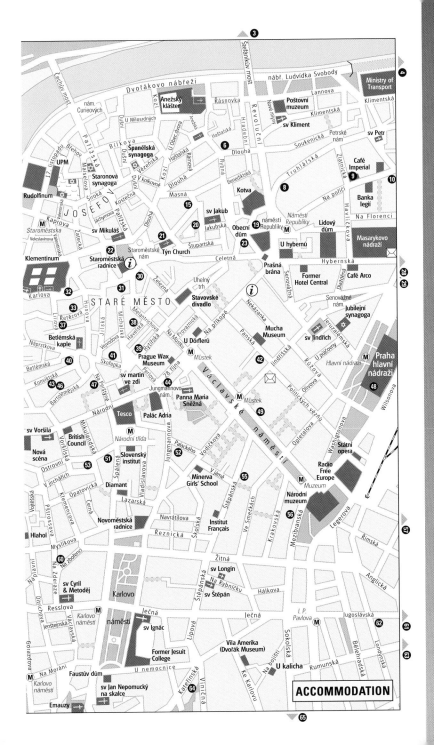

HRADČANY & MALÁ STRANA

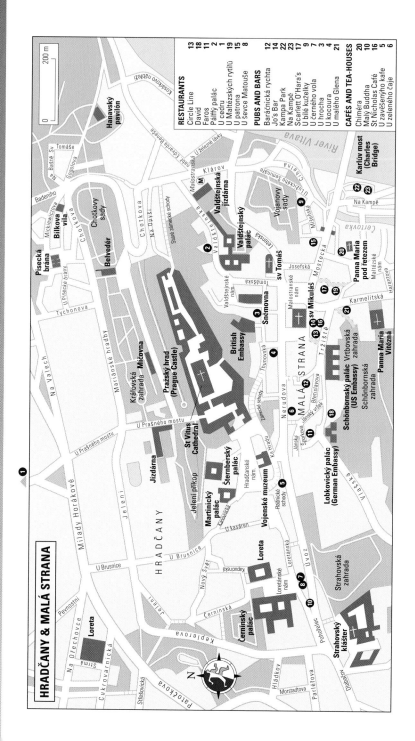

RESTAURANTS

Circle Line	13
David	18
Faros	11
Pálffy palác	2
U cedru	1
U Maltézských rytířů	19
U patrona	15
U Ševce Matouše	8

PUBS AND BARS

Baráčnická rychta	12
Jo's Bar	14
Kampa Park	22
Na Kampě	23
Scarlett O'Hara's	17
U bílé kuželky	9
U černého vola	7
U hrocha	3
U kocoura	4
U malého Glena	21

CAFÉS AND TEA-HOUSES

Chiméra	20
Malý Buddha	10
St Nicholas Café	16
U zavěšeného kafe	5
U zeleného čaje	6

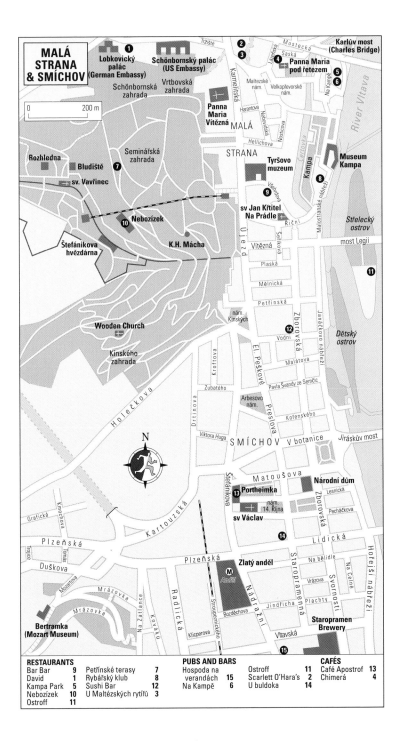

MALÁ STRANA & SMÍCHOV

Lobkovický palác (German Embassy) ❶
Schönbornský palác (US Embassy)
Schönbornská zahrada
Vrtbovská zahrada
Panna Maria Vítězná
MALÁ
STRANA
Rozhledna
Bludiště ❼
sv. Vavřinec
Seminářská zahrada
Tyršovo muzeum
Museum Kampa ❽
sv Jan Křtitel Na Prádle ❾
Nebozízek ❿
Štefánikova hvězdárna
K.H. Mácha
Vítězná
Plaská
Mělnická
Petřinská
Wooden Church
Kinského zahrada
nám. Kinských
Dětský ostrov
Vodní
SMÍCHOV
Zubatého
Arbesovo nám.
Viktora Huga
Matoušova
Portheimka ❭❸
nám. 14. Října
sv Václav
Národní dům
Zlatý anděl
M Anděl
Staropramen Brewery
Bertramka (Mozart Museum)
Tržiště
Mostecká
Saská
Panna Maria pod řetezem ❹ ❺ ❻
Karlův most (Charles Bridge)
Maltézské nám.
Velkopřevorské nám.
River Vltava
Střelecký ostrov
most Legii ❶❶
Jiráskův most
Na Kampě
Malostranské nábřeží

RESTAURANTS		PUBS AND BARS		CAFÉS	
Bar Bar	9	Petřínské terasy	7	Hospoda na		Ostroff	11	Café Apostrof	13
David	1	Rybářský klub	8	verandách	15	Scarlett O'Hara's	2	Chimerá	4
Kampa Park	5	Sushi Bar	12	Na Kampě	6	U buldoka	14		
Nebozízek	10	U Maltézských rytířů	3						
Ostroff	11								

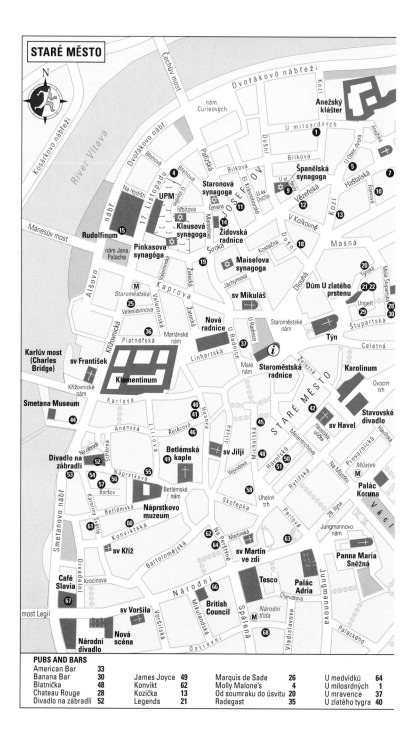

STARÉ MĚSTO

N

River Vltava

Čechův most

Dvořákovó nábřeží

Kosárkovo nábřeží

Dvořákovo nábř.

Mánesův most

nám. Curieových

Anežský klášter

U milosrdných ❶

Dušní

Bilkova

Španělská synagoga

U Obecního dvora ❺

❼

Haštalská

17. listopadu

Na rejdišti

nábř.

Břehová

Břehová

Pařížská

Bilkova

U st. Židov.

❾

U sv. Ducha

El Kramáriho

Věžeňská ❶❷

Kozí ❶❸

Ramová ❶⓪

UPM ❹

Staronová synagoga

hřbitova

olizova L

Cervená

Maiselova

❶❶

❶❹

Klausová synagóga

Židovská radnice

V Kolkovně

Masná

Rudolfinum ❶❺

nám Jana Palacha

Pinkasova synagóga

Siroká

Kostečná

Dušní ❶❽

Dlouhá

Týnská ❷⓪

Malá Štupartská

❷❶❷❷

Alšovo

Kaprova

Žatecka

Valentinská

❶❾

Maiselova synagoga

Jáchymova

Dům U zlatého prstenu

Ungelt ❷❾

❷❽❸⓪

Staroměstska Ⓜ

❷❺

Veleslavínova

Valentinská

Žatecka

sv Mikuláš

Staroměstské nám.

Týn

Štupartská

Celetná

❸❻

Platnéřská

Mariánské nám

Nová radnice

U Radnice ❸❼

ⓘ

Linhartská

Malé nám

Staroměstská radnice

STARÉ MĚSTO

Železná

Karolinum

Ovocný trh

Karlův most (Charles Bridge)

sv František

Křižovnická

Křížovnické nám

Klementinum

Karlova

Husova

Jilská

Michalská

Melantrichova

sv Havel

Havelská ulička

Havelská

Stavovské divadlo

Havířská

Smetana Museum ❹❹

Anenská

Liliová

❹⓪

❹❶

Řetězová

❹❻

sv Jiljí

Vejvodova

Havelská

❹❽

❹❺

❺⓪

❺❶

Rytířská

Na Můstku

Ⓜ Můstek

Palác Koruna

Václ

Divadlo na zábradlí

Na zábradlí

Stříbrná

❺❷

Náprstkova

❺❹

❺❸

❺❺

❺❻

❺❼

Boršov

Betlémská kaple ❹❾

Betlémské nám

Konviktská

Karolíny Světlé

Betlémská

Skořepka

❺❽

Uhelný trh

Perlová

28. října

Jungmannovo nám

Náprstkovo muzeum

Smetanovo nábř.

most Legií

Divadelní

Krocínova

❻❶

Konviktská

❻⓪

sv Kříž

Bartolomějská

Na perštýně

❻❷

❻❹

Martinská

sv Martin ve zdi

❻❸

Panna Maria Sněžná

Café Slavia ❻❼

Národní

❻❻

sv Voršila

Nová scéna

Národní divadlo

Voršilská

Mikulandská

British Council

Spálená

❻❽

Ⓜ Národní třída

Tesco

Palác Adria

Charvátova

Jungmannova

Vladislavova

Národní

Ostrovní

Palackého

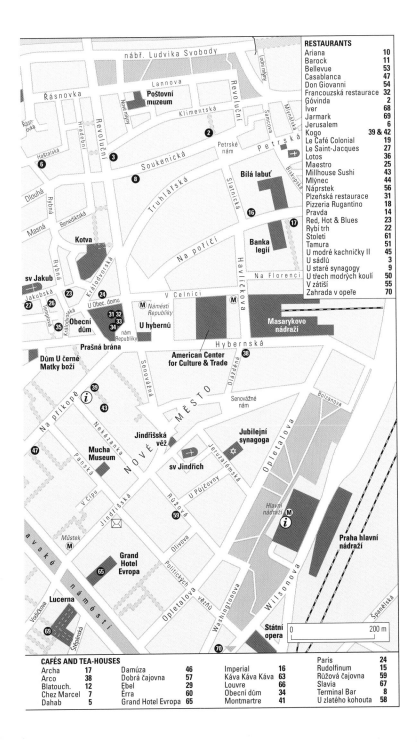

RESTAURANTS

Ariana	10
Barock	11
Bellevue	53
Casablanca	47
Don Giovanni	54
Francouzská restaurace	32
Góvinda	2
Iver	68
Jarmark	69
Jerusalem	6
Kogo	39 & 42
Le Café Colonial	19
Le Saint-Jacques	27
Lotos	36
Maestro	25
Millhouse Sushi	43
Mlýnec	44
Náprstek	56
Plzeňská restaurace	31
Pizzeria Rugantino	18
Pravda	14
Red, Hot & Blues	23
Rybí trh	22
Stoleti	61
Tamura	51
U modré kachničky II	45
U sádlů	3
U staré synagogy	9
U třech modrých koulí	50
V zátiší	55
Zahrada v opeře	70

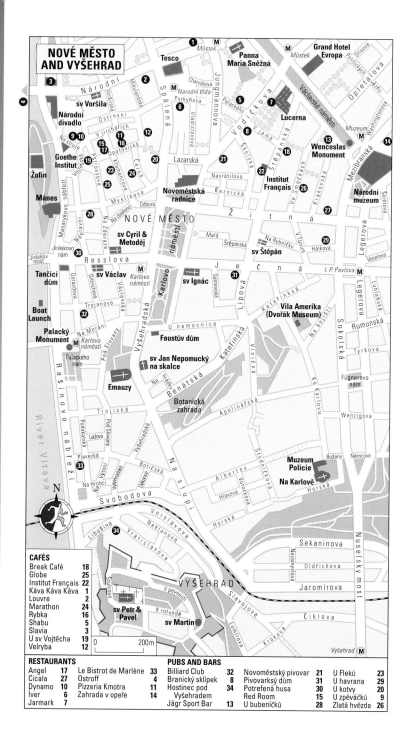

NOVÉ MĚSTO AND VYŠEHRAD

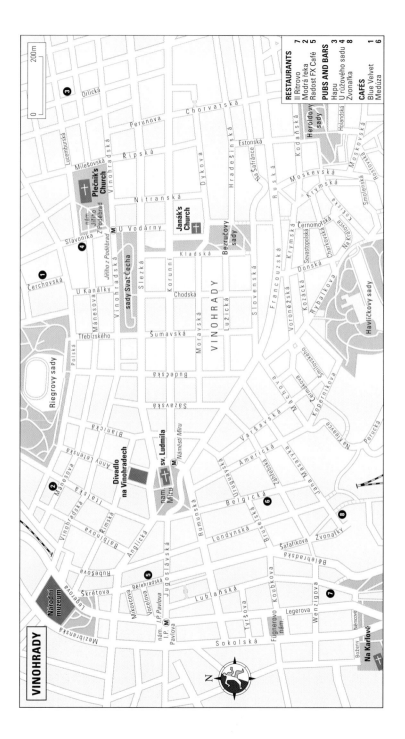

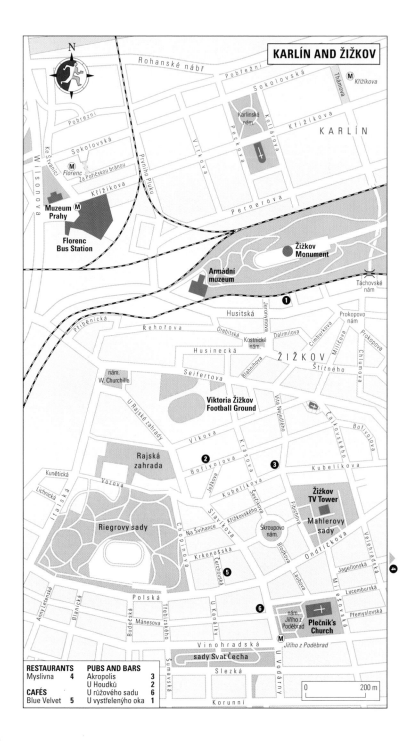

KARLÍN AND ŽIŽKOV

RESTAURANTS
Myslivna 4

CAFÉS
Blue Velvet 5

PUBS AND BARS
Akropolis 3
U Houdků 2
U růžového sadu 6
U vystřeleného oka 1

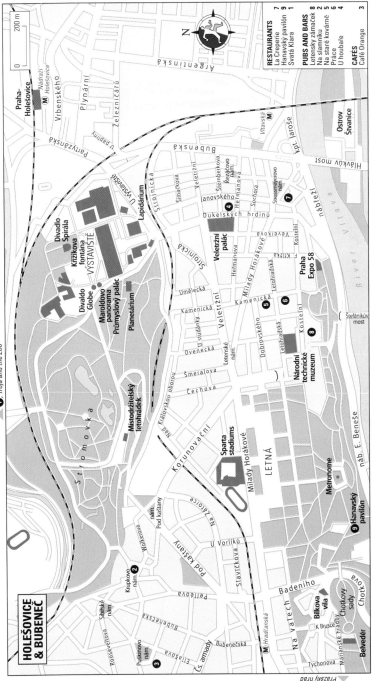

HOLEŠOVICE & BUBENEČ

0 — 200 m

N

1 Troja and the Zoo

Praha-Holešovice

M Nádraží Holešovice

Partyzánská
Vrbenského
Plynární
Železničářů

Stromovka

VÝSTAVIŠTĚ
Divadlo Spirála
Křižíkova fontána
Divadlo Globe
Maroldovo panorama
Průmyslový palác
Planetárium
Lapidárium

U Výstaviště

Mistodržitelský letohrádek

Na Ovenecká
Nad Královskou oborou
Kamenická
Umělecká
Čechova
Šmeralova
Letenské nám.
Na studány

Kaupkovo nám. 2
Wolkerova
Pod kaštany
Na Zátorce
Pod kaštany
U Vorlíků
Slavíčkova

Sibiřské nám.
Roosveltova
Bubenečská
Pelléova

Puškinovo nám. 3
Eliášova
Čs. armády
Bubenečská

M Hradčanská
Mariánské hradby
K Brusce
Na valech
Badeniho
Tychonova

Bílkova vila
Chotkovy sady
Chotkova
Belvedér

Korunovační
Milady Horákové
Sparta stadiums
LETNÁ
Metronome
Hanavský pavilón 9
nábř. E. Beneše

Stromnická
Šimáčkova
Veletržní
Šternberkova
Rezekovo nám.
Hermanova
Sochoří
Dukelských hrdinů 4
Janovského

Bubenská
BUBENEČ

M Vltavská

Strojnická
Veletržní palác
Heřmanova
Veletržní
Milady Horákové
Kamenická 5
Dobrovského
Letohradská
Kostelní 8
Národní technické muzeum
Kamenická 6
Letohradská
Křižíka
Veverkova
Kostelní
Praha Expo 58

Stefánikův most
Štefánikův most

River Vltava

Kpt. Jaroše
Strossmayerovo nám. 7
nábřeží
Hlávkův most

Ostrov Štvanice

M

Argentinská

Pražský hrad

RESTAURANTS
La Creperie   7
Hanavský pavilón   9
Svatá Klara   1

PUBS AND BARS
Letenský zámeček   8
Na slamníku   2
Na staré kovárně   5
Práce   6
U houbaře   4

CAFÉS
Café Orange   3

TRANSPORT SYSTEM

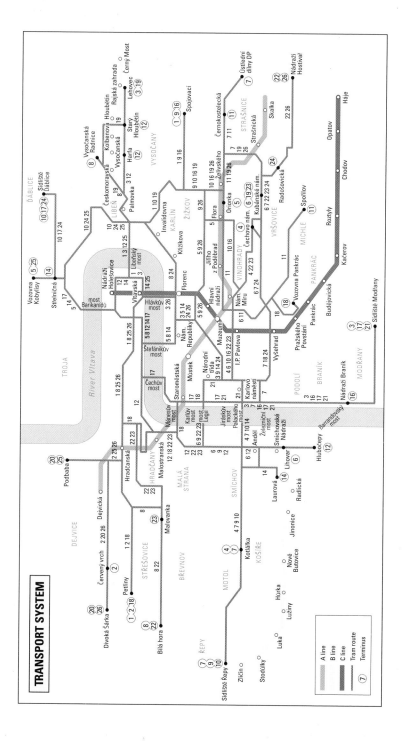